CLIFFS

Test of English as a Foreign Language

PREPARATION GUIDE

by

Michael A. Pyle, M.A.

and

Mary Ellen Muñoz Page, M.A.

Series Editor
Jerry Bobrow, Ph.D.

INCORPORATED
LINCOLN, NEBRASKA   68501

ACKNOWLEDGMENTS

We are indebted to many for providing us incentive and support during the time that we were writing this manuscript. We dedicate this book to our families, including Maria, Maria Elena, Rita, Louie, and our parents; their understanding and support during the many months of writing was essential.

We are also grateful to Dr. Clyde C. Clements, Jr., Dean of Community Education at Santa Fe Community College, for providing us the opportunity to organize a class for test preparation and supporting us in our quest to write this book. Special thanks are due Dr. Patricia Byrd, Assistant Director of the University of Florida's English Language Institute, for providing us classroom space, equipment, students, publicity, and encouragement. We wish to thank Dr. Manuel López Figuera, María Lopez de Pyle, Dr. Felipe Sierra, Dr. José Zaglul, and Paul F. Schmidt for writing materials for the practice tests.

We also wish to thank Jerry Bobrow of Bobrow Test Preparation Services for recommending our book and Michele Spence of Cliffs Notes, Inc., for her invaluable assistance in editing.

We are indebted to our students, who acted as our critics while we were preparing the materials.

We have revised this book several times since it was first written. The changes in this edition are extensive to parallel the 1995 changes to the TOEFL. We are now indebted to even more people who provided reading and listening passages or reviewed materials for us. They include Margarita Bardgett, Elizabeth Eschbach, Joe Romero, Sherry Keyes, Harry Gebert, and Dr. Dana Griffin, III. Michael Pyle is especially thankful for all the help his wife María provided in suggesting materials and typing. In addition to the superb editing work of Michele Spence, the authors were very fortunate to be provided the editing expertise of Linnea Fredrickson.

Neither the authors nor Cliffs Notes, Inc., is affiliated with Educational Testing Service or involved in the development or administration of the TOEFL. Neither the directions nor any sample questions were provided or approved by Educational Testing Service.

ISBN 0-8220-2081-5

FIFTH EDITION

© Copyright 1995 by Michael A. Pyle and Mary Ellen Muñoz Page

Previous editions © Copyright 1991, 1986, 1983, 1982 by

Michael A. Pyle and Mary Ellen Muñoz

All Rights Reserved

Printed in U.S.A.

CONTENTS

PART I: INTRODUCTION

PART II: ANALYSIS OF EXAM AREAS

Ability Tested • Basic Skills Necessary
Directions • Suggested Approach with Samples

PART III: SUBJECT AREA REVIEWS
with
Exercises and Mini-Tests

PART IV: PRACTICE-REVIEW-ANALYZE-PRACTICE
Six Full-Length Practice Tests

PART V: LISTENING COMPREHENSION SCRIPTS, ANSWERS, AND EXPLANATIONS FOR PRACTICE TESTS 1 THROUGH 6

PART VI: TEST OF WRITTEN ENGLISH

Ability Tested • Basic Skills Necessary
• General Information •

PREFACE

Your TOEFL scores make the difference! And better scores result from thorough preparation. Therefore, your study time must be used most effectively. You need the most comprehensive test preparation guide that you can realistically complete in a reasonable time. It must be thorough, direct, precise, and easy to use, giving you all the information you need to do your best on the TOEFL.

In keeping with the fine tradition of Cliffs Notes, leading experts in the field of test preparation and teaching English as a second language have developed this guide as part of a series to provide excellent test preparation materials. The testing strategies, techniques, and materials were researched, developed, tested, and evaluated at Santa Fe Community College and the University of Florida's English Language Institute.

Part I of this guide gives you basic information on the TOEFL and a Successful Overall Approach to taking the test.

Part II includes a thorough analysis of all question types for the three sections of the test, test-taking techniques and strategies, and a Patterned Plan of Attack for each area.

Part III provides an intensive grammar review, review of style problems in written English, and a survey of problem vocabulary and prepositions. Make full use of the six mini-tests and the fifty-nine exercises that are included with the reviews to chart your progress and your understanding.

Part IV contains six full-length practice tests, very similar in format to the Institutional administration of TOEFL. Take these tests under testing conditions, exactly as you will on the day of the actual test. Follow time allotments carefully.

Part V includes cross-referenced answer keys, scoring sheets, listening comprehension scripts, and answers and explanations for the six practice tests. Use the cross-referenced answer keys to guide you to review sections. After each practice test, be sure to review those areas in which you had difficulty. The listening comprehension scripts will give you quick reference for any question with which you had a problem. Use all of the techniques and study tools provided. Your ability and confidence will grow with each practice test.

Part VI: If you will be taking the TOEFL at an administration that includes an essay writing section, review all of the material in Part VI. Practice writing essays on the sample topics provided. Have the practice essays graded by a composition teacher.

Allow yourself as much study time as possible. Study over several months, if you can, slowly and methodically, in conjunction with your regular study of English.

HOW TO USE THIS BOOK

This guide is ideal for either individual or classroom use. To use this material most effectively, it is sometimes best not to simply begin at the beginning and go through to the end. Pace yourself. Make full use of the cross-referenced answers, table of contents, index, and clearly organized review for efficient study throughout your TOEFL preparation. The following suggestions have proven helpful for many students.

1. Carefully read all of the introductory material found in Part I.

2. Read Part II concerning Ability Tested, Basic Skills Necessary, Directions, and Suggested Approach with Samples for each of the question types in the three test sections.

3. Decide how many weeks of study time you will have before the actual TOEFL or, if there is a class, how many class sessions will be scheduled.

4. Divide the total number of pages in the Part III Grammar Review by the number of weeks before the TOEFL or the number of class sessions involved. Study this number of pages and do the accompanying exercises each week or session.

5. Divide memorizing tasks, such as the lists of irregular verbs and verbal idioms and the remaining review material in Part III in the same way.

6. When you are about halfway through the review, stop. Now carefully reread the Suggested Approach to each question type (Part II) and review once again the Successful Overall Approach (Part I).

7. Now take Practice Test 1. It will contain some familiar and some unfamiliar material. Use the listening comprehension cassette

xiv

tapes included with this guide. Chart your test results carefully. Allow yourself time to return to the sections of the review that you have not fully understood.

8. Take the other five practice tests in the same way, at predetermined intervals, while you continue your study of the Part III review materials.

9. If you will be taking the TOEFL at an administration that includes an essay writing section, review all of the material in Part VI, Test of Written English. Practice writing essays on the sample topics provided. Have the practice essays graded by a composition teacher.

STUDY GUIDE CHECKLIST

____ 1. Read the Bulletin of Information for TOEFL and TSE (see page 11 for address).

____ 2. Become familiar with the Format of Recent TOEFL Exams, page 3.

____ 3. Familiarize yourself with the answers to Questions Commonly Asked about the TOEFL, page 8.

____ 4. Learn the techniques of a Successful Overall Approach, page 12.

____ 5. Carefully study the Analysis of Exam Areas for each of the three test sections, beginning on page 17.

____ 6. Begin your study of the review material in Part III, do the accompanying exercises, take the mini-tests for each section, and restudy sections that give you trouble.

____ 7. Strictly observing time allotments, take Practice Test 1, in its entirety, beginning on page 315.

____ 8. Check your answers and analyze your results, beginning on page 498.

____ 9. Fill out the Analysis-Scoring Sheet to pinpoint your mistakes, page 500.

____ 10. While referring to each item of Practice Test 1, study ALL the answers and explanations as well as the listening comprehension script, beginning on page 501. Replay the cassette and listen carefully for questions you missed. Use the cross-referenced answer keys.

____ 11. Continue your study of the review material given in Part III.

____ 12. Repeat this process with Practice Tests 2, 3, 4, 5, and 6.

____ 13. If your TOEFL administration includes an essay section, review all of Part VI and write practice essays as directed.

____ 14. Go over "Final Preparation," page 655.

PART I: Introduction

FORMAT OF RECENT TOEFL EXAMS
LENGTH AND NUMBER OF QUESTIONS

Subject Area	Time	Number of Questions
Listening Comprehension	30 minutes (approx.)	50 questions
Structure and Written Expression	25 minutes	40 questions
Reading Comprehension	55 minutes	50 questions
Total	110 minutes	140 questions

NOTE: Consult the Bulletin of Information for TOEFL and TSE. Time limits may change from time to time.

FORM OF TOEFL

Section 1: Listening Comprehension
Part A: Short conversations. The conversations are between two people. After each conversation, a third voice will ask a question about what was said. You must find the answer to the question in the test book.
Part B: Longer conversations. The conversations are between two people. After each conversation, a third voice will ask some questions about what was said. You must find the answers to the questions in the test book.
Part C: Oral readings. These may be about any subject. There are several questions about each reading or conversation. You must find the answers to the questions in the test book.
Section 2: Structure and Written Expression
Part A: Multiple choice answers to complete sentences. You must choose the best way to complete the sentence *in formal written English.*
Part B: Sentences have four words or phrases underlined. You must choose the *one* underlined part that is *incorrect* in formal written English.
Section 3: Reading Comprehension
You must read selections in the test book and answer questions based on what is *stated* or *implied* in the readings.

GENERAL DESCRIPTION

Use of TOEFL by Colleges and Universities

TOEFL, Test of English as a Foreign Language, is probably the most often used examination in the admissions process of foreign students to colleges and universities in the United States. However, these schools often do not consider the TOEFL score as the only criterion for admission. They may also consider the student's grades in schools which he or she previously attended and the records from any intensive English program in which the student was enrolled. All this depends on the school's admission criteria.

The score which is acceptable to a given school also depends on the regulations for that particular school. Some schools require 450, some 500, some 550 or 600. If you find that a school requires no TOEFL score, or a very low score, it is probable that the school does not have extensive experience with foreign students, and you may find that it would be better to attend a different school. Remember that admission to a school is not the end of the battle, but the beginning. You must be able to understand enough English to make good grades in competition with native English-speaking students. This is what TOEFL tests, and this is why schools consider TOEFL a valuable examination.

Administration of TOEFL

There are different administrations of TOEFL: Institutional Testing Program (ITP) and Friday and Saturday Testing Programs. The format is basically the same; however, there are distinctions as described below.

Institutional Testing Program (ITP)

This administration is generally given only to students in intensive English programs. It is a service offered by these programs to their students but is an actual TOEFL given in previous Friday and Saturday administrations.

You can register for an ITP administration only at an institution at which the test is given and only if you are a student at the

4

institution. You *cannot* register for this administration of TOEFL through Educational Testing Service.

Scores for this type of the exam are reported in roster form only to the institution at which the exam was taken. You will not receive a form entitled "Examinee's Score Record" as you would in the other administrations. In fact, the institution that administers the exam may not accept the score for admission purposes. Some institutions use these scores for internal purposes in their intensive English programs only. You should check with the individual institution regarding the acceptability of this administration for admission purposes.

Friday and Saturday Testing Programs

The Friday and Saturday Testing Programs are distinguished from the ITP because both result in official score reports, unlike the ITP. The Friday Testing Program was previously called the Special Center Testing Program, and the Saturday Testing Program was previously called the International Testing Program. Each exam is offered six times each year. Thus, one exam in the Friday and Saturday Testing Programs is administered each month in many locations.

Any foreign student can take these examinations. Applications are available from Educational Testing Service at the addresses listed on page 11 of this book. The application comes with the Bulletin of Information for TOEFL and TSE (the United States and Canada Edition or the Overseas Edition, depending on where you will take the exam).

You may *not* register for either of these tests at the institution in which the exam is given; instead, you must send the application directly to Educational Testing Service. Generally, the deadline for application is about six weeks before the exam, but it is wise to register well in advance because the testing centers are often full before the deadline.

Scores for these administrations are sent to the test taker and to any colleges or universities to which the student is applying approximately five weeks after the exam. Any school in the United States that requires TOEFL for admission will accept the score for either of these administrations.

The Determination of the TOEFL Score

Your test score is determined by adding the total number of correct answers in each section and then changing these "raw scores" into "converted scores." The raw score is the total number correct in each section. The converted score is different for each examination. It is based on the difficulty of the test. There is no way that you can use any simple mathematics to determine the converted score.

The "total converted score" is then determined by adding the three converted scores and multiplying the result by 3⅓ (or multiplying by 10 and dividing by 3).

In Part V of this guide, there is a scale to convert your practice test scores from raw scores to converted scores. The scale is NOT one that has been produced by Educational Testing Service, but is quite similar to its scoring scale, adjusted slightly to account for possible differences in difficulty level. It is intended only to give you a *general idea* of what your total score might be. *Do not assume that it is exactly like that of the TOEFL that you are going to take.*

Sections of the TOEFL

There are now only three sections on the TOEFL. An additional section may be added in the future. There have been experimental sections on the examination from time to time. ETS uses these experimental sections to determine how well a given type of question tests a student's knowledge of English. When there is such a section, the score for that section is *not* included in the computation of your TOEFL score.

Test of Written English (TWE)

Certain administrations of TOEFL include a separate writing test known as the Test of Written English. This test is currently given at four Friday and Saturday administrations each year. You must consult your Bulletin of Information to determine if it is included in the administration you intend to take. If it is included, you will be required to take the TWE at that administration. The score is not incorporated into the total TOEFL score but is included as a separate score on the report sent to the institutions receiving your score report.

In this test, the examinee is given one topic on which to write an essay. The essays are read by composition specialists who assign scores based on a six-point scoring guide. Each essay is read by at least two readers, who review the essay independently. The scores assigned by the readers are then averaged.

Information on the TWE is provided in the same bulletin you will receive for TOEFL and TSE. Strategies and practice material for the writing test are presented in Part VI of this book.

Test of Spoken English (TSE)

The Test of Spoken English is not addressed in this book. It is a test intended to measure proficiency in spoken English. It is administered twelve times a year on the same dates as certain Friday and Saturday administrations of the TOEFL test. It takes approximately thirty minutes. Complete information and practice questions are included in the Bulletin of Information for TOEFL and TSE, which is the same bulletin you will receive if you request an application for a Friday or Saturday testing administration.

QUESTIONS COMMONLY ASKED
ABOUT THE TOEFL

Q: WHO ADMINISTERS THE TOEFL?

A: The TOEFL is written and administered by Educational Testing Service (ETS) of Princeton, New Jersey.

Q: IS THERE A DIFFERENCE BETWEEN THE INSTITUTIONAL AND THE FRIDAY AND SATURDAY ADMINISTRATIONS OF TOEFL?

A: They are the same in difficulty and subject matter tested. The uses of the Institutional Administration are quite limited.

Q: CAN I TAKE THE TOEFL MORE THAN ONCE?

A: Yes. Previous scores will be reported, but most schools consider only the most recent score. Many students take TOEFL more than once.

Q: WHAT MATERIALS MAY I BRING TO THE TOEFL?

A: Bring your admission ticket or official authorization, your official identification document, a completed photo file record with a recent photo attached. (For information on the above, see the Bulletin.) Also bring three or four sharpened medium-soft (Number 2 or HB) black lead pencils, a good clean eraser, and a watch (but alarms are not permitted).

Q: WHAT MATERIALS MAY I NOT BRING?

A: You may not bring any paper, food, calculators, dictionaries (or any other books), tape recorders, or cameras.

Q: IF NECESSARY, MAY I CANCEL MY SCORE?

A: Yes. You may cancel your score on the day of the test by completing the score cancellation section of your TOEFL answer sheet, or you can contact ETS by any of the methods mentioned in the Bulletin, but in any event, you *must* follow up any contact to cancel scores with a *written, signed* request to TOEFL/TSE Score Cancellations, P.O. Box 6151, Princeton, NJ 08541-6151, USA.

Q: SHOULD I GUESS ON THE TOEFL?

A: Yes. There is no penalty on TOEFL for incorrect answers, so DO NOT LEAVE ANY SPACES BLANK on your answer sheet. Of course, it is best to eliminate the answers that you are sure are not correct, and then choose among the remaining answers. Some educators suggest that if you have many spaces blank when time is almost up on a section, you *may* slightly improve your score by choosing one letter and filling in all the spaces with that answer rather than randomly choosing answers.

Q: HOW SHOULD I PREPARE FOR THE TOEFL?

A: You should study all the material in this book, and complete all the exercises and practice tests. Also, be sure that you know the directions for each section and know the format of the test. Be sure to consult the TOEFL bulletin in case of changes in format.

Q: WHEN IS THE TOEFL ADMINISTERED?

A: The TOEFL is administered every month in some areas. Consult the TOEFL bulletin for the administration dates of areas near you.

Q: IS TOEFL ADMINISTERED ONLY IN THE UNITED STATES?

A: No. TOEFL is administered in many countries. You can receive information on foreign locations by writing to the TOEFL office and asking for the Overseas Edition of the TOEFL bulletin.

Q: HOW AND WHEN SHOULD I REGISTER FOR TOEFL?

A: Most schools with foreign students have copies of the TOEFL bulletin and application form. If your school does not, write to the TOEFL office and request the application form. Remember to register as early as possible before the deadline date in the bulletin. There are a limited number of seats in the testing center. When you fill out the application form, be sure you make a note of your registration number, (printed in red at the top right of the application form.) You will need this number if you need to contact the TOEFL office about your registration.

Q: SHOULD I ORDER THE "TOEFL SAMPLE TEST" OR "TEST PREPARATION KIT" LISTED IN THE BULLETIN OF INFORMATION?

A: Yes. For additional practice after you have finished using this book, it would be a very good idea to order and use these items.

Q: IS WALK-IN REGISTRATION PROVIDED?

A: No. You MUST register in advance.

Q: ONCE I HAVE RECEIVED MY CONFIRMATION TICKET, MAY I CHANGE THE DATE?

A: Changes in test dates are *not* allowed. If you decide to take the test on a day other than the one that you originally applied for, you must submit a new application with the total fees. You may then request a partial refund for the original amount within sixty days of the original test date.

Q: CAN I CHANGE THE TEST CENTER ONCE MY APPLICATION HAS BEEN CONFIRMED?

A: Test center changes are no longer permitted. If you cannot attend the test center you are scheduled for on the date of your test, you may go to another center on that date. If space and test materials are available, you *may* be permitted to take this test.

Q: CAN I RECEIVE A REFUND IF I DO NOT TAKE THIS TEST?

A: If you did not enter the test center and did not take the test, you are eligible for a partial refund. Consult the TOEFL bulletin for details.

Q: IF I FINISH A SECTION BEFORE TIME IS CALLED, CAN I GO TO ANOTHER SECTION?

A: No. During the time allotted for a given section, you must work only on questions in that section. If you are found working on another section, your score may be canceled.

Q: WHAT SHOULD I DO IF I MISPLACE ANSWERS ON MY ANSWER SHEET?

A: To avoid this problem, you should check your answer sheet every ten questions to be sure that if you have skipped a question in the test booklet, you have also skipped it on the answer sheet. If you find that you have misplaced a number of answers, DON'T ERASE THEM. Simply raise your hand and ask for another answer sheet to finish the test beginning in the place that you realized the mistake. After the examination, a proctor will assist you in correcting your answer sheet.

Q: CAN I ERASE AN ANSWER THAT I FEEL IS WRONG?
A: Yes, but it is very important to erase mistakes completely. Before you go to the test, be sure that your erasers are clean so that they will not smudge the paper. If there are two marks for one question on the answer sheet, even if you have tried to erase the incorrect one, the question will not be counted.

Q: HOW SHOULD I MARK MY ANSWER SHEET?
A: Be sure to fill in the answer spaces correctly and completely and to fill in only one answer for each question.

Correct—   Ⓐ ● © Ⓓ
Incorrect— ⬤ Ⓑ ⓒ̸ Ⓓ
Incorrect— Ⓐ ⊗ © Ⓓ

Q: HOW CAN I CONTACT EDUCATIONAL TESTING SERVICE?
A: General Information: TOEFL/TSE Services
P.O. Box 6151
Princeton, NJ 08541-6151 USA

To Obtain Bulletins: TOEFL/TSE Publications
P.O. Box 6154
Princeton, NJ 08541-6154 USA

To Register: TOEFL/TSE Registration Office
P.O. Box 6152
Princeton, NJ 08541-6152 USA

Telephone Number: (609) 771-7100 (8:30 a.m. to 4:30 p.m.)

Fax Phone Number: (609) 771-7681

TAKING THE TOEFL: A SUCCESSFUL
OVERALL APPROACH

Every second counts when you are taking a standardized test such as the TOEFL. Avoid wasting that time. One way that you can save time is by not reading the directions for each section. If you know the directions for each section, and the format looks similar to the format of that section in this guide and the TOEFL handbook, it is suggested that you begin work immediately. While the other examinees are reading the directions, you can answer several questions. Of course, if the section looks at all unfamiliar, check the directions to be sure there has not been a change.

Many who take the TOEFL don't get the score that they are entitled to because they spend too much time dwelling on hard questions, leaving insufficient time to answer the easy questions they can get right. Don't let this happen to you. Use the following system in Sections 2 and 3 to mark your answer sheet:

1. Answer easy questions immediately.
2. Place a "+" next to any problem that seems solvable but is too time-consuming.
3. Place a "−" next to any problem that seems impossible. Act quickly. Don't waste time deciding whether a problem is a "+" or a "−."

After working all the problems you can do immediately, go back and work your "+" problems. If you finish them, try your "−" problems (sometimes when you come back to a problem that seemed impossible you will suddenly realize how to solve it).

Your answer sheet should look something like this after you finish working your easy questions:

```
 1. Ⓐ ● Ⓒ Ⓓ
+2. Ⓐ Ⓑ Ⓒ Ⓓ
 3. Ⓐ Ⓑ ● Ⓓ
−4. Ⓐ Ⓑ Ⓒ Ⓓ
+5. Ⓐ Ⓑ Ⓒ Ⓓ
```

MAKE SURE TO ERASE YOUR "+" AND "−" MARKS BEFORE YOUR TIME IS UP. The scoring machine may count extraneous marks as wrong answers. THE TOEFL BULLETIN STATES THAT YOU MAY NOT MARK IN YOUR TEST BOOK.

By using this overall approach, you are bound to achieve your best possible score.

PART II: Analysis of Exam Areas

This section is designed to introduce you to each TOEFL area by carefully reviewing the

1. Ability Tested
2. Basic Skills Necessary
3. Directions
4. Suggested Approach with Samples

This section features the PATTERNED PLAN OF ATTACK for each subject area and emphasizes important test-taking techniques and strategies and how to apply them to a variety of problem types.

SECTION 1: LISTENING COMPREHENSION

The Listening Comprehension section is always first in the examination and it is in three parts. It typically lasts 30 to 35 minutes and contains 50 questions.

Ability Tested

This section tests your ability to understand and interpret *spoken* English.

Basic Skills Necessary

It is necessary to have a good "ear" for English, which can only be obtained with a great deal of practice. You must be able to distinguish between words that sound similar and be able to comprehend entire sentences, not just single words or phrases. Notetaking, underlining, and crossing out in the test book are *not allowed*. You must be able to listen only and then choose your answer.

PART A

DIRECTIONS

In Part A, you will hear short conversations between two speakers. At the end of each conversation, a third voice will ask a question about what was said. The question will be *spoken* just one time. After you hear a conversation and the question about it, read the four possible answers and decide which one would be the best answer to the question you have heard. Then, on your answer sheet, find the number of the problem and mark your answer.

Suggested Approach with Samples

You will always hear three different voices in this section, generally, but not always, alternating between male and female. *Sample:*

You will hear: Man: I don't feel like going out tonight.
                            Let's just stay home instead.
                Woman: OK, but I was looking forward to
                            seeing that new movie about Alca-
                            traz.
                Third Voice: What does the man want to do
                            tonight?

You will read: (A) go to a party
                            (B) stay home
                            (C) see a movie
                            (D) sleep

Answer (B) means most nearly the same as what the man said he
would like to do. Therefore, you should choose answer (B).

Remember that it is best to glance at the four possible answers
before you hear the conversation. In this way, you can often listen
specifically for the particular information that you know will answer
the question. Several types of questions often appear in this section.

1. What does _____ mean?
2. What does _____ imply about _____?
3. What will _____ probably do?
4. What are the speakers talking about?
5. What did _____ suggest that _____ do?
6. What does _____ think about _____?
7. What had _____ assumed about _____?

Sample: You see that the answers to a question are

   (A) Ill   (B) Well   (C) Exhausted   (D) Angry

You know that the question will be about how someone feels, and
you should listen for that.

PART B

DIRECTIONS

In Part B, you will hear longer conversations. After each
conversation, you will be asked some questions. The conversations
and questions will be *spoken* just one time. They will not be written

out for you, so you will have to listen carefully in order to understand and remember what the speaker says.

When you hear a question, read the four possible answers in your test book and decide which one would be the best answer to the question you have heard. Then, on your answer sheet, find the number of the problem and fill in the space that corresponds to the letter of the answer you have chosen.

Suggested Approach with Samples

You will always hear three different voices in this section, generally, but not always, alternating between male and female. The third voice will ask you several questions after each conversation. *Sample:*

You will hear:	Woman:	This is my first semester in Orange Lake. What is there to do for recreation in the summer?
	Man:	It seems that I'm always studying at the unversity. But when I do get some time, my friends and I play tennis, go swimming and boating at the lake, or picnic at the park in the Ocala National Forest.
	Woman:	Is the park very far from here?
	Man:	It's about a half an hour away and easy to find. It's right on the state highway.
	Woman:	Is there a restaurant in the park?
	Man:	There's a snack bar, but we usually take a cooler of sandwiches, fruit, and soft drinks, and eat in the picnic area.
	Woman:	What else is there to do in the park?
	Man:	You can swim in the enclosed area, or go tubing in the river that runs through the park, or you can take a tour through the underground caves located at the far end of the park.

Woman:	What's tubing?
Man:	Oh. Sorry. Everybody around here knows what it is. Remember how old car and truck tires had rubber inner tubes inside? Well you sit in one of those and just float downstream. There's a tram at the bottom to take you back up. The water is quite cold, but you get used to it.
Woman:	What does it cost?
Man:	It's only about $4 to get into the park, and everything else is free, except if you don't have a tube, you need to rent one. They're only a couple of dollars.
Woman:	That really sounds great to me.
Third Voice:	Which of the following activities is NOT mentioned as being available in the national park?

You will read:

(A) Tubing.
(B) Swimming.
(C) Volleyball.
(D) Picnicking.

Answer (C) was not mentioned in the conversation as being an activity available in the national park. Therefore, you should choose answer (C). More questions will follow.

You will hear: Third Voice: Which of the following is true about tubing at the park?

You will read:

(A) It is done in a plugged up old tire.
(B) The water is chilly.
(C) The water flows upstream.
(D) You must be prepared to walk back up the river with your inner tube.

From the conversation you learn that an inner tube is used for tubing, not a plugged up old tire (A), you know water does not flow upstream (C), and you learn that a tram can take you back upstream so you don't have to walk (D). The answer is (B), the water is chilly, but the man says you get used to it.

Again, it is best to glance at the possible answer choices before you hear the reading in order to get an indication of the topic of the reading. Before the conversation, the speaker will tell you which question numbers will refer to that particular selection.

Remember not to take notes or write in your test booklet in any way during the Listening Comprehension section.

PART C

DIRECTIONS

In Part C, you will hear several talks. After each talk, you will be asked some questions. The talks and questions will be *spoken* just one time. They will not be written out for you, so you will have to listen carefully in order to understand and remember what the speaker says.

When you hear a question, read the four possible answers in your test book and decide which one would be the best answer to the question you have heard. Then, on your answer sheet, find the number of the problem and fill in the space that corresponds to the letter of the answer you have chosen.

Suggested Approach with Samples

In this section you will hear talks, lectures, announcements, explanations, and news stories on various subjects. One speaker will deliver the talk and another speaker will ask a number of questions about what was said. *Sample:*

You will hear: Woman: Welcome, everyone! I'm glad to see you all here this afternoon. Cross-country skiing is a fabulous sport for mind, body, and spirit. It gets you outdoors in the wintertime in beautiful places like this, and the repetitive rhythm washes away your worries. The hills and turns—when you become more advanced students—will provide excitement, and your arm, back, and leg movements will give you a top-notch cardiovascular workout.

Today we're going to go out on a short trail where you will learn the basic diagonal stride, the step-turn, and how to stop. First, the basic diagonal stride. This is a lot like walking, so that's what we'll do, simply walk on our skis. Lean a bit forward, slide your left ski forward, and give a little push downward and backward on your right pole. Now slide your right ski forward and give a little push with your left pole. Your arms should alternate with your leg movements, just as when you're striding down a sidewalk with your arms swinging. As you become more sure of your balance, we'll go a tiny bit faster and you'll see how your weight will come still farther forward. You'll begin to kick off of your skis to gain more glide, using the friction provided by the wax that we put under your foot. For now, let's just travel along the trail for a few hundred yards, so you can get the feel of moving around on your skis.

Man: Where did this talk most likely take place?

You will read:

    (A) On a frozen lake.
    (B) At a ski resort.
    (C) At a health spa.
    (D) In a national forest.

While any of the answers might be true, the place where this skiing lesson is being delivered is *most likely* at a ski resort (B). Other questions will follow. Here is one more sample question.

You will hear: Man: What does wax do for cross-country skiing?

You will read:

    (A) It provides friction.
    (B) It provides glide.
    (C) It makes the ski surface shiny.
    (D) It prevents falling.

The ski instructor never mentioned shiny skis or falling down, so eliminate (C) and (D). You'll have to remember that wax on the ski beneath the skier's foot provided friction to kick against so the skier could gain more glide—after the kick. Therefore, the answer is (A), provides friction.

Again, it is best to glance at the possible answer choices before you hear the reading in order to get an indication of the topic of the reading. Before the talk, the speaker will tell you which question numbers will refer to that particular talk.

Remember not to take notes or write in your test booklet in any way during the Listening Comprehension section.

HOW TO PREPARE FOR THE LISTENING COMPREHENSION SECTION

Besides the methods mentioned here, there is actually no way to "study" for listening comprehension. It is necessary to tune your ear to English. Speak to native English speakers as often as possible. Also you should

1. Watch news and weather reports on television or listen to them on the radio.

2. Make telephone calls to recorded messages such as weather reports, time of day, or movie theaters.
3. Attend lectures at your school or in your city.
4. Make use of the language laboratory if your school has one.

Practice for the Listening Comprehension section is included in this guide in the practice tests. Use the cassettes included with this book to take practice tests 1 through 6. All scripts are included in Part V. Remember the suggestions listed here when you take these tests. If you miss a question, ALWAYS study the script. Look up any words you don't know and study grammatical expressions that have caused you trouble.

A PATTERNED PLAN OF ATTACK

Listening Comprehension

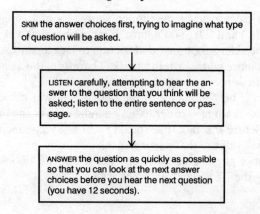

SKIM the answer choices first, trying to imagine what type of question will be asked.

LISTEN carefully, attempting to hear the answer to the question that you think will be asked; listen to the entire sentence or passage.

ANSWER the question as quickly as possible so that you can look at the next answer choices before you hear the next question (you have 12 seconds).

SECTION 2: STRUCTURE AND WRITTEN EXPRESSION

The structure and written expression section includes two question types, Part A, Structure, and Part B, Written Expression. This section typically lasts 25 minutes and contains approximately 40 questions.

Ability Tested

The grammar section of the TOEFL tests your ability to recognize *formal written English*. Many things that are acceptable in spoken English are *not* acceptable in formal written English. You must choose the most economical, mature, and correct way of stating each sentence in this section.

Basic Skills Necessary

You need to know correct grammar well enough that an error will be immediately evident.

PART A

DIRECTIONS

This section is designed to measure your ability to recognize language that is appropriate for standard written English. There are two types of questions in this section, with special directions for each type. Questions 1–15 are incomplete sentences. Beneath each sentence you will see four words or phrases, marked (A), (B), (C), and (D). Choose the *one* word or phrase that best completes the sentence. Then, on your answer sheet, find the number of the question and fill in the space that corresponds to the letter of the answer you have chosen. Fill in the space so that the letter inside the oval cannot be seen.

Suggested Approach with Samples

• Notice that the directions call for recognition of language that is appropriate for standard WRITTEN English.
• Notice that you are to choose the ONE word or phrase that BEST completes the sentence. There might be other possible ways of completing the sentence, but only one way is the *best* way.

For Part A questions you should

1. Read the entire sentence, inserting the (A) answer.
2. If that is not correct, try to discover WHY it is incorrect.
3. If you can discover why (A) is incorrect, proceed to answer (B), (C), and (D).
4. If you still are not sure, try to remember a formula for the sentence.
5. If you cannot find the correct answer, eliminate the obviously incorrect answers and GUESS.

Samples:

1. I wish you would tell me _____.
   (A) who is being lived next door
   (B) who does live in the next door
   (C) who lives next door
   (D) who next door was living

When you read the sentence with (A), you can immediately eliminate that answer because *is being lived* is an impossible verbal structure when used with *who*. A *life* may be lived. A *person* may not. *Live* usually does not take a complement and therefore cannot be passive. (B) can also be eliminated because *does* and *in the* are not necessary in this sentence. You will realize by now that the required phrase must be [subject + verb + (complement) + (modifier)]. (D) is incorrect because it does not follow that order. (C) is correct (it has no complement because *live* does not require a complement).

2. During the Daytona 500, the lead car _____, leaving the others far behind.
   (A) forwarded rapidly
   (B) advanced rapidly
   (C) advanced forward quickly
   (D) advanced in a rapidly manner

When you read the sentence with (A), you see that a verb is necessary after *the lead car,* but you know that *forward* is not a verb here. Thus (A) is incorrect. If you realize that *advanced* in (B) is a suitable verb for the sentence, and it is correctly modified by the adverb *rapidly,* you will not have to look further for the correct answer. If you do not realize that (B) is correct and go on to (C), you will see that *advanced forward* is redundant (that is, *advance* means *move forward,* so it is not necessary to use the two words together). (D) is also incorrect because *rapidly* is used in the position of an adjective.

Be sure to review the additional strategies for elimination of incorrect answers in style questions beginning on page 229.

PART B

DIRECTIONS

In questions 16–40, each sentence has four underlined words or phrases. The four underlined parts of the sentence are marked (A), (B), (C), and (D). Identify the *one* underlined word or phrase that must be changed in order for the sentence to be correct. Then, on your answer sheet, find the number of the question and fill in the space that corresponds to the letter of the answer you have chosen.

Suggested Approach with Samples

• Again, remember that you are looking for correct WRITTEN English.
• Notice that you are looking for the one word or phrase that is INCORRECT, and thus must be changed to make the sentence correct.

For Part B questions you should

1. Read the entire sentence.
2. If an error does not become immediately evident, remember the formulas from this book and be sure that portions of the sentence fit the correct pattern.

Samples:

1. In the United States, there are much holidays throughout
      A   B   C

   the year.
   D

You should immediately notice that *much* modifies non-count nouns and that *holidays* is a count noun. Therefore, *much* is incorrect, and *many* would be correct. Therefore, (C) is the correct answer.

2. Tomatoes grows all year long in Florida.
      A   B   C   D

If you made a hasty decision before reading the entire sentence, you could choose answer (A) assuming that it must be singular because the verb *grows* is singular. But you see by the context of the entire sentence that the sentence is not speaking of a single tomato, and therefore (A) is not the correct answer. (B), then, is incorrect because it is a singular verb; it should be *grow*.

A PATTERNED PLAN OF ATTACK

Structure and Written Expression

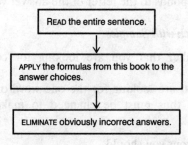

READ the entire sentence.

↓

APPLY the formulas from this book to the answer choices.

↓

ELIMINATE obviously incorrect answers.

SECTION 3: READING COMPREHENSION

This section contains reading passages followed by questions based on the reading. The section contains approximately 50 questions, and you will have 55 minutes to complete it.

Ability Tested

The Reading Comprehension section tests your ability to understand, interpret, and analyze reading passages on a variety of topics. The TOEFL stresses reading passages that are typical of those you will read in colleges and universities. This section also tests your knowledge of English vocabulary. You must find synonyms for selected words from the passage among the four answer choices that you are given.

Basic Skills Necessary

You must be able to read a passage containing rather complicated constructions and vocabulary and answer questions based on what you have read. This section requires a strong college-level vocabulary. A strong vocabulary cannot be developed instantly. It grows over a long period of time spent reading widely and learning new words. Knowing the meanings of prefixes, suffixes, and roots will help you to derive word meanings on the test.

DIRECTIONS

In this section, you will read a number of passages. Each one is followed by approximately ten questions about it. For questions 1–50, choose the *one* best answer, (A), (B), (C), or (D), to each question. Then, find the number of the question on your answer sheet, and fill in the space that corresponds to the letter of the answer you have chosen. Answer all of the questions following a passage on the basis of what is *stated* or *implied* in that passage.

Suggested Approach with Samples

• Be sure to answer questions based on what is *stated* or *implied* in the passage, even if it is a subject that you know a great deal about.

• Skim the questions first, noting words that give you clues about what to look for when you read the passage. Do not spend more than a few seconds doing this.

• Skim the passage, reading only the first sentence of each paragraph.

• Read the passage, noting main points, important conclusions, names, definitions, places, and numbers.

• For vocabulary questions, remember that you are looking for the word that means most nearly the same as the underlined word *as it is used in the reading passage.* Some words may have several definitions, but only one will fit the meaning as it is used in the passage.

• Read the sentences near the sentence containing the vocabulary word to find contextual clues to help you understand the meaning of the word.

• Learn prefixes, suffixes, and roots, and use them for clues on vocabulary questions. The answer choices will generally be the same part of speech as the word tested, but it is still beneficial to know whether it is a noun, verb, adjective, or adverb.

Samples

The majority of the reading selections will be factual readings from science, history, linguistics, or other areas. It is possible that a reading will show up on the TOEFL that you believe you know everything about. Perhaps something from your major field of study will appear. If this happens, you are lucky, but do not assume that you do not have to read it. Some information may not be exactly the same in the reading as you have supposed. Before you read anything, *look at the questions.* Do not spend time looking at all of the answer choices; simply glance at the answer choices so that you have an idea of what to look for. Do not try to look at an answer choice and then skim the reading looking for the answer. Generally, the words in the question and in the reading itself will not be the same and you will lose valuable time using this method. Look at the following example (remember to glance at the questions first).

Questions 1 through 4 are based on the following reading.

Athens and Sparta were the two most advanced Greek cities of the Hellenic period (750–338 B.C.). Both had a city-state type of government, and both took slaves from the peoples they conquered. However, the differences outweigh
(5) the similarities in these two ancient civilizations. Sparta was hostile, warlike (constantly fighting the neighboring cities), and military, while Athens catered more towards the democratic and cultural way of life. The latter city left its mark in the fields of art, literature, philosophy, and science, while
(10) the former passed on its totalitarianism and superior military traditions. The present system of a well-rounded education followed in the United States is based on the ancient Athenian idea. The Spartan system, on the other hand, was concerned only with military education.

1. All of the following are true EXCEPT
   (A) both cities had city-state types of government
   (B) both cities took slaves
   (C) both cities were advanced, but in different areas
   (D) both cities developed a well-rounded education

2. Which of the following was NOT mentioned as part of Athens' cultural heritage?
   (A) Totalitarianism   (C) Art
   (B) Well-rounded education   (D) Philosophy

3. Which of the following was borrowed from Athens by the United States?
   (A) Well-rounded education   (C) Totalitarianism
   (B) Military might   (D) Slavery

4. It can be inferred from this reading that
   (A) Athens and Sparta were friendly with each other
   (B) Athens was attacked by other warlike nations
   (C) Athens never fought other people
   (D) the cultural aspects of Athenian culture made a great impression on the world

Answers:

1. (D) You know from the second sentence that (A) and (B) are true. You will know from the entire reading that (C) is also true. The correct answer is (D). The reading said that Sparta was hostile and warlike, with no mention of its having a well-rounded education. The sixth sentence tells you that Athens had a rell-rounded education that had an influence on the United States.

2. (A) You must know the meanings of *the former* and *the latter*. Sentence 4 in this reading mentioned Sparta first and Athens second. Thus, if a subsequent sentence speaks of the former and the latter, the former is Sparta (the first) and the latter is Athens (the second). You will see from sentence 5 that the latter (Athens) left is mark in the fields of art and philosophy. Sentence 6 tells you that it was also important in the theory of well-rounded education. Sparta, not Athens, was involved in the idea of totalitarianism. Thus (A) is the answer as it was not mentioned as part of Athens' cultural heritage.

3. (A) This question is answered in sentence 6.

4. (D) Inference questions are difficult and appear frequently on the TOEFL. You must decide which of the answer choices you can assume to be true from the facts given in the reading selection. Again, it is important to eliminate answer choices which are obviously not correct. (A) may be true, but there is nothing in the reading selection to cause you to assume that it is. (C) is definitely not true. Sentence 2 says that both cities took slaves from the people they conquered. If they conquered people, they must have fought. (D) can be inferred from the statement in sentence 5 that the latter (Athens) *left its mark*.

Questions 5 through 9 are based on the following reading.

Finnish-born botanist William Nylander taught at the University of Helsinki for a number of years and later moved to Paris, where he lived until his death at the end of the nineteenth century. During the second half of the last
(5) century, he became a prominent figure in the field of lichenology.

Botanists from all over the world sent samples to his laboratory to be analyzed and classified. It can be said without exaggeration that four out of five lichens bear his
(10) name.

He was the first to realize the importance of using chemical reagents in the taxonomy of lichens. He selected the most common reagents used by the chemists of his time. Lichenologists all over the world still use these reagents,
(15) including tincture of iodine and hypochlorite, in their laboratories. During the first half of the twentieth century, a Japanese named Arahina added only one chemical product—P-Phenol diamines.

Nylander was also responsible for discovering that the
(20) atmosphere of big cities hindered the lichens' development and caused them to disappear. Now they are used to detect atmospheric pollution.

Nevertheless, he considered lichens to be simple plants and vehemently opposed the widely accepted modern theo-
(25) ries that lichens are a compound species formed by two discordant elements: algae and fungi.

5. Internationally renowned scientists sent lichen samples to Nylander because
   (A) he considered them to be simple plants
   (B) he used reagents to determine their use
   (C) he analyzed and classified them
   (D) he collected and preserved them

6. Which of the following is NOT true?
   (A) Nylander accepted his colleagues' theories on the composition of lichens.
   (B) Eighty percent of lichens bear Nylander's name.
   (C) Today lichens are used to detect atmospheric pollution.
   (D) Most botanists consider lichens to be a compound species.

7. All of the following are true about Nylander EXCEPT
   (A) he was the first to use chemical reagents in the taxonomy of lichens
   (B) he believed that lichens were simple plants
   (C) he was an esteemed lichenologist
   (D) he taught botany at the University of Paris

8. According to accepted nineteenth-century theories, which two elements form the composition of lichens?
   (A) Iodine and chemical reagents
   (B) Algae and fungi
   (C) Hypochlorite and iodine
   (D) Chemical reagents and atmospheric chemicals

9. How could William Nylander best be described?
   (A) Degenerate   (C) Ingenious
   (B) Domineering   (D) Anxious

Answers:

5. (C) Choice (B) is an incorrect statement because Nylander used reagents to *identify* lichens, not to determine their *use*. Choices (A), (C), and (D) are correct. Yet, only answer (C) answers the question *why* other scientists sent lichen samples to Nylander. This is explained in sentence 3. (C) is the correct answer.

6. (A) Choices (C) and (D) are true, and mentioned specifically in the reading. (B) is true because the reading says four out of five (80%) of lichens bear Nylander's name. However, (A) is not true, and is therefore the correct answer. The last paragraph states that he vehemently opposed the theories that lichens are a compound species.

7. (D) Choices (A), (B), and (C) are specifically stated in the reading. Sentence 1 says he taught at the University of Helsinki and then moved to Paris, but it does not say that he ever taught in Paris. Therefore, (D) is *not* true and is the correct answer.

8. (B) The last sentence of the reading verifies (B) as the correct answer.

9. (C) This is the correct answer because *ingenious* means *clever* or *showing great practical knowledge or intelligence.* Nylander was first to realize the importance of using chemical reagents and he discovered that atmospheric pollutions hindered the development of lichens. (A), (B), and (D) do not describe him as this reading does.

A PATTERNED PLAN OF ATTACK

Reading Comprehension

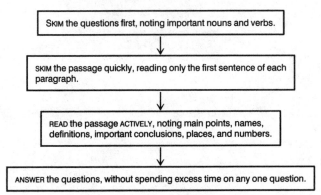

SKIM the questions first, noting important nouns and verbs.

↓

SKIM the passage quickly, reading only the first sentence of each paragraph.

↓

READ the passage ACTIVELY, noting main points, names, definitions, important conclusions, places, and numbers.

↓

ANSWER the questions, without spending excess time on any one question.

PART III: Subject Area Reviews
with
Exercises and Mini-Tests

The following pages are designed to give you an intensive review in English grammar, style in written English, problem vocabulary, and prepositions. Pace yourself. Learn a predetermined amount of material each week, depending on the study time you have available before the actual TOEFL. Do all the exercises and take all the mini-tests that follow each review section.

Be sure that you use the cross-referenced answer keys provided with each of the practice tests to refer back to this review and restudy rules and concepts that give you trouble. The table of contents and answer keys will direct you quickly to sections you need to go over again.

GRAMMAR REVIEW

1. RULES

A rule in grammar is a generalization. It is a formula that one makes to account for how a given grammatical construction *usually behaves*. A rule is *not* necessarily true in every instance. It is *generally* true. Don't be concerned if you see or hear something that does not coincide with a rule in this book.

In this guide:

Parentheses (   ) indicate optional usage when used in a rule.

Braces {   } indicate either one choice or the other.

$$\begin{Bmatrix} has \\ have \end{Bmatrix} = \text{either } have \text{ or } has$$

2. METHOD OF STUDY

The best method of improving your use of English grammar with this guide is to study the formulas and sample sentences. Then do the practice exercise at the end of each section. After each group of lessons, there is an exercise using grammatical points from the preceding explanations. If you still make errors, the practice test answer keys and the index give you the page number of the explanation to study again.

3. NORMAL SENTENCE PATTERN IN ENGLISH

subject	verb	complement	modifier
John and I	ate	a pizza	last night
We	studied	"present perfect"	last week

SUBJECT

The subject is the agent of the sentence in the active voice; it is the person or thing that performs or is responsible for the action of the sentence, and it normally precedes the verb. NOTE: *Every sentence in English must have a subject.* (In the case of commands, the subject [you] is understood.) The subject may be a single noun.

Coffee is delicious.

Milk contains calcium.

The subject may be a noun phrase. A noun phrase is a group of words ending with a noun. (It CANNOT begin with a preposition.)

The book is on the table.

That new red car is John's.

Examples of subjects:

We girls are not going to that movie.

George likes boats.

Mary, John, George, and I went to a restaurant last night.

The weather was very bad yesterday.

The chemistry professor canceled class today.

The bank closed at two o'clock.

It can act as a pronoun for a noun or can be the subject of an impersonal verb. As the subject of an impersonal verb, the pronoun is not actually used in place of a noun, but is part of an idiomatic expression.

It rains quite often here in the summer.

It is hard to believe that he is dead.

In some sentences, the true subject does not appear in normal subject position. *There* can act as a pseudo-subject and is treated like a subject when changing word order to a question. However, the true subject appears after the verb, and the number of the true subject controls the verb.

There ___was___ ___a fire___ in that building last month.
    verb (singular) *subject (singular)*

<u>Was</u> there <u>a fire</u> in that building last month?
verb   *subject*

There ___were___ ___many students___ in the room.
    verb (plural)   *subject (plural)*

<u>Were</u> there <u>many students</u> in the room?
verb   *subject*

VERB

The verb follows the subject in a declarative sentence; it generally shows the action of the sentence. NOTE: *Every sentence must have a verb.* The verb may be a single word.

John <u>drives</u> too fast.
They <u>hate</u> spinach.

The verb may be a verb phrase. A verb phrase consists of one or more auxiliaries and one main verb. The auxiliaries always precede the main verb.

John <u>is going</u> to Miami tomorrow.
    (auxiliary—*is*; main verb—*going*)

Jane <u>has been reading</u> that book.
    (auxiliaries—*has, been;* main verb—*reading*)

Examples of verbs and verb phrases:

She <u>will go</u> to Boston next week.
Jane <u>is</u> very tall.
She <u>must have gone</u> to the bank.
Joe <u>has gone</u> home.
Mary <u>is watching</u> television.
It <u>was raining</u> at six o'clock last night.

COMPLEMENT

A complement completes the verb. It is similar to the subject because it is usually a noun or noun phrase; however, it generally follows the verb when the sentence is in the active voice. NOTE: *Every sentence does not require a complement.* The complement CANNOT begin with a preposition. A complement answers the question what? or whom?

Examples of complements:

John bought a cake yesterday.	(*What* did John buy?)
Jill was driving a new car.	(*What* was Jill driving?)
He wants to drink some water.	(*What* does he want to drink?)
She saw John at the movies last night.	(*Whom* did she see at the movies?)
They called Mary yesterday.	(*Whom* did they call yesterday?)
He was smoking a cigarette.	(*What* was he smoking?)

MODIFIER

A modifier tells the time, place, or manner of the action. Very often it is a prepositional phrase. A prepositional phrase is a group of words that begins with a preposition and ends with a noun. NOTE: A modifier of time usually comes last if more than one modifier is present.

Examples of prepositional phrases:

in the morning, at the university, on the table

A modifier can also be an adverb or an adverbial phrase.

last night, hurriedly, next year, outdoors, yesterday

NOTE: *Every sentence does not require a modifier.* A modifier answers the question when? where? or how?

Examples of modifiers:

John bought a book
    at the bookstore.   (*Where* did John buy a book?)
    <small>modifier of place</small>

Jill was swimming in the pool   (*Where* was Jill swimming?)
                <small>modifier of place</small>

    yesterday .   (*When* was Jill swimming?)
    <small>modifier of time</small>

He was driving   very fast   .   (*How* was he driving?)
                <small>modifier of manner</small>

The milk is in the refrigerator.   (*Where* is the milk?)
            <small>modifier of place</small>

She drove the car
    on Main Street.   (*Where* did she drive?)
    <small>modifier of place</small>

We ate dinner
    at seven o'clock.   (*When* did we eat dinner?)
    <small>modifier of time</small>

NOTE: The modifier normally follows the complement, but not always. However, the modifier, especially when it is a prepositional phrase, usually cannot separate the verb and the complement.

Incorrect: She drove on the street the car .
                  <small>verb</small>   <small>complement</small>

Correct: She drove the car on the street.
                <small>verb</small>   <small>complement</small>

Exercise 1: Subject, Verb, Complement, and Modifier

Identify the subject, verb, complement, and modifier in each of the following sentences. Remember that not every sentence has a complement or modifier. *Examples*:

Jill / is buying / a new hat / in the store.
<small>subject   verb phrase   complement   modifier of place</small>

Betty / is shopping / downtown.
<small>subject   verb phrase   modifier of place</small>

1. George is cooking dinner tonight.
2. Henry and Marcia have visited the president.
3. We can eat lunch in this restaurant today.
4. Pat should have bought gasoline yesterday.
5. Trees grow.
6. It was raining at seven o'clock this morning.
7. She opened a checking account at the bank last week.
8. Harry is washing dishes right now.
9. She opened her book.
10. Paul, William, and Mary were watching television a few minutes ago.

4. THE NOUN PHRASE

The noun phrase is a group of words that ends with a noun. It can contain determiners (*the, a, this,* etc.), adjectives, adverbs, and nouns. It CANNOT begin with a preposition. Remember that both subjects and complements are generally noun phrases.

COUNT AND NON-COUNT NOUNS

A count noun is one that *can* be counted.

book—one book, two books, three books, . . .
student—one student, two students, three students, . . .
person—one person, two people, three people, . . .

A non-count noun is one that *cannot* be counted.

milk—you cannot say: one milk, two milks, . . .

It is possible, however, to count some non-count nouns if the substance is placed in a countable container.

glass of milk—one glass of milk, two glasses of milk, . . .

Some determiners can be used only with count or non-count nouns, while others can be used with either. Memorize the words in the following chart.

WITH COUNT NOUNS	WITH NON-COUNT NOUNS
a(n), the, some, any	the, some, any
this, that, these, those	this, that
none, one, two, three, . . .	none
many	much (usually in negatives or questions)
a lot of	a lot of
a $\left\{ \begin{matrix} \text{large} \\ \text{great} \end{matrix} \right\}$ number of	a large amount of
(a) few	(a) little
fewer . . . than	less . . . than
more . . . than	more . . . than

It is very important to know if a noun is count or non-count. Be sure that you know the plurals of irregular count nouns. The following list contains some irregular count nouns that you should know.

person–people	child–children	tooth–teeth
foot–feet	mouse–mice	man–men
woman–women		

The following list contains some non-count nouns that you should know.

sand	soap	physics	mathematics
news	mumps	air	politics
measles	information	meat	homework
food	economics	advertising*	money

*NOTE: Although *advertising* is a non-count noun, *advertisement* is a count noun. If you wish to speak of one particular advertisement, you must use this word.

There are too many advertisements during television shows.

There is too much advertising during television shows.

Some non-count nouns, such as *food, meat, money,* and *sand,* may be used as count nouns in order to indicate different types.

This is one of the foods that my doctor has forbidden me to eat.
  (indicates a particular type of food)

He studies meats.
  (for example, beef, pork, lamb, etc.)

The word *time* can be either countable or non-countable depending on the context. When it means an occasion, it is countable. When it means a number of hours, days, years, etc., it is non-countable.

We have spent too much time on this homework. (non-count)

She has been late for class six times this semester. (count)

To decide if a noun that you are not sure of is countable or non-countable, decide if you can say: *one* _____ or *a* _____. For example, you can say "one book," so it is a count noun. You cannot say "one money," so it is not a count noun. Also, of course, by the very nature of non-count nouns, a non-count noun can never be plural. Remember that, while some of the nouns in the list of non-count nouns appear to be plural because they end in -s, they are actually not plural.

Exercise 2: Count and Non-Count Nouns

Identify the following nouns as count nouns or non-count nouns according to their *usual* meaning.

television	atmosphere	food	cup
car	person	tooth	money
news	water	soap	hydrogen
geography	pencil	soup	minute

Exercise 3: Determiners

Choose the correct determiners in the following sentences.

1. He doesn't have (many/much) money.
2. I would like (a few/a little) salt on my vegetables.
3. She bought (that/those) cards last night.
4. There are (less/fewer) students in this room than in the next room.
5. There is (too much/too many) bad news on television tonight.
6. I do not want (these/this) water.
7. This is (too many/too much) information to learn.
8. A (few/little) people left early.
9. Would you like (less/fewer) coffee than this?
10. This jacket costs (too much/too many).

A AND *AN*

A or *an* can precede only singular count nouns; they mean *one*. They can be used in a general statement or to introduce a subject which has not been previously mentioned.

A baseball is round.   (general—means all baseballs)

I saw a boy in the street.   (We don't know which boy.)

An is used before words that begin with a vowel sound. *A* is used before words that begin with a consonant sound.

a book   an apple

Some words can be confusing because the spelling does not indicate the pronunciation.

a house   (begins with a consonant sound)
an hour   (begins with a vowel sound)
a university   (begins with a consonant sound)
an umbrella   (begins with a vowel sound)

The following words begin with a consonant sound and thus must *always* be preceded by *a*.

European	eulogy	euphemism	eucalyptus
house	home	heavy	half
uniform	university	universal	union

The following words begin with a vowel sound and thus must *always* be preceded by *an*.

hour	heir	herbal	honor
uncle	umbrella	unnatural	understanding

The initial sound of the word that immediately follows the indefinite article will determine whether it should be *a* or *an*.

an umbrella	a white umbrella
an hour	a whole hour

THE

The is used to indicate something that we already know about or something that is common knowledge.

The boy in the corner is my friend.	(The speaker and the listener know which boy.)
The earth is round.	(There is only one earth.)

With non-count nouns, one uses the article *the* if speaking in specific terms, but uses no article if speaking in general.

Sugar is sweet.	(general—all sugar)
The sugar on the table is from Cuba.	(specific—the sugar that is on the table)

Normally, plural count nouns, when they mean everything within a certain class, are not preceded by *the*.

Oranges are green until they ripen.   (all oranges)

Athletes should follow a well-balanced diet.   (all athletes)

Normally a proper noun is not preceded by an article unless there are several people or things with the same name and the speaker is specifying one of them.

There are three Susan Parkers in the telephone directory.

The Susan Parker that I know lives on First Avenue.

Normally words such as *breakfast, lunch, dinner, school, church, home, college,* and *work* do not use any article unless to restrict the meaning.

We ate breakfast at eight o'clock this morning.

We went to school yesterday.

Use the following generalizations as a guide for the use of the article *the*.

USE *THE* WITH	DON'T USE *THE* WITH
oceans, rivers, seas, gulfs, plural lakes the Red Sea, the Atlantic Ocean, the Persian Gulf, the Great Lakes	*singular lakes* Lake Geneva, Lake Erie
mountains the Rocky Mountains, the Andes	*mounts* Mount Vesuvius, Mount McKinley
earth, moon the earth, the moon	*planets, constellations* Venus, Mars, Earth, Orion

USE *THE* WITH	DON'T USE *THE* WITH
schools, colleges, universities when the phrase begins with school, etc. the University of Florida, the College of Arts and Sciences	*schools, colleges, universities when the phrase begins with a proper noun* Santa Fe Community College, Cooper's Art School, Stetson University
ordinal numbers before nouns the First World War, the third chapter	*cardinal numbers after nouns* World War One, chapter three
wars (except world wars) the Crimean War, the Korean War	
certain countries or groups of countries with more than one word (except Great Britain) the United States, the United Kingdom, the Central African Republic.	*countries preceded by New or an adjective such as a direction* New Zealand, South Africa, North Korea
	countries with only one word France, Sweden, Venezuela
	continents Europe, Africa, South America
	states Florida, Ohio, California
historical documents the Constitution, the Magna Carta	
ethnic groups the Indians, the Aztecs	
	sports baseball, basketball
	abstract nouns freedom, happiness
	general areas of subject matter mathematics, sociology
	holidays Christmas, Thanksgiving

Exercise 4: Articles

In the following sentences supply the articles (*a, an,* or *the*) if they are necessary. If no article is necessary, leave the space blank.

1. Jason's father bought him _____ bicycle that he had wanted for his birthday.
2. _____ Statue of Liberty was a gift of friendship from _____ France to _____ United States.
3. Rita is studying _____ English and _____ math this semester.
4. _____ judge asked _____ witness to tell _____ truth.
5. Please give me _____ cup of _____ coffee with _____ cream and _____ sugar.
6. _____ big books on _____ table are for my history class.
7. No one in _____ Spanish class knew _____ correct answer to _____ Mrs. Perez's question.
8. My _____ car is four years old, and it still runs well.
9. When you go to _____ store, please buy _____ bottle of _____ chocolate milk and _____ dozen oranges.
10. There are only _____ few seats left for _____ tonight's musical at _____ university.
11. John and Marcy went to _____ school yesterday and then studied in _____ library before returning home.
12. _____ Lake Erie is one of _____ five Great Lakes in _____ North America.
13. On our trip to _____ Spain, we crossed _____ Atlantic Ocean.
14. _____ Mount Rushmore is the site of _____ magnificent tribute to _____ four great American presidents.
15. What did you eat for _____ breakfast this morning?
16. Louie played _____ basketball and _____ baseball at _____ Boys' Club this year.
17. Rita plays _____ violin and her sister plays _____ guitar.
18. While we were in _____ Alaska, we saw _____ Eskimo village.
19. Phil can't go to _____ movies tonight because he has to write _____ essay.
20. David attended _____ Princeton University.
21. Harry has been admitted to _____ School of Medicine at _____ midwestern university.

22. Mel's grandmother is in _____ hospital, so we went to visit her _____ last night.
23. _____ political science class is taking _____ trip to _____ United Arab Emirates in _____ spring.
24. _____ Queen Elizabeth II is _____ monarch of _____ Great Britain.
25. _____ Declaration of Independence was drawn up in 1776.
26. Scientists sent _____ expedition to _____ Mars during _____ 1990s.
27. Last night there was _____ bird singing outside my house.
28. _____ chair that you are sitting in is broken.
29. _____ Civil War was fought in _____ United States between 1861 and 1865.
30. _____ Florida State University is smaller than _____ University of Florida.

OTHER

The use of the word *other* is often a cause of confusion for foreign students. Study the following formulas.

WITH COUNT NOUNS	WITH NON-COUNT NOUNS
an + *other* + singular noun (one more) another pencil = one more pencil	
the other + singular noun (last of the set) the other pencil = the last pencil present	
other + plural noun (more of the set) other pencils = some more pencils	*other* + non-count nouns (more of the set) other water = some more water
the other + plural noun (the rest of the set) the other pencils = all remaining pencils	*the other* + non-count noun (all the rest) the other water = the remaining water

NOTE: *Another* and *other* are nonspecific while *the other* is specific. If the subject is understood, one can omit the noun and keep the determiner and *other* so that *other* functions as a pronoun. If it is a plural count noun that is omitted, *other* becomes *others.* The word *other* can NEVER be plural if it is followed by a noun.

I don't want this book. Please give me <u>another</u>.
   (*another* = any other book—not specific)

I don't want this book. Please give me <u>the other</u>.
   (the *other* = the other book—specific)

This chemical is poisonous. <u>Others</u> are poisonous too.
   (*others* = other chemicals—not specific)

I don't want these books. Please give me <u>the others</u>.
   (*the others* = the other books—specific)

NOTE: Another way of substituting for the noun is to use *other* + *one* or *ones*.

I don't want this book. Please give me <u>another one</u>.
I don't want this book. Please give me <u>the other one</u>.
This chemical is poisonous. <u>Other ones</u> are poisonous too.
I don't want these books. Please give me the <u>other ones</u>.

Exercise 5: Other

Fill in the blanks with the appropriate form of *other*.

1. This pen isn't working. Please give me _____. (singular)
2. If you're still thirsty, I'll make _____ pot of coffee.
3. This dictionary has a page missing. Please give me _____. (the last one)
4. He does not need those books. He needs _____. (all the remaining)
5. There are thirty people in the room. Twenty are from Latin America and _____ are from _____ countries.
6. Six people were in the store. Two were buying meat. _____ was looking at magazines. _____ was eating a candy bar. _____ were walking around looking for more food. (notice the verbs)

7. This glass of milk is sour. _____ glass of milk is sour too.
8. The army was practicing its drills. One group was doing artillery practice. _____ was marching; _____ was at attention; and _____ was practicing combat tactics.
9. There are seven students from Japan. _____ are from Iran, and _____ are from _____ places.
10. We looked at four cars today. The first two were far too expensive, but _____ ones were reasonably priced.

NOTE: It is also possible to use the demonstrative articles *this, that, these,* and *those* as pronouns. It is correct to say *this one* and *that one;* however, it is not correct to say *these ones* or *those ones.* Simply use *these* or *those* as pronouns without adding *ones.*

This elevator is broken. That one is also broken. (*that one* = that elevator)

These glasses are dirty. Those are dirty also. (*those* = those glasses)

5. THE VERB PHRASE

As mentioned in item 3, the verb phrase consists of the main verb and any auxiliaries.

TENSES AND ASPECTS

- **simple present**—He walks to school every day.
- **simple past**—He walked to school yesterday.
- **present progressive** (continuous)—He is walking to school now.
- **past progressive** (continuous)—He was walking to school when he saw Jane.
- **present perfect**—He has walked to school several times.
- **past perfect**—He had walked to school before he hurt his foot.

Given here is a list of some of the common irregular verbs in English. It is very important that you know whether a verb is regular or irregular. You will notice that regular verbs are the same in the past tense and past participle; however, irregular verbs are very often different in these forms.

SIMPLE PRESENT TENSE	SIMPLE PAST TENSE	PAST PARTICIPLE	PRESENT PARTICIPLE
beat	beat	beaten	beating
begin	began	begun	beginning
bind	bound	bound	binding
bite	bit	bitten	biting
blow	blew	blown	blowing
break	broke	broken	breaking
bring	brought	brought	bringing
build	built	built	building
buy	bought	bought	buying
catch	caught	caught	catching
choose	chose	chosen	choosing
do	did	done	doing
drink	drank	drunk	drinking
drive	drove	driven	driving
eat	ate	eaten	eating
fall	fell	fallen	falling
feel	felt	felt	feeling
find	found	found	finding
fly	flew	flown	flying
forget	forgot	forgotten	forgetting
get	got	gotten	getting
give	gave	given	giving
hear	heard	heard	hearing
hide	hid	hidden	hiding
keep	kept	kept	keeping
know	knew	known	knowing
lead	led	led	leading
leave	left	left	leaving
lose	lost	lost	losing
make	made	made	making
meet	met	met	meeting
pay	paid	paid	paying
ride	rode	ridden	riding
run	ran	run	running
say	said	said	saying
see	saw	seen	seeing
sell	sold	sold	selling
send	sent	sent	sending
sing	sang	sung	singing

SIMPLE PRESENT TENSE	SIMPLE PAST TENSE	PAST PARTICIPLE	PRESENT PARTICIPLE
sink	sank	sunk	sinking
sit	sat	sat	sitting
speak	spoke	spoken	speaking
spend	spent	spent	spending
stand	stood	stood	standing
steal	stole	stolen	stealing
strive	strove (strived)	striven (striven)	striving
swim	swam	swum	swimming
take	took	taken	taking
teach	taught	taught	teaching
tear	tore	torn	tearing
tell	told	told	telling
think	thought	thought	thinking
throw	threw	thrown	throwing
understand	understood	understood	understanding
wear	wore	worn	wearing

You should also know that there is no change in the following verbs to indicate the different tenses.

SIMPLE PRESENT TENSE	SIMPLE PAST TENSE	PAST PARTICIPLE	PRESENT PARTICIPLE
bet	bet	bet	betting
bid	bid	bid	bidding
cost	cost	cost	costing
cut	cut	cut	cutting
fit	fit	fit	fitting
hit	hit	hit	hitting
put	put	put	putting
quit	quit	quit	quitting
read*	read	read	reading
shut	shut	shut	shutting
spread	spread	spread	spreading

*Read is prounced differently in the past tense and participle but is spelled the same.

SIMPLE PRESENT TENSE

This tense is usually not used to indicate present time. However, it is used to indicate present time (now) with the following stative verbs.

know	believe	hear	see	smell	wish
understand	hate	love	like	want	sound
have	need	appear	seem	taste	own

NOTE: The verbs listed above are almost never used in the present or past progressive (continuous), although it is possible in some cases.

Simple present is used to indicate a regular or habitual action.

John <u>walks</u> to school <u>every day</u>.

Examples of simple present tense:

They <u>understand</u> the problem <u>now</u>.	(stative verb)
Henry <u>always</u> <u>swims</u> in the evening.	(habitual action)
We <u>want</u> to leave <u>now</u>.	(stative verb)
The coffee <u>tastes</u> delicious.	(stative verb)
Mark <u>usually</u> <u>walks</u> to school.	(habitual action)
Your cough <u>sounds</u> bad.	(stative verb)

PRESENT PROGRESSIVE (CONTINUOUS)

Use the following rule to form the present progressive.

$$\text{subject} + \begin{Bmatrix} am \\ is \\ are \end{Bmatrix} + [\text{verb} + ing] \ldots$$

The present progressive is used to indicate present time (now) with all but the stative verbs listed previously.

John is eating dinner now.

It is also used to indicate future time.

We are leaving for the theater at seven o'clock.

Examples of present progressive:

The committee members are
    examining the material now.   (present time)

George is leaving for France
    tomorrow.   (future time)

Henry is walking to school
    tomorrow.   (future time)

The president is trying to
    contact his advisors now.   (present time)

The secretary is typing the
    letter now.   (present time)

We are flying to Venezuela
    next month.   (future time)

Exercise 6: Simple Present and Present Progressive

Choose either the simple present or present progressive in the following sentences.

1. Something _____ (smell) very good.
2. We _____ (eat) dinner at seven o'clock tonight.
3. He _____ (practice) the piano every day.
4. They _____ (drive) to school tomorrow.
5. I _____ (believe) you.
6. Maria _____ (have) a cold.
7. Jorge _____ (swim) right now.
8. John _____ (hate) smoke.
9. Jill always _____ (get) up at 6:00 A.M.
10. Jerry _____ (mow) the lawn now.

SIMPLE PAST TENSE

The simple past is used for a *completed* action that happened at *one specific time* in the past. The italicized words in the previous sentence are important because they show that simple past is not the same as past progressive or present perfect.

John <u>went</u> to Spain <u>last year</u>.
Bob <u>bought</u> a new bicycle <u>yesterday</u>.
Maria <u>did</u> her homework <u>last night</u>.
Mark <u>washed</u> the dishes <u>after dinner</u>.
We <u>drove</u> to the grocery store <u>this afternoon</u>.
George <u>cooked</u> dinner for his family <u>Saturday night</u>.

PAST PROGRESSIVE (CONTINUOUS)

Use the following rule to form the past progressive.

$$\text{subject} + \begin{Bmatrix} was \\ were \end{Bmatrix} + [\text{verb} + ing] \ldots$$

The past progressive is used to indicate:

• An action which was occurring in the past and was interrupted by another action. In this case, the general rule is:

when + subject$_1$ + simple past tense + subject$_2$ + past progressive . . .

OR

subject$_1$ + past progressive + *when* + subject$_2$ + simple past tense . . .

When Mark <u>came</u> home, Martha <u>was watching</u> television.

OR

Martha <u>was watching</u> television <u>when</u> Mark <u>came</u> home.

● Two actions occurring at the same time in the past. In this case, the following rules usually apply.

> subject₁ + past progressive + *while* + subject₂ + past progressive . . .

OR

> *while* + subject₁ + past progressive + subject₂ + past progressive . . .

Martha <u>was watching</u> television <u>while</u> John <u>was reading</u> a book.

OR

<u>While</u> John <u>was reading</u> a book, Martha <u>was watching</u> television.

NOTE: The following construction is also possible, but it is not as common as the preceding two.

> *while* + subject₁ + past progressive + subject₂ + simple past . . .

<u>While</u> Martha <u>was watching</u> television, John <u>read</u> a book.

● An action which was occurring at some specific time in the past.

Martha <u>was watching</u> television <u>at seven o'clock last night</u>.
What <u>were</u> you <u>doing</u> <u>at one o'clock this afternoon</u>?

Examples of past progressive:

John <u>was walking</u> to class <u>when</u> he <u>lost</u> his pen.
The student <u>was reading</u> <u>while</u> the professor <u>was speaking</u>.
George <u>was watching</u> television <u>when</u> his brother <u>called</u>.

Henry was eating a snack at midnight last night.

When Mary came home, her husband was cooking dinner.

Mark was driving on Main Street when his car broke down.

Exercise 7: *Simple Past Tense and Past Progressive*

Use either the simple past tense or the past progressive in the following sentences as appropriate.

1. Gene _____ (eat) dinner when his friend called.
2. While Maria was cleaning the apartment, her husband _____ (sleep).
3. At three o'clock this morning, Eleanor _____ (study).
4. When Mark arrived, the Johnsons _____ (have) dinner, but they stopped in order to talk to him.
5. John _____ (go) to France last year.
6. When the teacher _____ (enter) the room, the students were talking.
7. While Joan was writing the report, Henry _____ (look) for more information.
8. We _____ (see) this movie last night.
9. At one time, Mr. Roberts _____ (own) this building.
10. Jose _____ (write) a letter to his family when his pencil _____ (break).

PRESENT PERFECT

Use the following rule to form the present perfect.

subject + $\begin{Bmatrix} has \\ have \end{Bmatrix}$ + [verb in past participle] . . .

The present perfect is used to indicate:

- An action that happened at an indefinite time in the past.

  John has traveled around the world. (We don't known when.)

- An action that happened more than once in the past.

  George <u>has seen</u> this movie <u>three times</u>.

- An action that began in the past and is still occurring in the present.

  John <u>has lived</u> in the same house <u>for twenty years</u>. (He still lives there.)

OR

  John <u>has lived</u> in the same house <u>since 1975</u>. (He still lives there.)

If it is now 1995:

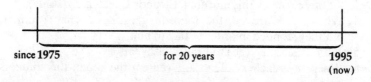

FOR/SINCE

Use *for* + duration of time: *for five hours, for thirty years, for ten minutes.* Use *since* + beginning time: *since 1975, since five o'clock, since January.*

YET/ALREADY

The adverbs *yet* and *already* are used to indicate that something has happened (or hasn't happened) at an unspecified time in the past. These adverbs are often used with the present perfect.

> *already*—affirmative sentences
> *yet*—negative sentences and questions

Note: *Already* usually appears between the auxiliary and the main verb; however, it can appear at the beginning or end of the sentence. *Yet* appears at the end of the sentence.

> subject + $\begin{Bmatrix} has \\ have \end{Bmatrix}$ + *already* + [verb in past participle] . . .

> subject + $\begin{Bmatrix} has \\ have \end{Bmatrix}$ + *not* + [verb in past participle] . . . + *yet* . . .

Examples of *yet* and *already*:

We have already written our reports.

We haven't written our reports yet.

Gabriel has already read the entire book.

The president hasn't decided what to do yet.

Sam has already recorded the results of the experiment.

Maria hasn't called her parents yet.

NOTE: Another option with the use of *yet* is sometimes possible. In this case, the verb is positive and the adverb *yet* does not appear at the end of the sentence.

> subject + $\begin{Bmatrix} has \\ have \end{Bmatrix}$ + *yet* + [verb in infinitive] . . .

John has yet to learn the material. = John hasn't learned the material yet.

We have yet to decide what to do with the money. = We haven't decided what to do with the money yet.

This use of *yet* should not be confused with the coordinating conjunction *yet*, which means *but*.

I don't have the money, yet I really need the computer.

My neighbors never have the time, yet they always want to do something on Saturday nights.

PRESENT PERFECT PROGRESSIVE (CONTINUOUS)

For an action that began in the past and is still occurring in the present (present perfect rules, third item), it is also possible to use the present perfect progressive (continuous). Use the following rule to form this aspect.

$$\text{subject} + \begin{Bmatrix} has \\ have \end{Bmatrix} + been + [\text{verb} + ing] \ldots$$

John has been living in the same house for twenty years. = John has lived in the same house for twenty years.

Examples of present perfect:

Jorge has already walked to school.
(indefinite time)
He has been to California three times.
(more than once)
Mary has seen this movie before.
(indefinite time)
They have been at home all day.
(not yet completed)
We haven't gone to the store yet.
(indefinite time)
John has worked in Washington for three years.

OR

John has been working in Washington for three years.
(not yet completed)

Exercise 8: Present Perfect and Simple Past

Use either the present perfect or the simple past in the following sentences.

1. John _____ (write) his report last night.
2. Bob _____ (see) this movie before.
3. Jorge _____ (read) the newspaper already.
4. Mr. Johnson _____ (work) in the same place for thirty-five years, and he is not planning to retire yet.
5. We _____ (begin; negative) to study for the test yet.
6. George _____ (go) to the store at ten o'clock this morning.
7. Joan _____ (travel) around the world.
8. Betty _____ (write) a letter last night.
9. Guillermo _____ (call) his employer yesterday.
10. We _____ (see; negative) this movie yet.

PAST PERFECT

Use the following rule to form the past perfect.

subject + *had* + [verb in past participle] . . .

The past perfect is used to indicate:

• An action that happened before another action in the past; there usually are two actions in the sentence.

John <u>had gone</u> to the store <u>before</u> he <u>went</u> home.
    1st action   *2nd action*

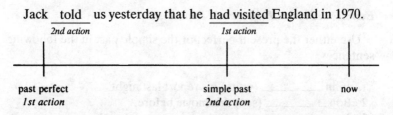

Jack told us yesterday that he had visited England in 1970.

The past perfect is usually used with *before, after,* or *when.* Study the following formulas.

> subject + past perfect + *before* + subject + simple past tense

John had gone to the store before he went home.

> subject + simple past tense + *after* + subject + past perfect

John went home after he had gone to the store.

> *before* + subject + simple past tense + subject + past perfect

Before John went home, he had gone to the store.

> *after* + subject + past perfect + subject + simple past tense

After John had gone to the store, he went home.

NOTE: The adverb *when* can be used in place of *before* or *after* in any of these four formulas without change in meaning. We still know which action happened first because of the use of past perfect.

• A state which continued for a time in the past, but stopped before now. Note that there is no connection with the present.

Abdu <u>had lived</u> in New York <u>for ten years</u> <u>before</u> he <u>moved</u> to California.

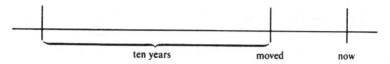

ten years   moved   now

PAST PERFECT PROGRESSIVE (CONTINUOUS)

This past perfect concept can also be conveyed by the past perfect progressive (continuous). Study the following rule.

> subject + *had* + *been* + [verb + *ing*] . . .

Abdu <u>had been living</u> in New York <u>for ten years</u> <u>before</u> he <u>moved</u> to California.

Examples of past perfect:

The professor <u>had reviewed</u> the material <u>before</u> he <u>gave</u> the quiz.

<u>After</u> Henry <u>had visited</u> Puerto Rico, he <u>went</u> to St. Thomas.

<u>Before</u> Ali <u>went</u> to sleep, he <u>had called</u> his family.

George <u>had worked</u> at the university <u>for forty-five years</u> <u>before</u> he <u>retired</u>.

OR

George <u>had been working</u> at the university <u>for forty-five years</u> <u>before</u> he <u>retired</u>.

<u>After</u> the committee members <u>had considered</u> the consequences, they <u>voted</u> on the proposal.

The doctor <u>had examined</u> the patient thoroughly <u>before</u> he <u>prescribed</u> the medication.

Exercise 9: Past Perfect and Simple Past

Supply the past perfect or simple past in the following sentences.

1. The policeman read the suspect his rights after he _____ (arrest) him.
2. After John _____ (wash) his clothes, he began to study.
3. George _____ (wait) for one hour before the bus came.
4. Maria _____ (enter) the university after she had graduated from the community college.
5. Jeannette _____ (wash) the pipettes after she had completed the experiment.
6. Jane sent a letter to her university after she _____ (receive) her scholarship check.
7. After the stewardesses had served lunch to the passengers, they _____ (sit) down.
8. The car _____ (flip) ten times before it landed on its roof.
9. We corrected our papers after we _____ (take) the quiz.
10. John _____ (live) in Miami for one year when his parents came to visit.

6. SUBJECT-VERB AGREEMENT

Remember that the subject and verb in a sentence must agree in person and number.

The <u>elevator</u> <u>works</u> very well.   The <u>elevators</u> <u>work</u> very well.
    singular   *singular*   *plural*   *plural*

SUBJECT SEPARATED FROM THE VERB

When taking the TOEFL, you must always check the subject and verb to be sure they agree. However, sometimes it is difficult to decide exactly what the subject is if the subject and verb are separated.

<u>The boys</u> in the room <u>are studying</u>.
   plural   *plural*

Very often, if the subject and verb are separated, they will be separated by a prepositional phrase. The prepositional phrase has no effect on the verb.

---

subject + [prepositional phrase] + verb

The study of languages is very interesting.
singular subject *singular verb*

Several theories on this subject have been proposed.
plural subject *plural verb*

The view of these disciplines varies from time to time.
singular subject *singular verb*

The danger of forest fires is not to be taken lightly.
singular subject *singular verb*

The effects of that crime are likely to be devastating.
plural subject *plural verb*

The fear of rape and robbery has caused many people to flee
singular subject *singular verb*

the cities.

The following expressions also have no effect on the verb.

| together with | along with |
| accompanied by | as well as |

The actress, along with her manager and some friends,
singular subject

is going to a party tonight.
singular verb

<u>Mr. Robbins</u>, accompanied by his wife and children,

<small>*singular subject*</small>

<u>is arriving</u> tonight.

<small>*singular verb*</small>

NOTE: If the conjunction *and* is used instead of one of these phrases, the verb would then be plural.

<u>The actress and her manager</u> <u>are going</u> to a party tonight.

<small>*plural subject*</small>　　　　　　　　<small>*plural verb*</small>

Exercise 10: Subject-Verb Agreement

Choose the correct form of the verb in parentheses in the following sentences.

1. John, along with twenty friends, (is/are) planning a party.
2. The picture of the soldiers (bring/brings) back many memories.
3. The quality of these recordings (is/are) not very good.
4. If the duties of these officers (isn't/aren't) reduced, there will not be enough time to finish the project.
5. The effects of cigarette smoking (have/has) been proven to be extremely harmful.
6. The use of credit cards in place of cash (have/has) increased rapidly in recent years.
7. Advertisements on television (is/are) becoming more competitive than ever before.
8. Living expenses in this country, as well as in many others, (is/are) at an all-time high.
9. Mr. Jones, accompanied by several members of the committee, (have/has) proposed some changes of the rules.
10. The levels of intoxication (vary/varies) from subject to subject.

WORDS THAT ALWAYS TAKE SINGULAR VERBS
AND PRONOUNS

Some words are often confused by students as being plural. The following words must be followed by singular verbs and pronouns in formal written English.

any +
  singular noun
anybody
anyone
anything
	no +
	  singular noun
	nobody
	no one
	nothing
		some +
		  singular noun
		somebody
		someone
		something

every + singular noun everybody everyone everything	each + singular noun either* neither*	

Either and *neither* are singular if they are not used with *or* and *nor*.

Everybody who has not purchased a ticket should be in this line.

Something was under the house.

If either of you takes a vacation now, we will not be able to finish the work.

Anybody who has lost his ticket should report to the desk. (note the singular pronoun)

No problem is harder to solve than this one.

Nobody works harder than John does.

NONE/NO

None can take either a singular or plural verb, depending on the noun which follows it.

none + of the + non-count noun + singular verb

None of the counterfeit <u>money</u> <u>has</u> been found.

> *none + of the +* plural count noun + plural verb

None of the <u>students</u> <u>have</u> finished the exam yet.

No can take either a singular or plural verb depending on the noun which follows it.

> $no + \begin{Bmatrix} \text{singular noun} \\ \text{non-count noun} \end{Bmatrix} +$ singular verb

No <u>example</u> <u>is</u> relevant to this case.

> *no* + plural noun + plural verb

No <u>examples</u> <u>are</u> relevant to this case.

EITHER/NEITHER

When *either* and *neither* are followed by *or* and *nor,* the verb may be singular or plural, depending on whether the noun following *or* and *nor* is singular or plural. If *or* or *nor* appears alone, the same rule applies. Study the following formulas.

> $\begin{Bmatrix} neither \\ either \end{Bmatrix} +$ noun $+ \begin{Bmatrix} nor \\ or \end{Bmatrix} +$ plural noun + plural verb

Neither John nor his friends are going to the beach today.
plural noun   plural verb

Either John or his friends are going to the beach today.
plural noun   plural verb

$$\begin{Bmatrix} neither \\ either \end{Bmatrix} + \text{noun} + \begin{Bmatrix} nor \\ or \end{Bmatrix} + \text{singular noun} + \text{singular verb}$$

Neither John nor   Bill   is going to the beach today.
singular noun singular verb

Either John or   Bill   is going to the beach today.
singular subject singular verb

Examples:

Neither John nor Jane is going to class today.
singular   singular

Neither Maria nor her friends are going to class today.
plural   plural

John or George is bringing the car.
singular   singular

Neither the boys nor Carmen has seen this movie before.
singular   singular

Neither the director nor the secretary wants to leave yet.
singular   singular

GERUNDS AS SUBJECTS

If a sentence begins with [verb + *ing*] (gerund), the verb must also be singular.

Knowing her has made him what he is.

Dieting is very popular today.

Not studying has caused him many problems.

Washing with a special cream is recommended for scalp infections.

Being cordial is one of his greatest assets.

Writing many letters makes her happy.

COLLECTIVE NOUNS

Also many words indicating a number of people or animals are singular. The following nouns are *usually singular*. In some cases they are plural if the sentence indicates that the individual members are acting separately.

Congress	family	group	committee	class
organization	team	army	club	crowd
government	jury	majority*	minority	public

Majority can be singular or plural. If it is alone it is usually singular; if it is followed by a plural noun, it is usually plural.

The majority believes that we are in no danger.

The majority of the students believe him to be innocent.

Examples of collective nouns:

The committee has met, and it has rejected the proposal.

The family was elated by the news.

The crowd was wild with excitement.

Congress has initiated a new plan to combat inflation.

The organization has lost many members this year.
Our team is going to win the game.

The following nouns are used to indicate groups of certain animals. It is not necessary to learn the nouns; however, they mean the same as *group* and thus are considered singular.

flock of birds, sheep   school of fish
herd of cattle   pride of lions
pack of dogs

The flock of birds is circling overhead.
The herd of cattle is breaking away.
A school of fish is being attacked by sharks.

Collective nouns indicating time, money, and measurements used as a whole are singular.

Twenty-five dollars is too much to pay for that shirt.
Fifty minutes isn't enough time to finish this test.
Twenty dollars is all I can afford to pay for that recorder.
Two miles is too much to run in one day.

A NUMBER OF / THE NUMBER OF

a number of + plural noun + plural verb . . .

the number of + plural noun + singular verb . . .

A number of students are going to the class picnic. (*a number of* = many)
The number of days in a week is seven.

A number of the applicants have already been interviewed.

The number of residents who have been questioned on this matter is quite small.

NOUNS THAT ARE ALWAYS PLURAL

The following nouns are always considered plural. They cannot be singular. In order to speak of them as singular, one must say "a pair of _____."

scissors	shorts	pants	jeans	tongs
trousers	eyeglasses	pliers	tweezers	

The pants are in the drawer.

A pair of pants is in the drawer.

The pliers were on the table.

The pair of pliers was on the table.

These scissors are dull.

This pair of scissors is dull.

THERE IS/THERE ARE

Remember that with sentences beginning with the existential *there*, the subject is actually after the verb.

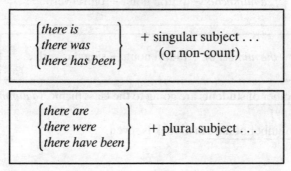

There is a storm approaching.
singular   singular

There have been a number of telephone calls today.
plural   plural

There was an accident last night.
singular   singular

There were too many people at the party.
plural   plural

There has been an increase in the importation of foreign cars.
singular   singular

There was water on the floor where he fell.
singular   non-count

Exercise 11: Subject-Verb Agreement

Choose the correct form of the verb in the following sentences.

1. Neither Bill nor Mary (is/are) going to the play tonight.
2. Anything (is/are) better than going to another movie tonight.
3. Skating (is/are) becoming more popular every day.
4. A number of reporters (was/were) at the conference yesterday.
5. Everybody who (has/have) a fever must go home immediately.
6. Your glasses (was/were) on the bureau last night.
7. There (was/were) some people at the meeting last night.
8. The committee (has/have) already reached a decision.
9. A pair of jeans (was/were) in the washing machine this morning.
10. Each student (has/have) answered the first three questions.
11. Either John or his wife (make/makes) breakfast each morning.
12. After she had perused the material, the secretary decided that everything (was/were) in order.
13. The crowd at the basketball game (was/were) wild with excitement.
14. A pack of wild dogs (has/have) frightened all the ducks away.
15. The jury (is/are) trying to reach a decision.
16. The army (has/have) eliminated this section of the training test.
17. The number of students who have withdrawn from class this quarter (is/are) appalling.
18. There (has/have) been too many interruptions in this class.

19. Every elementary school teacher (has/have) to take this examination.
20. Neither Jill nor her parents (has/have) seen this movie before.

7. PRONOUNS

There are five forms of pronouns in English: subject pronouns, complement pronouns (object pronouns), possessive pronouns, possessive adjectives, and reflexive pronouns.

SUBJECT PRONOUNS

Subject pronouns occur in the subject position of a sentence or after the verb *be*. Study the following list of subject pronouns.

		NOTE: Also use the subject pronoun after *than, as,* and *that*.
I	we	
you	you	
he		
she	they	
it		

<u>I</u> am going to the store.
subject

<u>We</u> have lived here for twenty years.
subject

It was <u>she</u> who called you. (after the verb *be*)

<u>She and I</u> have seen this movie before.
      subject

<u>George and I</u> would like to leave now.
       subject

<u>We students</u> are going to have a party.
       subject

NOTE: *We, you,* and *us* can be followed directly by a noun. In the above sentence *we students* makes it more clear exactly who *we* refers to.

COMPLEMENT PRONOUNS

Complement pronouns occur in complement position, whether they complement a verb or a preposition. Study the following list.

me	us
you	you
him	
her	them
it	

NOTE: *You* and *it* are the same for subject or complement position. The others are different.

They called ___us___ on the telephone.

complement

The teacher gave ___him___ a bad grade.

complement

John told ___her___ a story.

complement

The policeman was looking for ___him___ .

after preposition

To ___us___ , it seems like a good bargain.

after preposition

Mary is going to class with ___me___ .

after preposition

However, remember that many prepositions can also function as other parts of speech, like adverbs or conjunctions. Therefore, you must determine the part of speech of the word from context and not simply rely on your normal understanding of the word.

Janet will make her presentation   <u>after</u>   <u>him</u>   .

preposition   complement pronoun

Janet will make her presentation   <u>after</u>

conjunction

<u>he</u>   finishes his speech.

subject pronoun

clause

(A clause contains a subject and a verb. In the clause above, *he* is the subject and *finishes* is the verb.)

POSSESSIVE ADJECTIVES

Possessive adjectives are *not* the same as possessive pronouns. These simply modify, rather than replace, nouns; possessive pronouns replace nouns. Possessive forms indicate ownership. Study the following adjectives.

my	our
your	your
his	
her	their
its	

NOTE: Possessive adjectives are used to refer to parts of a body.

John is eating <u>his dinner</u>.
This is not <u>my book</u>.
The cat has injured <u>its foot</u>.
The boy broke <u>his arm</u> yesterday.
She forgot <u>her homework</u> this morning.
<u>My food</u> is cold.

NOTE: *Its* is not the same as *It's*. *It's* means *it is* or *it has*.

POSSESSIVE PRONOUNS

These pronouns cannot precede a noun. They are pronouns and thus replace the noun. The noun is understood from the context and is not repeated. Study the following pronouns.

NOTE: mine = *my* + noun; for example, *my book*
      yours = *your* + noun; for example, *your pen*
      hers = *her* + noun; for example, *her dress*

mine	ours
yours	yours
his	
hers	theirs
its	

NOTE: *His* and *its* are the same whether they precede a noun or not.

Examples of possessive pronouns:

This is my book.   This is mine.

Your teacher is the same as his teacher.   Yours is the same as his.

Her dress is green and my dress is red.   Hers is green and mine is red.

Our books are heavy.   Ours are heavy.

Their coats are too small.   Theirs are too small.

I forgot my homework.   I forgot mine.

REFLEXIVE PRONOUNS

These pronouns usually follow the verb and indicate that the subject is both giving and receiving the action. Study the following list.

myself	ourselves
yourself	yourselves
himself	
herself	themselves
itself	

NOTE: In the plural, the *self* changes to *selves*.

NOTE: Most forms are made by adding the suffix to the possessive adjective; however, *himself, itself,* and *themselves* are made by adding the suffix to the complement form. The forms *hisself* and *theirselves* are ALWAYS INCORRECT.

NOTE: John bought <u>him</u> a new car. (*him* = another person)

John bought <u>himself</u> a new car. (*himself* = John)

Examples of reflexive pronouns:

I washed <u>myself</u>.

He sent the letter to <u>himself</u>.

She served <u>herself</u> in the cafeteria.

We hurt <u>ourselves</u> playing football.

They were talking among <u>themselves</u>.

You can see the difference for <u>yourselves</u>.

Reflexive pronouns can also be used for emphasis. This means that the subject did the action alone. In this case, it normally follows the subject.

I <u>myself</u> believe that the proposal is good.

He <u>himself</u> set out to break the long distance flying record.

She prepared the nine-course meal <u>herself</u>.

The students <u>themselves</u> decorated the room.

You <u>yourself</u> must do this homework.

John <u>himself</u> bought these gifts.

NOTE: *by* + reflexive pronoun can also mean *alone*.

John washed the dishes <u>by himself</u> = John washed the dishes *alone*.

Exercise 12: Pronouns

Circle the correct form of the pronoun or possessive adjective in the following sentences.

1. I go to school with (he/him) every day.
2. I see (she/her/herself) at the Union every Friday.
3. She speaks to (we/us/ourselves) every morning.
4. Isn't (she/her) a nice person?
5. (He/Him) is going to New York on vacation.
6. (She/Her) and John gave the money to the boy.
7. (Yours/Your) record is scratched and (my/mine) is too.
8. I hurt (my/mine/the) leg.
9. John bought (himself/herself/hisself) a new coat.
10. (We/Us) girls are going camping over the weekend.
11. Mr. Jones cut (hisself/himself) shaving.
12. We like (our/ours) new car very much.
13. The dog bit (she/her) on the leg.
14. John (he/himself) went to the meeting.
15. You'll stick (you/your/yourself) with the pins if you are not careful.
16. Mary and (I/me) would rather go to the movies.
17. Everyone has to do (their/his) own research.
18. Just between you and (I/me), I don't like this food.
19. Monday is a holiday for (we/us) teachers.
20. (Her/Hers) car does not go as fast as (our/ours).

8. VERBS AS COMPLEMENTS

VERBS THAT ARE ALWAYS FOLLOWED BY THE INFINITIVE

Some verbs can take another verb as the complement instead of a noun. Sometimes the verb functioning as the complement must be in the infinitive (*to* + verb) and sometimes it must be in the gerund (verb + *ing*) form. The following verbs are always followed by the infinitive if the complement is a verb.

agree	attempt	claim	decide	demand
desire	expect	fail	forget	hesitate
hope	intend	learn	need	offer
plan	prepare	pretend	refuse	seem
strive	tend	want	wish	

John expects to begin studying law next semester.

Mary learned to swim when she was very young.

The budget committee decided to postpone this meeting.

The president will attempt to reduce inflation in the next four years.

The soldiers are preparing to attack the village.

Cynthia has agreed to act as a liaison between the two countries.

VERBS THAT ARE ALWAYS FOLLOWED BY THE GERUND

Other verbs must always be followed by the gerund. These verbs include:

admit	appreciate	avoid	can't help	consider
delay	deny	enjoy	finish	mind
miss	postpone	practice	quit	recall
report	resent	resist	resume	risk
suggest				

John admitted stealing the jewels.

We enjoyed seeing them again after so many years.

You shouldn't risk entering that building in its present condition.

Michael was considering buying a new car until the prices went up.

The Coast Guard <u>has reported</u> <u>seeing</u> another ship in the Florida Straits.

<u>Would</u> you <u>mind</u> <u>not smoking</u> in this office?

NOTE: These sentences are made negative by adding the negative particle *not* before the infinitive or gerund.

John <u>decided</u> <u>not to buy</u> the car.

We <u>regretted</u> <u>not going</u> to the party last night.

The following verbs can be followed by either the infinitive or the gerund with no change in meaning.

begin	can't stand	continue	dread
hate	like	love	prefer
regret	start	try	

He <u>started</u> <u>to study</u> after dinner.   OR   He <u>started</u> <u>studying</u> after dinner.

Joan <u>hates</u> <u>to ride</u> her bicycle to school.   OR   Joan <u>hates</u> <u>riding</u> her bicycle to school.

VERBS + PREPOSITIONS FOLLOWED BY THE GERUND

If a verb + preposition, adjective + preposition, noun + preposition, or preposition alone is followed directly by a verb, the verb will always be in the gerund form. The following list consists of verbs + prepositions.

approve of	be better off	count on	depend on
give up	insist on	keep on	put off
rely on	succeed in	think about	think of
worry about			

The following expressions contain the preposition *to*. The word *to* in these expressions must not be confused with the *to* in the infinitive. These verb + preposition expressions must also be followed by the gerund.

object to	look forward to	confess to

John gave up smoking because of his doctor's advice.
Mary insisted on taking the bus instead of the plane.
Fred confessed to stealing the jewels.
We are not looking forward to going back to school.
Henry is thinking of going to France in August.
You would be better off leaving now instead of tomorrow.

ADJECTIVES + PREPOSITIONS FOLLOWED BY THE GERUND

The following adjectives + prepositions are also followed by the gerund.

accustomed to intent on	afraid of interested in	capable of successful in	fond of tired of

Mitch is afraid of getting married now.
We are accustomed to sleeping late on weekends.
Jean is not capable of understanding the predicament.
Alvaro is intent on finishing school next year.
Craig is fond of dancing.
We are interested in seeing this film.

NOUNS + PREPOSITIONS FOLLOWED BY THE GERUND

The following nouns + prepositions are also followed by the gerund.

choice of	excuse for	intention of	method for
possibility of		reason for	(method of)

George has no excuse for dropping out of school.
There is a possibility of acquiring this property at a good price.
There is no reason for leaving this early.
Connie has developed a method for evaluating this problem.

Any time a preposition is followed directly by a verb, the verb will be in the gerund form.

After leaving the party, Ali drove home.
He should have stayed in New York instead of moving to Maine.

ADJECTIVES FOLLOWED BY THE INFINITIVE

The following adjectives are always followed by the infinitive form of the verb and never by the gerund.

anxious	boring	dangerous	hard
eager	easy	good	strange
pleased	prepared	ready	able*
usual	common	difficult	

*Able means the same as capable in many instances, but the grammar is very different. While able is followed by the infinitive, capable is followed by of + [verb + ing].

These students are not yet able to handle such difficult problems.
These students are not yet capable of handling such difficult problems.

Examples of adjectives followed by infinitives:

Mohammad is <u>eager</u> <u>to see</u> his family.

It is <u>dangerous</u> <u>to drive</u> in this weather.

We are <u>ready</u> <u>to leave</u> now.

It is <u>difficult</u> <u>to pass</u> this test.

It is <u>uncommon</u> <u>to find</u> such good crops in this section of the country.

Ritsuko was <u>pleased</u> <u>to be</u> admitted to the college.

Some verbs can be followed by either the infinitive or the gerund, but the meaning changes.

stop   remember   forget

John <u>stopped</u> <u>studying</u>.   (John is not going to study anymore.)

John <u>stopped</u> <u>to study</u>.   (John stopped doing something in order to study.)

Exercise 13: Verbs as Complements

Choose the correct form of the verb in parentheses in the following sentences.

1. The teacher decided (accepting/to accept) the paper.
2. They appreciate (to have/having) this information.
3. His father doesn't approve of his (going/to go) to Europe.
4. We found it very difficult (reaching/to reach) a decision.
5. Donna is interested in (to open/opening) a bar.
6. George has no intention of (to leave/leaving) the city now.
7. We are eager (to return/returning) to school in the fall.
8. You would be better off (to buy/buying) this car.
9. She refused (to accept/accepting) the gift.
10. Mary regrets (to be/being) the one to have to tell him.
11. George pretended (to be/being) sick yesterday.
12. Carlos hopes (to finish/finishing) his thesis this year.

13. They agreed (to leave/leaving) early.
14. Helen was anxious (to tell/telling) her family about her promotion.
15. We are not ready (to stop/stopping) this research at this time.
16. Henry shouldn't risk (to drive/driving) so fast.
17. He demands (to know/knowing) what is going on.
18. She is looking forward to (return/returning) to her country.
19. There is no excuse for (to leave/leaving) the room in this condition.
20. Gerald returned to his home after (to leave/leaving) the game.

PRONOUNS BEFORE THE GERUND OR INFINITIVE

In cases where the infinitive is used as a complement, any noun or pronoun directly preceding it will be in the *complement form*. Some common verbs which are followed by the infinitive and which often require an indirect object are listed here.

allow	ask	beg	convince	expect	instruct
invite	order	permit	persuade	prepare	promise
remind	urge	want			

subject + verb + complement form $\begin{Bmatrix} \text{pronoun} \\ \text{noun} \end{Bmatrix}$ + [*to* + verb] . . .

Joe asked Mary to call him when she woke up.
We ordered him to appear in court.
I urge you to reconsider your decision.
They were trying to persuade him to change his mind.
The teacher permitted them to turn their assignments in late.
You should prepare your son to take this examination.

However, before the gerund, a noun or pronoun must appear in the *possessive form*.

$$\text{subject} + \text{verb} + \begin{Bmatrix} \text{possessive form of noun} \\ \text{possessive adjective} \end{Bmatrix} + [\text{verb} + ing] \dots$$

We understand your not being able to stay longer.

He regrets her leaving.

We are looking forward to their coming next year.

We don't approve of John's buying this house.

We resent the teacher's not announcing the test sooner.

We object to their calling at this hour.

Exercise 14: Pronouns with Verbs as Complements

Choose the correct form of the pronoun in each of the following sentences.

1. Richard is expecting (us/our) to go to class tomorrow.
2. You shouldn't rely on (him/his) calling you in the morning.
3. They don't approve of (us/our) leaving early.
4. George asked (me/my) to call him last night.
5. We understand (him/his) having to leave early.
6. John resented (George/George's) losing the paper.
7. We object to (the defense attorney/the defense attorney's) calling the extra witness.
8. We are expecting (Henry/Henry's) to call us.
9. They are looking forward to (us/our) visiting them.
10. Susan regrets (John/John's) being in trouble.

9. THE VERB *NEED*

The verb *need* is followed by the infinitive only if an animate being is the subject. If an inanimate object is the subject of this verb, the verb is followed by a gerund or the verb *be* plus the past participle.

$$\text{animate being as subject} + [\text{verb in infinitive}] \dots$$

John and his brother <u>need</u> <u>to paint</u> the house.

My friend <u>needs</u> <u>to learn</u> Spanish.

He <u>will need</u> <u>to drive</u> alone tonight.

---

inanimate object as subject + $\begin{Bmatrix} \text{[verb} + ing] \\ to\ be + \text{[verb in past participle]} \end{Bmatrix} \cdots$

The grass <u>needs</u> <u>cutting</u>.   OR   The grass <u>needs</u> <u>to be cut</u>.

The television <u>needs</u> <u>repairing</u>.   OR   The television <u>needs to</u> <u>be repaired</u>.

The composition <u>needs</u> <u>rewriting</u>.   OR   The composition <u>needs</u> <u>to be rewritten</u>.

IN NEED OF

It is also possible to use the expression *in need of* in some cases instead of using *need* as a verb. Because *need* is not a verb in this case, it must be preceded by the verb *be*. Study the following rule.

---

subject + *be* + *in need of* + noun . . .

Jill <u>is</u> <u>in need of</u> <u>money</u>.   (Jill needs money.)

The roof <u>is</u> <u>in need of</u> <u>repair</u>.   (The roof needs to be repaired.)

The organization <u>was</u> <u>in need of</u> <u>volunteers</u>.   (The organization needed volunteers.)

Exercise 15: Need

Supply the correct form of the verb after *need* in each of the following sentences.

1. It's too hot and my hair needs _____ (cut).
2. The flowers need to be _____ (water).
3. James needs _____ (see) a doctor soon.

4. Mary will need ____ (make) a new dress for the party.
5. His piano needs ____ (tune).
6. You will need ____ (be) here at eight.
7. The squeaky door needs to be ____ (oil).
8. I need ____ (go) shopping this afternoon.
9. They need ____ (study) harder for that test.
10. The house needs to be ____ (paint) soon.

10. QUESTIONS

Remember that, when forming a question, one must place the auxiliary or the verb *be* before the subject. If there is no auxiliary or *be*, one must use the correct form of *do, does,* or *did*. After *do, does,* or *did*, the simple form of the verb must be used. The tense and person are shown only by this auxiliary, not by the main verb.

YES/NO QUESTIONS

These are questions for which the answer is *yes* or *no*.

$$\left\{ \begin{array}{l} \text{auxiliary} \\ be \\ do, does, did \end{array} \right\} + \text{subject} + \text{verb} \ldots$$

Is Mary going to school today?
Was Mary sick yesterday?
Have you seen this movie before?
Will the committee decide on the proposal today?
Do you want to use the telephone?
Does George like peanut butter?
Did you go to class yesterday?

INFORMATION QUESTIONS

These are questions for which the answer is more than *yes* or *no;* there must be some information in the answer. There are three different rules in this part:

• *Who* or *what* in subject questions: A subject question is one in which the *subject is unknown.*

$$\begin{Bmatrix} who \\ what \end{Bmatrix} + \text{verb} + \text{(complement)} + \text{(modifier)}$$

<u>Who</u> <u>opened</u> the door?   (*Someone* opened the door.)
<u>What</u> <u>happened</u> last night?   (*Something* happened last night.)

NOTE: It is NOT CORRECT to say: <u>Who</u> <u>did open</u> the door?
<u>What</u> <u>did happen</u> last night?

• *Whom* and *what* in complement questions: A complement question is one in which the *complement is unknown.*

$$\begin{Bmatrix} whom \\ what \end{Bmatrix} + \begin{Bmatrix} \text{auxiliary} \\ do, \ does, \ did \end{Bmatrix} + \text{subject} + \text{verb} + \text{(modifier)}$$

NOTE: Although in speech, most people use *who* rather than *whom* in these questions, in correct written English, you should use *whom* to indicate that the question word comes from the complement position.

<u>Whom</u> <u>does</u> Ahmad <u>know</u> from Venezuela? (Ahmad knows *someone* from Venezuela.)

<u>What</u> <u>did</u> George <u>buy</u> at the store? (George bought *something* at the store.)

• *When, where, how,* and *why* questions: These questions are formed the same as complement questions.

$$\begin{Bmatrix} when \\ where \\ how \\ why \end{Bmatrix} + \begin{Bmatrix} \text{auxiliary} \\ be \\ do,\ does,\ did \end{Bmatrix} + \text{subject} + \text{(verb)} + \text{(complement)} + \text{(modifer)} \ldots$$

When did John move to Jacksonville?
Where does Mohammad live?
Why did George leave so early?
How did Maria get to school today?
Where has Henry gone?
When will Bertha go back to Mexico?

EMBEDDED QUESTIONS

An embedded question is one which is included in a sentence or another question. The word order is *not* that of typical questions, except for subject questions. Study the following rule.

subject + verb (phrase) + question word + subject + verb

NOTE: There *must not* be an auxiliary between the question word and the subject in an embedded question.

Question: Where will the meeting take place?
Embedded question: We haven't ascertained where
Q word

the meeting will take place.
subject   verb phrase

Question: Why did the plane land at the wrong airport?

Embedded question: The authorities cannot figure out
                     why the plane landed at the

Q word   subject   verb

                     wrong airport.

The following rule applies if the embedded question is embedded in another question.

---

auxiliary + subject + verb + question word + subject + verb

Do you know where he went?

Could you tell me what time it is?

NOTE: Question words can be single words or phrases. Phrases include: *whose* + noun, *how many, how much, how long, how often, what time,* and *what kind.*

The professor didn't know how many students would be in her afternoon class.

I have no idea how long the interview will take.

Do they know how often the bus runs at night?

Can you tell me how far the museum is from the college?

I'll tell you what kind of ice cream tastes best.

The teacher asked us whose book was on his desk.

NOTE: There is no change in the order of subject position questions because the question word is functioning as the subject.

Who will paint that picture?

They can't decide who will paint that picture?

Whose car is parked in the lot?

The police can't determine whose car is parked in the lot.

Exercise 16: Embedded Questions

Complete the following sentences making embedded questions from the questions given before each one. Example: Where did he go? I know <u>where he went</u>.

1. Who will be elected president? I'm not sure
   _____.

2. Whose book is it? They haven't discovered
   _____.

3. How much will it cost to repair the car? The mechanic told me
   _____.

4. How was the murder committed? The police are still trying to decide _____.

5. How tall is John? Do you know _____?

6. How well does she play the guitar? You can't imagine
   _____.

7. When will the next exam take place? Do you know
   _____?

8. Where did they spend their vacation? Angela told me
   _____.

9. Why are they buying a new house? I don't know
   _____.

10. How long does the class last? The catalog doesn't say
    _____.

TAG QUESTIONS

In a tag question, the speaker makes a statement, but is not completely certain of the truth, so he or she uses a tag question to verify the previous statement. Sentences using tag questions should have the main clause separated from the tag by a comma. The sentence will always end with a question mark. Observe the following rules.

1. Use the same auxiliary verb as in the main clause. If there is no auxiliary, use *do, does,* or *did.*

2. If the main clause is negative, the tag is affirmative; if the main clause is affirmative, the tag is negative.

3. Don't change the tense.

4. Use the same subject in the main clause and the tag. The tag must always contain the subject form of the pronoun.

5. Negative forms are usually contracted (*n't*). (If they are not, they follow the order auxiliary + subject + *not*: He saw this yesterday, <u>did he not</u>?)

6. *There is, there are,* and *it is* forms contain a pseudo-subject so the tag will also contain *there* or *it* as if it were a subject pronoun.

7. The verb *have* may be used as a main verb (I *have* a new car) or it may be used as an auxiliary (John *has gone* to class already). When it functions as a main verb in American English, the auxiliary forms *do, does,* or *did* must be used in the tag.

<u>There are</u> only twenty-eight days in February, <u>aren't there</u>?

<u>It's</u> raining now, <u>isn't it</u>? It <u>isn't</u> raining now, <u>is it</u>?

The <u>boys don't</u> have class tomorrow, <u>do they</u>?

<u>You and I talked</u> with the professor yesterday, <u>didn't we</u>?

<u>You won't</u> be leaving for another hour, <u>will you</u>?

<u>Jill and Joe have</u> been to Mexico, <u>haven't they</u>?

<u>You have</u> two children, <u>don't you</u>?

In *British English,* you would be correct to say:

<u>You have</u> two children, <u>haven't you</u>?

On TOEFL, which tests standard *American English,* you must use a form of *do* if *have* is the main verb in the sentence.

<u>She has</u> an exam tomorrow, <u>doesn't she</u>?

Exercise 17: Tag Questions

Finish these sentences by adding a tag question with the correct form of the verb and the subject pronoun.

1. You're going to school tomorrow, _____?
2. Gary signed the petition, _____?
3. There's an exam tomorrow, _____?
4. Beverly will be attending the university in September, _____?
5. She's been studying English for two years, _____?
6. It sure is sunny today, _____?
7. He should stay in bed, _____?
8. You can't play tennis today, _____?
9. There aren't any peaches left, _____?
10. We've seen that movie, _____?

11. AFFIRMATIVE AGREEMENT

When indicating that one person or thing does something and then adding that another does the same, use the word *so* or *too*. To avoid needless repetition of words from the affirmative statement, use the conjunction *and,* followed by a simple statement using *so* or *too*. The order of this statement will depend on whether *so* or *too* is used.

● When a form of the verb *be* is used in the main clause, the same tense of the verb *be* is used in the simple statement that follows.

$$\text{affirmative statement } (be) + and + \begin{cases} \text{subject} + \text{verb } (be) + too \\ so + \text{verb } (be) + \text{subject} \end{cases}$$

I am happy, and you are too.
I am happy, and so are you.

● When a compound verb (auxiliary + verb), for example, *will go, should do, has done, have written, must examine,* etc., occurs in the main clause, the auxiliary of the main verb is used in the simple statement, and the subject and verb must agree.

> affirmative statement + *and* + ⎧subject + auxiliary only + *too*⎫
> (compound verb)   ⎩*so* + auxiliary only + subject⎭

They <u>will work</u> in the lab tomorrow, and <u>you will</u> too.
They <u>will work</u> in the lab tomorrow, and <u>so will you</u>.

• When any verb except *be* appears without any auxiliaries in the main clause, the auxiliary *do, does,* or *did* is used in the simple statement. The subject and verb must agree and the tense must be the same.

> affirmative statement + *and* + ⎧subject + *do, does,* or *did* + *too*⎫
> (single verb except *be*)   ⎩*so* + *do, does,* or *did* + subject⎭

Jane goes to that school, and <u>my sister does</u> too.
Jane goes to that school, and <u>so does my sister</u>.

Additional examples:

John went to the mountains on his vacation, and <u>we did</u> too.
John went to the mountains on his vacation, and <u>so did we</u>.

I will be in New Mexico in August, and <u>they will</u> too.
I will be in New Mexico in August, and <u>so will they</u>.

He has seen her plays, and <u>the girls have</u> too.
He has seen her plays, and <u>so have the girls</u>.

We are going to the movies tonight, and <u>Suzy is</u> too.
We are going to the movies tonight, and <u>so is Suzy</u>.

She will wear a costume to the party, and <u>we will</u> too.
She will wear a costume to the party, and <u>so will we</u>.

Velázquez was a famous painter, and <u>Rubens was</u> too.
Velázquez was a famous painter, and <u>so was Rubens</u>.

Exercise 18: Affirmative Agreement

Supply the correct form of the verb for the simple statement in each of the following sentences.

1. Rose likes to fly, and her brother _____ too.
2. They will leave at noon, and I _____ too.
3. He has an early appointment, and so _____ I.
4. She has already written her composition, and so _____ her friends.
5. Their plane is arriving at nine o'clock, and so _____ mine.
6. I should go grocery shopping this afternoon, and so _____ my neighbor.
7. We like to swim in the pool, and they _____ too.
8. Our Spanish teacher loves to travel, and so _____ we.
9. He has lived in Mexico for five years, and you _____ too.
10. I must write them a letter, and she _____ too.

12. NEGATIVE AGREEMENT

Either and *neither* function in simple statements much like *so* and *too* in affirmative sentences. However, *either* and *neither* are used to indicate negative agreement. The same rules for auxiliaries, *be* and *do, does,* or *did* apply.

> negative statement + *and* $\begin{cases} \text{subject + negative auxiliary or } be + \textit{either} \\ \textit{neither} + \text{positive auxiliary or } be + \text{subject} \end{cases}$

I didn't see Mary this morning.   John didn't see Mary this morning.

I didn't see Mary this morning, and John didn't either.

I didn't see Mary this morning, and neither did John.

She won't be going to the conference.   Her colleagues won't be going to the conference.

She won't be going to the conference, and her colleagues won't either.

She won't be going to the conference, and neither will her colleagues.

John hasn't seen the new movie yet. I haven't seen the new movie yet.

John hasn't seen the new movie yet, and I haven't either.

John hasn't seen the new movie yet, and neither have I.

Exercise 19: Negative Agreement

Fill in the blanks with the correct form of *either* or *neither*.

1. The children shouldn't take that medicine, and _____ should she.
2. We don't plan to attend the concert, and _____ do they.
3. I don't like tennis, and he doesn't _____.
4. She didn't see anyone she knew, and _____ did Tim.
5. The Yankees couldn't play due to the bad weather, and _____ could the Angels.
6. Mary can't type well, and her sister can't _____.
7. I'm not interested in reading that book, and _____ is she.
8. They won't have to work on weekends, and we won't _____.
9. I can't stand listening to that music, and she can't _____.
10. Michael doesn't speak English, and his family doesn't _____.

Exercise 20: Negative Agreement

In the following sentences, supply the correct form of the missing verb.

1. That scientist isn't too happy with the project, and neither _____ her supervisors.
2. We can't study in the library, and they _____ either.
3. I haven't worked there long, and neither _____ you.
4. You didn't pay the rent, and she _____ either.
5. They didn't want anything to drink, and neither _____ we.
6. John shouldn't run so fast, and neither _____ you.
7. The students won't accept the dean's decision, and the faculty _____ either.
8. Your class hasn't begun yet, and neither _____ mine.
9. She couldn't attend the lecture, and her sister _____ either.
10. He didn't know the answer, and neither _____ I.

13. NEGATION

To make a sentence negative, add the negative particle *not* after the auxiliary or verb *be*. If there is no auxiliary or *be*, add the appropriate form of *do, does,* or *did* and place the word *not* after that.

John is rich.	John is not rich.
Sandra is going to Hawaii.	Sandra is not going to Hawaii.
Mark has seen Bill.	Mark has not seen Bill.
Mary can leave now.	Mary cannot leave now.

The following examples contain no auxiliary, and thus use *do, does,* or *did*.

Marvin likes spinach.	Marvin does not like spinach.
Isaac went to class.	Isaac did not go to class.
They want to leave now.	They do not want to leave now.

SOME/ANY

If there is a noun in the complement of a negative sentence, one should add the particle *any* before the noun. NOTE: the following rule applies to the use of *some* and *any*.

> *some*—affirmative sentences
> *any*—negative sentences and questions

John has some money.   John doesn't have any money.

It is also possible to make sentences such as this negative by adding the negative particle *no* before the noun. In this case, the verb CANNOT be negative.

John has no money.

HARDLY, BARELY, RARELY, SELDOM, ETC.

Remember that in an English sentence it is usually incorrect to have two negatives together. This is called a double negative and is not acceptable in standard English. The following words have a negative meaning and, thus, *must be used with a positive verb.*

$$\left.\begin{array}{l} hardly \\ barely \\ scarcely \end{array}\right\} \text{mean} \quad \begin{array}{c} almost\ nothing \\ or \\ almost\ not\ at\ all \end{array} \quad \left.\begin{array}{l} rarely \\ seldom \\ hardly\ ever \end{array}\right\} \text{mean } almost\ never$$

John <u>rarely</u> <u>comes</u> to class on time.   (John usually does not come to class on time.)

Jerry <u>hardly</u> <u>studied</u> last night.   (Jerry studied very little last night).

She <u>scarcely</u> <u>remembers</u> the accident.   (She almost doesn't remember the accident.)

We <u>seldom</u> <u>see</u> photos of these animals.   (We almost never see photos of these animals.)

Jane <u>barely</u> <u>arrived</u> on time.   (Jane almost didn't arrive on time.)

I <u>hardly</u> <u>ever</u> <u>go</u> to sleep before midnight.   (I usually don't go to sleep before midnight.)

14. COMMANDS

A command is an imperative statement. One person orders another to do something. It can be preceded by *please*. The understood subject is *you*. Use the simple form of the verb.

<u>Close</u> the door.   <u>Leave</u> the room.

Please <u>turn</u> off the light.   <u>Pay</u> your rent.

<u>Open</u> the window.   <u>Be</u> quiet.

NEGATIVE COMMANDS

A negative command is formed by adding the word *don't* before the verb.

Don't close the door.
Please don't turn off the light.
Don't open the window.

INDIRECT COMMANDS

Usually the verbs *order, ask, tell,* or *say* are used to indicate an indirect command. They are followed by the infinitive [*to* + verb]

John told Mary to close the door.
Jack asked Jill to turn off the light.
The teacher told Christopher to open the window.
Please tell Jaime to leave the room.
John ordered Bill to close his book.
The policeman ordered the suspect to be quiet.

NEGATIVE INDIRECT COMMANDS

To make an indirect command negative, add the particle *not* before the infinitive.

| subject + verb + complement + *not* + [verb in infinitive] |

John told Mary not to close the door.
Jack asked Jill not to turn off the light.
The teacher told Christopher not to open the window.
Please tell Jaime not to leave the room.
John ordered Bill not to close his book.

MINI-TEST 1: GRAMMAR ITEMS 3 THROUGH 14

Following is a mini-test containing questions on all the material up to this point in Section II, items 3 through 14. This mini-test is similar to Section II, Part B, of the TOEFL. You should review everything up to this point before attempting the mini-test. After you take the test, check your answers, and if you do not understand why a given answer is incorrect, study that section again.

DIRECTIONS

Each question on this mini-test consists of a sentence in which four words or phrases are underlined. The four underlined parts of the sentence are marked, A, B, C, D. You are to identify the *one* underlined word or phrase that *would not be acceptable in standard written English.* Circle the letter of the underlined portion which is not correct. *Example:*

The study of <u>these</u> animals <u>are</u> truly fascinating, and
           A   B

many books <u>have</u> been <u>written about them.</u>
          C   D

In this sentence, the verb *are* in answer B is incorrect because the subject is *study,* which is singular. Thus B is the correct answer. Remember that if a prepositional phrase separates a subject and verb, it has no effect on the verb.

<u>The study</u> [of these animals]   <u>is</u>   . . .
singular subject   *singular verb*

1. Buying clothes <u>are</u> often <u>a very time-consuming</u> practice
                A   B
    because <u>those</u> clothes that a person likes <u>are rarely the ones</u>
           C   D
    that fit him or her.

2. <u>Because</u> they had spent <u>too many</u> time <u>considering</u> the new
    A   B   C
contract, the students <u>lost the opportunity to lease</u> the
                                 D
apartment.

3. <u>These</u> televisions are <u>all too expensive</u> for <u>we to buy</u> at
   A   B   C
<u>this time</u>, but perhaps we will return later.
   D

4. After she <u>had bought</u> <u>himself</u> a new automobile, <u>she sold</u>
          A   B   C
<u>her</u> bicycle.
 D

5. The next <u>important</u> question we <u>have to decide</u> is when
        A   B
<u>do we have</u> to <u>submit</u> the proposal.
   C   D

6. George <u>has not</u> completed <u>the assignment</u> <u>yet</u>, and Maria
       A   B   C
<u>hasn't neither</u>.
    D

7. John decided <u>to buy</u> <u>in the morning a new car</u>, but
              A   B
<u>in the afternoon</u> he <u>changed his mind</u>.
     C   D

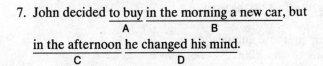

8. <u>Some of the plants</u> in this store require very <u>little care</u>, but this
        A   B
one needs <u>much more sunlight</u> than the <u>others ones</u>.
            C   D

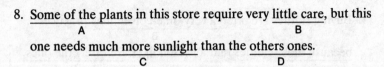

9. After George <u>had returned</u> <u>to his house,</u> <u>he</u> <u>was reading</u> a
   A   B C D
book.

10. <u>Many</u> theories on conserving the purity of water <u>has been</u>
    A   B
proposed, but <u>not one has</u> been <u>as widely accepted</u> as this one.
     C   D

11. <u>The food</u> that Mark is <u>cooking</u> in the kitchen <u>is smelling</u>
    A   B   C
<u>delicious.</u>
D

12. After John <u>eaten</u> dinner, <u>he wrote</u> <u>several letters</u> and
       A   B   C
<u>went to bed.</u>
D

13. The manager <u>has finished</u> <u>working</u> <u>on the report</u> last night,
         A   B   C
and now she will begin <u>to write</u> the other proposal.
         D

14. <u>Because</u> Sam and Michelle <u>had done</u> all of the work
    A   B
<u>theirselves,</u> they were <u>unwilling to give</u> the results to Joan.
C   D

15. Daniel said that <u>if he had to do</u> <u>another</u> homework tonight, he
         A   B
<u>would not be able</u> <u>to attend</u> the concert.
C   D

16. After <u>to take</u> the medication, <u>the patient</u> <u>became drowsy</u> and
      A   B   C
more <u>manageable.</u>
D

17. We insist on you leaving the meeting before any
            ___   _____   _____
             A   B   C
    further outbursts take place.
    _____
          D

18. It has been a long time since we have talked to John, isn't it?
       ___   _____ _____   _____
        A   B   C   D

19. Henry objects to our buying this house without the approval
                     _____ _____
                            A   B
    of our attorney, and John does so.
    _____   _____
           C   D

20. Rita enjoyed to be able to meet several members of Congress
                  _____ _____
                       A   B   C
    during her vacation.
           _____
                D

21. After being indicted for his part in a bank robbery,
    _____   ___
         A   B
    the reputed mobster decided find another attorney.
    _____   ____
         C   D

22. Harry's advisor persuaded his taking several courses which did
                              _____   _____
                                  A   B
    not involve much knowledge of mathematics.
    _____ _____
        C   D

23. The only teachers who were required to attend the meeting
    _____   _____   _____
        A   B   C
    were George, Betty, Jill, and me.
                                  __
                                  D

24. The work performed by these officers are not worth our paying
    _____ ___   _____
                 A   B   C
    them any longer.
    _____
         D

25. The president went fishing after he has finished with the
    $\overline{\text{A}}$ $\overline{\text{B}}$ $\overline{\text{C}}$ $\overline{\text{has finished}}$
                                                        D
    conferences.

26. Peter and Tom plays tennis every afternoon with
                    $\overline{\text{plays}}$ $\overline{\text{tennis}}$ $\overline{\text{afternoon}}$
                      A   B   C
    Mary and me.
    $\overline{\text{Mary and me.}}$
         D

27. There were a time that I used to swim five laps every day, but
         $\overline{\text{were}}$ $\overline{\text{used to swim}}$ $\overline{\text{day}}$
           A   A   C
    now I do not have enough time.
               $\overline{\text{have enough time.}}$
                        D

28. He was drink a cup of coffee when the telephone rang.
       $\overline{\text{was drink}}$ $\overline{\text{a cup}}$ $\overline{\text{when}}$ $\overline{\text{rang.}}$
          A   B   C   D

29. We called yesterday our friends in Boston to tell
       $\overline{\text{called}}$ $\overline{\text{yesterday our friends in Boston}}$ $\overline{\text{to tell}}$
          A   B   C
    them about the reunion that we are planning.
    $\overline{\text{them about}}$
        D

30. The children were playing last night outdoors when it began
                 $\overline{\text{were playing}}$ $\overline{\text{last night outdoors}}$ $\overline{\text{began}}$
                      A   B   C
    to rain very hard.
    $\overline{\text{to rain}}$ very hard.
        D

31. Those homework that your teacher assigned is due
    $\overline{\text{Those}}$ $\overline{\text{assigned}}$
      A   B
    on Tuesday unless you have made prior arrangements to turn
    $\overline{\text{on Tuesday}}$ $\overline{\text{have made}}$
         C   D
    it in late.

32. Please give me a few coffee and some donuts
           $\overline{\text{give me}}$ $\overline{\text{a few}}$ $\overline{\text{some donuts}}$
              A   B   C
    if you have any left.
    $\overline{\text{if you have any}}$ left.
           D

33. There are ten childs playing in the yard near her house, but
       A   B

    your child is not among them.
       C   D

34. People respected George Washington because he was
      A   B

    a honest man, and he turned out to be one of our greatest
        C   D

    military leaders.

35. He isn't driving to the convention in March, and
        A   B   C

    neither they are.
       D

36. Catherine is studying law at the university, and so does John.
              A   B   C   D

37. The company has so little money that it can't hardly operate
            A B   C   D

    anymore.

38. My cousin attends an university in the Midwest which
       A   B

    specializes in astronomy.
       C   D

39. The students were interested in take a field trip to The
            A   B   C

    National History Museum, but they were not able to raise
                         D

    enough money.

40. Because they have moved away, they hardly never go
      A   B   C

    to the beach anymore.
      D

41. <u>Us students</u> <u>would rather not attend</u> night classes in the
     A   B

summer, but <u>we</u> often <u>have to</u>.
       C   D

42. The policeman ordered <u>the suspect</u> to <u>don't remove</u> <u>his hands</u>
                       A   B   C

<u>from the</u> hood of the car.
   D

43. It was <u>him</u> <u>who</u> came running <u>into the classroom</u>
        A   B   C

<u>with the news</u>.
   D

44. <u>My brother</u> doesn't care how much <u>does the car cost</u> <u>because</u>
     A   B   C

<u>he is going to buy</u> it anyway.
     D

45. <u>Mary and her</u> sister <u>studied</u> biology <u>last year</u>, and
      A   B   C

<u>so does Jean</u>.
   D

46. Pete had <u>already saw</u> that musical <u>before</u> he <u>read</u> the reviews
            A   B   C

<u>about it</u>.
  D

47. There's <u>a</u> <u>new</u> Oriental restaurant <u>in town</u>, <u>isn't it</u>?
       A B   C   D

48. The government <u>has</u> decided <u>voting</u> <u>on the resolution</u> now
               A   B   C

<u>rather</u> than next month.
  D

49. The professor is thinking to go to the conference
                      ‾A‾   ‾‾B‾‾
    on aerodynamics next month.
        ‾‾‾C‾‾‾   ‾‾‾D‾‾‾

50. His father does not approve of him to go to the banquet
               ‾‾‾‾A‾‾‾‾   ‾‾‾‾B‾‾‾
    without dressing formally.
    ‾‾‾‾‾C‾‾‾‾ ‾‾‾D‾‾‾

15. MODAL AUXILIARIES

The modal auxiliaries have a number of different meanings. They are generally used to indicate something which is potential or uncertain. Remember that a modal is an auxiliary, and thus is NEVER used with *do, does,* or *did.* The modals include:

PRESENT TENSE	PAST TENSE
will	would (used to)
can	could
may	might
shall	should (ought to) (had better)
must (have to)	(had to)

NOTE: Words in parentheses ( ) indicate semi-modals. These have similar meanings to the modals, but are not grammatically the same.

NEGATION OF MODALS

To make a modal negative, add the particle *not* after the modal.

John would like to leave.   John would not like to leave.
     ‾‾‾‾‾‾‾‾‾‾   ‾‾‾‾‾‾‾‾‾‾‾‾‾

QUESTIONS WITH MODALS

To make a question, place the modal at the beginning of the sentence.

<u>Would</u> John <u>like</u> to leave?

NOTE: A modal is always directly followed by the simple form (verb word). This is the infinitive without *to*.

INFINITIVE	SIMPLE FORM
to be	be
to go	go
to have	have

This means that after a modal there can NEVER be: [verb + *ing*], [verb + *s*], past tense, or infinitive.

There are two ways that a modal can occur:

(1) modal + simple form of the verb

would be   could go   will have

(2) modal + *have* + [verb in past participle]

would have been   could have gone   will have had

NOTE: The word *have*, of course, must always be in the simple form after a modal; it can never be *has* or *had*.

WILL

Will indicates future certainty.

John <u>will begin</u> the job tomorrow.
Maria <u>will leave</u> in January.

CONDITIONAL SENTENCES

The modals *will, would, can,* and *could* often appear in conditional sentences. Usually conditional sentences contain the word *if.* There are two types of conditionals: the real (factual and habitual) and the unreal (contrary to fact or hypothetical). The real, or "future possible" as it is sometimes called, is used when the speaker expresses an action or situation which usually occurs, or will occur if the circumstances in the main clause are met.

Hypothetical situation: If I am not planning anything for this evening, when someone asks me if I want to go to the movies, I say:

If I have the time, I will go.
     X   Y

(I will go unless I don't have time.)
(If X is true, then Y is true.)

If my headache disappears, we can play tennis.
(I will play tennis unless I have a headache.)

However, the unreal condition expresses a situation (past, present, or future) that would take place or would have taken place if the circumstances expressed were or had been different now or in the past.

Hypothetical situation: If I don't have time to go to the movies, but I actually want to go, I say:

If I had the time, I would go.
(I know I don't have time, and therefore, I can't go to the movies.)
This sentence is contrary to fact because I *cannot* go.

If today were Saturday, we could go to the beach.
(Today is not Saturday, so we can't go to the beach.)

The *if* clause can come first or last in the sentence with no change in meaning. Notice that when the *if* clause comes first, it is followed by a comma.

If we <u>didn't have</u> to study, we <u>could</u> go out tonight.

OR

We <u>could</u> go out tonight <u>if</u> we <u>didn't have</u> to study.

(Both sentences mean: we can't go out tonight because we have to study.)

NOTE: The word *if* is generally not followed directly by the modal; the modal appears in the other part of the sentence unless there are two modals in one sentence.

> *if* + subject + conjugated verb . . . + modal . . .

OR

> subject + modal . . . + *if* . . . + conjugated verb . . .

NOTE: In the unreal condition, the past tense form of *be* is always *were* in a conditional sentence; it can NEVER be *was* in correct English.

If I were . . .	If we were . . .
If you were . . .	If you were . . .
If he were . . .	
If she were . . .	If they were . . .
If it were . . .	

Unreal conditional sentences are difficult for foreign students to understand because it seems that the truth value of a sentence is the opposite of the way the sentence appears. If a verb in an unreal conditional sentence is negative, the meaning is actually positive; if a verb is positive, the meaning is actually negative.

If I <u>were</u> rich, I <u>would travel</u> around the world.

(I am *not* rich).   (I'm *not* going to travel around the world.)

If he <u>were</u> sick, he <u>would stay</u> home today.

(He's *not* sick.)   (He's *not* going to stay home today.)

BUT

If I <u>hadn't been</u> in a hurry, I <u>wouldn't have spilled</u> the milk.

(I *was* in a hurry.)   (I *spilled* the milk.)

If the firemen <u>hadn't arrived</u> when they did, they <u>couldn't have</u> saved the house.

(The firemen *arrived* in time.)   (They *saved* the house.)

We <u>would have left</u> yesterday if it <u>hadn't snowed</u>.

(We *didn't leave* yesterday.)   (It *snowed*.)

The following rules will guide you in deciding which tense to use in conditional sentences. Remember:

> past perfect = *had* + [verb in past participle]
> modal + perfect = modal + *have* + [verb in past participle]

Remember that the following rules can be reversed. The *if* clause can go either at the beginning or in the middle of the sentence.

REAL CONDITIONS (POSSIBLY TRUE)

FUTURE TIME
if + subject + simple present tense . . . + $\begin{Bmatrix} will \\ can \\ may \\ must \end{Bmatrix}$ + [verb in simple form]

If I <u>have</u> the money, I <u>will buy</u> a new car.

We <u>will have</u> plenty of time to finish the project before dinner <u>if</u> it <u>is</u> only ten o'clock now.

HABITUAL

---

if + subject + simple present tense . . . + simple present tense . . .

If the doctor <u>has</u> morning office hours, he <u>visits</u> his patients in the hospital in the afternoon. (no modal)

John usually <u>walks</u> to school <u>if</u> he <u>has</u> enough time.

COMMAND

---

if + subject + simple present tense . . . + command form* . . .

---

*Remember that the command form consists of the simple form of the verb.

If you <u>go</u> to the Post Office, please <u>mail</u> this letter for me.

Please <u>call</u> me <u>if</u> you <u>hear</u> from Jane.

UNREAL CONDITIONS (NOT TRUE)

PRESENT OR FUTURE TIME

---

if + subject + simple past tense . . . + $\begin{Bmatrix} would \\ could \\ might \end{Bmatrix}$ + [verb in simple form]

If I <u>had</u> the time, I <u>would go</u> to the beach with you this weekend. (I *don't have* the time.)   (I'm *not going* to the beach with you.)

He <u>would tell</u> you about it <u>if</u> he <u>were</u> here. (He *won't tell* you about it.)   (He's *not here.*)

If he <u>didn't speak</u> so quickly, you <u>could understand</u> him. (He *speaks* very quickly.)   (You *can't understand* him.)

PAST TIME

if + subject + past perfect ... + $\begin{Bmatrix} would \\ could \\ might \end{Bmatrix}$ + *have* + [verb in past participle]

If we <u>had known</u> that you were there, we <u>would have written</u> you a letter.

(We *didn't know* that you were there.)   (We *didn't write* you a letter.)

She <u>would have sold</u> the house <u>if</u> she <u>had found</u> the right buyer.
(She *didn't sell* the house.)   (She *didn't find* the right buyer.)

<u>If</u> we <u>hadn't lost</u> our way, we <u>would have arrived</u> sooner.
(We *lost* our way.)   (We *didn't arrive* early.)

NOTE: It is also possible to indicate a past unreal condition without using the word *if*. In this case, the auxiliary *had* is placed before, rather than after, the subject. This clause will usually come first in the sentence.

---

had + subject + [verb in past participle] ...

<u>Had we known</u> that you were there, we <u>would have written</u> you a letter.

<u>Had she found</u> the right buyer, she <u>would have sold</u> the house.

The above rules indicate the most common methods of using tenses in conditional sentences. However, if the two actions clearly happened at quite different times, the verbs should show that difference.

Less common: If she <u>had seen</u> the movie, she <u>would tell</u> you.
                               past   *future*

More common: If she <u>had seen</u> the movie, she
                               past

                        <u>would have told</u> you.
                              past

AS IF/AS THOUGH

These conjunctions indicate something unreal or contrary to fact and thus are very similar in form to conditional sentences. The verb which follows these conjunctions must be in the past tense or past perfect. Remember that the past tense of *be* in a contrary to fact statement must be *were* and NEVER *was*.

---

subject + verb (present) + $\begin{Bmatrix} as\ if \\ as\ though \end{Bmatrix}$ + subject + verb (past) . . .

The old lady <u>dresses</u> <u>as if</u> it <u>were</u> winter even in the summer.
(It is *not* winter.)

Angelique <u>walks</u> <u>as though</u> she <u>studied</u> modeling.
(She *didn't* study modeling.)

He <u>acts</u> <u>as though</u> he <u>were</u> rich.
(He is *not* rich.)

---

subject + verb (past) + $\begin{Bmatrix} as\ if \\ as\ though \end{Bmatrix}$ + subject + verb (past perfect) . . .

Betty <u>talked</u> about the contest <u>as if</u> she <u>had won</u> the grand prize.
(She *didn't win* the grand prize.)

Jeff <u>looked</u> <u>as if</u> he <u>had seen</u> a ghost.
(He *didn't see* a ghost.)

He <u>looked</u> <u>as though</u> he <u>had run</u> ten miles.
(He *didn't run* ten miles.)

NOTE: The two preceding rules apply only when *as if* or *as though* indicates a contrary to fact meaning. At times, they do not have that meaning and then would not be followed by these tenses.

He looks <u>as if</u> he <u>has finished</u> the test.

(*Perhaps* he has finished.)

He looked <u>as though</u> he <u>was leaving</u>.

(*Perhaps* he was leaving.)

HOPE/WISH

These two verbs, while they are similar in meaning, are not at all the same grammatically. The verb *hope* is used to indicate something that possibly happened or will possibly happen. The verb *wish* is used to indicate something that definitely did not happen or definitely will not happen. The verb *hope* can be followed by any tense. The verb *wish* must NOT be followed by *any present tense verb or present tense auxiliary*. Be sure that you understand the difference in the following sentences with *wish* and *hope*.

We <u>hope</u> that they <u>will come</u>.   (We *don't know* if they are coming.)

We <u>wish</u> that they <u>could come</u>.   (They are *not* coming.)

We <u>hope</u> that they <u>came</u> yesterday.   (We *don't know* if they came.)

We <u>wish</u> that they <u>had come</u> yesterday.   (They *didn't* come.)

Remember that *wish* is very similar to a contrary to fact or unreal condition.

Present unreal condition: <u>If</u> I <u>were</u> rich, I would be very happy.

Present wish: I wish I <u>were</u> rich.

Past unreal condition: <u>If</u> you <u>had been</u> here last night, we would have enjoyed it.

Past wish: We wish that you <u>had been</u> here last night.

NOTE: In the following rules, notice that the word *that* is optional.

FUTURE WISH

subject* + *wish* + (*that*) + subject* + $\begin{Bmatrix} \textit{could} + \text{verb} \\ \textit{would} + \text{verb} \\ \textit{were} + [\text{verb} + \textit{ing}] \end{Bmatrix}$ . . .

---

*Subjects can be the same or different.

We <u>wish</u> that you <u>could come</u> to the party tonight.   (You *can't come.*)

I <u>wish</u> that you <u>would stop</u> saying that.   (You *probably won't stop.*)

She <u>wishes</u> that she <u>were coming</u> with us.   (She is *not coming* with us.)

PRESENT WISH

subject + *wish* + (*that*) + subject + simple past tense . . .

I <u>wish</u> that I <u>had</u> enough time to finish my homework.   (I *don't have* enough time.)

We <u>wish</u> that he <u>were</u> old enough to come with us. (He *is not* old enough.)

They <u>wish</u> that they <u>didn't have to go</u> to class today.   (They *have to* go to class.)

PAST WISH

subject + *wish* + (*that*) + subject + $\begin{Bmatrix} \text{past perfect} \\ \textit{could have} + [\text{verb in past participle}] \end{Bmatrix}$

I <u>wish</u> that I <u>had washed</u> the clothes yesterday.   (I *didn't wash* the clothes.)

She <u>wishes</u> that she <u>could have been</u> there.   (She *couldn't be* there.)

We <u>wish</u> that we <u>had had</u> more time last night.   (We *didn't have* more time.)

Exercise 21: Conditional Sentences

Supply the correct form of the verb in parentheses for each of the following sentences. Review the formulas if you have trouble.

1. Henry talks to his dog as if it _____ (understand) him.
2. If they had left the house earlier, they _____ (be; negative) so late getting to the airport that they could not check their baggage.
3. If I finish the dress before Saturday, I _____ (give) it to my sister for her birthday.
4. If I had seen the movie, I _____ (tell) you about it last night.
5. Had Bob not interfered in his sister's marital problems, there _____ (be) peace between them.
6. He would give you the money if he _____ (have) it.
7. I wish they _____ (stop) making so much noise so that I could concentrate.
8. She would call you immediately if she _____ (need) help.
9. Had they arrived at the sale early, they _____ (find) a better selection.
10. We hope that you _____ (enjoy) the party last night.
11. If you have enough time, please _____ (paint) the chair before you leave.
12. We could go for a drive if today _____ (be) Saturday.
13. If she wins the prize, it will be because she _____ (write) very well.
14. Mike wished that the editors _____ (permit) him to copy some of their material.
15. Joel wished that he _____ (spend) his vacation on the Gulf Coast next year.
16. I _____ (accept) if they invite me to the party.
17. If your mother _____ (buy) that car for you, will you be happy?

18. If he _____ (decide) earlier, he could have left on the afternoon flight.
19. Had we known your address, we _____ (write) you a letter.
20. If the roofer doesn't come soon, the rain _____ (leak) inside.
21. Because Rose did so poorly on the exam, she wishes that she _____ (study) harder last night.
22. My dog always wakes me up if he _____ (hear) strange noises.
23. If you _____ (see) Mary today, please ask her to call me.
24. If he _____ (get) the raise, it will be because he does a good job.
25. The teacher will not accept our work if we _____ (turn) it in late.
26. Mrs. Wood always talks to her tenth-grade students as though they _____ (be) adults.
27. If he had left already, he _____ (call) us.
28. If they had known him, they _____ (talk) to him.
29. He would understand it if you _____ (explain) it to him more slowly.
30. I could understand the French teacher if she _____ (speak) more slowly.

WOULD

Besides its use in conditional sentences, *would* can also mean a past time habit.

When David was young, he <u>would swim</u> once a day.

USED TO

In this usage, the expression *used to* means the same as *would*. *Used to* is always in this form; it can NEVER be *use to*. Also, there are two grammar rules for *used to*. Notice the difference in meaning as well as in grammar.

> subject + *used to* + [verb in simple form] ...

When David was young, he used to swim once a day. (past time habit)

$$\text{subject} + \begin{Bmatrix} be \\ get \end{Bmatrix} + used\ to + [\text{verb} + ing] \ldots$$

John is used to swimming every day. (He is accustomed to swimming every day.

John got used to swimming every day. (He became accustomed to swimming every day.)

NOTE: *Be used to* means to *be accustomed to,* and *get used to* means to *become accustomed to.*

The program director used to write his own letters. (past time habit)

George is used to eating at 7:00 P.M. (is accustomed to)

We got used to cooking our own food when we had to live alone. (became accustomed to)

Mary was used to driving to school. (was accustomed to)

The government used to restrict these pills. (past time habit)

The man is used to reading his newspaper in the morning. (is accustomed to)

Exercise 22: Used To

Supply the simple form or [verb + *ing*] as required in the following sentences.

1. I was used to _____ (eat) at noon when I started school.
2. He used to _____ (eat) dinner at five o'clock.
3. When I was young, I used to _____ (swim) every day.
4. He used to _____ (like) her, but he doesn't anymore.
5. Don't worry. Some day you will get used to _____ (speak) English.
6. Alvaro can't get used to _____ (study).
7. He used to _____ (dance) every night, but now he studies.
8. Adam is used to _____ (sleep) late on weekends.

9. Chieko is used to _____ (eat) American food now.
10. She finally got used to _____ (eat) our food.

WOULD RATHER

Would rather means the same as *prefer*, except that the grammar is different. *Would rather* must be followed by a verb, but *prefer* may or may not be followed by a verb.

John <u>would rather</u> <u>drink</u> Coca-Cola <u>than</u> orange juice.

John <u>prefers</u> <u>drinking</u> Coca-Cola <u>to</u> <u>drinking</u> orange juice.

OR

John <u>prefers</u> Coca-Cola <u>to</u> orange juice.

NOTE: *Would rather* is followed by *than* when two things are mentioned, but *prefer* is followed by *to*.

There are different rules for *would rather* depending on the number of subjects and the meaning of the sentence.

PRESENT
subject + *would rather* + [verb in simple form] . . .

Jim <u>would rather</u> <u>go</u> to class tomorrow than today.

PAST
subject + *would rather* + *have* + [verb in past participle]

John <u>would rather</u> <u>have</u> <u>gone</u> to class yesterday than today.

Would rather that, when used with two subjects in the present, can be followed by either the simple form of the verb or the past tense. It will be followed by the simple form when it has a subjunctive meaning (as explained in Grammar item 25). It will be followed by the past tense when the meaning of the sentence is "contrary to fact" just as that rule affects conditional sentences and the verb *wish*.

PRESENT SUBJUNCTIVE

subject$_1$ + *would rather that* + subject$_2$ + [verb in simple form]

I <u>would rather that</u> you <u>call</u> me tomorrow.
We <u>would rather that</u> he <u>take</u> this train.

PRESENT CONTRARY TO FACT

subject$_1$ + *would rather that* + subject$_2$ + [verb in simple past tense] . . .

Henry <u>would rather that</u> his girlfriend <u>worked</u> in the same department as he does.

(His girlfriend does *not* work in the same department.)

Jane <u>would rather that</u> it <u>were</u> winter now.

(It is *not* winter now.)

The following rule applies to *would rather* when there are two subjects and the time is past. In this case, the meaning must always be contrary to fact.

PAST CONTRARY TO FACT

subject$_1$ + *would rather that* + subject$_2$ + past perfect . . .

Jim <u>would rather that</u> Jill <u>had gone</u> to class yesterday.

(Jill did *not* go to class yesterday.)

Notice how each of the following sentences becomes negative. When there is only one subject and when you have a present subjunctive, simply place *not* before the verb.

John <u>would rather</u> <u>not go</u> to class tomorrow.
John <u>would rather</u> <u>not</u> <u>have gone</u> to class yesterday.
John <u>would rather that</u> you <u>not call</u> me tomorrow.

For the present and past contrary to fact sentences, use *didn't* + [verb in simple form] and *hadn't* + [verb in past participle] respectively.

Henry would rather that his girlfriend didn't work in the same department as he does.

(She *does* work in the same department.)

John would rather that Jill had not gone to class yesterday.

(Jill *went* to class yesterday.)

Examples of *would rather:*

Jorge would rather stay home tonight.

We would rather that you call tonight.

Mayra would rather drink coffee than Coke.

Ricardo would rather not be here.

Ritsuko would rather that we didn't leave now, but we must go to work.

Roberto would rather that we hadn't left yesterday.

Exercise 23: Would Rather

Fill in the blanks with the correct form of the verb in the following sentences.

1. We would rather _____ (stay) home tonight.
2. Mr. Jones would rather _____ (stay) home last night.
3. The policeman would rather _____ (work) on Saturday than on Sunday.
4. Maria would rather that we _____ (study) more than we do.
5. George would rather _____ (study; negative) tonight.
6. The photographer would rather _____ (have) more light.
7. The photographer would rather that we _____ (stand) closer together than we are standing.
8. Carmen would rather _____ (cook; negative) for the entire family.
9. She would rather that you _____ (arrive; negative) last night.
10. John would rather _____ (sleep) than worked last night.

WOULD LIKE

This expression is often used in invitations; it can also mean *want*. NOTE: It is NOT CORRECT to say: "Do you like . . . ?" to invite somebody to do something.

---

subject + *would like* + [*to* + verb] . . .

Would you like to dance with me?
I would like to visit Japan.
We would like to order now, please.
The president would like to be re-elected.
They would like to study at the university.
Would you like to see a movie tonight?

COULD/MAY/MIGHT

Although *could* is used in conditionals, it can also be used to mean possibility. In this case, *could, may,* or *might* mean the same. The speaker is not sure of the statement made when using these modals.

It might rain tomorrow.   It will *possibly* rain tomorrow.
It may rain tomorrow.   =   OR
It could rain tomorrow.   *Maybe* it will rain tomorrow.

NOTE: *Maybe* is a combination of *may* and *be,* but it is one word and is not an auxiliary. It means the same as *perhaps.*

Examples of *could, may,* and *might:*

The president said that there might be a strike next week.
I don't know what I'm doing tomorrow. I may go to the beach or I may stay home.

It might be warmer tomorrow.

I may not be able to go with you tonight.

I don't know where Jaime is. He could be at home.

SHOULD

This modal is used to indicate:

• A recommendation, advice, or obligation (see *must* for further explanation).

Henry should study tonight.

One should exercise daily.

Maria should go on a diet.

You should see a doctor about this problem.

• Expectation; used to indicate something that the speaker expects to happen.

It should rain tomorrow.   (I expect it to rain tomorrow.)

My check should arrive next week.   (I expect it to arrive next week.)

NOTE: The expressions *had better, ought to,* and *be supposed to* generally mean the same as *should* in either of the two definitions.

$$\text{subject} + \begin{cases} had\ better \\ should \\ ought\ to \\ be\ supposed\ to \end{cases} + \text{[verb in simple form]} \ldots$$

John should study tonight.

John had better study tonight.

John ought to study tonight.

John is supposed to study tonight.

MUST

This modal is used to indicate:

• Complete obligation; this is stronger than *should*. With *should* the person has some choice on whether or not to act, but with *must* the person has no choice.

One <u>must endorse</u> a check before one cashes it.

George <u>must call</u> his insurance agent today.

A pharmacist <u>must keep</u> a record of the prescriptions that are filled.

An automobile <u>must have</u> gasoline to run.

An attorney <u>must pass</u> an examination before practicing law.

This freezer <u>must be kept</u> at −20°.

• Logical conclusion; *must* is used to indicate that the speaker assumes something to be true from the facts that are available but is not absolutely certain of the truth.

John's lights are out.   He <u>must be</u> asleep.
(We assume that John is asleep because the lights are out.)

The grass is wet.   It <u>must be</u> raining.
(We assume that it is raining because the grass is wet.)

HAVE TO

This pseudo-modal means the same as *must* (meaning complete obligation).

George <u>has to call</u> his insurance agent today.

A pharmacist <u>has to keep</u> a record of the prescriptions that are filled.

For a past time obligation, it is necessary to use *had to*. *Must* CANNOT be used to mean a past obligation.

George <u>had to call</u> his insurance agent yesterday.

Mrs. Kinsey <u>had to pass</u> an examination before she could practice law.

MODALS + PERFECTIVE

You have already seen these in the section on conditionals; however, it is also possible to use other modals in this form. The modal + perfective is *usually used* to indicate past time.

> modal + *have* + [verb in past participle] . . .

NOTE: Remember that a modal is *always* followed by the simple form of the verb. Thus, *have* can *never* be *has* or *had*.

COULD/MAY/MIGHT + PERFECTIVE

Use any of these modals + perfective to indicate a past possibility. Remember that these modals also mean possibility in the present.

It <u>may have rained</u> last night, but I'm not sure.

The cause of death <u>could have been</u> bacteria.

John <u>might have gone</u> to the movies yesterday.

SHOULD + PERFECTIVE

This is used to indicate an obligation that was supposed to occur in the past, but for some reason it did not occur.

John <u>should have gone</u> to the post office this morning.

(He *did not go* to the post office.)

Maria <u>shouldn't have called</u> John last night.

(She *did call* him.)

The policeman <u>should have made</u> a report about the burglary.

(He *did not make* a report.)

NOTE: The expression *was/were supposed to* + [verb in simple form] means much the same as *should* + perfective.

John was supposed to go to the post office this morning.

(He *didn't* go.)

The policeman was supposed to make a report about the burglary.

(He *didn't make* a report.)

MUST + PERFECTIVE

This is NOT *used to indicate a past obligation.* Remember to use only *had to, should* + perfective, or *be supposed to* to indicate a past obligation. *Must* + perfective can *only* mean a logical conclusion in the past.

The grass is wet.   It must have rained last night.

    (It *probably rained* last night.)

Tony's lights are out.   He must have gone to sleep.

    (He *probably went* to sleep.)

Jane did very well on the exam.   She must have studied.

    (She *probably studied*.)

Sandra failed the test.   She must not have studied.

    (She *probably did not study*.)

Exercise 24: Must/Should + *Perfective*

Choose between *must* + perfective and *should* + perfective in the following sentences.

1. Henri was deported for having an expired visa. He _____ (have) his visa renewed.
2. Julietta was absent for the first time yesterday. She _____ (be) sick.
3. The photos are black. The X-rays at the airport _____ (damage) them.
4. Blanca got a parking ticket. She _____ (park; negative) in a reserved spot, since she had no permit.

5. Carmencita did very well on the exam. She _____ (study) very hard.

6. Jeanette did very badly on the exam. She _____ (study) harder.

7. German called us as soon as his wife had her baby. He _____ (be) very proud.

8. Eve had to pay $5.00 because she wrote a bad check. She _____ (deposit) her money before she wrote a check.

9. John isn't here yet. He _____ (forget) about our meeting.

10. Alexis failed the exam. He _____ (study; negative) enough.

Exercise 25: Modals + Perfective

Choose the correct answer in each of the following sentences according to meaning and tense.

1. If I had a bicycle, (I would/I will) ride it every day.

2. George (would have gone/would go) on a trip to Chicago if he had had time.

3. Marcela didn't come to class yesterday. She (will have had/may have had) an accident.

4. John didn't do his homework, so the teacher became very angry. John (must have done/should have done) his homework.

5. Sharon was supposed to be here at nine o'clock. She (must forget/must have forgotten) about our meeting.

6. Where do you think Juan is today? I have no idea. He (should have slept/may have slept) late.

7. George missed class today. He (might have had/might had had) an accident.

8. Robert arrived without his book. He (could have lost/would have lost) it.

9. Thomas received a warning for speeding. He (should have driven/shouldn't have driven) so fast.

10. Henry's car stopped on the highway. It (may run/may have run) out of gas.

16. ADJECTIVES AND ADVERBS

ADJECTIVES

Adjectives fall into two categories: descriptive and limiting. Descriptive adjectives are those which describe the color, size, or quality of a person or thing (noun or pronoun). Limiting adjectives place restrictions on the words they modify (quantity, distance, possession, etc.). NOTE: Only *these* and *those* are plural forms. All others remain the same whether the noun is singular or plural.

DESCRIPTIVE	LIMITING
beautiful	cardinal numbers (one, two)
large	ordinal numbers (first, second)
red	possessives (my, your, his)
interesting	demonstratives (this, that, these, those)
important	quantity (few, many, much)
colorful	articles (a, an, the)

When descriptive adjectives modify a singular countable noun, they are usually preceded by *a, an,* or *the.*

a pretty girl   an interesting story   the red dress

Adjectives normally precede the nouns they modify, or follow linking verbs. Adjectives modify only nouns, pronouns, and linking verbs. (See next section for an explanation of linking verbs.) NOTE: An adjective answers the question: What kind . . . ?

ADVERBS

Adverbs modify verbs (except linking verbs), adjectives, or other adverbs. Many descriptive adjectives can be changed to adverbs by adding -*ly* to the adjective base.

ADJECTIVES	ADVERBS
bright	brightly
careful	carefully
quiet	quietly

NOTE: The following words are also adverbs: *so, very, almost, soon, often, fast, rather, well, there, too.* An adverb answers the question: How . . . ?

John is reading <u>carefully</u>.　　　(*How* is John reading?)

Maria Elena speaks Spanish　　(*How* does she speak?)
<u>fluently</u>.

Rita drank <u>too</u> much coffee.　　(*How much* coffee did she drink?)

I don't play tennis <u>very</u> well.　　(*How well* do I play?)

He was driving <u>fast</u>.　　　　(*How* was he driving?)

She reviewed her notes　　　　(*How* did she review her
<u>carefully</u>.　　　　　　　　notes?)

Exercise 26: Adjectives and Adverbs

Circle the correct form in parentheses.

1. Rita plays the violin (good/well).
2. That is an (intense/intensely) novel.
3. The sun is shining (bright/brightly).
4. The girls speak (fluent/fluently) French.
5. The boys speak Spanish (fluent/fluently).
6. The table has a (smooth/smoothly) surface.
7. We must figure our income tax returns (accurate/accurately).
8. We don't like to drink (bitter/bitterly) tea.
9. The plane will arrive (soon/soonly).
10. He had an accident because he was driving too (fast/fastly).

ADJECTIVES WITH LINKING (COPULATIVE) VERBS

A special category of verbs connects or links the subject with the subject complement (predicate adjective). Unlike most verbs, these do not show action. They must be modified by adjectives, not adverbs.

be	appear	feel
become	seem	look
remain	sound	smell
stay		taste

Mary <u>feels</u> <u>bad</u> about her test grade.
Children <u>become</u> <u>tired</u> quite easily.
Lucy will <u>look</u> <u>radiant</u> in her new dress.
They <u>were</u> <u>sorry</u> to see us leave.
The flowers <u>smell</u> <u>sweet</u>.
The soup <u>tastes</u> <u>good</u>.

Be, become, and *remain* can be followed by noun phrases as well as adjectives.

They <u>remained</u>   <u>sad</u>   even though I tried to cheer them up.
                 adjective
Doug <u>remained</u> <u>chairman</u> of the board despite the opposition.
                noun
Children often <u>become</u> <u>bored</u> at meetings.
                      adjective
Christine <u>became</u> <u>class president</u> after a long, hard campaign.
                    noun phrase
Sally will <u>be</u> <u>happy</u> when she hears the good news.
            adjective
Ted will <u>be</u> <u>prom king</u> this year.
            noun phrase

Feel, look, smell, and *taste* may also be transitive verbs and take a direct object. When they function in this way, they become active and are modified by adverbs. Notice the following pairs of sentences. Those which take objects are active, and those which do not are linking.

The doctor <u>felt</u> <u>the leg</u> <u>carefully</u> to see if there were any broken
               object   *adverb*

    bones.

Mike <u>felt</u> <u>ecstatic</u> after passing his law school exam.
          adjective

Professor Ingells <u>looked at</u> <u>the exams</u> <u>happily</u>.
                   object   *adverb*

Joey does not <u>look</u> <u>happy</u> today.
             adjective

The lady is <u>smelling</u> <u>the flowers</u> <u>gingerly</u>.
             object   *adverb*

After being closed up for so long, the house <u>smells</u> <u>musty</u>.
                                       adjective

The chef <u>tasted</u> <u>the meat</u> <u>cautiously</u> before presenting it to the
            object   *adverb*

    king.

Your chocolate cake <u>tastes</u> <u>delicious</u>.
                      adjective

Exercise 27: Linking (Copulative) Verbs

Circle the correct form in parentheses.

1. Your cold sounds (terrible/terribly).
2. The pianist plays very (good/well).
3. The food in the restaurant always tastes (good/well).
4. The campers remained (calm/calmly) despite the thunderstorm.
5. They became (sick/sickly) after eating the contaminated food.

6. Professor Calandra looked (quick/quickly) at the students' sketches.
7. Paco was working (diligent/diligently) on the project.
8. Paul protested (vehement, vehemently) about the new proposals.
9. Our neighbors appeared (relaxed/relaxedly) after their vacation.
10. The music sounded too (noisy/noisily) to be classical.

17. COMPARISONS

Comparisons indicate degrees of difference with adjectives and adverbs, and may be equal or unequal.

EQUAL COMPARISONS

An equal comparison indicates that the two entities are (or are not, if negative) exactly the same. The following rule generally applies to this type of comparison.

$$\text{subject} + \text{verb} + as + \begin{Bmatrix} \text{adjective} \\ \text{adverb} \end{Bmatrix} + as + \begin{Bmatrix} \text{noun} \\ \text{pronoun} \end{Bmatrix}$$

NOTE: Sometimes you may see *so* instead of *as* before the adjective or adverb in negative comparisons.

He is <u>not as tall as</u> his father.

OR

He is <u>not so tall as</u> his father.

NOTE: Remember that the subject form of the pronoun will always be used after *as* in correct English.

Peter is as tall as <u>I</u>.   You are as old as <u>she</u>.

Examples of equal comparisons:

My book is as interesting as yours.	(adjective)
His car runs as fast as a race car.	(adverb)
John sings as well as his sister.	(adverb)
Their house is as big as that one.	(adjective)
His job is not as difficult as mine.	(adjective)

OR

His job is not so difficult as mine.
They are as lucky as we.   (adjective)

The same idea can also be conveyed in another way.

$$\text{subject} + \text{verb} + \textit{the same} + (\text{noun}) + \textit{as} + \begin{Bmatrix} \text{noun} \\ \text{pronoun} \end{Bmatrix}$$

NOTE: *As high as* means the same as *the same height as*.

My house is as high as his.
My house is the same height as his.

Be sure that you know the following adjectives and their corresponding nouns.

ADJECTIVES	NOUNS
heavy, light	weight
wide, narrow	width
deep, shallow	depth
long, short	length
big, small	size

NOTE: Remember that the opposite of *the same as* is *different from.* NEVER use *different than.*

My nationality is different from hers.
Our climate is different from Canada's.

Examples of *the same as* and *different from:*

These trees are <u>the same as</u> those.
He speaks <u>the same language as</u> she.
Her address is <u>the same as</u> Rita's.
Their teacher is <u>different</u> from ours.
My typewriter types <u>the same as</u> yours.
She takes <u>the same courses as</u> her husband.

UNEQUAL COMPARISONS

This type of comparative implies that the entities are comparable in a greater or lesser degree. The following rules generally apply to this type of comparative.

---

1. Add *-er* to the adjective base of most one- and two-syllable adjectives. (thick–thick*er*; cold–cold*er*; quiet–quiet*er*)

2. Use the form *more* + adjective for most three-syllable adjectives. (*more* beautiful, *more* important, *more* believable)

3. Use the form *more* + adjective for adjectives ending in the following suffixes: *-ed, -ful, -ing, -ish,* and *-ous.* (*more* hated, *more* useful, *more* boring, *more* stylish, *more* cautious)

4. Double the final consonant of one-syllable adjectives which end in a single consonant (except *w, x,* and *z*) and are preceded by a single vowel. (big–big*ger*, red–red*der*, hot–hot*ter*)

5. When an adjective ends in a consonant + *y*, change the *y* to *i* and add *-er.* (happy–happ*ier*, dry–dr*ier*)

NOTE: The *-er* suffix means exactly the same as *more*. Therefore, they can NEVER be used together. It is NOT CORRECT to say:

more prettier, more faster, more better

$$\text{subject + verb +} \begin{cases} \text{adjective + } er \\ \text{adverb + } er* \\ more \text{ + adjective/adverb} \\ less \text{ + adjective/adverb} \end{cases} + than + \begin{cases} \text{noun} \\ \text{pronoun} \end{cases}$$

*One can add *-er* to only a few adverbs: *faster, quicker, sooner,* and *later.*

NOTE: Remember always to use the subject form of the pronoun after *than.*

John's grades are <u>higher than</u> his sister's.	(adjective)
Today is <u>hotter than</u> yesterday.	(adjective)
This chair is <u>more comfortable than</u> the other.	(adjective)
He speaks Spanish <u>more fluently than</u> I.	(adverb)
He visits his family <u>less frequently than</u> she does.	(adverb)
This year's exhibit is <u>less impressive than</u> last year's.	(adjective)

Unequal comparisons can be further intensified by adding *much* or *far* before the comparative form.

$$\text{subject + verb +} \begin{cases} far \\ much \end{cases} + \begin{cases} \text{adjective} \\ \text{adverb} \end{cases} + er + than + \begin{cases} \text{noun} \\ \text{pronoun} \end{cases}$$

$$\text{subject + verb +} \begin{cases} far \\ much \end{cases} + \begin{cases} more \\ less \end{cases} + \begin{cases} \text{adjective} \\ \text{adverb} \end{cases} + than + \begin{cases} \text{noun} \\ \text{pronoun} \end{cases}$$

Harry's watch is <u>far more expensive</u> than mine.

That movie we saw last night was <u>much less interesting than</u> the one on television.

A watermelon is <u>much sweeter than</u> a lemon.

She dances <u>much more artistically than</u> her predecessor.

He speaks English <u>much more rapidly than</u> he does Spanish.

His car is <u>far better than</u> yours.

Nouns can also be used in comparisons. Be sure to use the determiners correctly depending on whether the adjectives are countable or noncountable.

$$\text{subject} + \text{verb} + as + \begin{Bmatrix} many \\ much \\ little \\ few \end{Bmatrix} + \text{noun} + as + \begin{Bmatrix} \text{noun} \\ \text{pronoun} \end{Bmatrix}$$

OR

$$\text{subject} + \text{verb} + \begin{Bmatrix} more \\ fewer \\ less \end{Bmatrix} + \text{noun} + than + \begin{Bmatrix} \text{noun} \\ \text{pronoun} \end{Bmatrix}$$

I have <u>more</u> <u>books</u> <u>than</u> she.

February has <u>fewer</u> <u>days</u> <u>than</u> March.

He earns <u>as</u> <u>much</u> <u>money</u> <u>as</u> his brother.

They have <u>as</u> <u>few</u> classes <u>as</u> we.

Their job allows them <u>less</u> <u>freedom</u> <u>than</u> ours does.

Before payday, I have <u>as</u> <u>little</u> <u>money</u> <u>as</u> my brother.

ILLOGICAL COMPARISONS

An illogical comparison is one in which unlike entities have been compared. Be sure that the items being compared are the same. These forms can be divided into three categories: possessives, *that of,* and *those of.*

Incorrect: His drawings are as perfect as his instructor.

(This sentence compares *drawings* with *instructor.*)

Correct: His drawings are as perfect as his <u>instructor's</u>.
            (*instructor's* = <u>instructor's drawings</u>)

Incorrect: The salary of a professor is higher than a secretary.
            (This sentence compares *salary* with *secretary*.)

Correct: The salary of a professor is higher than <u>that of</u> a secretary.
            (*that of* = the salary of)

Incorrect: The duties of a policeman are more dangerous than a teacher.
            (This sentence compares *duties* with *teacher*.)

Correct: The duties of a policeman are more dangerous than <u>those of</u> a teacher.
            (*those of* = the duties of)

Examples of logical comparisons:

John's car runs <u>better than</u> <u>Mary's</u>.
    (*Mary's* = <u>Mary's car</u>)

The climate in Florida is <u>as mild as</u> <u>that of</u> California.
    (*that of* = the climate of)

Classes in the university are <u>more difficult than</u> <u>those in</u> the college.
    (*those in* = the classes in)

The basketball games at the university are <u>better than</u> <u>those of</u> the high school.
    (*those of* = the games of)

Your accent is not <u>as strong as</u> <u>my mother's</u>.
    (*my mother's* = my mother's accent)

My sewing machine is <u>better than</u> <u>Jane's</u>.
    (*Jane's* = Jane's sewing machine)

IRREGULAR COMPARATIVES AND SUPERLATIVES

A few adjectives and adverbs have irregular forms for the comparative and superlative. Study them.

ADJECTIVE OR ADVERB	COMPARATIVE	SUPERLATIVE
far	{farther / further}	{farthest / furthest}
little	less	least
{much / many}	more	most
{good / well}	better	best
{bad / badly}	worse	worst

I feel <u>much better</u> today <u>than</u> I did last week.

The university is <u>farther than</u> the mall.

He has <u>less time</u> now <u>than</u> he had before.

Marjorie has <u>more books than</u> Sue.

This magazine is <u>better than</u> that one.

He acts <u>worse</u> now <u>than</u> ever before.

Exercise 28: Comparisons

Supply the correct form of the adjectives and adverbs in parentheses. Let *as* and *than* be your clues. Add any other words that may be necessary.

1. John and his friends left _____ (soon) as the professor had finished his lecture.
2. His job is _____ (important) than his friend's.
3. He plays the guitar _____ (well) as Andrés Segovia.
4. A new house is much _____ (expensive) than an older one.
5. Last week was _____ (hot) as this week.
6. Martha is _____ (talented) than her cousin.
7. Bill's descriptions are _____ (colorful) than his wife's.

8. Nobody is _____ (happy) than María Elena.
9. The boys felt _____ (bad) than the girls about losing the game.
10. A greyhound runs _____ (fast) than a Chihuahua.

Exercise 29: Comparisons

Supply *than, as,* or *from* in each of the following sentences.

1. The Empire State Building is taller _____ the Statue of Liberty.
2. California is farther from New York _____ Pennsylvania.
3. His assignment is different _____ mine.
4. Louie reads more quickly _____ his sisters.
5. No animal is so big _____ King Kong.
6. That report is less impressive _____ the government's.
7. Sam wears the same shirt _____ his teammates.
8. Dave paints much more realistically _____ his professor.
9. The twins have less money at the end of the month _____ they have at the beginning.
10. Her sports car is different _____ Nancy's.

MULTIPLE NUMBER COMPARATIVES

Number multiples can include: *half, twice, three times, four times,* etc. Study the following rule.

subject + verb + number multiple + *as* + {*much* / *many*} + (noun) + *as* + {noun / pronoun}

NOTE: It is *incorrect* to say: "twice more than," etc.

This encyclopedia costs twice as much as the other one.

At the clambake last week, Fred ate three times as many oysters as Barney.

Jerome has half as many records now as I had last year.

DOUBLE COMPARATIVES

These sentences begin with a comparative construction, and thus the second clause must also begin with a comparative.

> *the* + comparative + subject + verb + *the* + comparative + subject + verb

The <u>hotter</u> it is, <u>the more miserable</u> I feel.
The <u>higher</u> we flew, <u>the worse</u> Edna felt.
The <u>bigger</u> they are, <u>the harder</u> they fall.
The <u>sooner</u> you take your medicine, <u>the better</u> you will feel.
The <u>sooner</u> you leave, <u>the earlier</u> you will arrive at your destination.

> *the more* + subject + verb + *the* + comparative + subject + verb

The <u>more</u> you study, <u>the smarter</u> you will become.
The <u>more</u> he rowed the boat, <u>the farther</u> away he got.
The <u>more</u> he slept, <u>the more irritable</u> he became.

NO SOONER

If the expression *no sooner* appears at the beginning of a sentence, the word *than* must introduce the second clause. Note also that the auxiliary precedes the subject.

> *no sooner* + auxiliary + subject + verb + *than* + subject + verb

<u>No sooner</u> had we started out for California <u>than</u> it started to rain.
<u>No sooner</u> will he arrive <u>than</u> he will want to leave.
<u>No sooner</u> had she entered the building <u>than</u> she felt the presence of somebody else.

NOTE: *No longer* means *not anymore*. NEVER use *not longer* in a sentence that has this meaning.

John no longer studies at the university.
> (John *does not* study at the university *anymore*.)

Cynthia may no longer use the library because her card has expired.
> (Cynthia *may not* use the library *anymore*.)

POSITIVES, COMPARATIVES, AND SUPERLATIVES

Most descriptive adjectives have three forms: the positive (*happy*), the comparative (*happier*), and the superlative (*happiest*).

POSITIVE	COMPARATIVE	SUPERLATIVE
hot	hotter	hottest
interesting	more interesting	most interesting
sick	sicker	sickest
colorful	more colorful	most colorful

• The *positive* shows no comparison. It describes only the simple quality of a person, thing, or group.

The house is big.
The flowers are fragrant.

• The *comparative* involves *two* entities and shows a greater or lesser degree of differences between them.

My dog is smarter than yours.
Bob is more athletic than Richard.
Spinach is less appealing than carrots.

It is also possible to compare two entities without using *than*. In this case the expression *of the two* will usually appear someplace in the sentence.

> subject + verb + *the* + comparative + *of the two* + (noun)

OR

> *of the two* + (noun) + subject + verb + *the* + comparative

Harvey is the smarter of the two boys.

Of the two shirts, this one is the prettier.

Please give me the smaller of the two pieces of cake.

Of the two landscapes that you have shown me, this one is the more picturesque.

Of the two books, this one is the more interesting.

Remember:

> 2 entities–comparative
> 3 or more–superlative

• In the *superlative* degree, three or more entities are compared, one of which is superior or inferior to the others. The following rule applies.

$$\text{subject} + \text{verb} + \textit{the} + \begin{Bmatrix} \text{adjective} + \textit{est} \\ \textit{most} + \text{adjective} \\ \textit{least} + \text{adjective} \end{Bmatrix} + \begin{Bmatrix} \textit{in} + \text{singular count noun} \\ \textit{of} + \text{plural count noun} \end{Bmatrix}$$

John is the tallest boy in the family.

Deana is the shortest of the three sisters.

These shoes are the least expensive of all.

Of the three shirts, this one is the prettiest.

NOTE: After the expression *one of the* + superlative, be sure that the noun is plural and the verb is singular.

One of the greatest tennis players in the world is Bjorn Borg.

Kuwait is one of the biggest oil producers in the world.

Adverbs usually are not followed by *-er* or *-est*. Instead, they are compared by adding *more* or *less* for the comparative degree, and by adding *most* or *least* to form the superlative.

POSITIVE	COMPARATIVE	SUPERLATIVE
carefully	more carefully less carefully	most carefully least carefully
cautiously	more cautiously less cautiously	most cautiously least cautiously

Sal drove more cautiously than Bob.   (comparative)

Joe dances more gracefully than his partner.   (comparative)

That child behaves the most carelessly of all.   (superlative)

Irene plays the most recklessly of all.   (superlative)

Exercise 30: Comparisons

Select the correct form in parentheses in the following sentences.

1. Of the four dresses, I like the red one (better/best).
2. Phil is the (happier/happiest) person we know.
3. Pat's car is (faster/fastest) than Dan's.
4. This is the (creamier/creamiest) ice cream I have had in a long time.
5. This poster is (colorfuler/more colorful) than the one in the hall.
6. Does Fred feel (weller/better) today than he did yesterday?
7. This vegetable soup tastes very (good/well).
8. While trying to balance the baskets on her head, the woman walked (awkwarder/more awkwardly) than her daughter.

9. Jane is the (less/least) athletic of all the women.
10. My cat is the (prettier/prettiest) of the two.
11. This summary is (the better/the best) of the pair.
12. Your heritage is different (from/than) mine.
13. This painting is (less impressive/least impressive) than the one in the other gallery.
14. The colder the weather gets, (sicker/the sicker) I feel.
15. No sooner had he received the letter (when/than) he called Maria.
16. A mink coat costs (twice more than/twice as much as) a sable coat.
17. Jim has as (little/few) opportunities to play tennis as I.
18. That recipe calls for (many/much) more sugar than mine does.
19. The museum is the (farther/farthest) away of the three buildings.
20. George Washington is (famouser/more famous) than John Jay.

18. NOUNS FUNCTIONING AS ADJECTIVES

In English, many nouns can function as adjectives when they appear before other nouns (a wool coat, a gold watch, a history teacher). The first noun of the combination functions as an adjective, describing the second one, which functions as a noun. The nouns which function as adjectives are always in the singular even though they may modify a plural noun. Number-noun combinations always appear hyphenated.

We took a tour that lasted five weeks.

(*Weeks* functions as a noun in this sentence.)

We took a five-week tour.
  adjective   *noun*

His subscription to that magazine is for two years.

(*Years* functions as a noun in this sentence.)

He has a two-year subscription to that magazine.
  adjective   *noun*

That student wrote a report that was <u>ten pages</u> long.

(*Pages* functions as a noun in this sentence.)

That sudent wrote a <u>ten-page</u> <u>report</u>.
adjective   noun

These shoes cost <u>twenty dollars</u>.

(*Dollars* functions as a noun in this sentence.)

These are <u>twenty-dollar</u> <u>shoes</u>.
adjective   noun

Exercise 31: Nouns Functioning as Adjectives

In each of the following sets, choose the appropriate form for the blank in the second sentence.

Example: Her call to California lasted ten minutes.

                 She made a <u>ten-minute call</u> to California.

1. Sam's new apartment is in a building which has twelve stories.
   Sam's new apartment is in a _____ building.
2. We teach languages.
   We are _____ teachers.
3. My parents saw a play in three acts last night.
   My parents saw a _____ play last night.
4. The manager said that the sale would last for two days.
   The manager said that it would be a _____ sale.
5. Hal bought a tool set containing 79 pieces.
   Hal bought a _____ tool set.
6. Margie has a bookcase with five shelves.
   Margie has a _____ bookcase.
7. I need two cans of tomatoes that weigh 16 ounces each.
   I need two _____ cans of tomatoes.
8. I'm looking for a pressure cooker that holds six quarts.
   I'm looking for a _____ pressure cooker.
9. He is a specialist at building houses made of bricks.
   He is a specialist at building _____ houses.
10. Mrs. Jansen just bought her daughter a bicycle with ten speeds.
    Mrs. Jansen just bought her daughter a _____ bicycle.

19. *ENOUGH* WITH ADJECTIVES, ADVERBS, AND NOUNS

Enough changes positions depending on whether it is modifying a noun, an adjective, or an adverb. When modifying an adjective or an adverb, *enough* follows.

$$\begin{Bmatrix} \text{adjective} \\ \text{adverb} \end{Bmatrix} + enough$$

Are those french fries <u>crisp</u> <u>enough</u> for you?
    adjective

She speaks Spanish <u>well</u> <u>enough</u> to be an interpreter.
    adverb

It is not <u>cold</u> <u>enough</u> to wear a heavy jacket.
    adjective

When modifying a noun, *enough* precedes the noun.

$$enough + \text{noun}$$

Do you have <u>enough</u> <u>sugar</u> for the cake?
    noun

Jake bought <u>enough</u> <u>red paint</u> to finish the barn.
    noun phrase

He does not have <u>enough</u> <u>money</u> to attend the concert.
    noun

NOTE: The noun that is modified by *enough* may sometimes be deleted with no change in meaning.

I forgot my money. Do you have <u>enough</u>?
(We understand that the speaker means "enough money.")

Exercise 32: **Enough**

In the following sentences, choose the correct form in parentheses.

1. There were not (enough people/people enough) to have the meeting.
2. Allen has learned (enough French/French enough) to study in France next year.
3. Do you have (enough time/time enough) to talk now?
4. She drove (enough fast/fast enough) to win the race.
5. Mike will graduate from law school (enough soon/soon enough) to join his father's firm.
6. We arrived (enough early/early enough) to have some coffee before class began.
7. It has rained (enough hard/hard enough) to flood the low-lying areas.
8. You should type (enough slowly/slowly enough) that you will not make an error.
9. He has just (enough flour/flour enough) to bake that loaf of bread.
10. There are (enough books/books enough) for each student to have one.

20. CAUSE CONNECTORS

This section demonstrates the usage of several grammatical devices which show cause.

BECAUSE/BECAUSE OF

Because (not followed by *of*) must always be followed by a clause. A clause standing alone is a complete sentence. (There must be a subject and a verb.) *Because of* is followed *only* by a noun or noun phrase. (There must NOT be a conjugated verb.)

$$\ldots because + \begin{Bmatrix} \text{subject} + \text{verb} \\ \textit{there} + \text{verb} + \text{subject} \end{Bmatrix}$$

$$\ldots because \ of + \text{noun (phrase)}$$

NOTE: *Because of* is often interchangeable with the expression *due to.*

Jan was worried because <u>it</u> <u>had started to rain</u>.
                           subject   *verb*

Jan was worried <u>because of the rain</u>.
                       noun phrase

The students arrived late because <u>there</u> <u>was</u> a <u>traffic jam</u>.
                                     verb   *subject*

The students arrived late <u>because of the traffic jam</u>.
                             noun phrase

We have to cut down on our driving because <u>there</u> <u>is</u> an
                                         verb

<u>oil shortage</u>.
subject

We have to cut down on our driving <u>because of</u>

<u>the oil shortage</u>.
noun phrase

NOTE: It is also possible for the cause clause to begin the sentence.

<u>Because of the rain</u>, we have canceled the party.

Exercise 33: **Because/Because Of**

Supply either *because* or *because of* as appropriate.

1. It was difficult to deliver the letter _____ the sender had written the wrong address on the envelope.
2. We decided to leave early _____ the party was boring.
3. Rescue attempts were temporarily halted _____ the bad weather.
4. They visited their friends often _____ they enjoyed their company.
5. Paul cannot go to the football game _____ his grades.
6. Marcella was awarded a scholarship _____ her superior scholastic ability.
7. Nobody ventured outdoors _____ the hurricane warnings.
8. We plan to spend our vacation in the mountains _____ the air is purer there.
9. We have to drive around the bay _____ the bridge was destroyed in the storm.
10. The chickens have died _____ the intense heat.

PURPOSE AND RESULT (*SO THAT*)

Clauses showing purpose are followed by the conjunction *so that.* After *so that* is a result clause with both a subject and a verb. The time of the result clause must be future in relation to the time of the purpose clause.

> subject + verb + *so that* + subject + verb

NOTE: It is NOT correct in formal written English to eliminate *that* in these sentences, although it is possible in spoken English.

He studied very hard so that he could pass the test.

She is sending the package early so that it will arrive in time for her sister's birthday.

Damien is practicing the guitar so that he can play for the dance.

I am learning German so that I will be able to speak it when I go to Austria next summer.

Susan drove to Miami instead of flying so that she could save money.

Will you let me know about the party so that I can make plans to attend?

CAUSE AND EFFECT (*SO, SUCH*)

The following constructions are used to indicate a cause and effect (result) relationship.

$$\text{subject} + \text{verb} + so + \begin{Bmatrix} \text{adjective} \\ \text{adverb} \end{Bmatrix} + that + \text{subject} + \text{verb}$$

NOTE: Do NOT use a noun after *so*. See constructions below.

The soprano sang so well that she received a standing ovation.

Terry ran so fast that he broke the previous speed record.

Judy worked so diligently that she received an increase in salary.

The soup tastes so good that everyone will ask for more.

The little boy looks so unhappy that we all feel sorry for him.

The student had behaved so badly that he was dismissed from the class.

The rules for clauses including the intensive modifiers are:

$$\text{subject} + \text{verb} + so + \begin{Bmatrix} many \\ few \end{Bmatrix} + \text{plural count noun} + that + \text{subject} + \text{verb}$$

The Smiths had so many children that they formed their own baseball team.

I had so few job offers that it wasn't difficult to select one.

$$\text{subject} + \text{verb} + so + \begin{Bmatrix} much \\ little \end{Bmatrix} + \text{non-count noun} + that + \text{subject} + \text{verb}$$

He has invested <u>so</u> <u>much</u> <u>money</u> in the project <u>that</u> he cannot abandon it now.

The grass received <u>so</u> <u>little</u> <u>water</u> <u>that</u> it turned brown in the heat.

---

subject + verb + *such* + *a* + adjective + singular count noun + *that* . . .

OR

---

subject + verb + *so* + adjective + *a* + singular count noun + *that* . . .

NOTE: *Such* + *a* + adjective is the more common of the two.

It was <u>such</u> <u>a</u> <u>hot</u> <u>day</u> <u>that</u> we decided to stay indoors.
OR
It was <u>so</u> <u>hot</u> <u>a</u> <u>day</u> <u>that</u> we decided to stay indoors.

It was <u>such</u> <u>an</u> <u>interesting</u> <u>book</u> <u>that</u> he couldn't put it down.
OR
It was <u>so</u> <u>interesting</u> <u>a</u> <u>book</u> <u>that</u> he couldn't put it down.

---

subject + verb + *such* + adjective + { plural count noun / non-count noun } + *that* + subject + verb

---

She has <u>such</u> <u>exceptional</u> <u>abilities</u> <u>that</u> everyone is jealous of her.
*plural count
noun*

They are <u>such</u> <u>beautiful</u> <u>pictures</u> <u>that</u> everybody will want one.
*plural count
noun*

Perry has had <u>such</u> <u>bad</u> <u>luck</u> <u>that</u> he's decided not to gamble.
*non-count
noun*

This is <u>such</u> <u>difficult</u> <u>homework</u> <u>that</u> I will never finish it.
non-count noun

NOTE: It is NOT possible to use *so* in the above rule.

Meanings:

It has been <u>such a long time</u> since I've seen him <u>that</u> I'm not sure
if I will remember him.

(I'm not sure if I will remember him *because* it has been a long
time.)

Cause: It has been a long time.

Effect: I'm not sure if I will remember him.

He has <u>so heavy a work load that</u> it is difficult for him to travel.

(It is difficult for him to travel *because* he has a heavy work
load.)

Cause: He has a very heavy work load.

Effect: It is difficult for him to travel.

Peter has <u>such long fingers that</u> he should play the piano.

(Peter should play the piano *because* he has very long fingers.)

Cause: Peter has very long fingers.

Effect: He should play the piano.

Professor Sands gives <u>such interesting lectures that</u> his classes are
never boring.

(Professor Sand's classes are never boring *because* he gives very
interesting lectures.)

Cause: Professor Sands gives very interesting lectures.

Effect: His classes are never boring.

This is <u>such tasty ice cream that</u> I'll have another helping.

(I'll have another helping of ice cream *because* it is very tasty.)

Cause: The ice cream is very tasty.

Effect: I'll have another helping.

Exercise 34: So/Such

Following the formulas, use either *so* or *such* in these sentences as appropriate.

1. The sun shone _____ brightly that Maria had to put on her sunglasses.
2. Dean was _____ a powerful swimmer that he always won the races.
3. There were _____ few students registered that the class was cancelled.
4. We had _____ wonderful memories of that place that we decided to return.
5. We had _____ good a time at the party that we hated to leave.
6. The benefit was _____ great a success that the promoters decided to repeat it.
7. It was _____ a nice day that we decided to go to the beach.
8. Jane looked _____ sick that the nurse told her to go home.
9. Those were _____ difficult assignments that we spent two weeks finishing them.
10. Ray called at _____ an early hour that we weren't awake yet.
11. The book looked _____ interesting that he decided to read it.
12. He worked _____ carefully that it took him a long time to complete the project.
13. We stayed in the sun for _____ a long time that we became sunburned.
14. There were _____ many people on the bus that we decided to walk.
15. The program was _____ entertaining that nobody wanted to miss it.

MINI-TEST 2: GRAMMAR ITEMS 15 THROUGH 20

DIRECTIONS

Each question on this mini-test consists of a sentence in which four words or phrases are underlined. The four underlined parts of the sentence are marked A, B, C, D. You are to identify the *one* underlined word or phrase that *would not be acceptable in standard written English*. Circle the letter of the underlined portion which is not correct.

1. Children enjoy telling and listening to ghosts stories, especially
                     A   B   C

   on Halloween night.
        D

2. At the rate the clerks were processing the applications, Harry
                             A

   figured that it will take four hours for his to be reviewed.
            B   C   D

3. No one would have attended the lecture if you told
                    A   B

   the truth about the guest speaker.
        C   D

4. We had better to review this chapter carefully because we will
             A   B

   have some questions on it on our test tomorrow.
        C   D

5. The little boy's mother bought him a five-speeds racing bicycle
     A   B   C

   for his birthday.
     D

6. Despite the time of the year, yesterday's temperature was
     A   B

   enough hot to turn on the air conditioning.
     C   D

7. The Andersons just had an enclosed bricks patio built
   _____   _____   _____
        A   B   C
   after fighting off the insects for two months.
   _____
         D

8. Danny spent such enjoyable vacation in Europe this summer
               _____
                     A
   that he plans to return as soon as he saves enough money.
   _____ _____   _____
      B   C   D

9. Although the quantity was small, we had supplies enough to
   _____   ___   _____
      A   B   C
   finish the experiment.
          ___
           D

10. Kurt had so interesting and creative plans that everyone
              _____   _____
                    A   B
    wanted to work on his committee.
    _____   __
       C   D

11. If Rudy would have studied German in college, he would not
            _____   _____
                    A   B
    have found the scientific terminology
               _____
                     C
    so difficult to understand.
    _____
                D

12. I have to depositing this money in my checking account or else
              _____   _____
                   A   B
    the check I just wrote will bounce.
               _____ _____
                   C   D

13. We wish today was sunny so that we could spend the day
                    ___   _____   _____
                     A   B   C
    in the country communing with nature.
    _____
          D

14. Paul did <u>so</u> well in his speech today <u>that</u> he
      A   B
<u>should have rehearsed</u> it many times <u>this past week</u>.
         C   D

15. Bess is used <u>to fly</u> after <u>having crossed</u> the continent
               A   B
<u>many times</u> during the <u>past decade</u>.
    C   D

16. Our Spanish professor would like <u>us</u> <u>spending</u> more time
                                  A B
<u>in the</u> laboratory <u>practicing</u> our pronunciation.
  C   D

17. Sam used to <u>living</u> in Oklahoma, <u>but</u> his company
            A   B
<u>had him transferred</u> to a <u>better position</u> in Georgia.
      C   D

18. The bolder <u>the matador's</u> display <u>in the arena</u> became,
            A   B
louder the audience expressed <u>its</u> approval of his presentation.
 C   D

19. Hal's new <u>sports</u> car <u>costs</u> <u>much more</u> than his <u>friend Joel</u>.
         A   B   C   D

20. Max would rather <u>to be fishing</u> <u>from this boat</u> in the lake
                A   B
<u>than</u> sitting <u>at his desk</u> in the office.
  C   D

21. Sally <u>must have called</u> her sister last night, but she
         A
<u>arrived</u> home <u>too late</u> to call <u>her</u>.
  B   C   D

22. If a crisis <u>would occur</u>, <u>those unfamiliar</u> with <u>the</u> procedures
                A   B   C

    would not know <u>how to handle</u> the situation.
                      D

23. <u>Standing among</u> so many strangers, <u>the frightened</u> child began
           A   B

    <u>to sob</u> <u>uncontrollable</u>.
     C   D

24. The teacher <u>tried to make</u> the classes enjoyable experiences
                  A

    for the students <u>so</u> they <u>would take a greater</u> interest
                   B   C

    <u>in the</u> subject.
      D

25. Whenever students asked <u>for help</u> or guidance, the counselor
                          A

    <u>would advise</u> them or <u>refer them</u> to someone who <u>will</u>.
        B   C   D

26. Anybody <u>who plans</u> <u>to attend</u> the meeting <u>ought send</u> a short
            A   B   C

    note <u>to the</u> chairperson.
       D

27. The teachers and the administrators are having

    <u>such difficult</u> time <u>agreeing</u> on a contract for
       A   B

    <u>the forthcoming year</u> that the teachers <u>may go on strike</u>.
          C   D

28. Mary <u>usually arrives</u> <u>at the office</u> at nine o'clock, but
            A   B

    <u>because</u> the storm, she was two hours <u>late</u>.
      C   D

29. Our new television came with a ninety-days warranty
                              A   B
    on all electrical components.
    C   D

30. It is difficult to get used to sleep in a tent after having a soft,
            A   B   C
    comfortable bed to lie on.
                    D

31. The director felt badly about not giving Mary the position
                     A   B
    that she had sought with his company.
    C   D

32. Tom and Mark hope go skiing in the mountains this weekend
                       A   B
    if the weather permits.
    C   D

33. The political candidate talked as if she has already
    A   B
    been elected to the presidency.
    C   D

34. The salad tasted so well that my brother returned to the
                     A   B
    salad bar for another helping.
    C   D

35. Even though she looks very young, she is twice older than my
    A   B   C
    twenty-year-old sister.
    D

36. Despite his smiling face, the second-place contestant is
    A   B   C
    more sadder than the winner.
    D

37. I do not believe that I <u>have ever seen</u> as many expensive cars
                                      A

<u>than</u> <u>were</u> in <u>that shopping center.</u>
 B   C   D

38. <u>The</u> members of the orchestra <u>had to arrived</u> an hour
     A   B

<u>prior to the performance</u> <u>for a short</u> rehearsal.
           C   D

39. We thought our cameras were <u>the same</u>, but <u>his is</u> different
                                      A   B

<u>than</u> the one that I <u>bought.</u>
 C   D

40. If Monique had not attended <u>the</u> conference, she
                                 A

<u>never would meet</u> her old friend Dan, <u>whom</u> she
        B   C

<u>had not seen</u> in years.
     D

41. <u>Having lived</u> here <u>for</u> seven years, my friend is used to
        A   B

<u>speak</u> English with <u>all her</u> classmates.
   C   D

42. No one in our office <u>wants</u> to drive to work any more
                          A

<u>because of</u> there <u>are</u> always traffic jams <u>at rush hour.</u>
    B   C   D

43. That novel is <u>definitely</u> a <u>dense-packed</u> narrative, but
                     A   B

<u>one which requires</u> a vast knowledge of cultural background or
        C

<u>an</u> excellent encyclopedia.
 D

44. Louise is <u>the more</u> capable <u>of the</u> three girls <u>who have</u> tried
             A   B   C
    out for the part <u>in the play</u>.
                      D

45. They <u>played</u> <u>so good</u> game of tennis last night <u>that</u> they
           A   B   C
    surprised <u>their</u> audience.
              D

46. I would rather <u>that</u> they <u>do not travel</u> during <u>the bad</u> weather,
                   A   B   C
    but they insist that <u>they must return</u> home today.
                          D

47. <u>Among us</u> students are <u>many foreigners</u> <u>who</u> attend
      A   B   C
    <u>languages</u> classes at the south campus.
      D

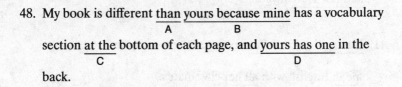

48. My book is different <u>than</u> <u>yours because mine</u> has a vocabulary
                        A   B
    section <u>at the</u> bottom of each page, and <u>yours has one</u> in the
               C   D
    back.

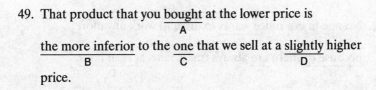

49. That product that you <u>bought</u> at the lower price is
                     A
    <u>the more inferior</u> to <u>the one</u> that we sell at a <u>slightly</u> higher
            B   C   D
    price.

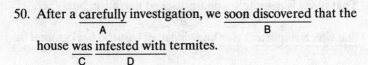

50. After a <u>carefully</u> investigation, we <u>soon discovered</u> that the
           A   B
    house <u>was</u> <u>infested with</u> termites.
            C   D

21. PASSIVE VOICE

A sentence can be either in the active or passive voice. In an "active" sentence, the subject performs the action. In a "passive" sentence, the subject receives the action. To make an active sentence into a passive sentence, follow these steps.

1. Place the complement of the active sentence at the beginning of the passive sentence.
2. If there are any auxiliaries in the active sentence, place them immediately after the new subject agreeing in number with the subject.
3. Insert the verb *be* after the auxiliary or auxiliaries in the same form as the main verb in the active sentence.
4. Place the main verb from the active sentence after the auxiliaries and *be* in the past participle.
5. Place the subject of the active sentence after the verb in the passive sentence preceded by the preposition *by*. (This can be eliminated completely if it is not important or is understood.)

Study the following possible word orders for passive voice.

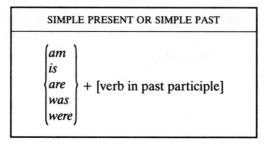

SIMPLE PRESENT OR SIMPLE PAST

$$\left.\begin{array}{l} am \\ is \\ are \\ was \\ were \end{array}\right\} + \text{[verb in past participle]}$$

Active: Hurricanes destroy a great deal of property each year.
           subject   present   complement

Passive: A great deal of property is destroyed by hurricanes each
           singular subject   be past participle

year.

Active: The tornado destroyed thirty houses.
             subject   *past*   *complement*

Passive: Thirty houses were destroyed by the tornado.
             plural subject   *be* *past participle*

PRESENT PROGRESSIVE OR PAST PROGRESSIVE

$$\left. \begin{array}{l} am \\ is \\ are \\ was \\ were \end{array} \right\} + being + [\text{verb in past participle}]$$

Active: The committee is considering several new proposals.
             subject   *present progressive*   *complement*

Passive: Several new proposals are being considered
             plural subject   *auxiliary* *be* *past participle*

by the committee.

Active: The committee was considering
             subject   *past progressive*

several new proposals.
             complement

Passive: Several new proposals were being considered
             plural subject   *auxiliary* *be* *past participle*

by the committee.

PRESENT PERFECT OR PAST PERFECT

$$\left\{\begin{matrix} has \\ have \\ had \end{matrix}\right\} + been + \text{[verb in past participle]}$$

Active: The company has ordered some new equipment.
               subject   *present perfect*   *complement*

Passive: Some new equipment has been ordered
               singular subject   *auxiliary* *be* *past participle*

           by the company.

Active: The company had ordered
               subject   *past perfect*

           some new equipment before the strike began.
                   complement

Passive: Some new equipment had been ordered
               subject   *auxiliary* *be* *past participle*

           by the company before the strike began.

MODALS

modal + *be* + [verb in past participle]

Active: The manager should sign these contracts today.
               subject   *modal + verb*   *complement*

Passive: These contracts should be   signed
               subject   *modal* *be* *past participle*

           by the manager today.

```
┌─────────────────────────────────────────────────────┐
│                 MODALS + PERFECT                      │
├─────────────────────────────────────────────────────┤
│   modal + have + been + [verb in past participle]     │
└─────────────────────────────────────────────────────┘
```

Active: <u>Somebody</u> <u>should have called</u> <u>the president</u> this
            subject   *modal + perfect*   *complement*
morning.

Passive: <u>The president</u> <u>should</u> <u>have</u> <u>been</u> <u>called</u> this
            subject   *modal*   *have*   *be* *past participle*
morning.

Exercise 35: Passive Voice

Change the following sentences from active to passive voice.

1. Somebody calls the president every day.
2. John is calling the other members.
3. Martha was delivering the documents to the department.
4. The other members have repealed the amendment.
5. The delegates had received the information before the recess.
6. The teacher should buy the supplies for this class.
7. Somebody will call Mr. Watson tonight.
8. The fire has caused considerable damage.
9. The company was developing a new procedure before the bankruptcy hearings began.
10. John will have received the papers by tomorrow.

22. CAUSATIVE VERBS

The causative verbs are used to indicate that one person causes a second person to do something for the first person. One can cause somebody to do something for him or her by paying, asking, or forcing the person. The causative verbs are: *have, get, make.*

HAVE/GET

The clause following *have* or *get* may be active or passive. Study the following rules.

(1) ACTIVE
subject + *have* + complement + [verb in simple form] . . . *(any tense)* *(usually person)*

(2) ACTIVE
subject + *get* + complement + [verb in infinitive] . . . *(any tense)* *(usually person)*

(3) PASSIVE
subject + $\begin{Bmatrix} have \\ get \end{Bmatrix}$ + complement + [verb in past participle] . . . *(any tense)* *(usually thing)*

(1) Mary had John wash the car. (John washed the car.) active
(2) Mary got John to wash the car. (John washed the car.) active
(3) Mary got the car washed. (The car was washed by
     Mary had the car washed. somebody.) passive

Examples of active clauses in causative sentences:

The president had his advisors arrange a press conference.
George is getting his teachers to give him a make-up exam.
Mary has had a friend type all of her papers.
John is having his father contact the officials.
The editor had the contributors attend a composition workshop.
Morris got his dog to bring him the newspaper.

Examples of passive clauses in causative sentences:

James has his shirts cleaned at the drycleaners.

Pat is having her car repaired this week.

Anna got her paper typed by a friend.

The president is having a press conference arranged by his advisors.

Mary got her husband arrested. (Exception: a person is the complement, but the second clause is passive.)

Rick was having his hair cut when John called.

MAKE

Make can be followed only by a clause in the active voice. It is stronger than *have* or *get*. It means *force*.

> subject + *make* + complement + [verb in simple form] . . .
> *(any tense)*

The robber made the teller give him the money.

(The robber *forced* the teller *to give* him the money.)

NOTE: *force* + complement + [verb in infinitive]

Examples of *make:*

The manager made the salesmen attend the conference.

The teacher always makes the children stay in their seats.

George made his son be quiet in the theater.

The president is making his cabinet members sign this document.

The teacher had made the students' parents sign release forms before he let the students jump on the trampoline.

LET

Let is usually added to the list of causatives in grammar textbooks. It is not actually causative. It means *allow* or *permit*. Notice the difference in grammar.

> subject + *let* + complement + [verb in simple form] . . .

> subject + $\begin{Bmatrix} permit \\ allow \end{Bmatrix}$ + complement + [verb in infinitive] . . .

NOTE: *Let* is NOT INTERCHANGEABLE WITH *leave,* which means *to go away.*

Examples:

John let his daughter swim with her friends.
(John allowed his daughter to swim with her friends.)
(John permitted his daughter to swim with her friends.)
The teacher let the students leave class early.
The policeman let the suspect make one phone call.
Dr. Jones is letting the students hand in the papers on Monday.
Mrs. Binion let her son spend the night with a friend.
We are going to let her write the letter.
Mr. Brown always lets his children watch cartoons on Saturday
  mornings.

HELP

Help is not actually a causative verb either, but is generally considered with causative verbs in grammar textbooks. It is usually followed by the simple form, but can be followed by the infinitive in some cases. It means *assist.*

$$\text{subject} + \textit{help} + \text{complement} + \begin{Bmatrix} [\text{verb in simple form}] \\ [\text{verb in infinitive}] \end{Bmatrix}$$

John helped Mary wash the dishes.
Jorge helped the old woman with the packages (to) find a taxi.
The teacher helped Carolina find the research materials.

Exercise 36: Causative Verbs

Use the correct form of the verb in parentheses in each of the following sentences.

1. The teacher made Juan _____ (leave) the room.
2. Toshiko had her car _____ (repair) by a mechanic.
3. Ellen got Marvin _____ (type) her paper.
4. I made Jane _____ (call) her friend on the telephone.
5. We got our house _____ (paint) last week.
6. Dr. Byrd is having the students _____ (write) a composition.
7. The policemen made the suspect _____ (lie) on the ground.
8. Mark got his transcripts _____ (send) to the university.
9. Maria is getting her hair _____ (cut) tomorrow.
10. We will have to get the Dean _____ (sign) this form.
11. The teacher let Al _____ (leave) the classroom.
12. Maria got Ed _____ (wash) the pipettes.
13. She always has her car _____ (fix) by the same mechanic.
14. Gene got his book _____ (publish) by a subsidy publisher.
15. We have to help Janet _____ (find) her keys.

23. RELATIVE CLAUSES

THE RELATIVE PRONOUN

A relative clause is used to form one sentence from two separate sentences. The relative pronoun replaces one of two identical noun phrases and relates the clauses to each other. The relative pronouns and their uses are listed here.

PRONOUN	USE IN FORMAL ENGLISH
that	things
which	things
who	people
whom	people
whose	usually people

NOTE: In speaking, *that* can be used for people, but NOT in formal written English.

The relative pronoun completely replaces a duplicate noun phrase. *There can be no regular pronoun along with the relative pronoun.*

Incorrect: This is the book that I bought it at the bookstore.

Correct: This is the book that I bought at the bookstore.

Remember that a sentence with a relative clause can always be reduced to two separate sentences, so each clause *must contain a verb.*

We bought the stereo. The stereo had been advertised at a re-
duplicate noun phrase
duced price.

We bought the stereo that had been advertised at a reduced price.

John bought a boat. The boat cost thirty thousand dollars.
John bought a boat that cost thirty thousand dollars.

George is going to buy the house. We have been thinking of buying the house.
George is going to buy the house that we have been thinking of buying.

John is the man. We are going to recommend John for the job.
John is the man whom we are going to recommend for the job.

WHO/WHOM

Who is used when the noun phrase being replaced is in the subject position of the sentence. *Whom* is used when it is from the complement position. NOTE: In speech, *whom* is rarely used, but it should be used when appropriate in formal written English. If you have difficulty deciding whether *who* or *whom* should be used, remember the following rule.

> ... *who* + verb ...
> ... *whom* + noun ...

Consider the following sentences.

The men are angry.

The men are in this room.

These sentences can also be considered as:

The men [the men are in this room] are angry.
           subject

The men who are in this room are angry.

The men are angry. I don't like the men.

The men [I don't like the men] are angry.
                    complement

The men whom I don't like are angry.

We also use the form *whom* after a preposition. In this case, the preposition should also be moved to the position before *whom* in formal written English.

The men are angry. The woman is talking to the men.

The men [the woman is talking to the men] are angry.
                              complement of
                              preposition

The men to whom the woman is talking are angry.

However, if the preposition is part of a combination such as a two-word verb, meaning that the preposition cannot reasonably be moved away from the verb, it will remain with the verb.

RESTRICTIVE AND NONRESTRICTIVE CLAUSES

A relative clause can be either restrictive or nonrestrictive. A restrictive clause is one that cannot be omitted from a sentence if the sentence is to keep its original meaning. A nonrestrictive clause contains additional information which is not required to give the meaning of the sentence. A nonrestrictive clause is set off from the other clause by commas and a restrictive clause is not. *Who, whom,* and *which* can be used in restrictive or nonrestrictive clauses. *That* can be used *only in restrictive clauses.* Normally, *that* is the preferred word to use in a restrictive clause, although *which* is acceptable. TOEFL does not test the use of *which* and *that* in restrictive clauses.

Examples of restrictive and nonrestrictive clauses:

Restrictive: Weeds that float to the surface should be removed before they decay.

(We are not speaking of all weeds, only those that float to the surface. Thus, the sentence is restrictive; if "that float to the surface" were omitted, the sentence would have a different meaning.)

Nonrestrictive: My car, which is very large, uses too much gasoline.

(The fact that my car is very large is additional information and not important to the rest of the sentence. Notice that it is not possible to use the pronoun *that* in place of *which* in this sentence.)

Examples of relative clauses:

Dr. Jones is the only doctor whom I have seen about this problem.

Hurricanes that are born off the coast of Africa often prove to be the most deadly.

Teachers who do not spend enough time on class preparation often have difficulty explaining new lessons.

This rum, which I bought in the Virgin Islands, is very smooth.

Film that has been exposed to X-rays often produces poor photographs.

The woman to whom we gave the check has left.

WHOSE

This relative pronoun indicates possession.

The board was composed of citizens. The citizens' dedication was evident.

The board was composed of citizens whose dedication was evident.

James [James's father is the president of the company] has received a promotion.

James, whose father is the president of the company, has received a promotion.

John found a cat. The cat's leg was broken.

John found a cat whose leg was broken.

Harold [Harold's car was stolen last night] is at the police station.

Harold, whose car was stolen last night, is at the police station.

The company [the company's employees are on strike] is closing down for two weeks.

The company, whose employees are on strike, is closing down for two weeks.

The dentist is with a child. The child's teeth are causing some problems.

The dentist is with a child whose teeth are causing some problems.

The president [the president's advisors have quit] is giving a press conference.

The president, whose advisors have quit, is giving a press conference.

Exercise 37: Relative Clauses

Combine the following individual sentences into single sentences with relative clauses.

1. The last record [the record was produced by this company] became a gold record.
2. Checking accounts [the checking accounts require a minimum balance] are very common now.
3. The professor [you spoke to the professor yesterday] is not here today.
4. John [John's grades are the highest in the school] has received a scholarship.
5. Felipe bought a camera. The camera has three lenses.
6. Frank is the man. We are going to nominate Frank for the office of treasurer.
7. The doctor is with a patient. The patient's leg was broken in an accident.
8. Jane is the woman. Jane is going to China next year.
9. Janet wants a typewriter. The typewriter self-corrects.
10. This book [I found the book last week] contains some useful information.
11. Mr. Bryant [Mr. Bryant's team has lost the game] looks very sad.
12. James wrote an article. The article indicated that he disliked the president.
13. The director of the program [the director graduated from Harvard University] is planning to retire next year.
14. This is the book. I have been looking for this book all year.
15. William [William's brother is a lawyer] wants to become a judge.

OPTIONAL RELATIVE CLAUSE REDUCTION

In restrictive relative clauses, it is possible to omit the relative pronoun and the verb *be* (along with any other auxiliaries) in the following cases.

- Before relative clauses in the passive voice:

  This is the Z value <u>which was obtained</u> from the table areas under the normal curve.

  OR

  This is the Z value <u>obtained</u> from the table areas under the normal curve.

- Before prepositional phrases:

  The beaker <u>that is on the counter</u> contains a solution.

  OR

  The beaker <u>on the counter</u> contains a solution.

- Before progressive (continuous) verb structures:

  The girl <u>who is running</u> down the street might be in trouble.

  OR

  The girl <u>running</u> down the street might be in trouble.

It is also possible to omit the relative pronoun and the verb *be* in nonrestrictive clauses before noun phrases.

  Mr. Jackson, <u>who is a professor</u>, is traveling in the Mideast this year.

  Mr. Jackson, <u>a professor</u>, is traveling in the Mideast this year.

Exercise 38: Relative Clause Reduction

Reduce the relative clauses in the following sentences.

1. George is the man who was chosen to represent the committee at the convention.
2. All of the money that was accepted has already been released.

3. The papers that are on the table belong to Patricia.
4. The man who was brought to the police station confessed to the crime.
5. The girl who is drinking coffee is Mary Allen.
6. John's wife, who is a professor, has written several papers on this subject.
7. The man who is talking to the policeman is my uncle.
8. The book that is on the top shelf is the one that I need.
9. The number of students who have been counted is quite high.
10. Leo Evans, who is a doctor, eats in this restaurant every day.

24. *THAT*—OTHER USES

OPTIONAL *THAT*

The word *that* has several uses besides its use in relative clauses. One such use is as a conjunction. Sometimes when *that* is used as a conjunction it is optional, and sometimes it is obligatory. *That* is usually *optional* after the following verbs.

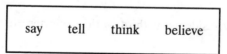

| say | tell | think | believe |

John said <u>that</u> he was leaving next week.

OR

John said he was leaving next week.

Henry told me <u>that</u> he had a lot of work to do.

OR

Henry told me he had a lot of work to do.

OBLIGATORY *THAT*

That is usually *obligatory* after the following verbs when introducing another clause.

mention	declare	report	state

The mayor declared that on June the first he would announce the results of the search.

George mentioned that he was going to France next year.

The article stated that this solution was flammable.

THAT CLAUSES

Some clauses, generally introduced by noun phrases, also contain *that*. These clauses are reversible.

It is well known that many residents of third world countries are dying.

OR

That many residents of third world countries are dying is well known.

NOTE: If a sentence begins with a *that* clause, be sure that both clauses contain a verb.

It surprises me that John would do such a thing.

OR

That John would do such a thing surprises me.

It wasn't believed until the fifteenth century that the earth revolves around the sun.

OR

That the earth revolves around the sun wasn't believed until the fifteenth century.

It is obvious <u>that</u> the Williams boy is abusing drugs.

OR

<u>That</u> the Williams boy is abusing drugs is obvious.

25. SUBJUNCTIVE

The subjunctive in English is the simple form of the verb when used after certain verbs indicating that one person wants another person to do something. The word *that* must always appear in subjunctive sentences. If it is omitted, most of the verbs are followed by the infinitive.

We <u>urge that</u> he <u>leave</u> now.
We <u>urge</u> him <u>to leave</u> now.

Study the following list of verbs.

advise	demand	prefer	require
ask	insist	propose	stipulate
command	move	recommend	suggest
decree	order	request	urge

NOTE: The verb *want* itself is not one of these verbs.

In the following rule, *verb* indicates one of the above verbs.

> subject +   verb   + *that* + subject + [verb in simple form]. . .
>   *(any tense)*

The judge <u>insisted that</u> the jury <u>return</u> a verdict immediately.
The university <u>requires that</u> all its students <u>take</u> this course.
The doctor <u>suggested that</u> his patient <u>stop</u> smoking.

Congress <u>has decreed that</u> the gasoline tax <u>be</u> abolished.

We <u>proposed that</u> he <u>take</u> a vacation.

I <u>move that</u> we <u>adjourn</u> until this afternoon.

The simple form of the verb is also used after impersonal expressions with the same meaning as the above verbs. The adjectives that fit into this formula include the following.

advised	necessary	recommended	urgent
important	obligatory	required	imperative
mandatory	proposed	suggested	

In the following rule, *adjective* indicates one of the above adjectives.

it + *be* + adjective + *that* + subject + [verb in simple form] . . .
(any
tense)

<u>It is necessary that</u> he <u>find</u> the books.

<u>It was urgent that</u> she <u>leave</u> at once.

<u>It has been proposed that</u> we <u>change</u> the topic.

<u>It is important that</u> you <u>remember</u> this question.

<u>It has been suggested that</u> he <u>forget</u> the election.

<u>It was recommended that</u> we <u>wait</u> for the authorities.

Exercise 39: Subjunctive

Correct the errors in the following sentences; if there are no errors, write *correct.*

1. The teacher demanded that the student left the room.
2. It was urgent that he called her immediately.
3. It was very important that we delay discussion.
4. She intends to move that the committee suspends discussion on this issue.

5. The king decreed that the new laws took effect the following month.
6. I propose that you should stop this rally.
7. I advise you take the prerequisites before registering for this course.
8. His father prefers that he attends a different university.
9. The faculty stipulated that the rule be abolished.
10. She urged that we found another alternative.

26. INCLUSIVES

The expressions *not only . . . but also, both . . . and,* and *as well as* mean *in addition to.* Like entities must be used together (noun with noun, adjective with adjective, etc.). All forms must be parallel.

NOT ONLY . . . BUT ALSO

The correlative conjunctions *not only . . . but also* must be used as a pair in joining like entities. The word *also* can be omitted, but it is preferable not to omit it.

$$\text{subject} + \text{verb} + \textit{not only} + \begin{Bmatrix} \text{noun} \\ \text{adjective} \\ \text{adverb} \\ \text{prepositional phrase} \end{Bmatrix} + \textit{but also} + \begin{Bmatrix} \text{noun} \\ \text{adjective} \\ \text{adverb} \\ \text{prepositional phrase} \end{Bmatrix}$$

OR

$$\text{subject} + \textit{not only} + \text{verb} + \textit{but also} + \text{verb}$$

Robert is <u>not only</u> <u>talented</u> <u>but also</u> <u>handsome</u>.
             adjective   *adjective*

Beth plays <u>not only</u> <u>the guitar</u> <u>but also</u> <u>the violin</u>.
                          noun   *noun*

He writes <u>not only</u> <u>correctly</u> <u>but also</u> <u>neatly</u>.
                         adverb   *adverb*

Maria excels <u>not only</u> <u>in mathematics</u> <u>but also</u> <u>in science</u>.
prepositional phrase   *prepositional phrase*

Paul Anka <u>not only</u> <u>plays</u> the piano <u>but also</u> <u>composes</u> music.
verb   *verb*

Make sure that the *not only* clause immediately precedes the phrase
to which it refers. Notice the following examples.

Incorrect: He is <u>not only famous</u> in Italy <u>but also</u> in Switzerland.

Correct: He is <u>famous not only</u> in Italy <u>but also</u> in Switzerland.

NOTE: If there is only one adjective, it usually precedes the *not only*
clause. In the above sentence, the adjective *famous* refers both to
Italy and to Switzerland.

AS WELL AS

The following rules apply to this conjunction.

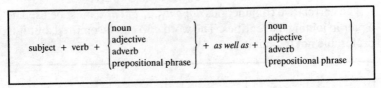

OR

subject + verb + *as well as* + verb . . .

Robert is <u>talented</u> as well as <u>handsome</u>.
adjective   *adjective*

Beth plays <u>the guitar</u> as well as <u>the violin</u>.
noun   *noun*

He writes <u>correctly</u> as well as <u>neatly</u>.
adverb   *adverb*

Marta excels <u>in mathematics</u> <u>as well as</u> <u>in science</u> .
      prepositional phrase   *prepositional phrase*

Paul Anka <u>plays</u> the piano <u>as well as</u> <u>composes</u> music.
        verb   *verb*

NOTE: When using *as well as* to indicate a compound subject, the phrase should be set off by commas. The verb will agree with the principal subject, NOT with the noun closest to it.

<u>The teacher</u>, <u>as well as</u> her students, <u>is going</u> to the concert.

<u>My cousins</u>, <u>as well as</u> Tim, <u>have</u> a test tomorrow.

BOTH . . . AND

These correlative conjunctions appear as a pair in a sentence. They follow the same rule as the one given for *not only . . . but also*.

Robert is <u>both</u> <u>talented</u> <u>and</u> <u>handsome</u>.
            adjective   *adjective*

Beth plays <u>both</u> <u>the guitar</u> <u>and</u> <u>the violin</u>.
                noun   *noun*

He writes <u>both</u> <u>correctly</u> <u>and</u> <u>neatly</u>.
                adverb   *adverb*

Marta excels <u>both</u> <u>in mathematics</u> <u>and</u> <u>in science</u> .
                  prepositional phrase   *prepositional phrase*

Paul Anka <u>both</u> <u>plays</u> the piano <u>and</u> <u>composes</u> music.
              verb   *verb*

NOTE: It is NOT CORRECT to use *both* and *as well as* in the same sentence.

Exercise 40: Inclusives

Supply the missing connectors (*not only . . . but also, both . . . and,* or *as well as*) in the following sentences.

1. Julia speaks _____ Spanish but also French.
2. She bought the yellow sweater _____ the beige skirt.

3. They have houses _____ in the country and in the city.
4. He is not only industrious _____ ingenious.
5. Her children have American cousins _____ Spanish ones.
6. Their European tour includes _____ Germany and Austria but also Switzerland.
7. He bandaged the arm both tightly _____ quickly.
8. Clark not only practices law _____ teaches it.
9. Tom Tryon was a playwright _____ an actor.
10. The bride's bouquet included roses _____ orchids.

27. KNOW/KNOW HOW

Study the following rules concerning the use of the verb *know*. *Know how* is usually used to indicate that one has the skill or ability to do something. Thus, it is *usually* followed by a verb, and when it is, the verb must be in the infinitive.

> subject + *know how* + [verb in infinitive] . . .

Know by itself, on the other hand, is usually followed by a noun, a prepositional phrase, or a sentence.

> subject + *know* + { noun
> prepositional phrase
> sentence }

Bill knows how to play tennis well.
Maggie and her sister know how to prepare Chinese food.
Do you know how to get to Jerry's house from here?
Jason knew the answer to the teacher's question.
No one knows about Roy's accepting the new position.
I didn't know that you were going to France.

Exercise 41: **Know/Know How**

Choose the correct form of *know* or *know how* in these sentences.

1. The fourth graders _____ to multiply.
2. How many people here _____ to ski?
3. We _____ about Mary's engagement to James.
4. The chemistry students _____ the formula for salt.
5. Although he has been driving for fifteen years, he doesn't _____ to change a tire properly.
6. Leon _____ that his friends would react to his proposition.
7. Nobody _____ to get to the turnpike yesterday.
8. The owner of the store was away, but she _____ about the robbery.
9. We _____ to type before we entered the university.
10. He doesn't _____ to dance, but he tries.

28. CLAUSES OF CONCESSION

Clauses of concession (yielding) show a contrast between two ideas. They are introduced by *although, even though, though, despite,* or *in spite of.*

DESPITE/IN SPITE OF

These are prepositions which can be used interchangeably. They mean the same as *although,* etc.; however, the grammar is different. They can go at the beginning or in the middle of a sentence.

$$\begin{Bmatrix} despite \\ in\ spite\ of \end{Bmatrix} + \text{noun phrase}$$

Despite his physical handicap, he has become a successful businessman.

In spite of his physical handicap, he has become a successful businessman.

Jane will be admitted to the university <u>despite</u> <u>her bad grades.</u>
Jane will be admitted to the university <u>in spite of</u> <u>her bad grades.</u>

ALTHOUGH/EVEN THOUGH/THOUGH

These are subordinate conjunctions used to connect two clauses. Notice how the grammar is different from that of *despite* and *in spite of*.

$$\left\{ \begin{array}{l} \textit{although} \\ \textit{even though} \\ \textit{though} \end{array} \right\} + \text{subject} + \text{verb} + \text{(complement)} \dots$$

<u>Although</u> <u>he has a physical handicap,</u> he has become a successful businessman.

Jane will be admitted to the university <u>even though</u> <u>she has bad grades.</u>

Additional examples of phrases and clauses of concession:

<u>In spite of</u> <u>the bad weather,</u> we are going to have a picnic.
<small>noun phrase</small>

The child ate the cookie <u>even though</u>
<u>his mother had told him not to.</u>
<small>subject + verb</small>

<u>Although</u> <u>the weather was very bad,</u> we had a picnic.
<small>subject + verb</small>

The committee voted to ratify the amendment <u>despite</u>
<u>the objections.</u>
<small>noun phrase</small>

<u>Though</u> <u>he had not finished the paper,</u> he went to sleep.
<small>subject + verb</small>

She attended the class <u>although</u> <u>she did not feel alert.</u>
<small>subject + verb</small>

Exercise 42: Clauses of Concession

Change these sentences to incorporate the expressions in parentheses.

1. Despite her dislike for coffee, she drank it to keep herself warm. (although)
2. Mary will take a plane, even though she dislikes flying. (in spite of)
3. In spite of Marcy's sadness at losing the contest, she managed to smile. (although)
4. We took many pictures though the sky was cloudy. (despite)
5. Despite her poor memory, the old woman told interesting stories to the children. (even though)
6. Though he has been absent frequently, he has managed to pass the test. (in spite of)
7. Nancy told me the secret, despite having promised not to do so. (though)
8. We plan to buy a ticket for the drawing although we know we will not win a prize. (even though)
9. In spite of the high prices, my daughters insist on going to the movies every Saturday. (even though)
10. He ate the chocolate cake even though he is on a diet. (in spite of)

29. PROBLEM VERBS

The verbs *lie/lay, rise/raise,* and *sit/set* cause problems even for native English speakers. The solution to the problem is to remember which verbs are transitive (verbs that take a complement) and which are intransitive (verbs that do not take a complement).

INTRANSITIVE			
rise	rose	risen	rising
lie	lay	lain	lying
sit	sat	sat	sitting

TRANSITIVE			
raise lay set	raised laid set	raised laid set	raising laying setting

RISE

This verb means to *get up, move up under one's own power* (without the help of someone else), *increase*. Notice that there is *no* complement.

The sun rises early in the summer.

When the bell rings, the students rise from their seats.

When oil and water mix, oil rises to the top.

Jim rose early so that he could play golf before the others.

It must be late; the moon has risen.

Prices have risen more than ten percent in a very short time.

RAISE

The verb means to *lift* or *elevate an object;* or to *increase something.* It must have a complement.

The students raise their hands in class.
          complement

The weightlifter raises the barbells over his head.
                  complement

The crane raised the car out of the lake.
          complement

After studying very hard, John raised his grades substantially.
                          complement

Mr. Daniels <u>has raised</u> <u>his tenants' rent</u> another fifteen dollars.
complement

The OPEC countries <u>have raised</u> <u>the price</u> of oil.
complement

LIE

This verb means to *rest, repose,* or to *be situated in a place.* It is often used with the preposition *down.* NOTE: This verb should not be confused with the verb *lie, lied, lied,* which means to *say something that is not true.*

The university <u>lies</u> in the western section of town.

If the children are tired, they should <u>lie down</u> for a nap.

María Elena <u>lay</u> on the beach for three hours yesterday sunbathing.

The old dog just <u>lay</u> on the grass watching the children at play.

Don't disturb Mary; she <u>has lain down</u> for a rest.

That old rug <u>had lain</u> in the corner for many years before it was put in the garage.

LAY

This verb means to *put somebody or something on a surface.*

Don't <u>lay</u> <u>your clothes</u> on the bed.
complement

The boy <u>lays</u> <u>his books</u> on the table every day.
complement

The enemy soldiers <u>laid down</u> <u>their weapons</u> and surrendered.
complement

The children <u>laid</u> <u>their toys</u> on the floor when they had finished
complement

using them.

The students had laid their compositions on the teacher's desk
complement

before the bell rang.

The nurse laid the baby in the crib.
complement

SIT

This verb means to *take a seat*. It is also often used with the preposition *down*.

We are going to sit in the fifth row at the opera.
Bullfight fans sit in the shade because it is cool.
Because the weather was nice, we sat on the patio.
After swimming, Bob sat on the beach to dry off.
Nobody has sat through as many boring lectures as Pete has.
They have sat in the same position for two hours.

SET

This verb means to *put somebody or something on a surface or in a place*. It is often interchangeable with *lay* or *put* except in certain idiomatic expressions like *set the table*.

The little girl helps her father set the table every night.
complement

The carpenters set their tools in the box at noon and go to lunch.
complement

The botanist set her plants in the sun so that they would grow.
complement

After carrying her son from the car, the mother set   him   in
complement

his crib.

Don't <u>set</u> <u>the chocolate</u> near the oven or it will melt.
complement

No sooner had they <u>set</u> <u>the roast</u> in the oven, than the electricity
complement

went out.

IDIOMATIC EXPRESSIONS WITH *SET, LAY* AND *RAISE*

The company had to <u>lay off</u> <u>twenty-five employees</u> because of a
production slowdown.

Dr. Jacobs <u>has set</u> <u>many broken bones</u> in plaster casts.

John <u>set</u> <u>his alarm</u> for six o'clock.

The chef is hoping that the <u>Jell-O</u> <u>will set</u> quickly.

While playing with matches, the children <u>set</u> <u>fire</u> to the sofa.

That farmer <u>raises</u> <u>chickens</u> for a living.

Exercise 43: Problem Verbs

Circle the correct form of the verb in parentheses and underline
the complement if there is one. Remember that complements do
not begin with prepositions.

1. You will see on the map that the Public Auditorium (lies/lays)
   north of the lake.
2. My dog loves to (sit/set) in the sun.
3. The delivery boy (lay/laid) the groceries on the table.
4. After the heavy rain, the water in the lake (raised/rose) another
   two feet.
5. The paper hangers decided to (raise/rise) the picture a few
   more inches.
6. He was exhausted so he decided to (lie/lay) down for a little
   while.
7. The workers were (lying/laying) cement for the patio when it
   began to rain.
8. The soldier (rose/raised) the flag when he heard the bugle
   blow.
9. In chemistry class, we learned that hot air (rises/raises).
10. They tried to (set/sit) the explosives carefully on the floor.

MINI-TEST 3: GRAMMAR ITEMS 21 THROUGH 29

DIRECTIONS

Each question on this mini-test consists of a sentence in which four words or phrases are underlined. The four underlined parts of the sentences are marked A, B, C, D. You are to identify the *one* underlined word or phrase that *would not be acceptable in standard written English.* Circle the letter of the underlined portion which is not correct.

1. Writers <u>like</u> William Shakespeare and Edgar Allan Poe <u>are</u> not

A   B   C

only prolific <u>but too interesting</u>.

                        D

2. James's counselor recommended that <u>he should take</u> a foreign

                                        A

language <u>in his</u> freshman year instead <u>of waiting</u> until

            B   C

<u>the following year</u>.

         D

3. Although Mark <u>has been cooking</u> for many years, he <u>still</u>

                    A   B

doesn't <u>know</u> to prepare French foods

           C

<u>in the traditional manner</u>.

            D

4. It is most important that <u>he</u> <u>speaks</u> to <u>the</u> dean before <u>leaving</u>

                          A   B   C   D

for his vacation.

5. <u>Visitors</u> were not permitted <u>entering</u> the park after dark

    A   B

<u>because of</u> the lack <u>of</u> security and lighting.

      C   D

6. I need <u>both</u> <u>fine</u> brown sugar as well <u>as</u> powdered sugar
        A   B   C
<u>to bake</u> a Hawaiian cake.
  D

7. <u>In spite</u> Nellie's fear of heights, she decided <u>to fly</u> with a group
   A   B
of her classmates <u>to the Bahamas</u> during <u>the</u> spring recess.
                    C   D

8. Let Nancy and <u>her</u> <u>to make</u> all the plans for the party, and you
              A   B
and I <u>will provide</u> <u>the refreshments</u> and entertainment.
         C   D

9. After <u>rising</u> the flag <u>to commemorate</u> <u>the holiday</u>, the mayor
       A   B   C
gave a <u>long speech.</u>
      D

10. <u>The</u> general commanded <u>the Officers' Club</u> be <u>off limits</u> to
  A   B   C
<u>the new</u> recruits.
  D

11. Louie got his sister <u>read</u> his class assignment, and then asked
                  A
her <u>to write</u> the report <u>for him</u> because he did not have
    B   C
<u>enough time.</u>
  D

12. Marcy said that she <u>knew how</u> the procedures for doing the
                  A
experiment, but when we began <u>to work</u> in the laboratory, she
                              B
found <u>that</u> she was <u>mistaken.</u>
     C   D

13. News of Charles Lindbergh's famous transatlantic flight in
    <u>　</u>
    A

    1927 <u>spread</u> rapidly <u>despite of</u> the lack of <u>an</u> international
         B   C   D

    communication system.

14. It <u>was</u> suggested that Pedro <u>studies</u> the material
       A   B

    <u>more thoroughly</u> before <u>attempting to pass</u> the exam.
           C   D

15. The piano teacher requires <u>that</u> her student <u>practices</u> at least
                                 A   B

    <u>forty-five minutes</u> every day <u>in preparation for</u> next week's
            C   D

    recital.

16. Marie's cousin is <u>studied</u> law <u>at</u> <u>one of the</u> ivy-league
                        A   B   C

    universities <u>in the East</u>.
                       D

17. If you <u>set</u> <u>in that position</u> for too long, <u>you may</u> get a cramp
            A   B   C

    <u>in your leg</u>.
         D

18. The president mentioned <u>to</u> the cabinet members <u>he</u> was going
                             A   B

    <u>to negotiate</u> a new treaty <u>with the foreign minister</u>.
          C   D

19. The conquerors stole not only <u>the</u> gold and silver
                                    A

    <u>that were needed</u> to replenish the <u>badly</u> depleted treasury but
            B   C

    also the supplies that were vital to the colonists <u>as well</u>.
                                                          D

20. <u>Despite</u> the roadblock, the police allowed <u>us enter</u> the
      A   B
    restricted area <u>to search</u> <u>for our friends</u>.
                          C   D

21. Did you <u>know how</u> that the actors' strike <u>will delay</u> the
               A   B
    beginning <u>of the new</u> television season and <u>cause the</u>
                  C   D
    cancellation of many contracts?

22. We should <u>have been informed</u> Janis <u>about</u> the change in
                      A   B
    plans <u>regarding</u> our <u>weekend trip</u> to the mountains.
            C   D

23. When we arrived <u>at the</u> store <u>to purchase</u> the dishwasher
                      A   B
    <u>advertise</u> in the newspaper, we learned that all the
       C
    dishwashers had <u>been sold</u>.
                      D

24. That manufacturer is not only <u>raising</u> his prices <u>but</u> also
                               A   B
    <u>decreasing</u> the production of his product <u>as well</u>.
       C   D

25. The director encouraged them <u>work</u> in committees <u>to plan</u>
                              A   B
    <u>a more effective</u> advertising campaign <u>for the new</u> product.
            C   D

26. Jason's professor had him <u>to rewrite</u> his thesis <u>many times</u>
                             A   B
    before <u>allowing him</u> to present <u>it to the committee</u>.
            C   D

27. Mr. Harris will <u>be divided</u> the biology class <u>into two sections</u> to
                    A   B   C

    prevent <u>overcrowding</u> in his classroom.
                D

28. <u>Hundreds of</u> houses and <u>other</u> buildings <u>were destroying</u> by
         A   B   C

    the <u>raging</u> tropical storm which later developed into a
         D

    hurricane.

29. Maribel <u>has registered</u> for both the afternoon anthropology
               A

    class <u>as well as</u> <u>the</u> evening <u>sociology lecture</u>.
          B   C   D

30. Food prices have <u>raised</u> <u>so rapidly</u> in the past few months <u>that</u>
                      A   B   C

    some families have been <u>forced to alter their eating habits</u>.
                                  D

31. The man, <u>of whom the</u> red car is <u>parked</u> in front <u>of our house</u>,
              A   B   C

    is a prominent physician in this town.
         D

32. <u>Although</u> her severe pain, Pat decided <u>to come</u> to the meeting
         A   B

    <u>so that</u> there <u>would be</u> a quorum.
        C   D

33. The proposal <u>has repealed</u> after a <u>thirty-minute</u> discussion and
                  A   B

    a <u>number</u> of objections <u>to its failure</u> to include our district.
        C   D

34. He is the <u>only</u> candidate <u>who</u> the faculty members voted
            A   B
    <u>not to retain</u> <u>on the list</u> of eligible replacements for Professor
          C   D
    Kotey.

35. <u>In spite</u> of the <u>tenants' objections</u>, the apartment manager
      A   B
    decided <u>to rise</u> the rent <u>by forty dollars</u> per month.
          C   D

36. This class, <u>that is a</u> <u>prerequisite for</u> microbiology, is <u>so difficult</u>
            A   B   C
    that I <u>would rather drop it</u>.
           D

37. The doctor <u>told Mr. Anderson that</u>, <u>because of</u> his severe
                  A   B
    cramps, he should <u>lay</u> in bed <u>for a few</u> days.
                 C   D

38. If you had <u>sat</u> the plant <u>in a cooler</u> location, <u>the leaves</u> would
             A   B   C
    not <u>have burned</u>.
         D

39. Dr. Harder, <u>which</u> is the professor for this class, <u>will be</u> absent
          A   A
    <u>this week</u> because <u>of illness</u>.
      C   D

40. <u>Despite of</u> a language barrier, <u>humans</u> have managed to
      A   B
    communicate <u>with others</u> through sign language, <u>in which</u>
               C   D
    certain motions stand for letters, words, or ideas.

41. This class <u>has canceled</u> because <u>too few</u> students
             A   B   C
    <u>had registered</u> before registration closed.
      D

42. After Allan <u>had searched</u> <u>for</u> twenty minutes, he realized that
                A   B
    his jacket had been <u>laying</u> on the table <u>the entire time</u>.
                 C   D

43. The problems that <u>discovered</u> <u>since</u> the initial research
                    A   B
    <u>had been completed</u> caused the committee members <u>to table</u>
         C   D
    the proposal temporarily.

44. The doctor suggested that he <u>lay</u> <u>in bed</u> for <u>several</u> days as a
                        A   B   C
    precaution against <u>further damage</u> to the tendons.
                   D

45. Dr. Alvarez was <u>displeased</u> because the student
              A
    <u>had turned in an unacceptable</u> report, <u>so</u> he made him
            B   C
    <u>to rewrite</u> it.
      D

46. The projector director <u>stated he</u> believed <u>it was necessary</u>
                       A   B
    <u>to study</u> the proposals for several more months
      C
    <u>before making a decision</u>.
             D

47. <u>Although</u> the danger that he might <u>be injured</u>, Boris
      A   B

   <u>bravely entered the</u> burning house in order to save
          C

   <u>the youngster</u>.
      D

48. <u>That</u> these students <u>have improved</u> their grades
     A   C

   <u>because of their</u> <u>participation in</u> the test review class.
       C   D

49. <u>Despite Martha's attempts</u> <u>to rise</u> her test score, she did not
             A   B

   receive <u>a high enough</u> score <u>to be accepted</u> by the law school.
           C   D

50. <u>That</u> Mr. Jones is not prepared to teach this course is not
     A

   <u>doubted</u>; however, at this late date <u>it is not likely that</u> we will
     B   C

   be <u>able finding</u> a replacement.
       D

STYLE IN WRITTEN ENGLISH

Written English is not always the same as spoken English. In spoken English, many people are not careful about the way they word sentences. As mentioned previously, the grammar section of the TOEFL tests your knowledge of *formal written English.* Many questions involve simple grammatical rules such as those that you've just studied. However, many questions, especially those in Part A, involve more than simple grammar. They are concerned with style; you must choose the clearest, most concise, best-stated answer. In some of these questions, several possible answers may contain acceptable grammar, but one choice is better than the others because it is stylistically acceptable.

Following are some stylistic problems that often appear in grammar questions and some methods for eliminating incorrect answers.

1. COMMON STYLISTIC PROBLEMS THAT APPEAR IN GRAMMAR QUESTIONS

SEQUENCE OF TENSES

When two clauses make up a sentence, they show a time relationship based on certain time words and verb tenses. This relationship is called "sequence of tenses." The verb tense of the main clause will determine that of the dependent clause.

If the *main clause* is	then the *dependent clause* will be
present tense	(1) present progressive (2) *will, can,* or *may* + verb (3) past tense (4) present perfect

- By using a present progressive with a present tense, we show two *simultaneous* actions.

  I <u>see</u> that Harriet <u>is writing</u> her composition.
  <u>Do</u> you <u>know</u> who <u>is riding</u> the bicycle?

- These modals in the dependent clause indicate that the action takes place *after* that of the main verb. (*be going to* is also used in this pattern.)

  He says that he <u>will look</u> for a job next week.
  I <u>know</u> that she <u>is going</u> to win that prize.
  Mary <u>says</u> that she <u>can play</u> the piano.

- Past tenses in the dependent clause show that this action took place *before* that of the main clause.

  I <u>hope</u> he <u>arrived</u> safely.
  They <u>think</u> he <u>was</u> here last night.

- Use of the present perfect in the dependent clause indicates that the action took place at *an indefinite time before* that of the main clause.

  He <u>tells</u> us that he <u>has been</u> to the mountains before.
  We <u>know</u> that you <u>have spoken</u> with Mike about the party.

If the *main clause* is	then the *dependent clause* will be
past tense	(1) past progressive or simple past (2) *would*, *could*, or *might* + verb (3) past perfect

NOTE: NO PRESENT FORM can come after the past tense.

- Simple past or past progressive in the dependent clause indicates a *simultaneous* action with the main clause.

  I <u>gave</u> the package to my sister when she <u>visited</u> us last week.

Mike <u>visited</u> the Prado Art Museum while he <u>was studying</u> in Madrid.

• These modals in the dependent clause indicate that the action takes place *after* that of the main verb.

He <u>said</u> that he <u>would look</u> for a job next week.
Mary <u>said</u> that she <u>could play</u> piano.

• Past perfect in the dependent clause shows that the action occurred *before* that of the main clause.

I <u>hoped</u> he <u>had arrived</u> safely.
They <u>thought</u> he <u>had been</u> here last night.

Exercise 44: Sequence of Tenses

The following contain sentences with present tense verbs in the main clause. Change the main clause to past and adjust the dependent clause as necessary. *Example:*

We <u>hope</u> that he <u>will be</u> able to attend.
We <u>hoped</u> that he <u>would be</u> able to attend.

1. He says that he will finish the project by May.
2. Mark thinks he is going to win the award.
3. I hear that Kate has accepted a new position at the East Side Clinic.
4. Steve says that he will make the dessert for the party.
5. Lou tells his friends that they are good tennis players.
6. I realize that they are older than they look.
7. Mary Ellen says that she eats three well-balanced meals every day.
8. The student is asking the professor when the class will do the next experiment.
9. We hope that you can play tennis later.
10. We know that you may move to France next year.

SAY/TELL

These verbs have the same meaning; however, the grammar is different. If there is an indirect object (if we mention the person to whom the words are spoken), we use *tell*. If there is no indirect object, we use *say*. Study the following rules.

> subject + *say* + (*that*) + subject + verb . . .

> subject + *tell* + indirect object + (*that*) + subject + verb . . .

Tell can also be followed occasionally by a direct object. Always use *tell* before the following nouns whether there is an indirect object or not.

tell	$\begin{cases} \text{a story} \\ \text{a joke} \\ \text{a secret} \\ \text{a lie} \\ \text{the truth} \\ \text{(the) time} \end{cases}$

John told a story last night.

OR

John told us a story last night.

The little boy was punished because he told a lie.

OR

The little boy was punished because he told his mother a lie.

NOTE: Remember to use the appropriate sequence of tenses with *say* and *tell*.

Present: He <u>says</u> that he <u>is</u> busy today.
    He <u>says</u> that he <u>will be</u> busy today.

Past: He <u>said</u> that he <u>was</u> busy today.
    He <u>said</u> that he <u>would be</u> busy today.

Exercise 45: Say/Tell

Write the correct form of *say* or *tell* in the following sentences. Be careful to observe sequence of tenses.

1. Harvey _____ he would take us on a picnic today.
2. Pete _____ the children some funny stories now.
3. Who _____ you that he was going to New York?
4. When did you _____ Mary that the party would be?
5. My sister _____ us that it had snowed in her town last week.
6. No one in the second grade class could _____ time.
7. The comedian always _____ his friends funny jokes when he is at a party.
8. What time did you _____ that the lecture had begun?
9. Who _____ that we are having an exam tomorrow?
10. The judge instructed the witness to _____ the whole truth about the accident.
11. The little boy _____ a lie about not eating the cookies before lunch.
12. Hamlet _____, "To be or not to be, that is the question."
13. Our teacher _____ that we would not have any homework during the vacation.
14. Because he could not _____ time, the boy arrived home very late one evening.
15. I saw my friend in the library and _____ that I had wanted to talk to him.
16. Shaun _____ that he had already seen the movie.
17. Larry _____ that his friends would be going camping next week.
18. James _____ that he has already done his homework.

19. I wonder who _____ that blondes had more fun.
20. Never _____ a secret to a person who spreads gossip.

ANTECEDENTS OF PRONOUNS

If a pronoun is used in a sentence, there must be a noun of the same person and number before it. There must be one, and only one, antecedent to which the pronoun refers.

Examples of pronouns without antecedents:

Incorrect: Henry was denied admission to graduate school because <u>they</u> did not believe that he could handle the work load.

(The pronoun *they* does not have an antecedent in the sentence. The *graduate school* is a singular unit, and the members of its faculty are not mentioned.)

Correct: The <u>members</u> of the admissions committee denied Henry admission to graduate school because <u>they</u> did not believe that he could handle the work load.

(In this sentence, *they* refers to *members.*)

OR

Henry was denied admission to graduate school because the <u>members</u> of the admissions committee did not believe that he could handle the work load.

(Here the noun is given instead of the pronoun.)

Incorrect: George dislikes politics because he believes that <u>they</u> are corrupt.

(The pronoun *they* does not have an antecedent in this sentence. The word *politics* is singular, so *they* cannot refer to it.)

Correct: George dislikes politics because he believes that <u>politicians</u> are corrupt.

OR

George dislikes <u>politicians</u> because he believes that <u>they</u> are corrupt.

Examples of pronouns with unclear antecedents:

Incorrect: Mr. Brown told Mr. Adams that <u>he</u> would have to work all night in order to finish the report.

(It is not clear whether the pronoun <u>he</u> refers to Mr. Brown or Mr. Adams.)

Correct: According to Mr. Brown, <u>Mr. Adams</u> will have to work all night in order to finish the report.

OR

Mr. Brown said that, in order to finish the report, <u>Mr. Adams</u> would have to work all night.

Incorrect: Janet visited her friend every day while <u>she</u> was on vacation.

(The pronoun *she* could refer to either Janet or her friend.)

Correct: While <u>Janet</u> was on vacation, <u>she</u> visited her friend every day.

Exercise 46: Antecedents of Pronouns

Rewrite the following sentences so that each pronoun has a clear antecedent. If you have to supply a noun, use any noun that will make the sentence correct.

1. The dispute between the faculty and the administration was not resolved until they got better working conditions.
2. Ellen spotted her friend as she walked toward the Student Union.
3. Foreigners are easily impressed by the bullfighters as they march into the arena.
4. In their spare time, many great books have been written about the famous Greek and Roman heroes.
5. Dr. Byrd's book was accepted for publication because they thought it would be beneficial to students.

6. Bob and Helen hate flying because they make too much noise.
7. Casey was not admitted to the country club because they thought he was not socially acceptable.
8. Mary loves touring the country by train because it is so interesting.
9. The colonel was decorated for bravery, having fought them off.
10. The children were frightened because they made such eerie sounds.

THE PRONOUNS *ONE* AND *YOU*

If *one* (meaning a person in general) is used in a sentence, a subsequent pronoun referring to the same person must also be *one* or *he*. If *you* is used, the subsequent pronoun must also be *you*. *He* or *you* can be in the possessive, complement, or reflexive case.

$$one + verb \ldots \begin{cases} one \\ one's + \text{noun} \\ he* \\ his + \text{noun} \end{cases} + (\text{verb}) \ldots$$

*NOTE: Many times it is considered more appropriate to use *he or she* and similar expressions so that the masculine pronoun is not used exclusively. On the TOEFL, however, you need not worry about this problem. If a sentence begins with *one,* be sure that *you* or *they* DOES NOT follow.

If <u>one</u> takes this exam without studying, <u>one</u> is likely to fail.
If <u>one</u> takes this exam without studying, <u>he</u> is likely to fail.

<u>One</u> should always do <u>one's homework</u>.
<u>One</u> should always do <u>his homework</u>.

$$you + \text{verb} \dots + \left\{ \begin{array}{l} you \\ your \end{array} \right\} + (\text{verb}) \dots$$

If you take this exam without studying, you are likely to fail.

You should always do your homework.

NOTE: It is NEVER CORRECT to say:

If one takes this exam without studying,   you   are likely to

3rd person   2nd person

fail.

If one takes this exam without studying, they are likely to fail.

singular   plural

Additional examples for both forms:

One should never tell his secrets to a gossip if he wishes them to remain secret.

You should always look both ways before you cross the street.

If one wants to make a lot of money, he needs to work hard.

If one's knowledge of English is complete, he will be able to pass TOEFL.

If you do not want your test scores reported, you must request that they be canceled.

One should always remember his family.

ILLOGICAL PARTICIPIAL MODIFIERS (DANGLING PARTICIPLES)

A participial phrase (one containing a [verb + *ing*] without auxiliaries) can be used to join two sentences with a common subject. When the two phrases do not share a common subject, we call the participial phrase an illogical participial modifier. Actually, the subject of the participial phrase is understood rather than explicit. Consider the following sentence.

Incorrect: After jumping out of a boat, the shark bit the man.

               (We understand that the actual subject of the verb *jumping* is *the man;* therefore, immediately after the comma, we must mention *the man.*)

Correct: After jumping out of the boat, <u>the man</u> was bitten by a shark.

For clarity, introductory participial phrases must be followed immediately by the noun which is logically responsible for the action · of the participle. There is no written subject in the participial phrase; thus no change of subject is possible. Sometimes the participial phrase is preceded by a preposition. The following prepositions commonly precede participial phrases.

by	upon	before	after	while

<u>After preparing</u> the dinner, <u>Michelle</u> will read a book.

<u>By working</u> a ten-hour day for four days, <u>we</u> can have a long weekend.

<u>While reviewing</u> for the test, <u>Marcia</u> realized that she had forgotten to study the use of participial phrases.

If only the [verb + *ing*] appears in the participial phrase, the time of the sentence is determined by the tense of the verb in the main clause; the two actions generally occur simultaneously.

(preposition) + (*not*) + [verb + *ing*] . . . + noun + verb . . .

Present: <u>Practicing</u> her swing every day, <u>Tricia hopes</u> to get a job as a golf instructor.

Past: <u>Having</u> a terrible toothache, <u>Felipe called</u> the dentist for an appointment.

Future: <u>Finishing</u> the letter later tonight, <u>Sally will mail</u> it tomorrow morning.

The perfect form (*having* + [verb in past participle]) is used to indicate that the action of the participial phrase took place before that of the main verb.

(*not*) + *having* + [verb in past participle] . . . + noun + verb . . .

Having finished their supper, the boys went out to play.
(After the *boys* had finished . . .)

Having written his composition, Louie handed it to his teacher.
(After *Louie* had written . . .)

Not having read the book, she could not answer the question.
(Because *she* had not read . . .)

The participial phrase can also be used to express an idea in the passive voice, one in which the subject was not responsible for the action.

(*not*) + *having been* + [verb in past participle] . . . + noun + verb . . .

Having been notified by the court, Melissa reported for jury duty.
(After *Melissa* had been notified . . .)

Having been delayed by the snowstorm, Jason and I missed our connecting flight.
(After *we* had been delayed . . .)

Not having been notified of the change in meeting times, George arrived late.
(Because *he* had not been notified . . .)

Sometimes a participial modifier in passive voice is reduced by dropping the *having been* and using the past participle alone.

Illogical: Attacked by an angry mob, the gashes in the boy's throat were life-threatening.

(Note that *attacked* means the same as *having been attacked*. The actual subject of the verb *attacked* is the boy; therefore, reference to him must appear immediately after the comma.)

Correct: <u>Attacked</u> by an angry mob, <u>the boy</u> suffered life-threatening gashes in his throat.

Observe the corrected form of the following illogical participial modifiers. Remember that the noun appearing after the comma must be the logical subject of the participial modifier.

Illogical: Having apprehended the hijackers, they were whisked off to FBI headquarters by the security guards.

Correct: <u>Having apprehended</u> the hijackers, <u>the security guards</u> whisked them off to FBI headquarters.

(After *the guards* had apprehended the hijackers, the guards whisked . . .)

OR

<u>Having been apprehended</u>, <u>the hijackers</u> were whisked off to FBI headquarters by the security guards.

(After *the hijackers* had been apprehended, they were whisked . . .)

Illogical: Before singing the school song, a poem was recited.

Correct: <u>Before singing</u> the school song, <u>the students</u> recited a poem.

(Before *the students* sang . . .)

Illogical: Guiding us through the museum, a special explanation was given by the director.

Correct: <u>Guiding</u> us through the museum, <u>the director</u> gave us a special explanation.

(While *the director* was guiding us . . .)

Exercise 47: Illogical Participial Modifiers

Following the examples given above, correct these illogical participial modifiers. You may have to reword the main clause and add a subject.

1. Being thoroughly dissatisfied with the picture, it was hidden in the closet.
2. Seeing the advancing army, all valuables were hidden under the stairwell.
3. Plunging into the water, the drowning child was rescued.
4. Criticizing the defendant for his cruel behavior, the sentence was handed down by the judge.
5. After painting the car, it was given to the man's wife by the man.
6. Being an early riser, it was easy for Edna to adjust to her company's new summer schedule.
7. After winning the tennis match, the victory made Nancy jump for joy.
8. Having wandered through the mountain passes for days, an abandoned shack where they could take shelter was discovered by the hikers.
9. Being very protective of its young, all those who approach the nest are attacked by the mother eagle.
10. Before playing ball, a two-minute period of silence was observed by the baseball players for their recently deceased teammate.

PARTICIPLES AS ADJECTIVES

Very often, when there is no regular adjective form for a verb, the present or past participle of the verb can be used as an adjective. It is sometimes difficult for foreign students to decide whether to use the present [verb + *ing*] or past [verb + *ed*] or [verb + *en*] participle as an adjective.

The present participle [verb + *ing*] is used as an adjective when the noun it modifies performs or is responsible for an action. The verb is usually intransitive (it doesn't take an object) and the verb form of the sentence is the progressive (continuous) aspect.

The crying baby woke Mr. Binion.
 (The baby *was crying*).

The purring kitten snuggled close to the fireplace.
 (The kitten *was purring*.)

The blooming flowers in the meadow created a rainbow of colors.
 (The flowers *were blooming*.)

The past participle is used as an adjective when the noun it modifies is the receiver of the action. The sentence from which this adjective comes is generally in the passive aspect.

The sorted mail was delivered to the offices before noon.
 (The mail *had been sorted*.)

Frozen food is often easier to prepare than fresh food.
 (The food *had been frozen*.)

The imprisoned men were unhappy with their living conditions.
 (The men *had been imprisoned*.)

Other verbs such as *interest, bore, excite,* and *frighten* are even more difficult. The rule is basically the same as that given above. The [verb + *ing*] form is used when the noun causes the action and the [verb + *ed*] form is used when it receives the action. Compare the following groups of sentences.

The boring professor put the students to sleep.
The boring lecture put the students to sleep.
The bored students went to sleep during the boring lecture.

The child saw a frightening movie.
The frightened child began to cry.

Exercise 48: Participles as Adjectives

Choose the correct form of the participles used as adjectives in the following sentences.

1. The (breaking/broken) dishes lay on the floor.
2. The (trembling/trembled) children were given a blanket for warmth.
3. Compassionate friends tried to console the (crying/cried) children.
4. The (interesting/interested) tennis match caused a great deal of excitement.
5. When James noticed the (burning/burnt) building, he notified the fire department immediately.
6. The (exciting/excited) passengers jumped into the lifeboats when notified that the ship was sinking.
7. The (smiling/smiled) *Mona Lisa* is on display in the Louvre in Paris.
8. The wind made such (frightening/frightened) noises that the children ran to their parents' room.
9. The (frightening/frightened) hostages only wanted to be left alone.
10. We saw the (advancing/advanced) army from across town.
11. Mrs. Harris's (approving/approved) smile let us know that our speeches were well done.
12. Our representative presented the (approving/approved) plan to the public.
13. The (blowing/blown) wind of the hurricane damaged the waterfront property.
14. We were going to see the movie at the Center Theater, but our friends told us it was a (boring/bored) movie.
15. Mary's (cleaning/cleaned) service comes every Wednesday.
16. The (cleaning/cleaned) shoes were placed in the sun to dry.
17. We could not open the (locking/locked) door without a key.
18. As we entered the (crowding/crowded) room, I noticed my cousins.
19. Dr. Jameson told my brother to elevate his (aching/ached) foot.
20. The police towed away the (parking/parked) cars because they were blocking the entrance.

REDUNDANCY

A sentence in which some information is unnecessarily repeated is called redundant. Given here are some word combinations that are *always redundant,* and thus should NEVER be used.

advance forward *proceed forward* *progress forward*	*advance, proceed,* and *progress* all mean "to move in a forward direction"; thus, the word *forward* is not necessary
return back *revert back*	*return* and *revert* mean "to go back or to send back" so *back* is not necessary
sufficient enough	these words are identical; one or the other should be used
compete together	*compete* means "to take part in a contest against others"
reason . . . because	these words indicate the same thing; the correct pattern is *reason . . . that*
join together	*join* means "to bring together," "to put together" or "to become a part or member of," "to take place among"
repeat again	*repeat* means "to say again" (*re-* usually means "again")
new innovations	*innovation* means "a new idea"
matinee performance	*matinee* means "a performance in the afternoon"
same identical	these words are identical
two twins	*twins* means "two brothers or sisters"
the time when	*the time* and *when* indicate the same thing; one or the other should be used
the place where	*the place* and *where* indicate the same thing; one or the other should be used

Examples of correct sentences:

The army <u>advanced</u> after the big battle.

OR

The army <u>moved forward</u> after the big battle.

The peace talks <u>advanced</u>.

OR

The peace talks <u>progressed</u>.

We have <u>sufficient</u> money to buy the new dress.

They have <u>enough</u> time to eat a sandwich before going to work.

The teacher <u>proceeded</u> to explain the lesson.

John and his brother are <u>competing</u> in the running games.

The teacher asked us to <u>join</u> the students who were cleaning the room.

Mary <u>repeated</u> the question slowly so that Jim would understand.

Besides the two evening showings, there will also be a <u>matinee</u>.

The <u>reason</u> I want to take that class is <u>that</u> the professor is supposed to be very eloquent.

This is <u>where</u> I left him.

That was <u>the time</u> I hit a home run.

Exercise 49: Redundancy

Cross out the redundant word in each of the following sentences.

Example:

The carpenter joined the two beams together with long nails.
(~~Together~~ is the redundant word.)

1. After Jill had shown Tim how to insert the paper once, she repeated the operation again.
2. The twins have the same identical birthmarks on their backs.
3. I think we have sufficient enough information to write the report.
4. When the roads became too slippery, we decided to return back to the cabin and wait for the storm to subside.

5. Nobody could get out of work early enough to attend the matinee performance.
6. The mountain climbers proceeded forward on their long trek up the side of the mountain.
7. Rita and her sister competed together in the musical talent show.
8. I think that we should come up with a new innovation for doing this job.
9. The minister joined the bride and groom together in holy wedlock.
10. My cousins love to play with the two twins from across the street.

PARALLEL STRUCTURE

When information in a sentence is given in the form of a list or series, all components must be grammatically parallel or equal. There may be only two components or there may be many components in a list; however, if the first is, for example, an infinitive, the rest must also be infinitives. Consider the following correct and incorrect sentences.

Not parallel: Peter is <u>rich</u> , <u>handsome</u>, and
                         adjective   *adjective*

<u>many people like him</u>.
                    clause

Parallel: Peter is <u>rich</u> , <u>handsome</u>, and <u>popular</u>.
                     adjective   *adjective*   *adjective*

Not parallel: Mr. Henry is a <u>lawyer</u>, a <u>politician</u>, and
                                       noun   *noun*

<u>he teaches</u>.
                    clause

Parallel: Mr. Henry is a <u>lawyer</u>, a <u>politician</u>, and a <u>teacher</u>.
                                   noun   *noun*   *noun*

(Remember that a clause standing alone would be a complete sentence, meaning it has a subject and a verb.)

Not parallel: The soldiers approached the enemy camp <u>slowly</u>
                                                              adverb

and <u>silent</u>.
         adjective

Parallel: The soldiers approached the enemy camp <u>slowly</u>
                                                              adverb

and <u>silently</u>.
         adverb

Not parallel: She likes <u>to fish</u>, <u>swim</u>, and <u>surfing</u>.
                            infinitive *simple form*   *[verb + ing]*

Parallel: She likes <u>to fish</u>, <u>to swim</u>, and <u>to surf</u>.
                        infinitive   *infinitive*   *infinitive*

OR

She likes <u>fishing</u>, <u>swimming</u>, and <u>surfing</u>.
          [verb + ing]   *[verb + ing]*   *[verb + ing]*

Not parallel: When teenagers finish high school, they have

several choices: <u>going to college</u>, <u>getting a job</u>, or
                 verb + noun   *verb + noun*

the <u>army</u>.
      noun

Parallel: When teenagers finish high school, they have

several choices: <u>going to college</u>, <u>getting a job</u>, or
                 verb + noun   *verb + noun*

<u>joining the army</u>.
 verb + noun

Not parallel: Enrique <u>entered</u> the room, <u>sat</u> down, and
                          past   *past*

<u>is opening</u> his book.
 present progressive

Parallel: Enrique <u>entered</u> the room, <u>sat</u> down, and <u>opened</u>
                         past   *past*   *past*
           his book.

NOTE: If the sentence indicates that the different clauses definitely happened or will happen at different times, then this rule does not need to be followed. *For example:*

She <u>is</u> a senior, <u>studies</u> every day, and <u>will graduate</u> a
     present   *present*   *future*
      semester early.

Exercise 50: Parallel Structure

Change the following sentences so that they are parallel.

1. The puppy stood up slowly, wagged its tail, blinking its eyes, and barked.
2. Ecologists are trying to preserve our environment for future generations by protecting the ozone layer, purifying the air, and have replanted the trees that have been cut down.
3. The chief of police demanded from his assistants an orderly investigation, a well-written report, and that they work hard.
4. Marcia is a scholar, an athlete, and artistic.
5. Slowly and with care, the museum director removed the Ming vase from the shelf and placed it on the display pedestal.
6. The farmer plows the fields, plants the seeds, and will harvest the crop.
7. Abraham Lincoln was a good president and was self-educated, hard-working, and always told the truth.
8. Children love playing in the mud, running through puddles, and they get very dirty.
9. Collecting stamps, playing chess, and to mount beautiful butterflies are Derrick's hobbies.
10. Despite America's affluence, many people are without jobs, on welfare, and have a lot of debts.

TRANSFORMATION OF DIRECT AND INDIRECT OBJECTS

There are two ways of writing the objects of many verbs without changing the meaning of the sentence. The indirect object may occur after the direct object, preceded by a preposition, or it may occur before the direct object without being preceded by a preposition. The prepositions that are generally used in this structure are *for* and *to*.

NOTE: The indirect object is an animate object or objects to whom or for whom something is done. The direct object can be a person or a thing and is the first receiver of the action.

I gave the book to Dan .
       direct object indirect object

(*The book* is the direct object because the first action was that of taking the book in my hand, and the second action, the indirect one, was to give it to Dan.)

Not all verbs allow for this object transformation. Here are some that do.

bring	find	make	promise	tell
build	get	offer	read	write
buy	give	owe	sell	
cut	hand	paint	send	
draw	leave	pass	show	
feed	lend	pay	teach	

Some of these verbs can be followed by either the preposition *for* or *to,* while others must be followed by one or the other. The transformation means exactly the same as the sentence with the original preposition. Study the following rules.

$$\text{subject} + \text{verb} + \text{direct object} + \begin{Bmatrix} for \\ to \end{Bmatrix} + \text{indirect object}$$

$$\text{subject} + \text{verb} + \text{indirect object} + \text{direct object}$$

NOTE: In the second rule, where the indirect object precedes the direct object, NO preposition exists.

Correct: The director's secretary <u>sent the manuscript to them</u> last night.

Correct: The director's secretary <u>sent them the manuscript</u> last night.

Incorrect: The director's secretary <u>sent to them the manuscript</u> last night.

NOTE: If the direct object and the indirect object are both pronouns, the first rule is generally used.

Correct: They gave <u>it to us.</u>
Incorrect: They gave <u>us it.</u>

Additional examples:

John gave <u>the essay to his teacher.</u>
John gave <u>his teacher the essay.</u>

The little boy brought <u>some flowers for his grandmother.</u>
The little boy brought <u>his grandmother some flowers.</u>

I fixed <u>a drink for Maria.</u>
I fixed <u>Maria a drink.</u>

He drew <u>a picture</u> for <u>his mother</u>.
He drew <u>his mother</u> <u>a picture</u>.

He lent <u>his car</u> to <u>his brother</u>.
He lent <u>his brother</u> <u>his car</u>.

We owe <u>several thousand dollars</u> to <u>the bank</u>.
We owe <u>the bank</u> <u>several thousand dollars</u>.

NOTE: The verbs *introduce* and *mention* must use the preposition *to*.
The transformation is NOT POSSIBLE.

I introduced <u>John to Dr. Jackson</u>.
I introduced <u>Dr. Jackson to John</u>.
He mentioned <u>the party to me</u>.

Exercise 51: Transformation of Direct and Indirect Object

Rewrite these sentences placing the indirect object immediately after the verb and eliminating the preposition.

1. Mary showed the photographs to me.
2. I'll send the books to you next week.
3. My sister sent a game to my daughter for her birthday.
4. He brought the telegram to her this morning.
5. The author gave an autographed copy of his book to his friend.
6. They wrote a letter to us.
7. Louie drew a lovely picture for his mother.
8. She made a bookcase for her cousin.
9. That teacher taught grammar to us last year.
10. Mary handed the tray to her brother.

Exercise 52: Transformation of Direct and Indirect Object

Rewrite these sentences placing the direct object immediately after the verb and supplying the correct preposition.

1. John owes his friend the money.
2. My friends sent me a bouquet of flowers while I was in the hospital.
3. The clerk sold us the records.

4. They found him a good, inexpensive car.
5. Picasso painted his wife a beautiful portrait.
6. My father read us the newspaper article.
7. Pass me the salt, please.
8. She bought him a red jacket.
9. The girls couldn't wait to show us the bicycles.
10. The construction crew built them a house in four weeks.

ADVERBIALS AT THE BEGINNING OF A SENTENCE

It is sometimes possible to place adverbials at the beginning of a sentence. This indicates a stronger emphasis on the action than when the adverbial is in its normal position. If the adverbial appears at the beginning of a sentence, the grammar of the sentence is somewhat different.

Juan hardly remembers the accident that took his sister's life.

Hardly does Juan remember the accident that took his sister's life.

$$\left.\begin{array}{l} hardly \\ rarely \\ seldom \\ never \\ only \ldots \end{array}\right\} + \text{auxiliary} + \text{subject} + \text{verb} \ldots$$

Never have so many people been unemployed as today.
adverb auxiliary   subject   verb

(So many people have never been unemployed as today.)

Hardly had he fallen asleep when he began to dream of
adverb auxiliary subject verb
far-away lands.

(He had hardly fallen asleep when he began to dream . . .)

<u>Rarely</u> <u>have</u> <u>we</u> <u>seen</u> such an effective actor as he has proven
 adverb *auxiliary* *subject* *verb*

himself to be.

(We <u>have</u> rarely <u>seen</u> such an effective actor . . .)

<u>Seldom</u> <u>does</u> <u>class</u> <u>let</u> out early.
 adverb   *auxiliary* *subject* *verb*

(<u>Class</u> seldom <u>lets</u> out early.)

<u>Only by hard work</u> <u>will</u> <u>we</u> <u>be</u> able to accomplish this great
 adverb   *auxiliary* *subject* *verb*

task.

(We <u>will be able</u> to accomplish this great task <u>only by hard
 work</u>.)

Exercise 53: Adverbials at the Beginning of a Sentence

Change each of the following sentences so that the adverbial is at
the beginning of the sentence.

1. Jorge rarely forgets to do his homework.
2. Jane can finish this work only by staying up all night.
3. Henry had hardly started working when he realized that he
   needed to go to the library.
4. We have never heard so moving a rendition as this one.
5. Maria seldom missed a football game when she was in the
   United States.
6. We will be able to buy the car only with a bank loan.
7. We rarely watch television during the week.
8. He has never played a better game than he has today.
9. This professor seldom lets his students leave class early.
10. Jennifer had hardly entered the room when she felt the
    presence of another person.

2. ELIMINATION OF INCORRECT ANSWERS IN STYLE QUESTIONS

Very often in the Structure and Written Expression section of the TOEFL, especially in Part A, Structure, you will find that the questions cannot be solved simply by applying a single grammatical rule. In order to solve these questions, you should eliminate any possible answer choices which are incorrect until you arrive at the correct choice. Follow these steps in eliminating incorrect answers.

(1) Check each answer for faulty grammar. Look for:

  (a) subject/verb agreement
  (b) adjective/adverb usage
  (c) placement of modifiers
  (d) sequence of tenses
  (e) logical pronoun reference
  (f) parallel structure

(2) Eliminate answers that are verbose (wordy). The sentence should convey its meaning in the most concise way.

  (a) Avoid answers containing expressions like:

    John read the letter <u>in a thoughtful manner.</u>   (4 words)

    There is usually a less wordy adverb such as:

    John read the letter <u>thoughtfully.</u>   (1 word)

  (b) Avoid answers containing two words that have the same meaning.

(3) Eliminate answers which contain improper vocabulary.

  (a) Be sure that all words show the meaning of the sentence.
  (b) Be sure that two-word verbs are connected with the proper preposition. (These are covered in the next section, Problem Vocabulary and Prepositions.)

(4) Eliminate answer choices containing slang expressions. Slang is nonstandard vocabulary that is sometimes used in speech, but not considered correct in formal English. Some examples are:

really when it is used to mean "very"

bunch when it is used to mean "many"

any noun + *wise* when it is used to mean "in relation to _____"

EXAMPLES OF STYLE QUESTIONS

1. Before we can decide on the future uses of this drug, _____ .
   - (A) many more informations must be reviewed
   - (B) is necessary to review more information
   - (C) we must review much more information
   - (D) another information must to be reviewed

Analysis:
   - (A) 2 errors in grammar: *many* + non-count noun is not possible; a non-count noun *cannot* be plural (*information*).
   - (B) 1 grammar error: no subject.
   - (C) Correct.
   - (D) 2 grammar errors: *another* + non-count noun is not possible; a modal must be followed by the simple form (*must be reviewed*)

2. In this country, a growing concern about the possible hazardous effects of chemical wastes _____ .
   - (A) have resulted in a bunch of new laws
   - (B) has resulted in several new laws
   - (C) is causing the results of numerous new laws
   - (D) result in new laws

Analysis:

- (A) 1 grammar error and 1 improper use of vocabulary (slang): The subject is *concern,* which is singular, so *have* should be *has*. The word *bunch* is not acceptable in formal English.
- (B) Correct.
- (C) Verbose; has too many unnecessary words.
- (D) 2 grammar errors: *result* is plural and the subject is singular; it is not possible to have a plural adjective (*new laws*).

MINI-TEST 4: STYLISTIC PROBLEMS

Part A: Structure

DIRECTIONS

Each sentence in Part A is an incomplete sentence. Four words or phrases, marked (A), (B), (C), (D) are given beneath each sentence. You are to choose the *one* word or phrase that best completes the sentence. Remember to eliminate answers that are incorrect and to choose the one that would be correct in formal written English.

1. The defendant refused to answer the prosecutor's questions
   _____ .
   - (A) because he was afraid it would incriminate him
   - (B) for fear that they will incriminate him
   - (C) because he was afraid that his answers would incriminate him
   - (D) fearing that he will be incriminated by it

2. _____ will Mr. Forbes be able to regain control of the company.
   - (A) With hard work
   - (B) In spite of his hard work
   - (C) Only if he works hardly
   - (D) Only with hard work

3. Mrs. Walker has returned _____ .
   (A) a wallet back to its original owner
   (B) to its original owner the wallet
   (C) the wallet to its originally owner
   (D) the wallet to its original owner

4. The hospital owes _____ for the construction of the new wing.
   (A) the government twenty million dollars
   (B) for the government twenty million dollars
   (C) to the government twenty million dollars
   (D) twenty millions of dollars to the government

5. Maria _____ that she could not attend classes next week.
   (A) told to her professors
   (B) said her professors
   (C) told her professors
   (D) is telling her professors

6. Having been asked to speak at the convention, _____ .
   (A) some notes were prepared for Dr. Casagrande
   (B) Dr. Casagrande prepared some notes
   (C) the convention members were pleased to hear Dr. Casagrande
   (D) some notes were prepared by Dr. Casagrande

7. _____ so many people been out of work as today.
   (A) More than ever before
   (B) Never before have
   (C) In the past, there never have
   (D) Formerly, there never were

8. The artist was asked to show some paintings at the contest because _____ .
   (A) he painted very good
   (B) they believed he painted well
   (C) of their belief that he was an good artist
   (D) the judges had been told of his talents

9. Having finished lunch, _____ .
   (A) the detectives began to discuss the case
   (B) the case was discussed again by the detectives
   (C) they discussed the case
   (D) a bunch of detectives discussed the case

10. Ms. Sierra offered _____ because she had faith in his capabilities.
   (A) to Mr. Armstrong the position
   (B) Mr. Armstrong the position
   (C) the position for Mr. Armstrong
   (D) Mr. Armstrong to the position

11. _____ did Jerome accept the job.
   (A) Only because it was interesting work
   (B) Because it was interesting work
   (C) Only because it was interested work
   (D) The work was interesting

12. _____ were slowly lowered to the ground for medical attention.
   (A) The victims who were screaming and who were burning
   (B) The screaming burn victims
   (C) The screamed burnt victims
   (D) The victims who were burning screamed

13. This car has many features including _____ .
   (A) stereo, safety devices, air condition, and it saves gas
   (B) good music, safe devices, air conditioning, and gas
   (C) stereo, safety devices, air conditioned, and good gas
   (D) stereo, safety devices, air conditioning, and low gas mileage

14. The proposal was tabled _____ that it would be helpful.
    (A) temporarily because there was not sufficient evidence
    (B) because for the time being there were not sufficient evidence
    (C) because at the present time there was not sufficient evidence
    (D) temporarily because there was not sufficient enough evidence

15. Adams was dismissed from his position _____ .
    (A) because his financial records were improperly
    (B) because financewise he kept poor records
    (C) for keeping improper financial records
    (D) for keep financial records that were improper

Part B: Written Expression

DIRECTIONS

Each question on this mini-test consists of a sentence in which four words or phrases are underlined. The four underlined parts of the sentence are marked A, B, C, D. You are to identify the *one* underlined word or phrase that would not be acceptable *in standard written English*. Circle the letter of the underlined portion which is not correct.

16. <u>Some</u> Italian scholars <u>stressed</u> <u>the study of</u> grammar,
       A   B   C

    rhetoric, <u>learning about history</u>, and poetry.
                   D

17. When the tank car <u>carried</u> the <u>toxic</u> gas derailed, the firemen
                   A   B

    <u>tried</u> to isolate the village <u>from</u> all traffic.
      C   D

18. While the boys were <u>ice skating</u>, they <u>slip</u> on the thin ice and
                   A   B

    <u>fell</u> <u>into</u> the deep water.
     C   D

19. If motorists do <u>not observe</u> <u>the</u> traffic regulations, <u>they</u> will be
               A   B   C
   stopped, ticketed, and <u>have to pay a fine.</u>
                                D

20. Fred, who usually conducts <u>the choir rehearsals</u>, did not
                                    A
   <u>show up</u> last night because he <u>had</u> an accident
     B   C
   <u>on his way to the practice.</u>
             D

21. <u>A short time</u> before her operation <u>last</u> month, Mrs. Carlyle
        A   B
   <u>dreams</u> of her daughter who <u>lives overseas.</u>
     C   D

22. The atmosphere <u>in Andalucia</u> is open, warm, and
                A
   <u>gives a welcome feeling</u> to all <u>who</u> have <u>the good</u> fortune to
          B   C   D
   visit there.

23. <u>Now that</u> they have <u>successfully</u> passed the TOEFL, the
      A   B
   students <u>were</u> ready <u>to begin</u> their classes at the university.
           C   D

24. Being <u>that he was</u> a good swimmer, John jumped <u>into</u> the
            A   B
   water and <u>rescued</u> the <u>drowning</u> child.
           C   D

25. Some <u>of the</u> people were <u>standing</u> in the street <u>watched</u> the
        A   B   C
   parade, while <u>others</u> were singing songs.
             D

26. The carpenters tried to join together the pieces of the broken
    A   B   C
    beam, but found it impossible to do.
                       D

27. As soon as Pete had arrived, he told us that he will be leaving
                       A   B   C
    for London tomorrow after the board meeting.
                           D

28. In Rome, Venice, and other cities, there developed an
                          A   B
    intellectual movement called humanism, which is the
                                            C
    basis of the Renaissance.
     D

29. The teacher repeated the assignment again for the students,
    A   B
    since they had difficulty understanding what to do after he
         C
    had explained it the first time.
          D

30. The way we react to other people, the educational training we
            A
    received, and the knowledge we display are all part of our
       B   C
    cultural heritage.
        D

31. When you come after class this afternoon, we discussed
    A   B
    the possibility of your writing a research paper.
    C   D

32. Mantovani conducted the orchestra gracefully and with style
             A   B
    to the delight of his appreciative audience.
       C   D

33. Having <u>finished</u> his term paper <u>before the</u> deadline,
          A   B

    <u>it was delivered</u> to the professor <u>before</u> the class.
         C   D

34. <u>After learning</u> all the details <u>about the project</u>, the contractor
       A   B

    told <u>us them</u> at the <u>planning meeting</u>.
        C   D

35. The new student's progress <u>advanced forward</u> with <u>such</u> speed
                      A   B

    <u>that all</u> his teachers <u>were amazed</u>.
      C   D

36. After Mr. Peabody <u>had died</u>, the money from his estate
               A

    reverted <u>back</u> to the company <u>which</u> he <u>had served</u> as
        B   C   D

    president for ten years.

37. In the distance <u>could be seen</u> the <u>sleepy</u> little village with <u>their</u>
              A   B   C

    <u>closely clustered adobe houses</u> and red, clay-tile roofs.
             D

38. <u>Although</u> the weather was not perfect, <u>a bunch of</u> people
     A   B

    <u>turned out</u> <u>for the annual</u> parade.
      C   D

39. After she had dressed and <u>ate</u> breakfast, Lucy <u>rushed off</u>
                  A   B

    <u>to her</u> office for a meeting <u>with</u> her accountant.
     C   D

40. <u>After</u> the rain had <u>let out</u>, the Mitchells <u>continued</u>
     A   B   C

    <u>their hike</u> up the mountain.
     D

ANSWERS FOR EXERCISES 1 THROUGH 53 AND MINI-TESTS 1 THROUGH 4

Exercise 1: Subject, Verb, Complement, and Modifier

1. George / is cooking / dinner / tonight.
   subject   verb phrase   complement   modifier of time

2. Henry and Marcia / have visited / the president.
   subject   verb phrase   complement

3. We / can eat / lunch / in this restaurant / today.
   subject   verb phrase   complement   modifier of place   modifier of time

4. Pat / should have bought / gasoline / yesterday.
   subject   verb phrase   complement   modifier of time

5. Trees / grow.
   subject   verb

6. It / was raining / at seven o'clock this morning.
   subject   verb phrase   modifier of time

7. She / opened / a checking account / at the bank /
   subject   verb   complement   modifier of place
   last week.
   modifier of time

8. Harry / is washing / dishes / right now.
   subject   verb phrase   complement   modifier of time

9. She / opened / her book.
   subject   verb   complement

10. Paul, William, and Mary / were watching / television /
    subject   verb phrase   complement
    a few minutes ago.
    modifier of time

Exercise 2: Count and Non-Count Nouns

television (count)
car (count)
news (non-count)
geography (non-count)
atmosphere (non-count)
person (count)

water (non-count)
pencil (count)
food (non-count)
tooth (count)
soap (non-count)
soup (non-count)

cup (count)
money (non-count)
hydrogen (non-count)
minute (count)

Exercise 3: Determiners

1. much 2. a little 3. those 4. fewer 5. too much
6. this 7. too much 8. few 9. less 10. too much

Exercise 4: Articles

(∅ = nothing)

1. the
2. The, ∅, the
3. ∅, ∅
4. The, the, the
5. a, ∅, ∅, ∅
6. The, the
7. the *or* ∅, the, ∅
8. ∅
9. the, a, ∅, a
10. a, ∅, the

11. ∅, the
12. ∅, the, ∅
13. ∅, the
14. ∅, a *or* the, ∅
15. ∅
16. ∅, ∅, the
17. the *or* ∅, the *or* ∅
18. ∅, an
19. the, an
20. ∅

21. the, a
22. the, ∅
23. The *or* A, a, the, the
24. ∅, the, ∅
25. The
26. an, ∅, the
27. a
28. The
29. The, the
30. ∅, the

Exercise 5: Other

1. another *or* the other *or* another one *or* the other one
2. another
3. the other
4. the others
5. the others, other

6. Another, Another, The others
7. The other
8. Another, another, another *or* the other
9. Others, the others, other
10. the other

Exercise 6: Simple Present and Present Progressive

1. smells
2. are eating
3. practices
4. are driving
5. believe
6. has
7. is swimming
8. hates
9. gets
10. is mowing

Exercise 7: Simple Past Tense and Past Progressive

1. was eating
2. was sleeping (preferred) *or* slept
3. was studying
4. were having
5. went
6. entered
7. was looking (preferred) *or* looked
8. saw
9. owned
10. was writing, broke

Exercise 8: Present Perfect and Simple Past

1. wrote
2. has seen
3. has read
4. has worked
5. have not begun (haven't begun)
6. went
7. has traveled
8. wrote
9. called
10. have not seen (haven't seen)

Exercise 9: Past Perfect and Simple Past

1. had arrested
2. had washed
3. had waited
4. entered
5. washed
6. had received
7. sat
8. had flipped
9. had taken
10. had lived

Exercise 10: Subject-Verb Agreement

1. is
2. brings
3. is
4. aren't
5. have
6. has
7. are
8. are
9. has
10. vary

Exercise 11: Subject-Verb Agreement

1. is
2. is
3. is
4. were
5. has
6. were
7. were
8. has
9. was
10. has
11. makes
12. was
13. was
14. has
15. is
16. has
17. is
18. have
19. has
20. have

Exercise 12: Pronouns

1. him	6. She	11. himself	16. I
2. her	7. Your, mine	12. our	17. his
3. us	8. my	13. her	18. me
4. she	9. himself	14. himself	19. us
5. He	10. We	15. yourself	20. Her, ours

Exercise 13: Verbs as Complements

1. to accept	6. leaving	11. to be	16. driving
2. having	7. to return	12. to finish	17. to know
3. going	8. buying	13. to leave	18. returning
4. to reach	9. to accept	14. to tell	19. leaving
5. opening	10. being	15. to stop	20. leaving

Exercise 14: Pronouns with Verbs as Complements

1. us   2. his   3. our   4. me   5. his   6. George's
7. the defense attorney's   8. Henry   9. our   10. John's

Exercise 15: Need

1. cutting *or* to be cut	5. tuning *or* to be tuned	9. to study
2. watered	6. to be	10. painted
3. to see	7. oiled	
4. to make	8. to go	

Exercise 16: Embedded Questions

1. who will be elected president
2. whose book it is
3. how much it would cost to repair the car
4. how the murder was committed
5. how tall John is
6. how well she plays the guitar
7. when the next exam will take place
8. where they spent their vacation
9. why they are buying a new house
10. how long the class lasts

Exercise 17: Tag Questions

1. aren't you   2. didn't he   3. isn't there   4. won't she
5. hasn't she   6. isn't it   7. shouldn't he   8. can you
9. are there   10. haven't we

Exercise 18: Affirmative Agreement

1. does   2. will   3. do   4. have   5. is   6. should
7. do   8. do   9. have   10. must

Exercise 19: Negative Agreement

1. neither   2. neither   3. either   4. neither   5. neither
6. either   7. neither   8. either   9. either   10. either

Exercise 20: Negative Agreement

1. are   2. can't   3. have   4. didn't   5. did   6. should
7. won't   8. has   9. couldn't   10. did

MINI-TEST TEST 1: GRAMMAR ITEMS 3 THROUGH 14

1. (A) should be *is*. Use a singular verb when a [verb + *ing*] is the subject.
2. (B) should be *too much*. As used in this sentence, *time* is a non-count noun.
3. (C) should be *us*. It is the object of the preposition *for*.
4. (B) should be *herself*. The subject is *she;* the reflexive pronoun must agree with the subject
5. (C) should be *when we have to*. This is an embedded question; question word + subject + verb.
6. (D) should be *hasn't either*. Subject + auxiliary (negative) + *either*.
7. (B) should be a *new car in the morning*. Subject/verb/complement/modifier.
8. (D) should be *the others* or *the other ones*. *Other* is an adjective when it appears before a noun and cannot be plural.

9. (D) should be *read*. Use the simple past with the past perfect.

10. (B) should be *have been*. *Have been* agrees with the plural subject *many theories*.

11. (C) should be *smells*. Use the simple present tense for present time with stative (linking) verbs.

12. (A) should be *had eaten*. Use the past perfect for the past action that happened first.

13. (A) should be *finished*. Use the simple past because *last night* is a specific time in the past.

14. (C) should be *themselves*. *Theirselves* is NEVER correct.

15. (B) should be *any more*. *Another* cannot be used with non-count nouns such as *homework*.

16. (A) should be *taking*. Use the gerund [verb + *ing*] after a preposition.

17. (A) should be *your*. Use the possessive adjective before the gerund.

18. (D) should be *hasn't it*. The auxiliary in the main sentence is *has*.

19. (D) should be *John does too* or *so does John*. See the affirmative agreement rule.

20. (A) should be *being*. *Enjoy* + gerund.

21. (D) should be *to find*. *Decide* + infinitive.

22. (A) should be *him to take*. *Persuade* + complement pronoun + infinitive.

23. (D) should be *I*. Use subject pronouns after the verb *be*.

24. (B) should be *is*. *Is* agrees with the singular subject *the work*.

25. (D) should be *had finished*. There were two actions in the past. First he finished the conference, then he went fishing.

26. (A) should be *play*. *Play* (the plural form of the verb) agrees with the plural subject *Peter and Tom*.

27. (A) should be *was*. The singular *was* agrees with the singular subject *a time*.

28. (A) should be *was drinking*. This is the past progressive:

$$\begin{Bmatrix} was \\ were \end{Bmatrix} + [\text{verb} + ing]$$

29. (D) should be *our friends in Boston yesterday*. Subject/verb/complement/modifier.

30. (B) should be *outdoors last night*. Modifier of place + modifier of time.
31. (A) should be *that*. *Homework* is a non-count noun and cannot be used with the plural *those*.
32. (B) should be *a little*. *Coffee* is a non-count noun and cannot be used with *few*.
33. (B) should be *children*. The plural of *child* is *children*.
34. (C) should be *an honest man*. Use the article *an* before words beginning with a vowel sound.
35. (D) should be *neither are they* or *they aren't either*. See the rule for negative agreement.
36. (D) should be *so is John*. *Is* agrees with the auxiliary *is* in the main sentence.
37. (D) should be *can hardly*. *Hardly* is negative and is always used with a positive verb.
38. (B) should be *a university*. The article *a* is used before words that begin with a consonant sound.
39. (C) should be *in taking*. Use the gerund after a preposition.
40. (C) should be *hardly ever*. *Hardly* is a negative word and cannot be used with another negative.
41. (A) should be *we*. *We students* is the subject of the sentence.
42. (B) should be *not to remove*. See the rule for negative indirect commands.
43. (A) should be *he*. Use subject pronouns after the verb *be*.
44. (B) should be *the car costs*. This is an embedded question; question word + subject + verb.
45. (D) should be *so did Jean*. *Did* agrees in tense (past) with the main sentence verb *studied*.
46. (A) should be *seen*. This is past perfect. *Had* + [verb in past participle].
47. (D) should be *isn't there*. When *there* appears in the subject position of a sentence, it is also used in the tag question.
48. (B) should be *to vote*. *Decide* + infinitive.
49. (B) should be *of going*. *Think of* or *think about* + [verb + *ing*]; NEVER use *think* + infinitive.
50. (B) should be *his going*. Use a possessive adjective and gerund after a preposition.

Exercise 21: Conditional Sentences

1. understood *or* could understand
2. would not have been
3. will give
4. would have told
5. would have been
6. had
7. would stop
8. needed
9. would have found
10. enjoyed
11. paint
12. were
13. writes
14. would permit *or* had permitted
15. could spend
16. will accept
17. buys
18. had decided
19. would have written
20. will leak *or* may leak
21. had studied
22. hears
23. see
24. gets
25. turn
26. were
27. would have called
28. would have talked
29. explained
30. spoke

Exercise 22: Used To

1. eating 2. eat 3. swim 4. like 5. speaking
6. studying 7. dance 8. sleeping 9. eating 10. eating

Exercise 23: Would Rather

1. stay 2. have stayed 3. work 4. studied 5. not study
6. have 7. stood 8. not cook 9. had not arrived
10. have slept

Exercise 24: Must/Should + *Perfective*

1. should have had
2. must have been
3. must have damaged
4. should not have parked
5. must have studied
6. should have studied
7. must have been
8. should have deposited
9. must have forgotten
10. must not have studied

Exercise 25: Modals + *Perfective*

1. I would
2. would have gone
3. may have had
4. should have done
5. must have forgotten
6. may have slept
7. might have had
8. could have lost
9. shouldn't have driven
10. may have run

Exercise 26: Adjectives and Adverbs

1. well   2. intense   3. brightly   4. fluent   5. fluently
6. smooth   7. accurately   8. bitter   9. soon   10. fast

Exercise 27: Linking (Copulative) Verbs

1. terrible   2. well   3. good   4. calm   5. sick   6. quickly
7. diligently   8. vehemently   9. relaxed   10. noisy

Exercise 28: Comparisons

1. as soon   2. more important   3. as well   4. more expensive
5. as hot   6. more talented   7. more colorful   8. happier
9. worse   10. faster

Exercise 29: Comparisons

1. than   2. than   3. from   4. than   5. as
6. than   7. as   8. than   9. than   10. from

Exercise 30: Comparisons

1. best
2. happiest
3. faster
4. creamiest
5. more colorful
6. better
7. good
8. more awkwardly
9. least
10. prettier
11. the better
12. from
13. less impressive
14. the sicker
15. than
16. twice as much as
17. few
18. much
19. farthest
20. more famous

Exercise 31: Nouns Functioning as Adjectives

1. twelve-story   2. language   3. three-act   4. two-day
5. 79-piece   6. five-shelf   7. 16-ounce   8. six-quart
9. brick   10. ten-speed

Exercise 32: Enough

1. enough people
2. enough French
3. enough time
4. fast enough
5. soon enough
6. early enough
7. hard enough
8. slowly enough
9. enough flour
10. enough books

Exercise 33: **Because/Because of**

1. because   2. because   3. because of   4. because
5. because of   6. because of   7. because of   8. because
9. because   10. because of

Exercise 34: **So/Such**

1. so   2. such   3. so   4. such   5. so   6. so   7. such   8. so
9. such   10. such   11. so   12. so   13. such   14. so   15. so

MINI-TEST 2: GRAMMAR ITEMS 15 THROUGH 20

1. (B) should be *ghost*. *Ghost* is an adjective in this sentence modifying the noun *stories* and thus cannot be in the plural form.
2. (B) should be *would take*. The correct sequence of tenses is *were . . . would take*.
3. (B) should be *had told*. This is a past unreal condition. *Would have attended . . . had told*.
4. (A) should be *review*. *Had better* + [verb in simple form].
5. (C) should be *five-speed*. *Five-speed* is an adjective modifying the noun *bicycle*.
6. (C) should be *hot enough*. Adjective + *enough*.
7. (C) should be *brick*. *Brick* is an adjective in this sentence modifying the noun *patio*.
8. (A) should be *such an enjoyable*. *Such* + (*a*) + adjective + singular count noun.
9. (C) should be *enough supplies*. *Enough* + noun.
10. (A) should be *such*. *Such* + adjective + noun (noun = *plans*).
11. (A) should be *had studied*. NEVER use *would* immediately after *if*.
12. (A) should be *deposit*. *Have to* + [verb in simple form].
13. (A) should be *were*. NEVER use *was* after the verb *wish*.
14. (C) should be *must have rehearsed*. This is a logical conclusion in the past (meaning "probably rehearsed").
15. (A) should be *flying*. *Be used to* + [verb + *ing*].
16. (B) should be *to spend*. *Would like* + (complement) + infinitive.
17. (A) should be *live*. *Used to* + [verb in simple form].

18. (C) should be *the louder*. This is a double comparative ("the bolder the . . . display, the louder . . . its approval").

19. (D) should be *his friend Joel's*. The original sentence makes an illogical comparison (comparing the *car* with *Joel*). What should be compared are *Hal's sports car* with *Joel's sports car*. NOTE: *Sports car* is an exception to the rule calling for a singular adjective before a noun.

20. (A) should be *be fishing*. *Would rather* + [verb in simple form].

21. (A) should be *should have called*. This is an unfulfilled past obligation (meaning "she did not call").

22. (A) should be *occurred*. NEVER use *would* immediately after *if*.

23. (D) should be *uncontrollably*. An adverb must modify the verb *sob*, not an adjective. (*How* did the child sob?)

24. (B) should be *so that*. Use *so that* + result clause.

25. (D) should be *would*. The sequence of tenses should be *would advise . . . would*.

26. (C) should be *ought to send*. *Ought to* + [verb in simple form].

27. (A) should be *such a difficult time*. *Such* + (*a*) + adjective + singular count noun.

28. (C) should be *because of*. *Because of* + noun (phrase).

29. (B) should be *ninety-day warranty*. *Ninety-day* is functioning as an adjective of the noun *warranty*.

30. (B) should be *to sleeping*. *Get used to* + [verb + *ing*].

31. (A) should be *bad*. *Feel* is a stative (linking) verb and is modified by an adjective, not an adverb.

32. (A) should be *to go*. *Hope* + infinitive.

33. (B) should be *had*. *As if* indicates an unreal (contrary-to-fact) idea. Use the same rule as for a past unreal condition.

34. (A) should be *so good*. *Taste* is a stative (linking) verb and is modified by an adjective, not an adverb.

35. (C) should be *as old as*. This is a multiple number comparative.

36. (D) should be *sadder than*. It is not correct to use *more* + adjective + *er* at the same time.

37. (B) should be *as*. *As many* + adjective + noun + *as*.

38. (B) should be *had to arrive*. *Have to* + [verb in simple form].

39. (C) should be *from*. The correct idiom is *different from*.

40. (B) should be *never would have met* or *would never have met*. This is a past unreal condition.

41. (C) should be *speaking*. *Be used to* + [verb + *ing*].

42. (B) should be *because*. *Because* + sentence.
43. (B) should be *densely packed*. Use an adverb (*densely*) to modify an adjective (*packed*). (*How* is it packed?)
44. (A) should be *the most*. Use the superlative with more than two.
45. (B) should be *so good a game* or *such a good game*. Cause/effect.
46. (B) should be *did not*. Subject₁ + *would rather that* + subject₂ + [verb in past tense]. The sentence is contrary to fact. They *are* traveling during the bad weather.
47. (D) should be *language*. *Language* is functioning as an adjective modifying the noun *classes* and cannot be plural.
48. (A) should be *from*. The correct idiom is *different from*.
49. (B) should be *inferior*. This adjective can be used in only the positive form, not the comparative or superlative.
50. (A) should be *careful*. This should be an adjective because it is modifying the noun *investigation*. (*What kind* of investigation was it?)

Exercise 35: Passive Voice

1. The president is called (by somebody) every day.
2. The other members are being called by John.
3. The documents were being delivered to the department by Martha.
4. The amendment has been repealed by the other members.
5. The information had been received by the delegates before the recess.
6. The supplies for this class should be bought by the teacher.
7. Mr. Watson will be called (by somebody) tonight.
8. Considerable damage has been caused by the fire.
9. A new procedure was being developed by the company before the bankruptcy hearings began.
10. The papers will have been received by John by tomorrow.

Exercise 36: Causative Verbs

1. leave	5. painted	9. cut	13. fixed
2. repaired	6. write	10. to sign	14. published
3. to type	7. lie	11. leave	15. find
4. call	8. sent	12. to wash	

Exercise 37: Relative Clauses

The word *which* shown in parentheses in these answers indicates optional acceptable answers. In each such case, *that* is the preferred choice, but *which* is not incorrect.

1. The last record that (which) was produced by this company became a gold record.
2. Checking accounts that (which) require a minimum balance are very common now.
3. The professor to whom you spoke yesterday is not here today.
4. John, whose grades are the highest in the school, has received a scholarship.
5. Felipe bought a camera that (which) has three lenses.
6. Frank is the man whom we are going to nominate for the office of treasurer.
7. The doctor is with a patient whose leg was broken in an accident.
8. Jane is the woman who is going to China next year.
9. Janet wants a typewriter that (which) self-corrects.
10. This book, which I found last week, contains some useful information.
11. Mr. Bryant, whose team has lost the game, looks very sad.
12. James wrote an article that (which) indicated that he disliked the president.
13. The director of the program, who graduated from Harvard University, is planning to retire next year.
14. This is the book that (which) I have been looking for all year.
15. William, whose brother is a lawyer, wants to become a judge.

Exercise 38: Relative Clause Reduction

1. George is the man chosen to represent the committee at the convention.
2. All the money accepted has already been released.
3. The papers on the table belong to Patricia.
4. The man brought to the police station confessed to the crime.
5. The girl drinking coffee is Mary Allen.
6. John's wife, a professor, has written several papers on this subject.

7. The man talking to the policeman is my uncle.
8. The book on the top shelf is the one I need.
9. The number of students counted is quite high.
10. Leo Evans, a doctor, eats in this restaurant every day.

Exercise 39: Subjunctive

1. The teacher demanded that the student *leave* the room.
2. It was urgent that he *call* her immediately.
3. Correct.
4. She intends to move that the committee *suspend* discussion on this issue.
5. The king decreed that the new laws *take* effect the following month.
6. I propose that you *stop* this rally.
7. I advise *that* you take the prerequisites before registering for this course *or* I advise you *to take* the prerequisites before registering for this course.
8. His father prefers that he *attend* a different university.
9. Correct.
10. She urged that we *find* another alternative.

Exercise 40: Inclusives

1. not only   2. as well as   3. both   4. but also   5. as well as
6. not only   7. and   8. but also   9. as well as   10. as well as

Exercise 41: Know/Know How

1. know how   2. know how   3. know   4. know   5. know how
6. knew   7. knew how   8. knew   9. knew how   10. know how

Exercise 42: Clauses of Concession

1. Although she disliked coffee, she drank it to keep herself warm.
2. Mary will take a plane in spite of her dislike of flying.
3. Although Marcy was sad after losing the contest, she managed to smile.
4. We took many pictures despite the cloudy sky.
5. Even though she had a poor memory, the old woman told interesting stories to the children.

6. In spite of his frequent absences, he has managed to pass the test.
7. Nancy told me the secret though she had promised not to do so.
8. We plan to buy a ticket for the drawing even though we know we will not win a prize.
9. Even though the prices are high, my daughters insist on going to the movies every Saturday.
10. He ate the chocolate cake in spite of his diet.

Exercise 43: Problem Verbs

1. lies
2. sit
3. laid
   (complement = *the groceries*)
4. rose
5. raise
   (complement = *the picture*)
6. lie
7. laying
   (complement = *cement*)
8. raised
   (complement = *the flag*)
9. rises
10. set
   (complement = *the explosives*)

MINI-TEST 3: GRAMMAR ITEMS 21 THROUGH 29

(∅ = nothing)

1. (D) should be *but also interesting. Not only . . . but also.*
2. (A) should be *he take. Recommend that* + [verb in simple form].
3. (C) should be *know how. Know how* + [verb in infinitive].
4. (B) should be *speak. It is important that* + [verb in simple form.].
5. (B) should be *to enter. Permit* + infinitive.
6. (A) should be ∅. It is redundant to say *both . . . as well as.*
7. (A) should be *in spite of* or *despite.*
8. (B) should be *make. Let* + [verb in simple form].
9. (A) should be *raising. Raise* + complement (complement = *the flag*).
10. (B) should be *that the Officers' Club. Command that* + [verb in simple form].
11. (A) should be *to read. Get* + infinitive.
12. (A) should be *knew. Know* + noun; *know how* + verb.
13. (C) should be *despite* or *in spite of.*

14. (B) should be *study*. *It was suggested that* + [verb in simple form].
15. (B) should be *practice*. *Require that* + [verb in simple form].
16. (A) should be *studying*. The present progressive is *be* + [verb + *ing*].
17. (A) should be *sit*. There is no complement in the sentence.
18. (B) should be *that he*. After the verb *mention* one must use *that*.
19. (D) should be ∅. It is redundant to use *as well* after *not only* . . . *but also*.
20. (B) should be *us to enter*. *Allow* + infinitive.
21. (A) should be *know*. *Know* + sentence.
22. (A) should be *have informed*. The sentence is in the active voice and *should have been informed* is the passive form.
23. (C) should be *advertised* or *that had been advertised*. This is a relative clause in passive voice and can be reduced.
24. (D) should be ∅. It is redundant to use *as well* after *not only* . . . *but also*.
25. (A) should be *to work*. *Encourage* + infinitive.
26. (A) should be *rewrite*. *Have* + person complement + [verb in simple form]; causative.
27. (A) should be *divide*. The sentence is in the active voice, and *will be divided* is in the passive form.
28. (C) should be *were destroyed*. Passive voice.
29. (B) should be *and*. *Both* . . . *and*.
30. (A) should be *risen*. There is no complement.
31. (A) should be *whose*. Use the possessive relative pronoun.
32. (A) should be *in spite of* or *despite*. *Although* + sentence:
$$\begin{Bmatrix} in\ spite\ of \\ despite \end{Bmatrix} + noun\ phrase.$$
33. (A) should be *was repealed* or *has been repealed*. Passive voice.
34. (B) should be *whom*. Use the complement relative pronoun (. . . they voted not to retain *him*).
35. (C) should be *to raise*. Complement = *the rent*.
36. (A) should be *which*. This is a nonrestrictive relative clause and must use *which*, not *that*.
37. (C) should be *lie*. There is no complement in this sentence.
38. (A) should be *set*. Complement = *the plant*.
39. (A) should be *who*. *Which* is used with things, *who* with people.

40. (A) should be *despite* or *in spite of*.
41. (A) should be *has been canceled*. Passive voice.
42. (C) should be *lying*. There is no complement in this sentence.
43. (A) should be *were discovered*. If a relative clause is reduced, the pronoun *that* must also be omitted.
44. (A) should be *lie*. There is no complement in this sentence.
45. (D) should be *rewrite*. *Make* + [verb in simple form].
46. (A) should be *stated that he*. *State that*.
47. (A) should be *in spite of* or *despite*. *The danger* is a noun phrase, and *although* must be followed by a sentence. *That he might be injured* is a relative clause.
48. (A) should be ∅. If a sentence begins with *that,* it must contain two clauses and thus two verbs.
49. (B) should be *to raise*. Complement = *her test score*.
50. (D) should be *able to find*. *Able* + infinitive.

Exercise 44: Sequence of Tenses

1. He *said* that he *would finish* the project by May.
2. Mark *thought* he *was going* to win the award.
3. I *heard* that Kate *had accepted* a new position at the East Side Clinic.
4. Steve *said* that he *would make* the dessert for the party.
5. Lou *told* his friends that they *were* good tennis players.
6. I *realized* that they *were* older than they *looked*.
7. Mary Ellen *said* that she *ate* three well-balanced meals every day.
8. The student *was asking* the professor when the class *would do* the next experiment.
9. We *hoped* that you *could play* tennis later.
10. We *knew* that you *might move* to France next year.

Exercise 45: Say/Tell

1. said	6. tell	11. told	16. said
2. is telling	7. tells	12. said	17. said
3. told	8. say	13. said	18. says
4. tell	9. says	14. tell	19. said
5. told	10. tell	15. said	20. tell

Exercise 46: Antecedents of Pronouns

Note that other choices are possible.

1. The dispute between the faculty and the administration was not resolved until the faculty (members) got better working conditions.
2. As Ellen walked toward the Student Union, she spotted her friend.
3. When the bullfighters march into the arena, foreigners are easily impressed.
4. In their spare time, authors have written many great books about the famous Greek and Roman heroes.
5. Dr. Byrd's book was accepted for publication because the publishers thought it would be beneficial to students.
6. Bob and Helen hate flying because planes make too much noise.
7. Casey was not admitted to the country club because the members thought he was not socially acceptable.
8. Mary loves touring the country by train because the countryside is so interesting.
9. The colonel was decorated for bravery, having fought off the enemy (soldiers).
10. The children were frightened because the animals (or any noun) made such eerie sounds.

Exercise 47: Illogical Participial Modifiers

Note that other choices are possible.

1. Being thoroughly dissatisfied with the picture, *Mary* (or any animate noun) hid it in the closet.
2. Seeing the advancing army, *the family* (or any animate noun) hid the valuables under the stairwell.
3. Plunging into the water, *the lifeguard* (or any animate noun) rescued the drowning child.
4. Criticizing the defendant for his cruel behavior, the judge handed down the sentence.
5. After painting the car, the man gave it to his wife.
6. Being an early riser, Edna adjusted easily to her company's new summer schedule.

7. After winning the match, Nancy jumped for joy.
8. Having wandered through the mountain passes for days, the hikers discovered an abandoned shack where they could take shelter.
9. Being very protective of its young, the mother eagle attacks all those who approach the nest.
10. Before playing ball, the baseball players observed a two-minute silence for their recently deceased teammate.

Exercise 48: Participles as Adjectives

1. broken	6. excited	11. approving	16. cleaned
2. trembling	7. smiling	12. approved	17. locked
3. crying	8. frightening	13. blowing	18. crowded
4. interesting	9. frightened	14. boring	19. aching
5. burning	10. advancing	15. cleaning	20. parked

Exercise 49: Redundancy

The redundant word is listed here.

1. again   2. identical *or* the same   3. enough *or* sufficient   4. back   5. performance   6. forward   7. together
8. new   9. together   10. two

Exercise 50: Parallel Structure

1. The puppy stood up slowly, wagged its tail, *blinked* its eyes, and barked. (past tense verbs)
2. Ecologists are trying to preserve our environment for future generations by protecting the ozone layer, purifying the air, and *replanting the trees* that have been cut down. (verbs + *ing*)
3. The chief of police demanded from his assistants an orderly investigation, a well-written report, and *hard work*. (adjective + noun)
4. Marcia is a scholar, an athlete, and *an artist*. (nouns)
5. Slowly and *carefully,* the museum director removed the Ming vase from the shelf and placed it on the display pedestal. (adverbs)

6. The farmer plows the fields, plants the seeds, and *harvests* the crop. (present tense verbs)
7. Abraham Lincoln was a good president—self-educated, hard working, and *honest*. (adjectives)
8. Children love playing in the mud, running through puddles, and *getting* very dirty. (verbs + *ing*)
9. Collecting stamps, playing chess, and *mounting* beautiful butterflies are Derrick's hobbies. (verbs + *ing* + nouns)
10. Despite America's affluence, many people are without jobs, on welfare, and *in debt*. (prepositional phrases)

Exercise 51: Transformation of Direct and Indirect Object

1. Mary showed *me* the photographs.
2. I'll send *you* the books next week.
3. My sister sent *my daughter* a game for her birthday.
4. He brought *her* the telegram this morning.
5. The author gave *his friend* an autographed copy of his book.
6. They wrote *us* a letter.
7. Louie drew *his mother* a lovely picture.
8. She made *her cousin* a bookcase.
9. That teacher taught *us* grammar last year.
10. Mary handed *her brother* the tray.

Exercise 52: Transformation of Direct and Indirect Object

1. John owes the money *to his friend*.
2. My friends sent a bouquet of flowers *to me* while I was in the hospital.
3. The clerk sold the records *to us*.
4. They found a good, inexpensive car *for him*.
5. Picasso painted a beautiful portrait *for his wife*.
6. My father read the newspaper article *to us*.
7. Pass the salt *to me* please.
8. She bought a red jacket *for him*.
9. The girls couldn't wait to show the bicycles *to us*.
10. The construction crew built a house *for them* in four weeks.

Exercise 53: Adverbials at the Beginning of a Sentence

1. Rarely does Jorge forget to do his homework.
2. Only by staying up all night can Jane finish this work.
3. Hardly had Henry started working when he realized that he needed to go to the library.
4. Never have we heard so moving a rendition as this one.
5. Seldom did Maria miss a football game when she was in the United States.
6. Only with a bank loan will we be able to buy the car.
7. Rarely do we watch television during the week.
8. Never has he played a better game than he has today.
9. Seldom does this professor let his students leave class early.
10. Hardly had Jennifer entered the room when she felt the presence of another person.

MINI-TEST 4: STYLISTIC PROBLEMS

For Part A of this mini-test, the answer key analyzes why each incorrect answer choice is incorrect.

Part A

1. (A) Style error. There is no antecedent for the pronoun *it*.
   (B) 2 style errors. *Refused . . . will* is an incorrect sequence of tenses; there is no antecedent for the pronoun *they*.
   (C) Correct.
   (D) 2 style errors. There is an incorrect sequence of tenses; there is no antecedent for the pronoun *it*.

2. (A) and (B) Style error. Because the structure of the sentence is auxiliary + subject + verb, the sentence must begin with an adverbial.
   (C) Vocabulary error. *Hardly* means "almost."
   (D) Correct

3. (A) Style error. It is redundant to say *return . . . back.*
   (B) Grammar error. When the indirect object precedes the direct object, no preposition is possible.
   (C) Grammar error. *Originally* is an adverb and is not correct because it modifies the noun *owner.*
   (D) Correct.

4. (A) Correct.
   (B) 2 grammar errors. It is not correct to use a preposition when the indirect object precedes the direct object; when *million* is preceded by a number, it cannot be plural (one million, two million).
   (C) Grammar error. It is not correct to use a preposition when the indirect object precedes the direct object.
   (D) 2 grammar errors. When *million* is preceded by a number, it cannot be plural, and when *million* is preceded by a number and followed by a noun, the preposition *of* is incorrect.

5. (A) Grammar error. *Tell* must be followed directly by the indirect object; there can be no preposition.
   (B) Grammar error. It is not correct to follow the verb *say* with the name of a person or people.
   (C) Correct.
   (D) Grammar error. *Is telling . . . could* is an incorrect sequence of tenses.

6. (A), (C), and (D) Style errors. These choices contain dangling participles. *Dr. Casagrande* is the subject of *having been asked,* and thus his name must follow the comma.
   (B) Correct.

7. (A) Grammar error. The only verb in the sentence is a past participle, *been,* and choice (A) contains no auxiliary verb.
   (B) Correct. Adverbial + auxiliary + subject + verb.
   (C) Grammar error. The choice uses incorrect word order.
   (D) Grammar error. The choice uses incorrect word order; *were* cannot be followed by the participle *been.*

8. (A) Grammar error. *Good* is an adjective and modifies the verb *painted;* it should always be *well*.
   (B) Style error. The pronoun *they* has no antecedent.
   (C) Style error. The pronoun *their* has no antecedent; *an* cannot precede a word beginning with a consonant sound.
   (D) Correct.

9. (A) Correct
   (B) Style error. This choice contains a dangling participle. *The detectives* is the subject of *having finished* and must immediately follow the comma.
   (C) Style error. The pronoun *they* has no antecedent.
   (D) Style error. *A bunch of* is slang and not appropriate in formal English.

10. (A) Grammar error. It is not correct to use a preposition when the indirect object precedes the direct object.
    (B) Correct.
    (C) Grammar error. *For* is the wrong preposition (*offer* something *to* somebody).
    (D) Grammar error. This choice uses incorrect word order.

11. (A) Correct.
    (B) Style error. Because the construction is auxiliary + subject + verb, the sentence must begin with an adverbial.
    (C) Grammar error. *Interested* should be *interesting*.
    (D) Style error. This choice uses incorrect word order.

12. (A) Style error. The choice is verbose, using too many unnecessary words (repeating *who were*).
    (B) Correct.
    (C) Grammar error. *Screamed* should be *screaming*.
    (D) Grammar error. The conjugated verb *screamed* immediately before the verb *were* is not possible.

13. (A) Improper word choice. It should read *air conditioning; and it saves gas* is not parallel.
    (B) Improper word choice. *Good music* does not mean the same as *stereo; a safe device* is a device that is safe, but a *safety device* is a device that makes something else safe; *gas* is not a "feature."
    (C) *Air conditioned* is improper word choice; *good gas* does not mean the same as *low gas mileage*.
    (D) Correct.

14. (A) Correct.
    (B) Grammar error. *Were* is plural and *evidence* is non-count.
    (C) Style error. *At the present time* is not correct because the sentence is in the past.
    (D) Style error. *Sufficient* and *enough* have the same meaning and when used together are redundant.

15. (A) Grammar error. *Improperly* is an adverb. An adverb cannot modify the noun *records*.
    (B) Style error. *Financewise* is not correct.
    (C) Correct.
    (D) Grammar error and style error. *For keeping* is correct, not *for keep* (preposition + [verb + ing]); *financial records that were improper* should be *improper financial records* because it is the more concise way of conveying the idea.

Part B

16. (D) should be *history*. *History* is parallel structure; noun, noun, noun.
17. (A) should be *carrying*. Use the present participle because the subject (*the tank car*) was involved in the action.
18. (B) should be *slipped*. The correct sequence of tenses is *were . . . slipped*.
19. (D) should be *fined*. For parallel structure, all past participles are required.
20. (C) should be *had had*. The past perfect should be used; the accident happened first.

21. (C) should be *dreamed*. Use past time because it happened last month.

22. (B) should be *welcoming*. For parallel structure, all adjectives are required.

23. (C) should be *are*. *Now* indicates present time.

24. (A) should be ∅. The wording is verbose. The sentence should read: *Being a good swimmer...*

25. (C) should be *watching*. *Were standing ... watching* is correct parallel structure.

26. (B) should be *join*. It is redundant to say *join together*.

27. (C) should be *would be leaving*. The correct sequence of tenses is *told ... would be*.

28. (C) should be *was*. *Was* (past) is the correct sequence of tenses because the sentence is in the past.

29. (B) should be ∅. It is redundant to say *repeat again*.

30. (B) should be *receive*. For parallel structure, *react ... receive ... display* (all present tense) is required.

31. (B) should be *will discuss*. The correct sequence of tenses is *come ... will discuss*.

32. (B) should be *stylishly*. Parallel structure requires *gracefully* (adverb) ... *stylishly* (adverb).

33. (C) should be *he delivered it*. A person is the subject of the verb *having finished*, and thus that person's name must appear immediately after the comma.

34. (C) should be *them to us*. Two pronouns cannot take the order of indirect object + direct object.

35. (A) should be *advanced*. It is redundant to say *advance forward*.

36. (B) should be ∅. It is redundant to say *revert back*.

37. (C) should be *its*. *Village* is singular, so the possessive pronoun must also be singular.

38. (B) should be *many*. *A bunch of* is slang.

39. (A) should be *eaten*. Parallel structure requires *had dressed and eaten*.

40. (B) should be *let up*. *Let up* means "to diminish"; *let out* means "to dismiss."

PROBLEM VOCABULARY AND PREPOSITIONS

This section contains information and exercises on commonly misused words, confusingly related words, use of prepositions, and two-word verbs. With each section are example sentences and exercises. The answers to the exercises will be found at the end of this section.

It should be noted that the material presented here may appear not only in the reading comprehension section of TOEFL but also in the grammar section and even in the listening comprehension section. Prior to July 1995, TOEFL contained a separate vocabulary section, but that has been eliminated. Vocabulary is tested in the reading comprehension section in order to provide contextual clues about the definitions. Therefore, you should take advantage of the fact that the words appear in context by using the clues contained in the reading passage to assist in choosing the correct synonym.

Memorizing long lists of words may result in frustration and is actually not very useful. There is no way to know which of the words you memorize will appear on TOEFL. Therefore, you should try to improve your vocabulary as you improve your English in general. The following suggestions will be useful in helping you improve your vocabulary.

1. Read well-written books, magazines, and newspapers. Magazines such as *Time* and *Newsweek,* for example, and major newspapers contain sophisticated vocabulary and grammatical constructions. Reading such materials is very useful.

2. Look up every word that is unfamiliar to you in the practice tests in this book and in other reading material. Keep a notebook of unfamiliar words. After looking up the word, write the word, the definition, and an original sentence in your notebook and study it often.

3. Study the problem vocabulary items and two-word verbs (verbal idioms) in this book.

4. Review your vocabulary word notebook often. Repetition will help you to remember the meaning of difficult words.

1. COMMONLY MISUSED WORDS

The following words are often misused by native English speakers as well as nonnative speakers. Sometimes the spellings are so similar that people fail to distinguish between them. Others are pronounced exactly the same, but they are spelled differently and have different meanings. Words in the latter category are called homonyms. Study the words, parts of speech (noun, verb, etc.), definitions, and sample sentences in this list.

ANGEL (noun)—a spiritual or heavenly being. The Christmas card portrayed a choir of *angels* hovering over the shepherds.

ANGLE (noun)—a figure formed by two lines meeting at a common point. The carpenters placed the planks at right *angles*.

CITE (verb)—quote as an example. In her term paper, Janis had to *cite* many references.

SITE (noun)—location. The corner of North Main and Mimosa Streets will be the *site* of the new shopping center.

SIGHT (a) (noun)—a device used to assist aim (of a gun or telescope). Through the *sight* of the rifle, the soldier spotted the enemy. (b) (noun)—view. Watching the landing of the space capsule was a pleasant *sight*. (c) (verb)—see. We *sighted* a ship in the bay.

COSTUME (noun)—clothing, typical style of dress. We all decided to wear colonial *costumes* to the Fourth of July celebration.

CUSTOM (noun)—a practice that is traditionally followed by a particular group of people. It is a *custom* in Western Europe for little boys to wear short pants to school.

DECENT (adjective)—respectable or suitable. When one appears in court, one must wear *decent* clothing.

DESCENT (noun) (a)—downward motion. The mountain climbers found their *descent* more hazardous than their ascent. (b)— lineage. Vladimir is of Russian *descent*.

DESSERT (noun) (desért)—the final course of a meal, usually something sweet. We had apple pie for *dessert* last night.

DESERT (noun) (désert)—a hot, dry place. It is difficult to survive in the *desert* without water.

DESERT (verb) (desért)—abandon. After *deserting* his post, the soldier ran away from the camp.

LATER (adverb)—a time in the future or following a previous action. We went to the movies and *later* had ice cream at Dairy Isle.

LATTER (adjective)—last of two things mentioned. Germany and England both developed dirigibles for use during World War II, the *latter* primarily for coastal reconnaissance. (*latter = England*)

LOOSE (adjective)—opposite of *tight*. After dieting, Marcy found that her clothes had become so *loose* that she had to buy a new wardrobe.

LOSE (verb) (a)—to be unable to find something. Mary *lost* her glasses last week. (b)—opposite of win. If Harry doesn't practice his tennis more, he may *lose* the match.

PASSED (verb—past tense of *pass*) (a)—elapse. Five hours *passed* before the jury reached its verdict. (b)—go by or beyond. While we were sitting in the park, several of our friends *passed* us. (c)—succeed. The students are happy that they *passed* their exams.

PAST (a) (adjective)—a time or event before the present. This *past* week has been very hectic for the students returning to the university. (b) (noun)—time before the present. In the *past*, he had been a cook, a teacher, and a historian.

PEACE (noun)—harmony or freedom from war. *Peace* was restored to the community after a week of rioting.

PIECE (noun)—part of a whole. Heidi ate a *piece* of chocolate cake for dessert.

PRINCIPAL (a) (noun)—director of an elementary or secondary school. The *principal* called a faculty meeting. (b) (adjective)—main or most important. An anthropologist, who had worked with the indigenous tribes in Australia, was the *principal* speaker at Friday's luncheon.

PRINCIPLE (noun)—fundamental rule or adherence to such a rule. Mr. Connors is a man who believes that truthfulness is the best *principle*.

QUIET (adjective)—serene, without noise. The night was so *quiet* that you could hear the breeze blowing.

QUITE (adverb) (a)—completely. Louise is *quite* capable of taking over the household chores while her mother is away. (b)—somewhat or rather. He was *quite* tired after his first day of classes.

QUIT (verb)—stop. Herman *quit* smoking on his doctor's advice.

STATIONARY (adjective)—nonmovable, having a fixed location. The weatherman said that the warm front would be *stationary* for several days.

STATIONERY (noun)—special writing paper. Lucille used only monogrammed *stationery* for correspondence.

THAN (conjunction)—used in unequal comparisons. Today's weather is better *than* yesterday's.

THEN (adverb)—a time following a previously mentioned time. First, Julie filled out her schedule; *then,* she paid her fees.

THEIR (adjective)—plural possessive adjective. *Their* team scored the most points during the game.

THERE (adverb) (a)—location away from here. Look over *there* between the trees. (b)—used with the verb *be* to indicate existence. *There* is a book on the teacher's desk.

THEY'RE (pronoun + verb)—contraction of *they* + *are*. *They're* leaving on the noon flight to Zurich.

TO (preposition)—toward, until, as far as. Go *to* the blackboard and write out the equation.

TWO (noun or adjective)—number following *one*. *Two* theories have been proposed to explain that incident.

TOO (adverb) (a)—excessively. This morning was *too* cold for the children to go swimming. (b)—also. Jane went to the movie, and we did *too*.

WEATHER (noun)—atmospheric conditions. Our flight was delayed because of bad *weather*.

WHETHER (conjunction)—if, indicates a choice. Because of the gas shortage, we do not know *whether* we will go away for our vacation or stay home.

WHOSE (pronoun)—possessive relative pronoun or adjective. The person *whose* name is drawn first will win the grand prize.

WHO'S (relative pronoun + verb)—contraction of *who* + *is* or *who* + *has*. *Who's* your new biology professor? Scott is the attorney *who's* been reviewing this case.

YOUR (adjective)—possessive of *you*. We are all happy about *your* accepting the position with the company in Baltimore.

YOU'RE (pronoun + verb)—contraction of *you* + *are*. *You're* going to enjoy the panorama from the top of the hill.

Exercise 54: Commonly Misused Words

Select the correct word in parentheses to complete the meaning of the sentence.

1. A beautiful (angle/angel) adorned their Christmas tree.
2. I have (your/you're) notes here, but I cannot find mine.
3. The rescuers were a welcome (cite/sight/site) for those trapped on the snow-covered mountain.
4. (Who's/Whose) supposed to supply the refreshments for to-night's meeting?
5. It is a (costume/custom) in the United States to eat turkey on Thanksgiving.
6. (Weather/Whether) we drive or fly depends on the length of our vacation.
7. Pasquale is of French (decent/descent), but his cousin is English.
8. Dr. Hipple will not be coming (to/two/too) the meeting because he has (to/two/too) many papers to grade.
9. Although my mother never eats (desert/dessert), I prefer something sweet.
10. I guess (their/there/they're) not interested because we have not heard from them.
11. Doris and Marge teach kindergarten; the (latter/later) works in Putnam.
12. Isaac Asimov's science books are more easily understood (than/then) most scientists'.

13. The fender on Sean's bike came (loose/lose) and had to be tightened.
14. Nobody had any (stationary/stationery), so we had to use notebook paper to write the letter.
15. The hikers had (passed/past) many hours waiting to be rescued.
16. Lisa had to (quiet/quit/quite) eating apples after the orthodontist put braces on her teeth.
17. After any war, the world desires a lasting (peace/piece).
18. Albert Einstein expressed his (principal/principle) of relativity.
19. Marcia was (quit/quiet/quite) tired after the long walk to class.
20. You must remember to (cite/site/sight) your references when you write a paper.

2. CONFUSINGLY RELATED WORDS

These are words that cause problems when the speaker is not able to distinguish between them. They are similar in meaning or pronunciation but CANNOT be used interchangeably. Learn the definition of each and its use before employing it in conversation.

ACCEPT (verb)—to take what is given. Professor Perez will *accept* the chairmanship of the humanities department.

EXCEPT (preposition)—excluding or omitting a thing or person. Everyone is going to the convention *except* Bob, who has to work.

ACCESS (noun)—availability, way of gaining entrance. The teachers had no *access* to the students' files, which were locked in the principal's office.

EXCESS (a) (adjective)—abundant, superfluous. We paid a surcharge on our *excess* baggage. (b) (noun)—extra amount. The demand for funds was in *excess* of the actual need.

ADVICE (noun)—opinion given to someone, counseling. If you heed the teacher's *advice,* you will do well in your studies.

ADVISE (verb)—act of giving an opinion or counsel. The Congress *advised* the president against signing the treaty at that time.

AFFECT (verb)—to produce a change in. The doctors wanted to see how the medication would *affect* the patient.

EFFECT (a) (noun)—end result or consequence. The children suffered no ill *effects* from their long plane ride. (b) (verb)—to produce as a result. To *effect* a change in city government we must all vote on Tuesday.

AGAIN (adverb)—repetition of an action, one more time. Mike wrote to the publishers *again,* inquiring about his manuscript.

AGAINST (preposition) (a)—in opposition to someone or something. The athletic director was *against* our dancing in the new gym. (b)—next to, adjacent. The boy standing *against* the piano is my cousin Bill.

ALREADY (adverb)—an action that happened at an indefinite time before the present. Jan's plane had *already* landed before we got to the airport.

ALL READY (noun + adjective)—prepared to do something. We are *all ready* to go boating.

AMONG (preposition)—shows a relationship or selection involving three or more entities. It was difficult to select a winner from *among* so many contestants.

BETWEEN (preposition)—shows a relationship or selection involving only two entities. *Between* writing her book *and* teaching, Mary Ellen had little time for anything else. NOTE: When *between* is followed by two nouns or noun phrases, the two nouns or noun phrases must be separated by *and* and never by *or.*

BESIDE (preposition)—next to. There is a small table *beside* the bed.

BESIDES (preposition or adverb)—in addition to, also, moreover. I have five history books here *besides* the four that I left at home.

ASIDE (adverb)—to one side. Harry sets money *aside* every payday for his daughter's education.

COMPARE (verb)—show similarities. Sue *compared* her new school with the last one she had attended.

CONTRAST (verb)—show differences. In her composition, Marta chose to *contrast* life in a big city with that of a small town.

CONSECUTIVE (adjective)—indicates an uninterrupted sequence. Today is the tenth *consecutive* day of this unbearable heat wave.

SUCCESSIVE (adjective)—indicates a series of separate events. The United States won gold medals in two *successive* Olympic Games.

CONSIDERABLE (adjective)—rather large amount or degree. Even though Marge had *considerable* experience in the field, she was not hired for the job.

CONSIDERATE (adjective)—thoughtful, polite. It was very *considerate* of Harry to send his hostess a bouquet of flowers.

CREDIBLE (adjective)—believable. His explanation of the rescue at sea seemed *credible.*

CREDITABLE (adjective)—worthy of praise. The fireman's daring rescue of those trapped in the burning building was a *creditable* deed.

CREDULOUS (adjective)—gullible. Rita is so *credulous* that she will accept any excuse you offer.

DETRACT (verb)—take away or lessen the value of a person or thing. Molly's nervousness *detracted* from her singing.

DISTRACT (verb)—cause a lack of mental concentration on what one is doing or the goals one has set. Please don't *distract* your father while he is balancing the checkbook.

DEVICE (noun)—an invention or plan. This is a clever *device* for cleaning fish without getting pinched by the scales.

DEVISE (verb)—invent, create, contrive. The general *devised* a plan for attacking the enemy camp at night while the soldiers were celebrating.

ELICIT (verb)—draw out, evoke. The prosecutor's barrage of questions finally *elicited* the truth from the witness.

ILLICIT (adjective)—unlawful. The politician's *illicit* dealings with organized crime caused him to lose his government position.

EMIGRANT (noun)—one who leaves one's own country to live in another. After World War II, many *emigrants* left Europe to go to the United States.

IMMIGRANT (noun)—one who comes to a new country to settle. The United States is a country composed of *immigrants.* NOTE: The verbs are *emigrate* and *immigrate.* It is possible to be both an emigrant and an immigrant at the same time as one leaves one's own country (emigrant) and arrives in another country (immigrant) to settle.

EXAMPLE (noun)—anything used to prove a point. Picasso's *Guernica* is an excellent *example* of expressionism in art.

SAMPLE (noun)—a representative part of a whole. My niece loves to go to the supermarket because the dairy lady always gives her a *sample* of cheese.

FORMERLY (adverb)—previously. He *formerly* worked as a professor, but now he is a physicist.

FORMALLY (adverb) (a)—an elegant way of dressing, usually a tuxedo for men and a long gown for women. At the resort we were required to dress *formally* for dinner every night. (b)—properly, officially. She has *formally* requested a name change.

HARD (adjective) (a)—difficult. The test was so *hard* that nobody passed. (b)—opposite of *soft.* The stadium seats were *hard,* so we rented a cushion. (adverb) (c)—with great effort. They worked *hard* on the project.

HARDLY (adverb)—barely, scarcely. He had so much work to do after the vacation that he *hardly* knew where to begin.

HELPLESS (adjective)—unable to remedy (an animate thing is helpless). Because I could not speak their language, I felt *helpless* trying to understand the tourists' plight.

USELESS (adjective)—worthless, unserviceable. An umbrella is *useless* in a hurricane.

HOUSE (noun) and **HOME** (noun) are many times used interchangeably, but there exists a difference in meaning. (a) *House* refers to the building or structure. The Chapmans are building a new *house* in Buckingham Estates. (b) *Home* refers to the atmosphere or feeling of domestic tranquility found in a house. *Home* is where the heart is.

IMAGINARY (adjective)—something not real that exists in one's imagination. Since Ralph has no brothers or sisters, he has created an *imaginary* playmate.

IMAGINATIVE (adjective)—showing signs of great imagination. *Star Wars* was created by a highly *imaginative* writer.

IMMORTAL (adjective)—incapable of dying. The *immortal* works of Shakespeare are still being read and enjoyed three centuries after their writing.

IMMORAL (adjective)—against the moral law, bad, evil. Their *immoral* behavior in front of the students cost the teachers their jobs.

IMPLICIT (adjective)—understood, but not specifically stated. Our supervisor has *implicit* faith in our ability to finish this project on time.

EXPLICIT (adjective)—expressed in a clear and precise manner. The professor gave *explicit* instructions for carrying out the research project.

INDUSTRIAL (adjective)—pertaining to industry. Paul had an *industrial* accident and was in the hospital for three months.

INDUSTRIOUS (adjective)—diligent, hard working. Mark was such an *industrious* student that he received a four-year scholarship to the university.

INFLICT (verb)—impose something unwelcome. Because the prisoners had created a riot and had assaulted several guards, the warden *inflicted* severe punishments on all the participants.

AFFLICT (verb)—cause physical or mental pain. During the Middle Ages, millions of people were *afflicted* by the plague.

INSPIRATION (noun)—stimulation to learn or discover. Thomas A. Edison, inventor of the phonograph, said that an idea was ninety-nine percent perspiration and one percent *inspiration*.

ASPIRATION (noun) (a)—ambition, desire, goal. Gail's lifelong *aspiration* has been that of becoming a doctor. (b)—expulsion of breath. To pronounce certain words, proper *aspiration* is necessary.

INTELLIGENT (adjective)—possessing a great deal of mental ability. Dan was so *intelligent* that he received good grades without ever having to study.

INTELLIGIBLE (adjective)—clear, easily understood. The science teacher's explanations were so *intelligible* that students had no problems doing their assignments.

INTELLECTUAL (a) (noun)—any person who possesses a great deal of knowledge. Because Fabian is an *intellectual,* he finds it difficult to associate with his classmates who are less intelligent. (b) (adjective)—wise. John was involved in an *intellectual* conversation with his old professor.

INTENSE (adjective)—extreme. Last winter's *intense* cold almost depleted the natural gas supply.

INTENSIVE (adjective)—concentrated. Before going to Mexico, Phil took an *intensive* course in Spanish.

LATE (a) (adjective or adverb)—not punctual. Professor Carmichael hates to see his students arrive *late.* (b) (adjective)—no longer living. Her *late* husband was the author of that book.

LATELY (adverb)—recently. I haven't seen Burt *lately.* He must be extremely busy with his research.

LEARN (verb)—obtain knowledge. The new cashier had to *learn* how to operate the computerized cash register.

TEACH (verb)—impart knowledge. The instructor is *teaching* us how to program computers.

LEND (verb) and **LOAN** (verb)—give something for temporary use with the promise of returning it. (*Lend* and *loan* as verbs may be used interchangeably.) Jill *loaned* (*lent*) me her red dress to wear to the dance.

BORROW (verb)—receive something for temporary use with the promise of returning it. I *borrowed* Jill's red dress to wear to the dance.

LIQUEFY (verb)—change to a watery or liquid state. The ice cream began to *liquefy* in the intense heat.

LIQUIDATE (verb)—eliminate, get rid of, change to cash. The foreign agents tried to *liquidate* the traitor before he passed the information to his contacts.

LONELY (adjective)—depressed feeling as a result of abandonment or being alone. After her husband's death, Debbie was very *lonely* and withdrawn.

ALONE (adjective)—physical state of solitude, unaccompanied. After losing in the Olympic tryouts, Phil asked to be left *alone*.

NEAR (preposition or adverb)—used to indicate a place not too far distant. My biology class meets *near* the Student Union.

NEARLY (adverb)—almost. We were *nearly* hit by the speeding car on the turnpike.

OBSERVATION (noun)—act of paying attention to or being paid attention. The ancient Egyptians' *observation* of the heavenly bodies helped them know when to plant and harvest.

OBSERVANCE (noun)—act of following custom or ceremony. There will be numerous parades and displays of fireworks in *observance* of Independence Day.

PERSECUTE (verb)—torture, harass. Throughout history many people have been *persecuted* for their religious beliefs.

PROSECUTE (verb)—in legal terms, to bring suit against or enforce a law through a legal process. Shoplifters will be *prosecuted* to the fullest extent of the law.

PRECEDE (verb)—to come before. Weather Service warnings *preceded* the hurricane.

PROCEED (verb)—continue an action after a rest period or interruption. After the fire drill, the teacher *proceeded* to explain the experiment to the physics class.

QUANTITY (noun)—used with non-count nouns to indicate amount, bulk. A large *quantity* of sand was removed before the archeologists found the prehistoric animal bones.

NUMBER (noun)—used with count nouns to designate individual amount. A *number* of artifacts were found at the excavation site.

REMEMBER (verb)—to recall or think of again. I do not *remember* what time he asked me to call. You don't *remember* me, do you?

REMIND (verb)—to cause (someone) to remember, to bring into (someone's) mind. Please *remind* me to call Henry at 7 o'clock tonight. Henry *reminds* me of my uncle.

SENSIBLE (adjective)—having good judgment. When it is raining hard, *sensible* people stay indoors.

SENSITIVE (adjective)—excitable, touchy, easily affected by outside influences. Stephen cannot be out in the sun very long because he has very *sensitive* skin and burns easily.

SPECIAL (adjective)—that which receives a lot of attention because of a distinct characteristic. Meyer's Department Store will have a *special* sale for their charge customers.

ESPECIALLY (adverb)—particularly. Rita is *especially* talented in the fine arts. She has a *special* talent for playing music by ear.

USE (noun)—act of putting into practice or service, application. The salesman said that regular *use* of fertilizer would ensure a greener, healthier lawn.

USAGE (noun)—way in which something is used. Norm Crosby's *usage* of English vocabulary in his comedy routine is hilarious.

Exercise 55: Confusingly Related Words

Select the word in parentheses that completes the meaning in each sentence.

1. Betty's insulting remark greatly (effected/affected) Kurt, who is a very sensitive person.
2. Detroit manufacturers hope to develop an easily attachable (device/devise) for the carburetor to improve gas mileage.
3. While doing the experiment, we asked the lab technician's (advice/advise).
4. After declaring bankruptcy, the company was forced to (liquefy/liquidate) its assets.
5. Keith's company's headquarters were (formerly/formally) located in Philadelphia.
6. (Especially/Special) attention must be given to the questions at the end of each chapter.
7. George was (among/between) those students selected to participate in the debate.
8. They were (already/all ready) to leave when a telegram arrived.
9. By asking many questions, the instructor tried to (elicit/illicit) information from the students.

10. You should not say things that might make a highly (sensitive/sensible) person upset.
11. The United States is a "melting pot," a land of (emigrants/immigrants).
12. A large (number/quantity) of whales beached and died last year because of ear problems.
13. When Louise set the table, she placed the silverware (besides/beside) the plates.
14. Mark is (sensible/sensitive) enough to swim close to shore.
15. In 1969 the astronauts who landed on the moon collected (examples/samples) of rocks and soil.
16. Maria has been working very (hardly/hard) on her thesis.
17. The government will (persecute/prosecute) the guilty parties for polluting the waters.
18. Every time Mariela travels with her children, she carries (access/excess) baggage.
19. Dante's (immoral/immortal) literary masterpieces are read in universities across the country.
20. An explanation will (precede/proceed) each section of the test.
21. Eric's courageous rescue of the drowning child was a (credulous/creditable) deed.
22. Perry's spare flashlight was (helpless/useless) the night of the storm because the batteries were corroded.
23. The gaudy decorations in the hall (detracted/distracted) from the beauty of the celebration.
24. Everything (accept/except) our swimwear is packed and ready to go.
25. "Your essay is very (imaginary/imaginative) and worthy of an 'A' grade," said Mrs. Jameson to her student.

3. USE OF PREPOSITIONS

Prepositions are difficult because almost every definition for a preposition has exceptions. The best way to learn them is to picture how they function in comparison with other prepositions and to study certain common uses and expressions using the various prepositions.

The following diagram will give you a general idea of how prepositions work. Often, however, the diagram will not help you to understand certain expressions containing prepositions. For the following expressions which are not self-explanatory, a definition is given in parentheses. Study the example sentences to understand the meaning of each expression. These prepositions and expressions are important in ALL sections of the TOEFL.

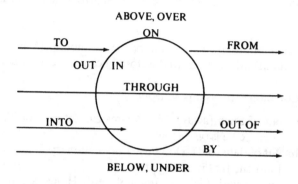

DURING

This preposition should be distinguished from *since* and *for*. *During* is usually followed by a noun indicating time. It indicates *duration* of time. *During our vacation,* we visited many relatives across the country. *During the summer,* we do not have to study.

FROM

This preposition generally means the opposite of *to* (see diagram). He came *from* Miami last night. (opposite of: He went *to* Miami.)

1. Common usage of *from: from* $\begin{Bmatrix} \text{a time} \\ \text{a place} \end{Bmatrix}$ *to* $\begin{Bmatrix} \text{a time} \\ \text{a place} \end{Bmatrix}$. He lived in Germany *from* 1972 *to* 1978. We drove *from* Atlanta *to* New York in one day.

2. Common expressions with *from:* from time to time (occasionally). We visit the art museum *from time to time.*

OUT OF

This preposition generally means the opposite of *into* (see diagram). He walked *out of* the room angrily when John admonished him.

1. Common usage of *out of: out of* + noun (to lack, to be without). Maria went to the store because she was *out of* milk.

2. Common expressions with *out of:*

   a. out of town (away). Mr. Adams cannot see you this week because he is *out of town.*
   b. out of date (old). Don't use that dictionary. It is *out of date.* Find one that is up to date.
   c. out of work (jobless, unemployed). Henry has been very unhappy since he has been *out of work.*
   d. out of the question (impossible). Your request for an extension of credit is *out of the question.*
   e. out of order (not functioning). We had to use our neighbor's telephone because ours was *out of order.*

BY

This preposition generally means to *go past a place* or to *be situated near a place.* We walked *by* the library on the way home. Your books are *by* the window.

1. Common usage of *by:*

   a. to indicate the agent in passive sentences. *Romeo and Juliet* was written *by* William Shakespeare.

b. *by* + specific time (before). We usually eat supper *by* six o'clock in the evening.

c. by bus/plane/train/ship/car/bike (indicates mode of travel) (see *on*, 1. b.). We traveled to Boston *by* train.

2. Common expressions with *by:*

a. by then (before a time in the past or future). I will graduate from the university in 1983. *By then,* I hope to have found a job.

b. by way of (via). We are driving to Atlanta *by way of* Baton Rouge.

c. by the way (incidentally). *By the way,* I've got two tickets for Saturday's game. Would you like to go with me?

d. by far (considerably). This book is *by far* the best on the subject.

e. by accident/by mistake (not intentionally, opposite of *on purpose*). Nobody will receive a check on Friday because the wrong cards were put into the computer *by accident.*

IN

This preposition generally means *inside a place or enclosure.* It is the opposite of *out* (see diagram). Dr. Jones is *in* his office.

1. Common usage of *in:*

a. in a room/building/drawer/closet (inside). Your socks are *in the drawer.*

b. *in* + month/year (see *on*, 1. a.). His birthday is *in January.* Peter will begin class *in 1997.*

c. in time (not late, early enough) (see *on time*, 2. a.). We arrived at the airport *in time* to eat before the plane left.

d. in the street (see *on*, 1. c.). The children were warned not to play *in the street.*

e. in the morning/afternoon/evening (see *at night*, 2. b.). I have a dental appointment *in the morning,* but I will be free *in the afternoon.*

f. in the past/future. *In the past,* attendance at school was not compulsory, but it is today.

g. in the beginning/end. Everyone seemed unfriendly *in the beginning,* but *in the end* everyone made friends.

h. in the way (obstructing) (see *on the way,* 2. d.). He could not park his car in the driveway because another car was *in the way.*

i. once in a while (occasionally). *Once in a while,* we eat dinner in a Chinese restaurant.

j. in no time at all (in a very short time). George finished his assignment *in no time at all.*

k. in the meantime (at the same time, meanwhile). We start school in several weeks, but *in the meantime,* we can take a trip.

l. in the middle. Grace stood *in the middle* of the room looking for her friend.

m. in the army/air force/navy. My brother was *in the army* for ten years.

n. in a row. We are going to sit *in the tenth row* of the auditorium.

o. in the event that (if). *In the event that* you win the prize, you will be notified by mail.

p. in case (if). I will give you the key to the house so you'll have it *in case* I arrive a little late.

q. (get) in touch with, (get) in contact with. It's very difficult to *get in touch with* Jenny because she works all day.

ON

This preposition generally means *a position above, but in contact with an object.* The records are *on* the table.

1. Common usage of *on:*

a. on a day/date (see *in,* 1. b.). I will call you *on Thursday.* His birthday is *on January 28.*

b. on $\begin{Bmatrix} a \\ the \end{Bmatrix}$ bus/plane/train/ship/bike (see *by,* 1. c.). It's too late to see Jane; she's already *on the plane.* I came to school this morning *on the bus.*

c. on a street (situation of a building) (see *in,* 2. d. and *at,* 1. a.). George lives *on 16th Avenue.*

d. on the floor of a building. Henri lives *on the fifteenth floor* of that building.

2. Common expressions with *on:*

a. on time (punctual, used for a scheduled event or appointment, more specific than *in time*) (see *in,* 2. c.). Despite the bad weather, our plane left *on time.*

b. on the corner (of two streets) (see *in,* 2. b.). Norman Hall is on the corner of 13th Street and 5th Avenue.

c. on the sidewalk. Don't walk in the street. Walk *on the sidewalk.*

d. on the way (enroute) (see *in,* 2. h.). We can stop at the grocery store *on the way* to their house.

e. on the right/left. Paul sits *on the left* side of the room and Dave sits *on the right.*

f. on television/(the) radio. The president's "State of the Union Address" will be *on television* and *on the radio* tonight.

g. on the telephone. Janet will be here soon; she is *on the telephone.*

h. on the whole (in general, all things considered). *On the whole,* the rescue mission was well executed.

i. on the other hand (however, nevertheless). The present perfect aspect is never used to indicate a specific time; *on the other hand,* the simple past tense is.

k. on sale (offered for sale). The house will go *on sale* this weekend (offered at a lower than normal price). The regular price of the radio is $39.95, but today it's *on sale* for $25.

l. on foot (walking). My car would not start so I came *on foot.*

AT

This preposition generally is used to indicate a general location. It is not as specific as *in*. Jane is *at* the bank.

1. Common usage of *at:*

   a. *at* + an address (see *on,* 1. c.). George lives *at 712 16th Avenue.*

   b. *at* + a specific time. The class begins *at 3:10.*

2. Common expressions with *at:*

   a. at home/school/work. From nine to five, Charles is *at work* and his roommate is *at school.* At night, they are usually *at home.*

   b. at night (see *in,* 2. e.). We never go out *at night* because we live too far from town.

   c. at least (at the minimum). We will have to spend *at least* two weeks doing the experiments.

   d. at once (immediately.) Please come home *at once.*

   e. at present/the moment (now). She is studying *at the moment.*

   f. at times (occasionally). *At times,* it is difficult to understand him because he speaks too fast.

   g. at first (initially). Jane was nervous *at first,* but later she felt more relaxed.

MISCELLANEOUS EXPRESSIONS WITH PREPOSITIONS

1. on the beach. We walked *on the beach* for several hours last night.

2. in place of (instead of). Sam is going to the meeting *in place of* his brother, who has to work.

3. for the most part (mainly). The article discusses, *for the most part,* the possibility of life on other planets.

4. in hopes of (hoping to). John called his brother *in hopes of* finding somebody to watch his children.

5. of course (certainly). *Of course,* if you study the material very thoroughly, you will have no trouble on the examination.
6. off and on (intermittently). It rained *off and on* all day yesterday.
7. all of a sudden (suddenly). We were walking through the woods when, *all of a sudden,* we heard a strange sound.
8. for good (forever). Helen is leaving Chicago *for good.*

Exercise 56: Use of Prepositions

Write the correct preposition in the following sentences. There may be several possible answers for some blanks.

__(1)__ the summer, we went __(2)__ the beach every day. We stayed __(3)__ a lovely motel right __(4)__ the beach. __(5)__ the morning we would get up __(6)__ 9:30, have breakfast, and then spend four hours __(7)__ the pool __(8)__ all the other guests. __(9)__ 1:00 we would have lunch __(10)__ our room. __(11)__ lunch we would eat something light like sandwiches and fruit. __(12)__ the afternoon we would return __(13)__ the pool area and sit __(14)__ the sun __(15)__ a while. __(16)__ night we would take long walks __(17)__ the beach or visit some friends who lived __(18)__ 520 Volusia Avenue __(19)__ Daytona Beach.

Many people from __(20)__ __(21)__ town stayed __(22)__ that motel. Like us, they had been coming __(23)__ that same motel __(24)__ 1975. Most __(25)__ them were __(26)__ Ohio. __(27)__ time __(28)__ time we would eat out __(29)__ a nice restaurant, where we did not have to wait long __(30)__ the waitress to serve us. __(31)__ July it is usually very crowded, but this year __(32)__ least, it was not as crowded as __(33)__ the past. Once __(34)__ a while we went __(35)__ the movies __(36)__ the theater __(37)__ the corner __(38)__ Las Olas Boulevard and Castillo Avenue. We arrived there __(39)__ no time __(40)__ all __(41)__ car. We sat __(42)__ the middle __(43)__ the theater, __(44)__ the twelfth row. The movie started __(45)__ 7:00 sharp, so we got there just __(46)__ time to buy some popcorn and find our seat. __(47)__ first, I thought I would not enjoy it, but __(48)__ the end, it turned __(49)__ to be a very interesting movie. __(50)__ the whole, it was an enjoyable evening.

We decided to get a Coke __(51)__ __(52)__ the machine, but unfortunately it was __(53)__ __(54)__ order. So __(55)__ place __(56)__ the Coke, we decided to get some ice cream __(57)__ the Dairy Isle which was located __(58)__ the corner __(59)__ Harper Ave. and Washington St.

__(60)__ returning __(61)__ our motel, I decided to finish reading my novel. It is __(62)__ far the most exciting book that Victoria Holt has ever written. __(63)__ the most part, her book deals __(64)__ a group __(65)__ archeologists who went __(66)__ Egypt __(67)__ hopes __(68)__ discovering some pharaoh's tomb. __(69)__ accident they uncovered a plot to smuggle the treasures __(70)__ __(71)__ Egypt. __(72)__ course the archeologists got __(73)__ touch __(74)__ the authorities, who had heard some rumors about smuggling off and __(75)__. All __(76)__ a sudden, one day the police showed up and caught them __(77)__ the act and arrested them.

4. VERBAL IDIOMS

A verbal idiom is a group of words, containing a verb, that has a meaning different from the meaning of any individual word within it. The following list of two- and three-word verbal idioms should be learned. Because they are idiomatic, you are less likely to find them in the grammar section of the TOEFL. Many of them, however, may appear in the listening comprehension section.

BREAK OFF—end. As a result of the recent, unprovoked attack, the two countries *broke off* their diplomatic relations.

BRING UP—raise, initiate. The county commissioner *brought up* the heated issue of restricting on-street parking.

CALL ON (a)—ask. The teacher *called on* James to write the equation on the blackboard. (b)—visit. The new minister *called on* each of the families of his church in order to become better acquainted with them.

CARE FOR (a)—like. Because Marita doesn't *care for* dark colors, she buys only brightly colored clothes. (b)—look after. My neighbors asked me to *care for* their children after school.

CHECK OUT (a)—borrow books, etc., from a library. I went to the library and *checked out* thirty books last night for my research paper. (b)—investigate. This photocopy machine is not working properly. Could you *check out* the problem?

CHECK OUT OF—leave. We were told that we had to *check out of* the hotel before one o'clock, or else we would have to pay for another day.

CHECK (UP) ON—investigate. The insurance company decided to *check up on* his driving record before insuring him.

CLOSE IN ON—draw nearer, approach. In his hallucinatory state, the addict felt that the walls were *closing in on* him.

COME ALONG WITH—accompany. June *came along with* her supervisor to the budget meeting.

COME DOWN WITH—become ill with. During the summer, many people *come down with* intestinal disorders.

COUNT ON—depend on, rely on. Maria was *counting on* the grant money to pay her way through graduate school.

DO AWAY WITH—eliminate, get rid of. Because of the increasing number of problems created after the football games, the director has decided to *do away with* all sports activities.

DRAW UP—write, draft (such as plans or contracts). A new advertising contract was *drawn up* after the terms had been decided.

DROP OUT OF—quit, withdraw from. This organization has done a great deal to prevent young people from *dropping out of* school.

FIGURE OUT—solve, decipher, interpret, understand. After failing to *figure out* his income tax return, Hal decided to see an accountant.

FIND OUT—discover. Erin just *found out* that her ancestors had come from Scotland, not Ireland.

GET BY—manage to survive. Despite the high cost of living, we will *get by* on my salary.

GET THROUGH (a)—finish. Jerry called for an earlier appointment because he *got through* with his project sooner than he had expected. (b)—manage to communicate. It is difficult to *get through* to someone who doesn't understand your language.

GET UP (a)—arise. Pete usually *gets up* early in the morning, but this morning he overslept. (b)—organize. Paul is trying to *get up* a group of square dancers to go to Switzerland.

GIVE UP—stop, cease. Helen *gave up* working for the company because she felt that the employees were not treated fairly.

GO ALONG WITH—agree. Mr Robbins always *goes along with* anything his employer wants to do.

HOLD ON TO—grasp, maintain. Despite moving to the Western world, Mariko *held on to* her Oriental ways.

HOLD UP (a)—rob at gunpoint. The convenience store was *held up* last night. (b)—endure or withstand pressure or use. Mrs. Jones *held up* very well after her husband's death. (c)—stop. Last night's accident *held up* rush hour traffic for two hours.

KEEP ON—continue. I *keep on* urging Rita to practice the violin, but she doesn't heed my advice.

LOOK AFTER—care for. After my aunt had died, her lawyer *looked after* my uncle's financial affairs.

LOOK INTO—investigate. Lynnette is *looking into* the possibility of opening a drugstore in Dallas as well as in Fort Worth.

PASS OUT/HAND OUT—distribute. The political candidate *passed out* campaign literature to her coworkers.

PASS OUT—faint. The intense heat in the garden caused Maria to *pass out*.

PICK OUT—select, choose. The judges were asked to *pick out* the essays that showed the most originality.

POINT OUT—indicate. Being a professional writer, Janos helped us by *pointing out* problems in style.

PUT OFF—postpone. Because Brian was a poor correspondent, he *put off* answering his letters.

RUN ACROSS—discover. While rummaging through some old boxes in the attic, I *ran across* my grandmother's wedding dress.

RUN INTO—meet by accident. When Jack was in New York, he *ran into* an old friend at the theater.

SEE ABOUT—consider, attend to. My neighbor is going to *see about* getting tickets for next Saturday's football game.

TAKE OFF—leave the ground to fly. Our flight to Toronto *took off* on schedule.

TAKE OVER FOR—substitute for. Marie had a class this afternoon, so Janet *took over for* her.

TALK OVER—discuss. The committee is *talking over* the plans for the homecoming dance and banquet.

TRY OUT (a)—test. General Mills asked us to *try out* their new product. (b)—audition for a play. Marguerite plans to *try out* for the lead in the new musical.

TURN IN (a)—submit. The students *turned in* their term papers on Monday. (b)—go to bed. After a long hard day, we decided to *turn in* early.

WATCH OUT FOR—be cautious or alert. While driving through that development, we had to *watch out for* the little children playing in the street.

Exercise 57: Verbal Idioms

Change the underlined words to incorporate two- and three-word verbs. Make all necessary tense changes. *Example:*

The senator <u>raised</u> the question of the treaty negotiations.
The senator <u>brought up</u> the question of the treaty negotiations.

1. Louis doesn't <u>like</u> peas unless they're mixed in with something else.
2. Because of the shortage of funds, we will have to <u>eliminate</u> all extracurricular activities.
3. Many teenagers <u>quit</u> school before graduation and regret it later.
4. Mike and Mary Ellen will be very happy when they <u>finish</u> writing their book.
5. Marsha was so upset by her fiancé's disloyalty that she <u>ended</u> their engagement.
6. The local convenience store was <u>robbed</u> last night and $225 was taken.

7. Thomas Jefferson was one of the men responsible for <u>writing</u> the Declaration of Independence.

8. I am trying to <u>interpret</u> this writing, but it is not easy.

9. <u>Continue</u> driving at 55 miles per hour if you want to save <u>gasoline</u> and prevent accidents.

10. Mrs. Davis <u>asked</u> me to serve as chairman of the entertainment committee.

11. Pete promised to <u>stop</u> smoking immediately.

12. The police are <u>approaching</u> the robbers' hideout.

13. María Elena will <u>take care of</u> the neighbors' children while they attend the school meeting.

14. Joey <u>became ill</u> with the measles just before his scout troop went to camp.

15. Mrs. Lastinger will <u>substitute</u> for the history teacher who is out of town.

16. The mountain climbers <u>grasped</u> the rope tightly to avoid falling.

17. We plan to <u>investigate</u> the possibility of spending a week at the seashore.

18. My mother <u>distributed</u> candy to the children last Halloween.

19. The manager said we had to <u>leave</u> the motel no later than noon.

20. Mike just <u>discovered</u> that his passport had expired three months previously.

21. When buying apples, remember to <u>select</u> only the firm, red ones.

22. We were counting on a raise in pay, but we'll have to <u>manage</u> without it.

23. Rita will <u>accompany</u> her sister to the Skating Palace on Saturday night.

24. The tour guide <u>indicated</u> the historical monuments of the city.

25. I knew I could <u>rely on</u> them to get the job done.

26. The dance had to be <u>postponed</u> because of the bad weather.

27. I accidently <u>met</u> an old friend in the shopping center last week.

28. The manager said he would <u>consider</u> hiring another secretary to take care of the backlog of work.

29. Last night Mr. Robbins <u>raised</u> the issue of student parking on city streets.

30. Henry was so upset at the sight of his injured daughter that he <u>fainted.</u>
31. Before making a decision on the project, the board of directors decided to <u>discuss</u> the matter.
32. Procter and Gamble is <u>testing</u> a new product and has sent everyone a sample.
33. All budget proposals had to be <u>submitted</u> by last Friday.
34. What time did you <u>awaken</u> this morning?
35. <u>Be careful of</u> speeding cars when you cross the street.

5. COMMON COMBINATIONS WITH PREPOSITIONS

Many nouns, verbs, and adjectives are generally followed by specific prepositions. However, there are many exceptions to any rule listing certain words which must appear with certain prepositions. This is something that one must learn from constant contact with and attention to the elements of a new language. Listed here are some nouns, verbs, and adjectives that USUALLY appear with the accompanying prepositions.

NOUNS + PREPOSITIONS

equivalent of	number of	example of
quality of	reason for	exception to
pair of	sample of	possibility of

NOTE: These nouns can be followed by either *of* or *for.*

fear	method	hatred	need	means

The <u>quality of</u> this photograph is poor.

I saw a <u>sample of</u> her work and was quite impressed.

They have yet to discover a new <u>method of/method for</u> analyzing this information.

VERBS + PREPOSITIONS

decide on	plan on	depend on
detract from	engage in	approve of
emerge from	pay for	succeed in
participate in	escape from	mingle with
confide in	remove from	rely on

NOTE: Do not confuse the *to* of an infinitive with *to* as a preposition. Some of these verbs can be followed either by an infinitive or by a preposition + gerund. We have decided *to stay* in the United States for several more weeks. We have decided *on staying* in the United States for several more weeks. Attending this seminar is *similar to working* in a laboratory.

Three dangerous criminals escaped from prison yesterday.

You can depend on Harry if you want the job done correctly.

He is going to participate in the demonstration next week.

ADJECTIVES + PREPOSITIONS

satisfied with	fond of	amenable to
divorced from	isolated from	inferior to
guilty of	afraid of	similar to
interested in	accustomed to	different from

William is quite fond of cooking Oriental food.

My employer says she is not satisfied with my performance.

Margaret is afraid of large dogs.

Keep in mind that other prepositions MAY be used with the above words in different contexts. Watch for prepositions when you read so that you can develop a "feel" for their use.

Some of the following exercises contain prepositions that have not been included in this list. See if you have acquired a native speaker's feel for them yet.

MINI-TEST 5: PROBLEM VOCABULARY AND PREPOSITIONS

DIRECTIONS

Select the correct word to complete each sentence.

1. Scientists are trying to (device/devise) an inexpensive substitute for gasoline.
2. On Halloween night, most children dress in (costumes/customs) and go from house to house asking for treats.
3. Mr. Miller's prejudice (of/toward) his neighbors caused him to be ostracized.
4. (Besides/Beside) geology, Herman is studying math, French, and literature.
5. Melanie said that she would arrive (later/latter) than the rest of us.
6. Despite his sore muscle, Paul planned on participating (with/in) the Olympic skating.
7. A fear (at/of) closed-in areas is called claustrophobia.
8. After being apprehended, all hijackers are (persecuted/prosecuted).
9. Mitzi didn't (loose/lose) any time in applying for the teaching position in math.
10. The letters were (already/all ready) for mailing when we realized that we had written the wrong addresses on the envelopes.
11. This report is (quite/quiet) complete and needs no revision.
12. Professor Baker teaches the same number of hours per week as Professor Jones, but the (later/latter) always looks more tired.
13. Ms. Davis asked us to help pass (out/up) some free (samples/examples).
14. Julie's skirt will be (to/too) (lose/loose) for her sister to wear.
15. Even though Marlon Brando had won an Oscar, he refused to (except/accept) it at the presentation ceremonies.

DIRECTIONS

In the following sentences, choose the form in parentheses that means the same as the underlined word or words.

16. Louis was <u>depending on</u> the Pittsburgh Steelers to win the championship. (picking out/counting on)

17. Dr. Clements <u>distributed</u> the materials at the deans' conference. (passed out/brought up)

18. Archeologists <u>continue</u> searching for buried Egyptian treasures. (keep on/do away with)

19. Four armed men <u>robbed</u> the bank last week and escaped with an undetermined amount of cash. (held up/pointed out)

20. We had to <u>postpone</u> the meeting because too many people had the flu. (drop out of/put off)

21. When Karen became ill, her colleagues had to <u>manage</u> without her. (get along/take off)

22. The department chairman <u>asked</u> his staff to help with the registration. (called on/counted on)

23. If we <u>terminate</u> our relations with that country, we'll have to find another supplier of raw materials. (break off/draw up)

24. After arriving at the check-in counter, Dennis <u>discovered</u> that he was in the wrong airport. (found out/pointed out)

25. Kevin <u>quit</u> the engineering program because he found it too difficult. (checked out of/dropped out of)

26. The gasoline fumes caused Mike to <u>faint</u>. (pass out/break off)

27. The baseball game had to be <u>postponed</u> because of the inclement weather. (put off/put on)

28. All bids for the project had to be <u>submitted</u> by November 1. (turned in/drawn up)

29. Because she is so tall, Sandy doesn't <u>like</u> high-heeled shoes. (care for/pick out)

30. My adviser <u>indicated</u> numerous errors in my proposal and told me to rewrite it. (figured out/pointed out)

MINI-TEST 6: PROBLEM VOCABULARY AND PREPOSITIONS

DIRECTIONS

Each question on this mini-test consists of a sentence in which four words or phrases are underlined. The four underlined parts of the sentence are marked A, B, C, D. You are to identify the *one* underlined word or phrase that *would not be acceptable in standard written English*. Circle the letter of the underlined portion which is not correct.

1. <u>Even though</u> the girls have <u>all ready</u> visited St. Augustine,

A   B

   <u>they</u> want <u>to return</u> to the Castillo de San Marcos.

C   D

2. <u>As a result of</u> his inconsistency <u>in represent</u> his constituents,

A   B

   the senator was not <u>reelected</u> <u>to the state legislature</u>.

C   D

3. <u>Knowing that</u> it would be <u>helpless</u> to continue <u>working</u> for a

A   B   C

   nearly bankrupt company, Louise decided to go away and find

   <u>another type</u> of employment.

D

4. <u>Excepting for</u> <u>the</u> graduate students, <u>everyone</u> will have

A   B   C

   <u>to take</u> the tests on the same day.

D

5. John <u>always</u> arrives <u>lately</u> for his chemistry class even though

A   B

   he <u>leaves</u> his dormitory <u>in plenty of time</u>.

C   D

6. Soon after Mel <u>has finished</u> his thesis, he will <u>leave</u> for

                      A   B

   Boston, <u>where</u> he has a job waiting <u>on him</u>.

        C   D

7. The Nelsons asked <u>us</u> to <u>look over</u> their plants for them while

                            A   B

   they were <u>away</u> <u>on vacation</u>.

           C   D

8. <u>The</u> refugees are very much <u>upset</u> because they <u>have been</u>

 A   B   C

   <u>deprived to</u> their homeland and their families.

   D

9. <u>According</u> the weatherman, <u>there is</u> a fifty percent chance of

     A   B

   rain <u>forecast</u> for today and a greater chance for

         C

   <u>over the weekend</u>.

        D

10. The athlete was disqualified <u>from</u> the tournament

     A   B

    <u>for</u> participating <u>at</u> an illegal demonstration.

 C   D

11. My English teacher said we <u>should write</u> another composition

                               A

    for tomorrow <u>related for</u> our experience <u>at</u> last

                  B   C

    <u>week's</u> workshop.

    D

12. If it <u>had not been</u> for the computerized register tape

        A

    <u>from the grocery</u> store, I <u>never</u> would have been able to

        B   C

    <u>figure on</u> my expenditures.

   D

13. Eric and his sister <u>won first prize</u> for the <u>most</u> elaborate
                              A   B
<u>customs</u> they had worn to <u>the Halloween</u> party.
     C   D

14. Our new office building <u>will be located</u> downtown
                                      A
<u>in the corner</u> <u>of</u> Euclid Avenue <u>and</u> East Ninth Street.
       B   C   D

15. <u>After checking out</u> the motor and the carburetor
            A
<u>for problems</u>, Jesse found that the noise <u>was caused</u> by a
       B   C
<u>lose</u> fan belt.
   D

16. The customer <u>said he</u> was interested <u>to purchase</u> <u>a</u> CD/ROM
                     A   B   C
reader <u>for</u> his office.
          D

17. <u>Because the committee was anxious</u> to attend the celebration,
                    A
<u>the</u> president dispensed <u>to reading</u> the <u>minutes</u>.
   B   C   D

18. <u>Scientists</u> were <u>interested about</u> the radioactivity <u>emanating</u>
        A   B   C
<u>from</u> the nuclear power plant.
   D

19. The coach was <u>depending for</u> his team <u>to win</u> the game
                        A   B
<u>so that</u> they would have a chance to play <u>in the Super Bowl</u>.
   C   D

20. $\underline{\text{Because it was faster}}$, John $\underline{\text{insisted in}}$ my $\underline{\text{taking}}$ the plane to
           A   B   C

     Miami $\underline{\text{instead of the train}}$.
                D

21. His $\underline{\text{highly}}$ $\underline{\text{imaginary}}$ composition won $\underline{\text{the}}$ judges' approval
            A   B   C

     and $\underline{\text{the first prize}}$ in the high school essay contest.
            D

22. The spring conference $\underline{\text{will be held}}$ $\underline{\text{in}}$ Milwaukee on three
                               A   B

     $\underline{\text{successive}}$ days, $\underline{\text{namely}}$ May 15, 16, and 17.
        C   D

23. Although Clyde is $\underline{\text{formally}}$ from Pennsylvania, he finds it
                      A

     $\underline{\text{difficult}}$ to $\underline{\text{get used to}}$ the cold winters we $\underline{\text{are having}}$.
        B   C   D

24. $\underline{\text{Admittance for}}$ the inauguration $\underline{\text{ceremonies}}$ was only
             A   B

     $\underline{\text{by}}$ special invitation $\underline{\text{of the}}$ committee.
      C   D

25. Paris $\underline{\text{has been}}$ well $\underline{\text{known about}}$ $\underline{\text{its}}$ famous monuments,
            A   B   C

     beautiful music, and wonderful restaurants $\underline{\text{for over}}$ one
                                                  D

     hundred years.

ANSWERS FOR EXERCISES 54 THROUGH 57 AND MINI-TESTS 5 AND 6

Exercise 54: Commonly Misused Words

1. angel	6. Whether	11. latter	16. quit
2. your	7. descent	12. than	17. peace
3. sight	8. to, too	13. loose	18. principle
4. Who's	9. dessert	14. stationery	19. quite
5. custom	10. they're	15. passed	20. cite

Exercise 55: Confusingly Related Words

1. affected	8. all ready	14. sensible	20. precede
2. device	9. elicit	15. samples	21. creditable
3. advice	10. sensitive	16. hard	22. useless
4. liquidate	11. immigrants	17. prosecute	23. detracted
5. formerly	12. number	18. excess	24. except
6. Special	13. beside	19. immortal	25. imaginative
7. among			

Exercise 56: Use of Prepositions

1. During 2. to 3. at 4. on 5. In 6. at 7. in (at, around, near) 8. with 9. At 10. in 11. For 12. In (During) 13. to 14. in 15. for 16. At 17. on (along) 18. at 19. in 20. out 21. of 22. at 23. to 24. since 25. of 26. from 27. From 28. to 29. at 30. for 31. In (During) 32. at 33. in 34. in 35. to 36. at 37. on 38. of 39. in 40. at 41. by 42. in 43. of 44. in 45. at 46. in 47. At 48. in 49. out 50. On 51. out 52. of 53. out 54. of 55. in 56. of 57. at 58. on (at) 59. of 60. After (Upon) 61. to 62. by 63. For 64. with 65. of 66. to 67. in 68. of 69. By 70. out 71. of 72. Of 73. in 74. with 75. on 76. of 77. in

Exercise 57: Verbal Idioms

1. care for	13. look after	24. pointed out
2. do away with	14. came down with	25. count on
3. drop out of	15. fill in	26. put off
4. get through	16. held on to	27. ran into
5. broke off	17. look into	28. see about
6. held up	18. passed out	29. brought up
7. drawing up	(handed out)	30. passed out
8. figure out	19. check out of	31. talk over
9. Keep on	20. found out	32. trying out
10. called on	21. pick out	33. turned in
11. give up	22. get by (get along)	34. get up (wake up)
12. closing in on	23. come along with	35. Watch out for

Mini-Test 5: Problem Vocabulary and Prepositions

1. devise	11. quite	21. get along
2. costumes	12. latter	22. called on
3. toward	13. out, samples	23. break off
4. Besides	14. too, loose	24. found out
5. later	15. accept	25. dropped out of
6. in	16. counting on	26. pass out
7. of	17. passed out	27. put off
8. prosecuted	18. keep on	28. turned in
9. lose	19. held up	29. care for
10. all ready	20. put off	30. pointed out

Mini-Test 6: Problem Vocabulary and Prepositions

1. (B) already
2. (B) in representing
3. (B) useless
4. (A) Except for
5. (B) late
6. (D) for him
7. (B) look after
   (take care of)
8. (D) deprived of
9. (A) According to
10. (D) in
11. (B) related to
12. (D) figure out
13. (C) costumes
14. (B) on the corner
15. (D) loose
16. (B) in purchasing
17. (C) with reading
18. (B) interested in
19. (A) depending on
20. (B) insisted on
21. (B) imaginative
22. (C) consecutive
23. (A) formerly
24. (A) Admittance to
25. (B) known for

PART IV: Practice-Review-Analyze-Practice
Six Full-Length Practice Tests

These practice tests are very similar to actual TOEFL examinations. The format, levels of difficulty, question structure, and number of questions are similar to those on the actual TOEFL. The actual TOEFL is copyrighted and may not be duplicated, and these questions are not taken directly from the actual tests.

You should take these tests under the same conditions you will face when you take the TOEFL. Find a quiet place where you can take the test in its entirety without being disturbed. Be sure to use the answer sheets provided for each test. Follow the time limits exactly. Remember that when the time for one section is over, you must go on to the next section of the test, and you may not return to any previous section. Remember not to leave any answers blank, as you are not penalized for guessing. The time limits for each section are:

Section 1: Listening Comprehension—approximately
30 minutes
Section 2: Structure and Written Expression—25 minutes
Section 3: Reading Comprehension—55 minutes

After you take each test, turn to Part V of this guide and follow the instructions for scoring your exam. Use the answers, the explanations, and the review cross-references to guide your study.

ANSWER SHEET FOR PRACTICE TEST 1
(Remove This Sheet and Use it to Mark Your Answers)

SECTION 1
LISTENING COMPREHENSION

SECTION 2
STRUCTURE AND WRITTEN EXPRESSION

SECTION 1

1 Ⓐ Ⓑ Ⓒ Ⓓ   26 Ⓐ Ⓑ Ⓒ Ⓓ
2 Ⓐ Ⓑ Ⓒ Ⓓ   27 Ⓐ Ⓑ Ⓒ Ⓓ
3 Ⓐ Ⓑ Ⓒ Ⓓ   28 Ⓐ Ⓑ Ⓒ Ⓓ
4 Ⓐ Ⓑ Ⓒ Ⓓ   29 Ⓐ Ⓑ Ⓒ Ⓓ
5 Ⓐ Ⓑ Ⓒ Ⓓ   30 Ⓐ Ⓑ Ⓒ Ⓓ

6 Ⓐ Ⓑ Ⓒ Ⓓ   31 Ⓐ Ⓑ Ⓒ Ⓓ
7 Ⓐ Ⓑ Ⓒ Ⓓ   32 Ⓐ Ⓑ Ⓒ Ⓓ
8 Ⓐ Ⓑ Ⓒ Ⓓ   33 Ⓐ Ⓑ Ⓒ Ⓓ
9 Ⓐ Ⓑ Ⓒ Ⓓ   34 Ⓐ Ⓑ Ⓒ Ⓓ
10 Ⓐ Ⓑ Ⓒ Ⓓ   35 Ⓐ Ⓑ Ⓒ Ⓓ

11 Ⓐ Ⓑ Ⓒ Ⓓ   36 Ⓐ Ⓑ Ⓒ Ⓓ
12 Ⓐ Ⓑ Ⓒ Ⓓ   37 Ⓐ Ⓑ Ⓒ Ⓓ
13 Ⓐ Ⓑ Ⓒ Ⓓ   38 Ⓐ Ⓑ Ⓒ Ⓓ
14 Ⓐ Ⓑ Ⓒ Ⓓ   39 Ⓐ Ⓑ Ⓒ Ⓓ
15 Ⓐ Ⓑ Ⓒ Ⓓ   40 Ⓐ Ⓑ Ⓒ Ⓓ

16 Ⓐ Ⓑ Ⓒ Ⓓ   41 Ⓐ Ⓑ Ⓒ Ⓓ
17 Ⓐ Ⓑ Ⓒ Ⓓ   42 Ⓐ Ⓑ Ⓒ Ⓓ
18 Ⓐ Ⓑ Ⓒ Ⓓ   43 Ⓐ Ⓑ Ⓒ Ⓓ
19 Ⓐ Ⓑ Ⓒ Ⓓ   44 Ⓐ Ⓑ Ⓒ Ⓓ
20 Ⓐ Ⓑ Ⓒ Ⓓ   45 Ⓐ Ⓑ Ⓒ Ⓓ

21 Ⓐ Ⓑ Ⓒ Ⓓ   46 Ⓐ Ⓑ Ⓒ Ⓓ
22 Ⓐ Ⓑ Ⓒ Ⓓ   47 Ⓐ Ⓑ Ⓒ Ⓓ
23 Ⓐ Ⓑ Ⓒ Ⓓ   48 Ⓐ Ⓑ Ⓒ Ⓓ
24 Ⓐ Ⓑ Ⓒ Ⓓ   49 Ⓐ Ⓑ Ⓒ Ⓓ
25 Ⓐ Ⓑ Ⓒ Ⓓ   50 Ⓐ Ⓑ Ⓒ Ⓓ

SECTION 2

1 Ⓐ Ⓑ Ⓒ Ⓓ   26 Ⓐ Ⓑ Ⓒ Ⓓ
2 Ⓐ Ⓑ Ⓒ Ⓓ   27 Ⓐ Ⓑ Ⓒ Ⓓ
3 Ⓐ Ⓑ Ⓒ Ⓓ   28 Ⓐ Ⓑ Ⓒ Ⓓ
4 Ⓐ Ⓑ Ⓒ Ⓓ   29 Ⓐ Ⓑ Ⓒ Ⓓ
5 Ⓐ Ⓑ Ⓒ Ⓓ   30 Ⓐ Ⓑ Ⓒ Ⓓ

6 Ⓐ Ⓑ Ⓒ Ⓓ   31 Ⓐ Ⓑ Ⓒ Ⓓ
7 Ⓐ Ⓑ Ⓒ Ⓓ   32 Ⓐ Ⓑ Ⓒ Ⓓ
8 Ⓐ Ⓑ Ⓒ Ⓓ   33 Ⓐ Ⓑ Ⓒ Ⓓ
9 Ⓐ Ⓑ Ⓒ Ⓓ   34 Ⓐ Ⓑ Ⓒ Ⓓ
10 Ⓐ Ⓑ Ⓒ Ⓓ   35 Ⓐ Ⓑ Ⓒ Ⓓ

11 Ⓐ Ⓑ Ⓒ Ⓓ   36 Ⓐ Ⓑ Ⓒ Ⓓ
12 Ⓐ Ⓑ Ⓒ Ⓓ   37 Ⓐ Ⓑ Ⓒ Ⓓ
13 Ⓐ Ⓑ Ⓒ Ⓓ   38 Ⓐ Ⓑ Ⓒ Ⓓ
14 Ⓐ Ⓑ Ⓒ Ⓓ   39 Ⓐ Ⓑ Ⓒ Ⓓ
15 Ⓐ Ⓑ Ⓒ Ⓓ   40 Ⓐ Ⓑ Ⓒ Ⓓ

16 Ⓐ Ⓑ Ⓒ Ⓓ
17 Ⓐ Ⓑ Ⓒ Ⓓ
18 Ⓐ Ⓑ Ⓒ Ⓓ
19 Ⓐ Ⓑ Ⓒ Ⓓ
20 Ⓐ Ⓑ Ⓒ Ⓓ

21 Ⓐ Ⓑ Ⓒ Ⓓ
22 Ⓐ Ⓑ Ⓒ Ⓓ
23 Ⓐ Ⓑ Ⓒ Ⓓ
24 Ⓐ Ⓑ Ⓒ Ⓓ
25 Ⓐ Ⓑ Ⓒ Ⓓ

CUT HERE

SECTION 3

READING COMPREHENSION

1 Ⓐ Ⓑ Ⓒ Ⓓ	26 Ⓐ Ⓑ Ⓒ Ⓓ
2 Ⓐ Ⓑ Ⓒ Ⓓ	27 Ⓐ Ⓑ Ⓒ Ⓓ
3 Ⓐ Ⓑ Ⓒ Ⓓ	28 Ⓐ Ⓑ Ⓒ Ⓓ
4 Ⓐ Ⓑ Ⓒ Ⓓ	29 Ⓐ Ⓑ Ⓒ Ⓓ
5 Ⓐ Ⓑ Ⓒ Ⓓ	30 Ⓐ Ⓑ Ⓒ Ⓓ
6 Ⓐ Ⓑ Ⓒ Ⓓ	31 Ⓐ Ⓑ Ⓒ Ⓓ
7 Ⓐ Ⓑ Ⓒ Ⓓ	32 Ⓐ Ⓑ Ⓒ Ⓓ
8 Ⓐ Ⓑ Ⓒ Ⓓ	33 Ⓐ Ⓑ Ⓒ Ⓓ
9 Ⓐ Ⓑ Ⓒ Ⓓ	34 Ⓐ Ⓑ Ⓒ Ⓓ
10 Ⓐ Ⓑ Ⓒ Ⓓ	35 Ⓐ Ⓑ Ⓒ Ⓓ
11 Ⓐ Ⓑ Ⓒ Ⓓ	36 Ⓐ Ⓑ Ⓒ Ⓓ
12 Ⓐ Ⓑ Ⓒ Ⓓ	37 Ⓐ Ⓑ Ⓒ Ⓓ
13 Ⓐ Ⓑ Ⓒ Ⓓ	38 Ⓐ Ⓑ Ⓒ Ⓓ
14 Ⓐ Ⓑ Ⓒ Ⓓ	39 Ⓐ Ⓑ Ⓒ Ⓓ
15 Ⓐ Ⓑ Ⓒ Ⓓ	40 Ⓐ Ⓑ Ⓒ Ⓓ
16 Ⓐ Ⓑ Ⓒ Ⓓ	41 Ⓐ Ⓑ Ⓒ Ⓓ
17 Ⓐ Ⓑ Ⓒ Ⓓ	42 Ⓐ Ⓑ Ⓒ Ⓓ
18 Ⓐ Ⓑ Ⓒ Ⓓ	43 Ⓐ Ⓑ Ⓒ Ⓓ
19 Ⓐ Ⓑ Ⓒ Ⓓ	44 Ⓐ Ⓑ Ⓒ Ⓓ
20 Ⓐ Ⓑ Ⓒ Ⓓ	45 Ⓐ Ⓑ Ⓒ Ⓓ
21 Ⓐ Ⓑ Ⓒ Ⓓ	46 Ⓐ Ⓑ Ⓒ Ⓓ
22 Ⓐ Ⓑ Ⓒ Ⓓ	47 Ⓐ Ⓑ Ⓒ Ⓓ
23 Ⓐ Ⓑ Ⓒ Ⓓ	48 Ⓐ Ⓑ Ⓒ Ⓓ
24 Ⓐ Ⓑ Ⓒ Ⓓ	49 Ⓐ Ⓑ Ⓒ Ⓓ
25 Ⓐ Ⓑ Ⓒ Ⓓ	50 Ⓐ Ⓑ Ⓒ Ⓓ

ANSWER SHEET FOR PRACTICE TEST 2
(Remove This Sheet and Use it to Mark Your Answers)

SECTION 1
LISTENING COMPREHENSION

SECTION 2
STRUCTURE AND WRITTEN EXPRESSION

1 Ⓐ Ⓑ Ⓒ Ⓓ	26 Ⓐ Ⓑ Ⓒ Ⓓ
2 Ⓐ Ⓑ Ⓒ Ⓓ	27 Ⓐ Ⓑ Ⓒ Ⓓ
3 Ⓐ Ⓑ Ⓒ Ⓓ	28 Ⓐ Ⓑ Ⓒ Ⓓ
4 Ⓐ Ⓑ Ⓒ Ⓓ	29 Ⓐ Ⓑ Ⓒ Ⓓ
5 Ⓐ Ⓑ Ⓒ Ⓓ	30 Ⓐ Ⓑ Ⓒ Ⓓ
6 Ⓐ Ⓑ Ⓒ Ⓓ	31 Ⓐ Ⓑ Ⓒ Ⓓ
7 Ⓐ Ⓑ Ⓒ Ⓓ	32 Ⓐ Ⓑ Ⓒ Ⓓ
8 Ⓐ Ⓑ Ⓒ Ⓓ	33 Ⓐ Ⓑ Ⓒ Ⓓ
9 Ⓐ Ⓑ Ⓒ Ⓓ	34 Ⓐ Ⓑ Ⓒ Ⓓ
10 Ⓐ Ⓑ Ⓒ Ⓓ	35 Ⓐ Ⓑ Ⓒ Ⓓ
11 Ⓐ Ⓑ Ⓒ Ⓓ	36 Ⓐ Ⓑ Ⓒ Ⓓ
12 Ⓐ Ⓑ Ⓒ Ⓓ	37 Ⓐ Ⓑ Ⓒ Ⓓ
13 Ⓐ Ⓑ Ⓒ Ⓓ	38 Ⓐ Ⓑ Ⓒ Ⓓ
14 Ⓐ Ⓑ Ⓒ Ⓓ	39 Ⓐ Ⓑ Ⓒ Ⓓ
15 Ⓐ Ⓑ Ⓒ Ⓓ	40 Ⓐ Ⓑ Ⓒ Ⓓ
16 Ⓐ Ⓑ Ⓒ Ⓓ	41 Ⓐ Ⓑ Ⓒ Ⓓ
17 Ⓐ Ⓑ Ⓒ Ⓓ	42 Ⓐ Ⓑ Ⓒ Ⓓ
18 Ⓐ Ⓑ Ⓒ Ⓓ	43 Ⓐ Ⓑ Ⓒ Ⓓ
19 Ⓐ Ⓑ Ⓒ Ⓓ	44 Ⓐ Ⓑ Ⓒ Ⓓ
20 Ⓐ Ⓑ Ⓒ Ⓓ	45 Ⓐ Ⓑ Ⓒ Ⓓ
21 Ⓐ Ⓑ Ⓒ Ⓓ	46 Ⓐ Ⓑ Ⓒ Ⓓ
22 Ⓐ Ⓑ Ⓒ Ⓓ	47 Ⓐ Ⓑ Ⓒ Ⓓ
23 Ⓐ Ⓑ Ⓒ Ⓓ	48 Ⓐ Ⓑ Ⓒ Ⓓ
24 Ⓐ Ⓑ Ⓒ Ⓓ	49 Ⓐ Ⓑ Ⓒ Ⓓ
25 Ⓐ Ⓑ Ⓒ Ⓓ	50 Ⓐ Ⓑ Ⓒ Ⓓ

1 Ⓐ Ⓑ Ⓒ Ⓓ	26 Ⓐ Ⓑ Ⓒ Ⓓ
2 Ⓐ Ⓑ Ⓒ Ⓓ	27 Ⓐ Ⓑ Ⓒ Ⓓ
3 Ⓐ Ⓑ Ⓒ Ⓓ	28 Ⓐ Ⓑ Ⓒ Ⓓ
4 Ⓐ Ⓑ Ⓒ Ⓓ	29 Ⓐ Ⓑ Ⓒ Ⓓ
5 Ⓐ Ⓑ Ⓒ Ⓓ	30 Ⓐ Ⓑ Ⓒ Ⓓ
6 Ⓐ Ⓑ Ⓒ Ⓓ	31 Ⓐ Ⓑ Ⓒ Ⓓ
7 Ⓐ Ⓑ Ⓒ Ⓓ	32 Ⓐ Ⓑ Ⓒ Ⓓ
8 Ⓐ Ⓑ Ⓒ Ⓓ	33 Ⓐ Ⓑ Ⓒ Ⓓ
9 Ⓐ Ⓑ Ⓒ Ⓓ	34 Ⓐ Ⓑ Ⓒ Ⓓ
10 Ⓐ Ⓑ Ⓒ Ⓓ	35 Ⓐ Ⓑ Ⓒ Ⓓ
11 Ⓐ Ⓑ Ⓒ Ⓓ	36 Ⓐ Ⓑ Ⓒ Ⓓ
12 Ⓐ Ⓑ Ⓒ Ⓓ	37 Ⓐ Ⓑ Ⓒ Ⓓ
13 Ⓐ Ⓑ Ⓒ Ⓓ	38 Ⓐ Ⓑ Ⓒ Ⓓ
14 Ⓐ Ⓑ Ⓒ Ⓓ	39 Ⓐ Ⓑ Ⓒ Ⓓ
15 Ⓐ Ⓑ Ⓒ Ⓓ	40 Ⓐ Ⓑ Ⓒ Ⓓ
16 Ⓐ Ⓑ Ⓒ Ⓓ	
17 Ⓐ Ⓑ Ⓒ Ⓓ	
18 Ⓐ Ⓑ Ⓒ Ⓓ	
19 Ⓐ Ⓑ Ⓒ Ⓓ	
20 Ⓐ Ⓑ Ⓒ Ⓓ	
21 Ⓐ Ⓑ Ⓒ Ⓓ	
22 Ⓐ Ⓑ Ⓒ Ⓓ	
23 Ⓐ Ⓑ Ⓒ Ⓓ	
24 Ⓐ Ⓑ Ⓒ Ⓓ	
25 Ⓐ Ⓑ Ⓒ Ⓓ	

CUT HERE

ANSWER SHEET FOR PRACTICE TEST 2
(Remove This Sheet and Use it to Mark Your Answers)

SECTION 3

READING COMPREHENSION

1 Ⓐ Ⓑ Ⓒ Ⓓ	26 Ⓐ Ⓑ Ⓒ Ⓓ
2 Ⓐ Ⓑ Ⓒ Ⓓ	27 Ⓐ Ⓑ Ⓒ Ⓓ
3 Ⓐ Ⓑ Ⓒ Ⓓ	28 Ⓐ Ⓑ Ⓒ Ⓓ
4 Ⓐ Ⓑ Ⓒ Ⓓ	29 Ⓐ Ⓑ Ⓒ Ⓓ
5 Ⓐ Ⓑ Ⓒ Ⓓ	30 Ⓐ Ⓑ Ⓒ Ⓓ
6 Ⓐ Ⓑ Ⓒ Ⓓ	31 Ⓐ Ⓑ Ⓒ Ⓓ
7 Ⓐ Ⓑ Ⓒ Ⓓ	32 Ⓐ Ⓑ Ⓒ Ⓓ
8 Ⓐ Ⓑ Ⓒ Ⓓ	33 Ⓐ Ⓑ Ⓒ Ⓓ
9 Ⓐ Ⓑ Ⓒ Ⓓ	34 Ⓐ Ⓑ Ⓒ Ⓓ
10 Ⓐ Ⓑ Ⓒ Ⓓ	35 Ⓐ Ⓑ Ⓒ Ⓓ
11 Ⓐ Ⓑ Ⓒ Ⓓ	36 Ⓐ Ⓑ Ⓒ Ⓓ
12 Ⓐ Ⓑ Ⓒ Ⓓ	37 Ⓐ Ⓑ Ⓒ Ⓓ
13 Ⓐ Ⓑ Ⓒ Ⓓ	38 Ⓐ Ⓑ Ⓒ Ⓓ
14 Ⓐ Ⓑ Ⓒ Ⓓ	39 Ⓐ Ⓑ Ⓒ Ⓓ
15 Ⓐ Ⓑ Ⓒ Ⓓ	40 Ⓐ Ⓑ Ⓒ Ⓓ
16 Ⓐ Ⓑ Ⓒ Ⓓ	41 Ⓐ Ⓑ Ⓒ Ⓓ
17 Ⓐ Ⓑ Ⓒ Ⓓ	42 Ⓐ Ⓑ Ⓒ Ⓓ
18 Ⓐ Ⓑ Ⓒ Ⓓ	43 Ⓐ Ⓑ Ⓒ Ⓓ
19 Ⓐ Ⓑ Ⓒ Ⓓ	44 Ⓐ Ⓑ Ⓒ Ⓓ
20 Ⓐ Ⓑ Ⓒ Ⓓ	45 Ⓐ Ⓑ Ⓒ Ⓓ
21 Ⓐ Ⓑ Ⓒ Ⓓ	46 Ⓐ Ⓑ Ⓒ Ⓓ
22 Ⓐ Ⓑ Ⓒ Ⓓ	47 Ⓐ Ⓑ Ⓒ Ⓓ
23 Ⓐ Ⓑ Ⓒ Ⓓ	48 Ⓐ Ⓑ Ⓒ Ⓓ
24 Ⓐ Ⓑ Ⓒ Ⓓ	49 Ⓐ Ⓑ Ⓒ Ⓓ
25 Ⓐ Ⓑ Ⓒ Ⓓ	50 Ⓐ Ⓑ Ⓒ Ⓓ

ANSWER SHEET FOR PRACTICE TEST 3
(Remove This Sheet and Use it to Mark Your Answers)

SECTION 1	SECTION 2
LISTENING COMPREHENSION	STRUCTURE AND WRITTEN EXPRESSION

SECTION 1

1 Ⓐ Ⓑ Ⓒ Ⓓ	26 Ⓐ Ⓑ Ⓒ Ⓓ
2 Ⓐ Ⓑ Ⓒ Ⓓ	27 Ⓐ Ⓑ Ⓒ Ⓓ
3 Ⓐ Ⓑ Ⓒ Ⓓ	28 Ⓐ Ⓑ Ⓒ Ⓓ
4 Ⓐ Ⓑ Ⓒ Ⓓ	29 Ⓐ Ⓑ Ⓒ Ⓓ
5 Ⓐ Ⓑ Ⓒ Ⓓ	30 Ⓐ Ⓑ Ⓒ Ⓓ
6 Ⓐ Ⓑ Ⓒ Ⓓ	31 Ⓐ Ⓑ Ⓒ Ⓓ
7 Ⓐ Ⓑ Ⓒ Ⓓ	32 Ⓐ Ⓑ Ⓒ Ⓓ
8 Ⓐ Ⓑ Ⓒ Ⓓ	33 Ⓐ Ⓑ Ⓒ Ⓓ
9 Ⓐ Ⓑ Ⓒ Ⓓ	34 Ⓐ Ⓑ Ⓒ Ⓓ
10 Ⓐ Ⓑ Ⓒ Ⓓ	35 Ⓐ Ⓑ Ⓒ Ⓓ
11 Ⓐ Ⓑ Ⓒ Ⓓ	36 Ⓐ Ⓑ Ⓒ Ⓓ
12 Ⓐ Ⓑ Ⓒ Ⓓ	37 Ⓐ Ⓑ Ⓒ Ⓓ
13 Ⓐ Ⓑ Ⓒ Ⓓ	38 Ⓐ Ⓑ Ⓒ Ⓓ
14 Ⓐ Ⓑ Ⓒ Ⓓ	39 Ⓐ Ⓑ Ⓒ Ⓓ
15 Ⓐ Ⓑ Ⓒ Ⓓ	40 Ⓐ Ⓑ Ⓒ Ⓓ
16 Ⓐ Ⓑ Ⓒ Ⓓ	41 Ⓐ Ⓑ Ⓒ Ⓓ
17 Ⓐ Ⓑ Ⓒ Ⓓ	42 Ⓐ Ⓑ Ⓒ Ⓓ
18 Ⓐ Ⓑ Ⓒ Ⓓ	43 Ⓐ Ⓑ Ⓒ Ⓓ
19 Ⓐ Ⓑ Ⓒ Ⓓ	44 Ⓐ Ⓑ Ⓒ Ⓓ
20 Ⓐ Ⓑ Ⓒ Ⓓ	45 Ⓐ Ⓑ Ⓒ Ⓓ
21 Ⓐ Ⓑ Ⓒ Ⓓ	46 Ⓐ Ⓑ Ⓒ Ⓓ
22 Ⓐ Ⓑ Ⓒ Ⓓ	47 Ⓐ Ⓑ Ⓒ Ⓓ
23 Ⓐ Ⓑ Ⓒ Ⓓ	48 Ⓐ Ⓑ Ⓒ Ⓓ
24 Ⓐ Ⓑ Ⓒ Ⓓ	49 Ⓐ Ⓑ Ⓒ Ⓓ
25 Ⓐ Ⓑ Ⓒ Ⓓ	50 Ⓐ Ⓑ Ⓒ Ⓓ

SECTION 2

1 Ⓐ Ⓑ Ⓒ Ⓓ	26 Ⓐ Ⓑ Ⓒ Ⓓ
2 Ⓐ Ⓑ Ⓒ Ⓓ	27 Ⓐ Ⓑ Ⓒ Ⓓ
3 Ⓐ Ⓑ Ⓒ Ⓓ	28 Ⓐ Ⓑ Ⓒ Ⓓ
4 Ⓐ Ⓑ Ⓒ Ⓓ	29 Ⓐ Ⓑ Ⓒ Ⓓ
5 Ⓐ Ⓑ Ⓒ Ⓓ	30 Ⓐ Ⓑ Ⓒ Ⓓ
6 Ⓐ Ⓑ Ⓒ Ⓓ	31 Ⓐ Ⓑ Ⓒ Ⓓ
7 Ⓐ Ⓑ Ⓒ Ⓓ	32 Ⓐ Ⓑ Ⓒ Ⓓ
8 Ⓐ Ⓑ Ⓒ Ⓓ	33 Ⓐ Ⓑ Ⓒ Ⓓ
9 Ⓐ Ⓑ Ⓒ Ⓓ	34 Ⓐ Ⓑ Ⓒ Ⓓ
10 Ⓐ Ⓑ Ⓒ Ⓓ	35 Ⓐ Ⓑ Ⓒ Ⓓ
11 Ⓐ Ⓑ Ⓒ Ⓓ	36 Ⓐ Ⓑ Ⓒ Ⓓ
12 Ⓐ Ⓑ Ⓒ Ⓓ	37 Ⓐ Ⓑ Ⓒ Ⓓ
13 Ⓐ Ⓑ Ⓒ Ⓓ	38 Ⓐ Ⓑ Ⓒ Ⓓ
14 Ⓐ Ⓑ Ⓒ Ⓓ	39 Ⓐ Ⓑ Ⓒ Ⓓ
15 Ⓐ Ⓑ Ⓒ Ⓓ	40 Ⓐ Ⓑ Ⓒ Ⓓ
16 Ⓐ Ⓑ Ⓒ Ⓓ	
17 Ⓐ Ⓑ Ⓒ Ⓓ	
18 Ⓐ Ⓑ Ⓒ Ⓓ	
19 Ⓐ Ⓑ Ⓒ Ⓓ	
20 Ⓐ Ⓑ Ⓒ Ⓓ	
21 Ⓐ Ⓑ Ⓒ Ⓓ	
22 Ⓐ Ⓑ Ⓒ Ⓓ	
23 Ⓐ Ⓑ Ⓒ Ⓓ	
24 Ⓐ Ⓑ Ⓒ Ⓓ	
25 Ⓐ Ⓑ Ⓒ Ⓓ	

CUT HERE

307

ANSWER SHEET FOR PRACTICE TEST 3
(Remove This Sheet and Use it to Mark Your Answers)

SECTION 3
READING COMPREHENSION

1 Ⓐ Ⓑ Ⓒ Ⓓ	26 Ⓐ Ⓑ Ⓒ Ⓓ
2 Ⓐ Ⓑ Ⓒ Ⓓ	27 Ⓐ Ⓑ Ⓒ Ⓓ
3 Ⓐ Ⓑ Ⓒ Ⓓ	28 Ⓐ Ⓑ Ⓒ Ⓓ
4 Ⓐ Ⓑ Ⓒ Ⓓ	29 Ⓐ Ⓑ Ⓒ Ⓓ
5 Ⓐ Ⓑ Ⓒ Ⓓ	30 Ⓐ Ⓑ Ⓒ Ⓓ
6 Ⓐ Ⓑ Ⓒ Ⓓ	31 Ⓐ Ⓑ Ⓒ Ⓓ
7 Ⓐ Ⓑ Ⓒ Ⓓ	32 Ⓐ Ⓑ Ⓒ Ⓓ
8 Ⓐ Ⓑ Ⓒ Ⓓ	33 Ⓐ Ⓑ Ⓒ Ⓓ
9 Ⓐ Ⓑ Ⓒ Ⓓ	34 Ⓐ Ⓑ Ⓒ Ⓓ
10 Ⓐ Ⓑ Ⓒ Ⓓ	35 Ⓐ Ⓑ Ⓒ Ⓓ
11 Ⓐ Ⓑ Ⓒ Ⓓ	36 Ⓐ Ⓑ Ⓒ Ⓓ
12 Ⓐ Ⓑ Ⓒ Ⓓ	37 Ⓐ Ⓑ Ⓒ Ⓓ
13 Ⓐ Ⓑ Ⓒ Ⓓ	38 Ⓐ Ⓑ Ⓒ Ⓓ
14 Ⓐ Ⓑ Ⓒ Ⓓ	39 Ⓐ Ⓑ Ⓒ Ⓓ
15 Ⓐ Ⓑ Ⓒ Ⓓ	40 Ⓐ Ⓑ Ⓒ Ⓓ
16 Ⓐ Ⓑ Ⓒ Ⓓ	41 Ⓐ Ⓑ Ⓒ Ⓓ
17 Ⓐ Ⓑ Ⓒ Ⓓ	42 Ⓐ Ⓑ Ⓒ Ⓓ
18 Ⓐ Ⓑ Ⓒ Ⓓ	43 Ⓐ Ⓑ Ⓒ Ⓓ
19 Ⓐ Ⓑ Ⓒ Ⓓ	44 Ⓐ Ⓑ Ⓒ Ⓓ
20 Ⓐ Ⓑ Ⓒ Ⓓ	45 Ⓐ Ⓑ Ⓒ Ⓓ
21 Ⓐ Ⓑ Ⓒ Ⓓ	46 Ⓐ Ⓑ Ⓒ Ⓓ
22 Ⓐ Ⓑ Ⓒ Ⓓ	47 Ⓐ Ⓑ Ⓒ Ⓓ
23 Ⓐ Ⓑ Ⓒ Ⓓ	48 Ⓐ Ⓑ Ⓒ Ⓓ
24 Ⓐ Ⓑ Ⓒ Ⓓ	49 Ⓐ Ⓑ Ⓒ Ⓓ
25 Ⓐ Ⓑ Ⓒ Ⓓ	50 Ⓐ Ⓑ Ⓒ Ⓓ

ANSWER SHEET FOR PRACTICE TEST 4
(Remove This Sheet and Use it to Mark Your Answers)

SECTION 1

LISTENING
COMPREHENSION

SECTION 2

STRUCTURE AND
WRITTEN EXPRESSION

CUT HERE

SECTION 1		SECTION 2	
1 Ⓐ Ⓑ Ⓒ Ⓓ	26 Ⓐ Ⓑ Ⓒ Ⓓ	1 Ⓐ Ⓑ Ⓒ Ⓓ	26 Ⓐ Ⓑ Ⓒ Ⓓ
2 Ⓐ Ⓑ Ⓒ Ⓓ	27 Ⓐ Ⓑ Ⓒ Ⓓ	2 Ⓐ Ⓑ Ⓒ Ⓓ	27 Ⓐ Ⓑ Ⓒ Ⓓ
3 Ⓐ Ⓑ Ⓒ Ⓓ	28 Ⓐ Ⓑ Ⓒ Ⓓ	3 Ⓐ Ⓑ Ⓒ Ⓓ	28 Ⓐ Ⓑ Ⓒ Ⓓ
4 Ⓐ Ⓑ Ⓒ Ⓓ	29 Ⓐ Ⓑ Ⓒ Ⓓ	4 Ⓐ Ⓑ Ⓒ Ⓓ	29 Ⓐ Ⓑ Ⓒ Ⓓ
5 Ⓐ Ⓑ Ⓒ Ⓓ	30 Ⓐ Ⓑ Ⓒ Ⓓ	5 Ⓐ Ⓑ Ⓒ Ⓓ	30 Ⓐ Ⓑ Ⓒ Ⓓ
6 Ⓐ Ⓑ Ⓒ Ⓓ	31 Ⓐ Ⓑ Ⓒ Ⓓ	6 Ⓐ Ⓑ Ⓒ Ⓓ	31 Ⓐ Ⓑ Ⓒ Ⓓ
7 Ⓐ Ⓑ Ⓒ Ⓓ	32 Ⓐ Ⓑ Ⓒ Ⓓ	7 Ⓐ Ⓑ Ⓒ Ⓓ	32 Ⓐ Ⓑ Ⓒ Ⓓ
8 Ⓐ Ⓑ Ⓒ Ⓓ	33 Ⓐ Ⓑ Ⓒ Ⓓ	8 Ⓐ Ⓑ Ⓒ Ⓓ	33 Ⓐ Ⓑ Ⓒ Ⓓ
9 Ⓐ Ⓑ Ⓒ Ⓓ	34 Ⓐ Ⓑ Ⓒ Ⓓ	9 Ⓐ Ⓑ Ⓒ Ⓓ	34 Ⓐ Ⓑ Ⓒ Ⓓ
10 Ⓐ Ⓑ Ⓒ Ⓓ	35 Ⓐ Ⓑ Ⓒ Ⓓ	10 Ⓐ Ⓑ Ⓒ Ⓓ	35 Ⓐ Ⓑ Ⓒ Ⓓ
11 Ⓐ Ⓑ Ⓒ Ⓓ	36 Ⓐ Ⓑ Ⓒ Ⓓ	11 Ⓐ Ⓑ Ⓒ Ⓓ	36 Ⓐ Ⓑ Ⓒ Ⓓ
12 Ⓐ Ⓑ Ⓒ Ⓓ	37 Ⓐ Ⓑ Ⓒ Ⓓ	12 Ⓐ Ⓑ Ⓒ Ⓓ	37 Ⓐ Ⓑ Ⓒ Ⓓ
13 Ⓐ Ⓑ Ⓒ Ⓓ	38 Ⓐ Ⓑ Ⓒ Ⓓ	13 Ⓐ Ⓑ Ⓒ Ⓓ	38 Ⓐ Ⓑ Ⓒ Ⓓ
14 Ⓐ Ⓑ Ⓒ Ⓓ	39 Ⓐ Ⓑ Ⓒ Ⓓ	14 Ⓐ Ⓑ Ⓒ Ⓓ	39 Ⓐ Ⓑ Ⓒ Ⓓ
15 Ⓐ Ⓑ Ⓒ Ⓓ	40 Ⓐ Ⓑ Ⓒ Ⓓ	15 Ⓐ Ⓑ Ⓒ Ⓓ	40 Ⓐ Ⓑ Ⓒ Ⓓ
16 Ⓐ Ⓑ Ⓒ Ⓓ	41 Ⓐ Ⓑ Ⓒ Ⓓ	16 Ⓐ Ⓑ Ⓒ Ⓓ	
17 Ⓐ Ⓑ Ⓒ Ⓓ	42 Ⓐ Ⓑ Ⓒ Ⓓ	17 Ⓐ Ⓑ Ⓒ Ⓓ	
18 Ⓐ Ⓑ Ⓒ Ⓓ	43 Ⓐ Ⓑ Ⓒ Ⓓ	18 Ⓐ Ⓑ Ⓒ Ⓓ	
19 Ⓐ Ⓑ Ⓒ Ⓓ	44 Ⓐ Ⓑ Ⓒ Ⓓ	19 Ⓐ Ⓑ Ⓒ Ⓓ	
20 Ⓐ Ⓑ Ⓒ Ⓓ	45 Ⓐ Ⓑ Ⓒ Ⓓ	20 Ⓐ Ⓑ Ⓒ Ⓓ	
21 Ⓐ Ⓑ Ⓒ Ⓓ	46 Ⓐ Ⓑ Ⓒ Ⓓ	21 Ⓐ Ⓑ Ⓒ Ⓓ	
22 Ⓐ Ⓑ Ⓒ Ⓓ	47 Ⓐ Ⓑ Ⓒ Ⓓ	22 Ⓐ Ⓑ Ⓒ Ⓓ	
23 Ⓐ Ⓑ Ⓒ Ⓓ	48 Ⓐ Ⓑ Ⓒ Ⓓ	23 Ⓐ Ⓑ Ⓒ Ⓓ	
24 Ⓐ Ⓑ Ⓒ Ⓓ	49 Ⓐ Ⓑ Ⓒ Ⓓ	24 Ⓐ Ⓑ Ⓒ Ⓓ	
25 Ⓐ Ⓑ Ⓒ Ⓓ	50 Ⓐ Ⓑ Ⓒ Ⓓ	25 Ⓐ Ⓑ Ⓒ Ⓓ	

ANSWER SHEET FOR PRACTICE TEST 4
(Remove This Sheet and Use it to Mark Your Answers)

SECTION 3

READING COMPREHENSION

1 Ⓐ Ⓑ Ⓒ Ⓓ	26 Ⓐ Ⓑ Ⓒ Ⓓ
2 Ⓐ Ⓑ Ⓒ Ⓓ	27 Ⓐ Ⓑ Ⓒ Ⓓ
3 Ⓐ Ⓑ Ⓒ Ⓓ	28 Ⓐ Ⓑ Ⓒ Ⓓ
4 Ⓐ Ⓑ Ⓒ Ⓓ	29 Ⓐ Ⓑ Ⓒ Ⓓ
5 Ⓐ Ⓑ Ⓒ Ⓓ	30 Ⓐ Ⓑ Ⓒ Ⓓ
6 Ⓐ Ⓑ Ⓒ Ⓓ	31 Ⓐ Ⓑ Ⓒ Ⓓ
7 Ⓐ Ⓑ Ⓒ Ⓓ	32 Ⓐ Ⓑ Ⓒ Ⓓ
8 Ⓐ Ⓑ Ⓒ Ⓓ	33 Ⓐ Ⓑ Ⓒ Ⓓ
9 Ⓐ Ⓑ Ⓒ Ⓓ	34 Ⓐ Ⓑ Ⓒ Ⓓ
10 Ⓐ Ⓑ Ⓒ Ⓓ	35 Ⓐ Ⓑ Ⓒ Ⓓ
11 Ⓐ Ⓑ Ⓒ Ⓓ	36 Ⓐ Ⓑ Ⓒ Ⓓ
12 Ⓐ Ⓑ Ⓒ Ⓓ	37 Ⓐ Ⓑ Ⓒ Ⓓ
13 Ⓐ Ⓑ Ⓒ Ⓓ	38 Ⓐ Ⓑ Ⓒ Ⓓ
14 Ⓐ Ⓑ Ⓒ Ⓓ	39 Ⓐ Ⓑ Ⓒ Ⓓ
15 Ⓐ Ⓑ Ⓒ Ⓓ	40 Ⓐ Ⓑ Ⓒ Ⓓ
16 Ⓐ Ⓑ Ⓒ Ⓓ	41 Ⓐ Ⓑ Ⓒ Ⓓ
17 Ⓐ Ⓑ Ⓒ Ⓓ	42 Ⓐ Ⓑ Ⓒ Ⓓ
18 Ⓐ Ⓑ Ⓒ Ⓓ	43 Ⓐ Ⓑ Ⓒ Ⓓ
19 Ⓐ Ⓑ Ⓒ Ⓓ	44 Ⓐ Ⓑ Ⓒ Ⓓ
20 Ⓐ Ⓑ Ⓒ Ⓓ	45 Ⓐ Ⓑ Ⓒ Ⓓ
21 Ⓐ Ⓑ Ⓒ Ⓓ	46 Ⓐ Ⓑ Ⓒ Ⓓ
22 Ⓐ Ⓑ Ⓒ Ⓓ	47 Ⓐ Ⓑ Ⓒ Ⓓ
23 Ⓐ Ⓑ Ⓒ Ⓓ	48 Ⓐ Ⓑ Ⓒ Ⓓ
24 Ⓐ Ⓑ Ⓒ Ⓓ	49 Ⓐ Ⓑ Ⓒ Ⓓ
25 Ⓐ Ⓑ Ⓒ Ⓓ	50 Ⓐ Ⓑ Ⓒ Ⓓ

ANSWER SHEET FOR PRACTICE TEST 5
(Remove This Sheet and Use it to Mark Your Answers)

SECTION 1	**SECTION 2**
LISTENING COMPREHENSION	STRUCTURE AND WRITTEN EXPRESSION

SECTION 1 — LISTENING COMPREHENSION

1 (A) (B) (C) (D)
2 (A) (B) (C) (D)
3 (A) (B) (C) (D)
4 (A) (B) (C) (D)
5 (A) (B) (C) (D)

6 (A) (B) (C) (D)
7 (A) (B) (C) (D)
8 (A) (B) (C) (D)
9 (A) (B) (C) (D)
10 (A) (B) (C) (D)

11 (A) (B) (C) (D)
12 (A) (B) (C) (D)
13 (A) (B) (C) (D)
14 (A) (B) (C) (D)
15 (A) (B) (C) (D)

16 (A) (B) (C) (D)
17 (A) (B) (C) (D)
18 (A) (B) (C) (D)
19 (A) (B) (C) (D)
20 (A) (B) (C) (D)

21 (A) (B) (C) (D)
22 (A) (B) (C) (D)
23 (A) (B) (C) (D)
24 (A) (B) (C) (D)
25 (A) (B) (C) (D)

26 (A) (B) (C) (D)
27 (A) (B) (C) (D)
28 (A) (B) (C) (D)
29 (A) (B) (C) (D)
30 (A) (B) (C) (D)

31 (A) (B) (C) (D)
32 (A) (B) (C) (D)
33 (A) (B) (C) (D)
34 (A) (B) (C) (D)
35 (A) (B) (C) (D)

36 (A) (B) (C) (D)
37 (A) (B) (C) (D)
38 (A) (B) (C) (D)
39 (A) (B) (C) (D)
40 (A) (B) (C) (D)

41 (A) (B) (C) (D)
42 (A) (B) (C) (D)
43 (A) (B) (C) (D)
44 (A) (B) (C) (D)
45 (A) (B) (C) (D)

46 (A) (B) (C) (D)
47 (A) (B) (C) (D)
48 (A) (B) (C) (D)
49 (A) (B) (C) (D)
50 (A) (B) (C) (D)

SECTION 2 — STRUCTURE AND WRITTEN EXPRESSION

1 (A) (B) (C) (D)
2 (A) (B) (C) (D)
3 (A) (B) (C) (D)
4 (A) (B) (C) (D)
5 (A) (B) (C) (D)

6 (A) (B) (C) (D)
7 (A) (B) (C) (D)
8 (A) (B) (C) (D)
9 (A) (B) (C) (D)
10 (A) (B) (C) (D)

11 (A) (B) (C) (D)
12 (A) (B) (C) (D)
13 (A) (B) (C) (D)
14 (A) (B) (C) (D)
15 (A) (B) (C) (D)

16 (A) (B) (C) (D)
17 (A) (B) (C) (D)
18 (A) (B) (C) (D)
19 (A) (B) (C) (D)
20 (A) (B) (C) (D)

21 (A) (B) (C) (D)
22 (A) (B) (C) (D)
23 (A) (B) (C) (D)
24 (A) (B) (C) (D)
25 (A) (B) (C) (D)

26 (A) (B) (C) (D)
27 (A) (B) (C) (D)
28 (A) (B) (C) (D)
29 (A) (B) (C) (D)
30 (A) (B) (C) (D)

31 (A) (B) (C) (D)
32 (A) (B) (C) (D)
33 (A) (B) (C) (D)
34 (A) (B) (C) (D)
35 (A) (B) (C) (D)

36 (A) (B) (C) (D)
37 (A) (B) (C) (D)
38 (A) (B) (C) (D)
39 (A) (B) (C) (D)
40 (A) (B) (C) (D)

CUT HERE

ANSWER SHEET FOR PRACTICE TEST 5
(Remove This Sheet and Use it to Mark Your Answers)

SECTION 3

READING COMPREHENSION

1 Ⓐ Ⓑ Ⓒ Ⓓ	26 Ⓐ Ⓑ Ⓒ Ⓓ
2 Ⓐ Ⓑ Ⓒ Ⓓ	27 Ⓐ Ⓑ Ⓒ Ⓓ
3 Ⓐ Ⓑ Ⓒ Ⓓ	28 Ⓐ Ⓑ Ⓒ Ⓓ
4 Ⓐ Ⓑ Ⓒ Ⓓ	29 Ⓐ Ⓑ Ⓒ Ⓓ
5 Ⓐ Ⓑ Ⓒ Ⓓ	30 Ⓐ Ⓑ Ⓒ Ⓓ
6 Ⓐ Ⓑ Ⓒ Ⓓ	31 Ⓐ Ⓑ Ⓒ Ⓓ
7 Ⓐ Ⓑ Ⓒ Ⓓ	32 Ⓐ Ⓑ Ⓒ Ⓓ
8 Ⓐ Ⓑ Ⓒ Ⓓ	33 Ⓐ Ⓑ Ⓒ Ⓓ
9 Ⓐ Ⓑ Ⓒ Ⓓ	34 Ⓐ Ⓑ Ⓒ Ⓓ
10 Ⓐ Ⓑ Ⓒ Ⓓ	35 Ⓐ Ⓑ Ⓒ Ⓓ
11 Ⓐ Ⓑ Ⓒ Ⓓ	36 Ⓐ Ⓑ Ⓒ Ⓓ
12 Ⓐ Ⓑ Ⓒ Ⓓ	37 Ⓐ Ⓑ Ⓒ Ⓓ
13 Ⓐ Ⓑ Ⓒ Ⓓ	38 Ⓐ Ⓑ Ⓒ Ⓓ
14 Ⓐ Ⓑ Ⓒ Ⓓ	39 Ⓐ Ⓑ Ⓒ Ⓓ
15 Ⓐ Ⓑ Ⓒ Ⓓ	40 Ⓐ Ⓑ Ⓒ Ⓓ
16 Ⓐ Ⓑ Ⓒ Ⓓ	41 Ⓐ Ⓑ Ⓒ Ⓓ
17 Ⓐ Ⓑ Ⓒ Ⓓ	42 Ⓐ Ⓑ Ⓒ Ⓓ
18 Ⓐ Ⓑ Ⓒ Ⓓ	43 Ⓐ Ⓑ Ⓒ Ⓓ
19 Ⓐ Ⓑ Ⓒ Ⓓ	44 Ⓐ Ⓑ Ⓒ Ⓓ
20 Ⓐ Ⓑ Ⓒ Ⓓ	45 Ⓐ Ⓑ Ⓒ Ⓓ
21 Ⓐ Ⓑ Ⓒ Ⓓ	46 Ⓐ Ⓑ Ⓒ Ⓓ
22 Ⓐ Ⓑ Ⓒ Ⓓ	47 Ⓐ Ⓑ Ⓒ Ⓓ
23 Ⓐ Ⓑ Ⓒ Ⓓ	48 Ⓐ Ⓑ Ⓒ Ⓓ
24 Ⓐ Ⓑ Ⓒ Ⓓ	49 Ⓐ Ⓑ Ⓒ Ⓓ
25 Ⓐ Ⓑ Ⓒ Ⓓ	50 Ⓐ Ⓑ Ⓒ Ⓓ

ANSWER SHEET FOR PRACTICE TEST 6
(Remove This Sheet and Use it to Mark Your Answers)

SECTION 1
LISTENING COMPREHENSION

SECTION 2
STRUCTURE AND WRITTEN EXPRESSION

SECTION 1

1 Ⓐ Ⓑ Ⓒ Ⓓ	26 Ⓐ Ⓑ Ⓒ Ⓓ
2 Ⓐ Ⓑ Ⓒ Ⓓ	27 Ⓐ Ⓑ Ⓒ Ⓓ
3 Ⓐ Ⓑ Ⓒ Ⓓ	28 Ⓐ Ⓑ Ⓒ Ⓓ
4 Ⓐ Ⓑ Ⓒ Ⓓ	29 Ⓐ Ⓑ Ⓒ Ⓓ
5 Ⓐ Ⓑ Ⓒ Ⓓ	30 Ⓐ Ⓑ Ⓒ Ⓓ
6 Ⓐ Ⓑ Ⓒ Ⓓ	31 Ⓐ Ⓑ Ⓒ Ⓓ
7 Ⓐ Ⓑ Ⓒ Ⓓ	32 Ⓐ Ⓑ Ⓒ Ⓓ
8 Ⓐ Ⓑ Ⓒ Ⓓ	33 Ⓐ Ⓑ Ⓒ Ⓓ
9 Ⓐ Ⓑ Ⓒ Ⓓ	34 Ⓐ Ⓑ Ⓒ Ⓓ
10 Ⓐ Ⓑ Ⓒ Ⓓ	35 Ⓐ Ⓑ Ⓒ Ⓓ
11 Ⓐ Ⓑ Ⓒ Ⓓ	36 Ⓐ Ⓑ Ⓒ Ⓓ
12 Ⓐ Ⓑ Ⓒ Ⓓ	37 Ⓐ Ⓑ Ⓒ Ⓓ
13 Ⓐ Ⓑ Ⓒ Ⓓ	38 Ⓐ Ⓑ Ⓒ Ⓓ
14 Ⓐ Ⓑ Ⓒ Ⓓ	39 Ⓐ Ⓑ Ⓒ Ⓓ
15 Ⓐ Ⓑ Ⓒ Ⓓ	40 Ⓐ Ⓑ Ⓒ Ⓓ
16 Ⓐ Ⓑ Ⓒ Ⓓ	41 Ⓐ Ⓑ Ⓒ Ⓓ
17 Ⓐ Ⓑ Ⓒ Ⓓ	42 Ⓐ Ⓑ Ⓒ Ⓓ
18 Ⓐ Ⓑ Ⓒ Ⓓ	43 Ⓐ Ⓑ Ⓒ Ⓓ
19 Ⓐ Ⓑ Ⓒ Ⓓ	44 Ⓐ Ⓑ Ⓒ Ⓓ
20 Ⓐ Ⓑ Ⓒ Ⓓ	45 Ⓐ Ⓑ Ⓒ Ⓓ
21 Ⓐ Ⓑ Ⓒ Ⓓ	46 Ⓐ Ⓑ Ⓒ Ⓓ
22 Ⓐ Ⓑ Ⓒ Ⓓ	47 Ⓐ Ⓑ Ⓒ Ⓓ
23 Ⓐ Ⓑ Ⓒ Ⓓ	48 Ⓐ Ⓑ Ⓒ Ⓓ
24 Ⓐ Ⓑ Ⓒ Ⓓ	49 Ⓐ Ⓑ Ⓒ Ⓓ
25 Ⓐ Ⓑ Ⓒ Ⓓ	50 Ⓐ Ⓑ Ⓒ Ⓓ

SECTION 2

1 Ⓐ Ⓑ Ⓒ Ⓓ	26 Ⓐ Ⓑ Ⓒ Ⓓ
2 Ⓐ Ⓑ Ⓒ Ⓓ	27 Ⓐ Ⓑ Ⓒ Ⓓ
3 Ⓐ Ⓑ Ⓒ Ⓓ	28 Ⓐ Ⓑ Ⓒ Ⓓ
4 Ⓐ Ⓑ Ⓒ Ⓓ	29 Ⓐ Ⓑ Ⓒ Ⓓ
5 Ⓐ Ⓑ Ⓒ Ⓓ	30 Ⓐ Ⓑ Ⓒ Ⓓ
6 Ⓐ Ⓑ Ⓒ Ⓓ	31 Ⓐ Ⓑ Ⓒ Ⓓ
7 Ⓐ Ⓑ Ⓒ Ⓓ	32 Ⓐ Ⓑ Ⓒ Ⓓ
8 Ⓐ Ⓑ Ⓒ Ⓓ	33 Ⓐ Ⓑ Ⓒ Ⓓ
9 Ⓐ Ⓑ Ⓒ Ⓓ	34 Ⓐ Ⓑ Ⓒ Ⓓ
10 Ⓐ Ⓑ Ⓒ Ⓓ	35 Ⓐ Ⓑ Ⓒ Ⓓ
11 Ⓐ Ⓑ Ⓒ Ⓓ	36 Ⓐ Ⓑ Ⓒ Ⓓ
12 Ⓐ Ⓑ Ⓒ Ⓓ	37 Ⓐ Ⓑ Ⓒ Ⓓ
13 Ⓐ Ⓑ Ⓒ Ⓓ	38 Ⓐ Ⓑ Ⓒ Ⓓ
14 Ⓐ Ⓑ Ⓒ Ⓓ	39 Ⓐ Ⓑ Ⓒ Ⓓ
15 Ⓐ Ⓑ Ⓒ Ⓓ	40 Ⓐ Ⓑ Ⓒ Ⓓ
16 Ⓐ Ⓑ Ⓒ Ⓓ	
17 Ⓐ Ⓑ Ⓒ Ⓓ	
18 Ⓐ Ⓑ Ⓒ Ⓓ	
19 Ⓐ Ⓑ Ⓒ Ⓓ	
20 Ⓐ Ⓑ Ⓒ Ⓓ	
21 Ⓐ Ⓑ Ⓒ Ⓓ	
22 Ⓐ Ⓑ Ⓒ Ⓓ	
23 Ⓐ Ⓑ Ⓒ Ⓓ	
24 Ⓐ Ⓑ Ⓒ Ⓓ	
25 Ⓐ Ⓑ Ⓒ Ⓓ	

313

ANSWER SHEET FOR PRACTICE TEST 6
(Remove This Sheet and Use it to Mark Your Answers)

SECTION 3
READING COMPREHENSION

1 Ⓐ Ⓑ Ⓒ Ⓓ	26 Ⓐ Ⓑ Ⓒ Ⓓ
2 Ⓐ Ⓑ Ⓒ Ⓓ	27 Ⓐ Ⓑ Ⓒ Ⓓ
3 Ⓐ Ⓑ Ⓒ Ⓓ	28 Ⓐ Ⓑ Ⓒ Ⓓ
4 Ⓐ Ⓑ Ⓒ Ⓓ	29 Ⓐ Ⓑ Ⓒ Ⓓ
5 Ⓐ Ⓑ Ⓒ Ⓓ	30 Ⓐ Ⓑ Ⓒ Ⓓ
6 Ⓐ Ⓑ Ⓒ Ⓓ	31 Ⓐ Ⓑ Ⓒ Ⓓ
7 Ⓐ Ⓑ Ⓒ Ⓓ	32 Ⓐ Ⓑ Ⓒ Ⓓ
8 Ⓐ Ⓑ Ⓒ Ⓓ	33 Ⓐ Ⓑ Ⓒ Ⓓ
9 Ⓐ Ⓑ Ⓒ Ⓓ	34 Ⓐ Ⓑ Ⓒ Ⓓ
10 Ⓐ Ⓑ Ⓒ Ⓓ	35 Ⓐ Ⓑ Ⓒ Ⓓ
11 Ⓐ Ⓑ Ⓒ Ⓓ	36 Ⓐ Ⓑ Ⓒ Ⓓ
12 Ⓐ Ⓑ Ⓒ Ⓓ	37 Ⓐ Ⓑ Ⓒ Ⓓ
13 Ⓐ Ⓑ Ⓒ Ⓓ	38 Ⓐ Ⓑ Ⓒ Ⓓ
14 Ⓐ Ⓑ Ⓒ Ⓓ	39 Ⓐ Ⓑ Ⓒ Ⓓ
15 Ⓐ Ⓑ Ⓒ Ⓓ	40 Ⓐ Ⓑ Ⓒ Ⓓ
16 Ⓐ Ⓑ Ⓒ Ⓓ	41 Ⓐ Ⓑ Ⓒ Ⓓ
17 Ⓐ Ⓑ Ⓒ Ⓓ	42 Ⓐ Ⓑ Ⓒ Ⓓ
18 Ⓐ Ⓑ Ⓒ Ⓓ	43 Ⓐ Ⓑ Ⓒ Ⓓ
19 Ⓐ Ⓑ Ⓒ Ⓓ	44 Ⓐ Ⓑ Ⓒ Ⓓ
20 Ⓐ Ⓑ Ⓒ Ⓓ	45 Ⓐ Ⓑ Ⓒ Ⓓ
21 Ⓐ Ⓑ Ⓒ Ⓓ	46 Ⓐ Ⓑ Ⓒ Ⓓ
22 Ⓐ Ⓑ Ⓒ Ⓓ	47 Ⓐ Ⓑ Ⓒ Ⓓ
23 Ⓐ Ⓑ Ⓒ Ⓓ	48 Ⓐ Ⓑ Ⓒ Ⓓ
24 Ⓐ Ⓑ Ⓒ Ⓓ	49 Ⓐ Ⓑ Ⓒ Ⓓ
25 Ⓐ Ⓑ Ⓒ Ⓓ	50 Ⓐ Ⓑ Ⓒ Ⓓ

PRACTICE TEST 1

SECTION 1
LISTENING COMPREHENSION

Time: Approximately 30 Minutes
50 Questions

Section 1 has three parts. Each part has its own set of directions. Do not take notes while listening or make any marks on the test pages. Notetaking, underlining, or crossing out will be considered cheating on the actual TOEFL exam. Answer the questions following the conversations or talks based on what the speakers have *stated* or *implied*.

For Practice Test 1, insert your Listening Comprehension cassette in your tape player. On the actual TOEFL, you will be given extra time to go on to the next page when you finish a page in the Listening Comprehension section. In the following test, however, you will have only the 12 seconds given after each question. Turn the page as soon as you have marked your answer. Start your cassette now.

Part A

DIRECTIONS

In Part A, you will hear short conversations between two speakers. At the end of each conversation, a third voice will ask a question about what was said. The question will be *spoken* just one time. After you hear a conversation and the question about it, read the four possible answers and decide which one would be the best answer to the question you have heard. Then, on your answer sheet, find the number of the problem and mark your answer.

315

1. (A) She's tired of teaching.
   (B) She was dismissed from her job.
   (C) She's changing jobs.
   (D) The school is too hot.

2. (A) She got up later than usual.
   (B) The bus was late.
   (C) She forgot her class.
   (D) Her clock was wrong.

3. (A) The weather report.
   (B) The traffic report.
   (C) Directions to Interstate 4.
   (D) Their disgust with careless drivers.

4. (A) She thinks his lectures are boring.
   (B) She thinks his tests are too long.
   (C) She doesn't like his choice of test questions.
   (D) She doesn't think he prepares well enough.

5. (A) A movie.   (C) A soccer game.
   (B) A documentary.   (D) A comedy.

6. (A) America.   (C) Switzerland.
   (B) England.   (D) Sweden.

7. (A) She had not applied to Stetson.
   (B) She had not worked very hard.
   (C) She was certain to be admitted.
   (D) She was not likely to be admitted.

8. (A) She got scratched in the wild berry bushes.
   (B) She got cut at the wild picnic celebration.
   (C) She was allergic to the fruit that she had eaten.
   (D) She was trying to get a suntan at the picnic.

9. (A) Wiwtner.   (B) Wittner.   (C) Wittmer.   (D) Iitner.

10. (A) Go out of town.
    (B) Help the woman prepare for her meeting.
    (C) Work with the woman.
    (D) Work when the woman was supposed to work.

11. (A) 5   (B) 3   (C) 2   (D) 8

12. (A) She went to the wrong class.
    (B) She was late for class because she got lost.
    (C) She missed the class.
    (D) She had some trouble finding the class, but she arrived on time.

13. (A) The man is not sure which type of flowers April sent.
    (B) April received many kinds of flowers.
    (C) The man received many kinds of flowers from April.
    (D) The man appreciated April's sending him flowers.

14. (A) William slept all the way from Georgia to New York.
    (B) George didn't sleep at all on the trip.
    (C) William was half asleep all the time that he was driving.
    (D) William didn't sleep at all on the trip.

15. (A) Too many people came to the meeting.
    (B) There were not enough people at the meeting to inspect the documents.
    (C) The man had expected more people to come to the meeting.
    (D) There were not enough seats for all the people.

16. (A) He sold no magazines.
    (B) He sold only one magazine.
    (C) He has never sold as many magazines as he sold today.
    (D) He sold five magazines at one house.

317

17. (A) Frank told the contractor to do the work in spite of the cost.
    (B) Frank told the contractor that the price was too high.
    (C) Frank cannot afford the work on his house.
    (D) Frank repaired his own house.

18. (A) He studied last night because he had to.
    (B) He tried to study last night, but the material was too hard.
    (C) He couldn't study last night because he was very tired.
    (D) He studied last night because he was bored.

19. (A) She goes to a movie every year.
    (B) She hasn't gone to a movie yet this year, but last year she did.
    (C) She doesn't go to a movie unless she has the time.
    (D) She hasn't seen a movie for a long time.

20. (A) He turned around to answer the teacher's question.
    (B) He is an intelligent student.
    (C) He must have been embarrassed.
    (D) He looked in the red book for the answer to the question.

21. (A) On a train.   (C) On a plane.
    (B) On a boat.   (D) On a bus.

22. (A) She is going on vacation.
    (B) She is leaving her job temporarily for health reasons.
    (C) During the summer, she often misses work because of illness.
    (D) She is sick of working all the time.

23. (A) She is disappointed with the results.
    (B) She likes her job very much.
    (C) She is hoping for some improvements in her workplace.
    (D) She is very pleased with the outcome of her meeting.

24. (A) He said he was sorry that he had not announced the test sooner.
    (B) He was sorry that he had forgotten to bring the tests to class.
    (C) He was sorry that he hadn't given the test earlier.
    (D) He said he was sorry that he had not given the results of the test sooner.

25. (A) She is taking a leave of absence from her job because of her health.
    (B) She is not going to return to her job.
    (C) She is right to quit her job.
    (D) She did very good work, but now she is quitting her job.

26. (A) John will be able to buy groceries.
    (B) John doesn't have enough money to buy groceries.
    (C) John wouldn't buy groceries even if he had enough money.
    (D) John can't find his grocery money.

27. (A) Eighty people came to the rally.
    (B) Forty people came to the rally.
    (C) One hundred sixty people came to the rally.
    (D) One hundred people came to the rally.

28. (A) They are going to meet Fred and Mary at the movies if they have time.
    (B) They went to the movies with Fred and Mary, but the theater was closed.
    (C) They couldn't meet Fred and Mary at the movies because they didn't have any money.
    (D) Fred and Mary were supposed to meet them at the movies, but their car broke down.

29. (A) He was supposed to give the awards at the banquet, but he didn't.
    (B) He was given an award, but he refused it.
    (C) He didn't go to the banquet.
    (D) He went to the awards banquet, but he refused to give a speech.

30. (A) He is out of sugar.
    (B) He puts only sugar in his coffee.
    (C) There isn't enough sugar in his coffee.
    (D) He likes sugar, but the coffee he is drinking has too much.

GO ON TO PART B

Part B

DIRECTIONS

In Part B, you will hear longer conversations. After each conversation, you will be asked some questions. The conversations and questions will be *spoken* just one time. They will not be written out for you, so you will have to listen carefully in order to understand and remember what the speaker says.

When you hear a question, read the four possible answers in your test book and decide which one would be the best answer to the question you have heard. Then, on your answer sheet, find the number of the problem and fill in the space that corresponds to the letter of the answer you have chosen.

31. (A) In a clothing store.
    (B) In customs.
    (C) At a bank.
    (D) In a liquor store.

32. (A) 1   (B) 2   (C) 3   (D) 4

33. (A) To make a list of her purchases.
    (B) To open her suitcase.
    (C) To pay $300 duty.
    (D) To show him the bottles of wine.

34. (A) Plants.   (B) Wine.   (C) Meat.   (D) Cash.

35. (A) *The Incredible Adventures of the Martians.*
    (B) *Mission to Mars.*
    (C) *Martian Renaissance.*
    (D) *Captivating Tales of Mars.*

36. (A) Science fiction.   (C) Biography.
    (B) Adventure.   (D) Documentary.

37. (A) One year.   (C) Five years.
    (B) Three years.   (D) Seven years.

38. (A) The crew had some incredible adventures on Mars.
    (B) The crew met some real Martians.
    (C) The Martians captured the crew.
    (D) The ship carried an all-male crew.

GO ON TO PART C

Part C

DIRECTIONS

In Part C, you will hear several talks. After each talk, you will be asked some questions. The talks and questions will be *spoken* just one time. They will not be written out for you, so you will have to listen carefully in order to understand and remember what the speaker says.

When you hear a question, read the four possible answers in your test book and decide which one would be the best answer to the question you have heard. Then, on your answer sheet, find the number of the problem and fill in the space that corresponds to the letter of the answer you have chosen.

39. (A) Spain.
    (B) Latin America.
    (C) Florida.
    (D) America.

40. (A) Soccer.
    (B) Handball.
    (C) Football.
    (D) Horse racing.

41. (A) Jai alai is one of the fastest-moving games.
    (B) Jai alai requires a great deal of skill and endurance.
    (C) Jai alai can be played as singles or doubles.
    (D) It is illegal to bet on Florida jai alai games.

42. (A) Baseball.
    (B) Ping-Pong.
    (C) Handball.
    (D) Badminton.

43. (A) Multiple telegraph.
    (B) Telephone.
    (C) Aviation.
    (D) Acoustics.

44. (A) Acoustical science.
    (B) Aviation.
    (C) Adventure.
    (D) Architecture.

45. (A) He worked very hard, but never achieved success.
    (B) He spent so many years working in aviation because he wanted to be a pilot.
    (C) He dedicated his life to science and the well-being of humankind.
    (D) He worked with the deaf so that he could invent the telephone.

46. (A) Bell was born in the eighteenth century.
    (B) Bell worked with the deaf.
    (C) Bell experimented with the science of acoustics.
    (D) Bell invented a multiple telegraph.

47. (A) 100   (B) 25   (C) 35   (D) 50

48. (A) It is less expensive than term insurance.
    (B) It can have a fixed premium for life.
    (C) It may result in the insured's being able to discontinue premium payments.
    (D) It may result in retirement income.

49. (A) Because the insured must pay for the agent's retirement fund.
    (B) Because it is pure insurance.
    (C) Because part of the money is invested.
    (D) Because it is based on the age of the insured.

50. (A) It is inexpensive.
    (B) One can borrow from the fund that is built up.
    (C) The premium is paid by the interest.
    (D) It requires an easier medical examination than does cash value insurance.

STOP. THIS IS THE END OF THE LISTENING COMPREHENSION SECTION. GO ON TO SECTION 2.

SECTION 2
STRUCTURE AND WRITTEN EXPRESSION

Time: 25 Minutes
40 Questions

Part A

DIRECTIONS

Questions 1–15 are incomplete sentences. Beneath each sentence you will see four words or phrases, marked (A), (B), (C), and (D). Choose the *one* word or phrase that best completes the sentence. Then, on your answer sheet, find the number of the question and fill in the space that corresponds to the letter of the answer you have chosen. Fill in the space so that the letter inside the oval cannot be seen.

1. After the funeral, the residents of the apartment building
_____.
  (A) sent faithfully flowers all weeks to the cemetery
  (B) sent to the cemetery each week flowers faithfully
  (C) sent flowers faithfully to the cemetery each week
  (D) sent each week faithfully to the cemetery flowers

2. Because the first pair of pants did not fit properly, he asked for
_____.
  (A) another pants
  (B) others pants
  (C) the others ones
  (D) another pair

3. The committee has met and _____.
   - (A) they have reached a decision
   - (B) it has formulated themselves some opinions
   - (C) its decision was reached at
   - (D) it has reached a decision

4. Alfred Adams has not _____.
   - (A) lived lonelynessly in times previous
   - (B) never before lived sole
   - (C) ever lived alone before
   - (D) before lived without the company of his friends

5. John's score on the test is the highest in the class; _____.
   - (A) he should study last night
   - (B) he should have studied last night
   - (C) he must have studied last night
   - (D) he must had to study last night

6. Henry will not be able to attend the meeting tonight because _____.
   - (A) he must to teach a class
   - (B) he will be teaching a class
   - (C) of he will teach a class
   - (D) he will have teaching a class

7. Having been served lunch, _____.
   - (A) the problem was discussed by the members of the committee
   - (B) the committee members discussed the problem
   - (C) it was discussed by the committee members the problem
   - (D) a discussion of the problem was made by the members of the committee

8. Florida has not yet ratified the amendment, and _____.
   - (A) several other states hasn't either
   - (B) neither has some of the others states
   - (C) some other states also have not either
   - (D) neither have several other states

9. The chairman requested that _____.
   - (A) the members studied more carefully the problem
   - (B) the problem was more carefulnessly studied
   - (C) with more carefulness the problem could be studied
   - (D) the members study the problem more carefully

10. California relies heavily on income from fruit crops, and _____.
    - (A) Florida also
    - (B) Florida too
    - (C) Florida is as well
    - (D) so does Florida

11. The professor said that _____.
    - (A) the students can turn over their reports on the Monday
    - (B) the reports on Monday could be received from the students by him
    - (C) the students could hand in their reports on Monday
    - (D) the students will on Monday the reports turn in

12. This year will be difficult for this organization because _____.
    - (A) they have less money and volunteers than they had last year
    - (B) it has less money and fewer volunteers than it had last year
    - (C) the last year it did not have as few and little volunteers and money
    - (D) there are fewer money and volunteers that in the last year there were

13. The teachers have had some problems deciding _____.
    (A) when to the students they shall return the final papers
    (B) when are they going to return to the students the final papers
    (C) when they should return the final papers to the students
    (D) the time when the final papers they should return for the students

14. She wanted to serve some coffee to her guests; however, _____.
    (A) she hadn't many sugar
    (B) there was not a great amount of the sugar
    (C) she did not have much sugar
    (D) she was lacking in amount of the sugar

15. There has not been a great response to the sale, _____?
    (A) does there
    (B) hasn't there
    (C) hasn't it
    (D) has there

GO ON TO PART B

Part B

DIRECTIONS

In questions 16–40, each sentence has four underlined words or phrases. The four underlined parts of the sentence are marked (A), (B), (C), and (D). Identify the *one* underlined word or phrase that must be changed in order for the sentence to be correct. Then, on your answer sheet, find the number of the question and fill in the space that corresponds to the letter of the answer you have chosen.

16. The main office of the factory can be found in Maple Street in
        A   B C   D
    New York City.

17. Because there are less members present tonight than there
                      A   B
    were last night, we must wait until the next meeting to vote.
     C   D

18. David is particularly fond of cooking, and he often cooks
              A   B   C
    really delicious meals.
     D

19. The progress made in space travel for the early 1960s is
         A   B   C   D
    remarkable.

20. Sandra has not rarely missed a play or concert since she
                 A   B   C
    was seventeen years old.
         D

21. The governor has not decided how to deal with the new
     A   B   C
    problems already.
         D

22. There was a very interesting news on the radio this morning
         A B   C
    about the earthquake in Italy.
     D

23. The professor had already given the homework assignment
                                      A
    when he had remembered that Monday was a holiday.
           B   C   D

24. Having been beaten by the police for striking an officer,
                       A   B
    the man will cry out in pain.
         C   D

25. This table is not sturdy enough to support a television, and
                    A   B
    that one probably isn't neither.
      C   D

26. The bridge was hitting by a large ship during a sudden storm
                    A   B   C
    last week.
     D

27. The company representative sold to the manager a
         A   B
    sewing machine for forty dollars.
      C   D

28. The taxi driver told the man to don't allow his disobedient son
            A   B   C
    to hang out the window.
         D

29. These televisions are quite popular in Europe, but those ones
                         A   B   C
    are not.
     D

30. Harvey seldom pays his bills on time, and his brother does too.
                  A   B   C   D

31. The price of crude oil used to be a great deal lower than now,
         A   B   C
    wasn't it?
       D

329

32. When <u>an</u> university formulates <u>new regulations</u>, <u>it</u>
         A   B   C

    <u>must relay its</u> decision to the students and faculty.
            D

33. Jim was <u>upset</u> last night <u>because</u> he <u>had to do</u> too
             A   B   C

    many <u>homeworks</u>.
         D

34. There <u>is</u> some <u>scissors</u> <u>in</u> the desk drawer <u>in</u> the bedroom if
         A   B   C   D

    you need them.

35. The Board of Realtors doesn't have any <u>informations</u>
                                          A

    <u>about</u> the <u>increase</u> <u>in rent for</u> this area.
      B   C   D

36. George is not <u>enough intelligent</u> <u>to pass</u> <u>this</u> <u>economics</u> class
                    A   B   C   D

    without help.

37. There were so <u>much</u> people trying to leave
    <u>   </u>
         A   B

    the <u>burning</u> building <u>that</u> the police had a great deal of trouble
           C   D

    controlling them.

38. John lived <u>in</u> New York <u>since</u> 1960 to 1975, but he <u>is now living</u>
            A   B   C

    <u>in</u> Detroit.
    D

39. The fire began <u>in</u> the <u>fifth</u> floor <u>of</u> the hotel, but it
                A   B   C

    soon <u>spread</u> to adjacent floors.
        D

40. Mrs. Anderson bought <u>last week a new sports car</u>; <u>however</u>,
                                     A   B

   she <u>has yet to learn</u> <u>how to operate</u> the manual gearshift.
             C   D

STOP. THIS IS THE END OF THE STRUCTURE AND WRITTEN EXPRESSION SECTION. IF YOU FINISH BEFORE TIME IS UP, CHECK YOUR WORK ON PARTS A AND B OF THIS SECTION ONLY. DO NOT WORK ON ANY OTHER SECTION OF THE TEST.

SECTION 3
READING COMPREHENSION

Time: 55 Minutes
50 Questions

DIRECTIONS

In this section, you will read a number of passages. Each one is followed by approximately ten questions about it. For questions 1–50, choose the *one* best answer, (A), (B), (C), or (D), to each question. Then, find the number of the question on your answer sheet, and fill in the space that corresponds to the letter of the answer you have chosen. Answer all of the questions following a passage on the basis of what is *stated* or *implied* in that passage.

Questions 1 through 10 are based on the following passage.

The Stone Age was a period of history which began in approximately 2 million B.C. and lasted until 3000 B.C. Its name was derived from the stone tools and weapons that modern scientists found. This period was divided into the
(5) Paleolithic, Mesolithic, and Neolithic Ages. During the first period (2 million to 8000 B.C.), the first hatchet and use of fire for heating and cooking were developed. As a result of the Ice Age, which evolved about 1 million years into the Paleolithic Age, people were forced to seek shelter in caves,
(10) wear clothing, and develop new tools.

During the Mesolithic Age (8000 to 6000 B.C.), people made crude pottery and the first fish hooks, took dogs hunting, and developed the bow and arrow, which were used until the fourteenth century A.D.
(15) The Neolithic Age (6000 to 3000 B.C.) saw humankind domesticating sheep, goats, pigs, and cattle, being less nomadic than in previous eras, establishing permanent settlements, and creating governments.

1. Into how many periods was the Stone Age divided?
   (A) 2   (B) 3   (C) 4   (D) 5

2. In line 3, the word "derived" is closest in meaning to
   (A) originated   (C) hallucinated
   (B) destroyed   (D) discussed

3. Which of the following was developed earliest?
   (A) Fish hook   (C) Bow and arrow
   (B) Hatchet   (D) Pottery

4. Which of the following developments is NOT related to the conditions of the Ice Age?
   (A) Farming   (C) Living indoors
   (B) Clothing   (D) Using fire

5. The word "crude" in line 12 is closest in meaning to
   (A) extravagant   (C) vulgar
   (B) complex   (D) primitive

6. The author states that the Stone Age was so named because
   (A) it was very durable like stone
   (B) the tools and weapons were made of stone
   (C) there was little vegetation
   (D) the people lived in stone caves

7. In line 17, "nomadic" is closest in meaning to
   (A) sedentary   (C) primitive
   (B) wandering   (D) inquisitive

8. With what subject is the passage mainly concerned?
   (A) The Neolithic Age   (C) The Stone Age
   (B) The Paleolithic Age (D) The Ice Age

9. Which of the following best describes the Mesolithic Age?
   (A) People were inventive.
   (B) People stayed indoors all the time.
   (C) People were warriors.
   (D) People were crude.

10. In line 17, the word "eras" is closest in meaning to
    (A) families   (B) periods   (C) herds   (D) tools

Questions 11 through 23 are based on the following passage.

Hot boning is an energy-saving technique for the meat processing industry. It has received significant attention in recent years when increased pressure for energy conservation has accentuated the need for more efficient methods of
(5) processing the bovine carcass. Cooling an entire carcass requires a considerable amount of refrigerated space, since bone and trimmable fat are cooled along with the muscle. It is also necessary to space the carcasses adequately in the refrigerated room for better air movement and prevention
(10) of microbial contamination, thus adding to the volume requirements for carcass chillers.

Conventional handling of meat involves holding the beef sides in the cooler for 24 to 36 hours before boning. Chilling in the traditional fashion is also associated with a loss of
(15) carcass weight ranging from 2 percent to 4 percent due to evaporation of moisture from the meat tissue.

Early excision, or hot boning, of muscle prerigor followed by vacuum packaging has several potential advantages. By removing only the edible muscle and fat prerigor, refrigera-
(20) tion space and costs are minimized, boning labor is decreased, and storage yields increased. Because hot boning often results in the toughening of meat, a more recent approach, hot boning following electrical stimulation, has been used to reduce the necessary time of rigor mortis.

(25) Some researchers have found this method beneficial in maintaining tender meat, while others have found that the meat also becomes tough after electrical stimulation.

11. The word "accentuated" in line 4 is closest in meaning to
    (A) de-emphasized
    (B) speeded up
    (C) caused
    (D) highlighted

12. All of the following are mentioned as drawbacks of the conventional method of boning EXCEPT
    (A) Storage space requirements
    (B) Energy waste
    (C) Loss of carcass weight
    (D) Toughness of meat

13. In line 3, the word "pressure" is nearest in meaning to
    (A) urgency
    (B) weight
    (C) flavor
    (D) cooking texture

14. Hot boning is becoming very popular because
    (A) it causes meat to be very tender
    (B) it helps conserve energy and is less expensive than conventional methods
    (C) meat tastes better when the bone is adequately seared along with the meat
    (D) it reduces the weight of the carcass

15. In line 11, "carcass chiller" is nearest in meaning to
    (A) a refrigerator for the animal body
    (B) a method of boning meat
    (C) electrical stimulation of beef
    (D) early excision

16. In line 17, "early excision" is closest in meaning to
    (A) vacuum packaging
    (B) hot boning
    (C) carcass chilling
    (D) electrical stimulation

17. The toughening of meat during hot boning has been combatted by
    (A) following hot boning with electrical stimulation
    (B) tenderizing the meat
    (C) using electrical stimulation before hot boning
    (D) removing only the edible muscle and fat prerigor

18. The word "bovine" in line 5 is nearest in meaning to
    (A) cold   (C) beef
    (B) electrically stimulated   (D) pork

19. The word "this" in line 25 refers to
    (A) hot boning
    (B) hot boning following electrical stimulation
    (C) rigor mortis
    (D) removing edible muscle and fat prerigor

20. In line 5, the word "carcass" is closest in meaning to
    (A) deboned meat   (C) refrigerator
    (B) body   (D) fat

21. The word "considerable" in line 6 is closest in meaning to
    (A) frigid   (B) kind   (C) lesser   (D) substantial

22. One reason it is recommended to remove bones before refrigerating is that
    (A) it makes the meat more tender
    (B) the bones are able to be used for other purposes
    (C) it increases chilling time
    (D) it saves cooling space by not refrigerating parts that will be discarded

23. The word "trimmable" in line 7 is nearest in meaning to
    (A) unsaturated   (C) unhealthy
    (B) removable   (D) chillable

Questions 24 through 31 are based on the following passage.

In 1920, after some thirty-nine years of problems with disease, high costs, and politics, the Panama Canal was officially opened, finally linking the Atlantic and Pacific Oceans by allowing ships to pass through the fifty-mile canal
(5) zone instead of traveling some seven thousand miles around Cape Horn. It takes a ship approximately eight hours to complete the trip through the canal and costs an average of fifteen thousand dollars, one tenth of what it would cost an average ship to round the Horn. More than fifteen thousand
(10) ships pass through its locks each year.

The French initiated the project but sold their rights to the United States, which actually began the construction of the project. The latter will control it until the end of the twentieth century when Panama takes over its duties.

24. Who currently controls the Panama Canal?
    (A) France   (C) Panama
    (B) United States   (D) Canal Zone

25. The word "locks" in line 10 is closest in meaning to
    (A) securities   (C) lakes
    (B) latches   (D) canal gates

26. On the average, how much would it cost a ship to travel around Cape Horn?
    (A) $1,500   (B) $15,000   (C) $150,000   (D) $1,500,000

27. In what year was construction begun on the canal?
    (A) 1881   (B) 1920   (C) 1939   (D) 1999

28. It can be inferred from this passage that
    (A) the canal is a costly project which should be reevaluated
    (B) despite all the problems involved, the project is beneficial
    (C) many captains prefer to sail around Cape Horn because it is less expensive
    (D) problems have made it necessary for three governments to control the canal over the years

29. In line 3, the word "linking" is closest in meaning to
    (A) controlling   (C) detaching
    (B) dispersing   (D) joining

30. In line 11, "initiated" is nearest in meaning to
    (A) purchased   (C) forfeited
    (B) launched   (D) forced

31. All of the following are true EXCEPT
    (A) it costs so much to pass through the locks because very few ships use them
    (B) the United States received the rights to the canal from the French
    (C) a ship can pass through the canal in only eight hours
    (D) passing through the canal saves thousands of miles of travel time around Cape Horn

Questions 32 through 41 are based on the following passage.

    In 776 B.C., the first Olympic Games were held at the foot of Mount Olympus to honor the Greeks' chief god, Zeus. The warm climate for outdoor activities, the need for preparedness in war, and their lifestyle caused the Greeks
(5) to create competitive sports. Only the elite and military could participate at first, but later the games were open to all free Greek males who had no criminal record. The Greeks emphasized physical fitness and strength in their education of youth. Therefore, contests in running, jump-

338

(10) ing, discus and javelin throwing, boxing, and horse and chariot racing were held in individual cities, and the winners competed every four years at Mount Olympus. Winners were greatly honored by having olive wreaths placed on their heads and having poems sung about their deeds.

(15) Originally these contests were held as games of friendship, and any wars in progress were halted to allow the games to take place. They also helped to strengthen bonds among competitors and the different cities represented.

The Greeks attached so much importance to the games

(20) that they calculated time in four-year cycles called "Olympiads," dating from 776 B.C. The contests coincided with religious festivities and constituted an all-out effort on the part of the participants to please the gods. Any who disobeyed the rules were dismissed and seriously punished.

(25) These athletes brought shame not only to themselves, but also to the cities they represented.

32. Which of the following is NOT true?
    (A) Winners placed olive wreaths on their own heads.
    (B) The games were held in Greece every four years.
    (C) Battles were interrupted to participate in the games.
    (D) Poems glorified the winners in song.

33. The word "elite" in line 5 is closest in meaning to
    (A) aristocracy   (C) intellectuals
    (B) brave   (D) muscular

34. Why were the Olympic Games held?
    (A) To stop wars
    (B) To honor Zeus
    (C) To crown the best athletes
    (D) To sing songs about the athletes

35. Approximately how many years ago did these games originate?
    (A) 800 years   (C) 2,300 years
    (B) 1,200 years   (D) 2,800 years

36. What conclusion can we draw about the ancient Greeks?
    (A) They were pacifists.
    (B) They believed athletic events were important.
    (C) They were very simple.
    (D) They couldn't count, so they used "Olympiads" for dates.

37. What is the main idea of this passage?
    (A) Physical fitness was an integral part of the lives of the ancient Greeks.
    (B) The Greeks severely punished those who did not participate in physical fitness programs.
    (C) The Greeks had always encouraged everyone to participate in the games.
    (D) The Greeks had the games coincide with religious festivities so that they could go back to war when the games were over.

38. In line 14, the word "deeds" is closest in meaning to
    (A) accomplishments   (C) documents
    (B) ancestors   (D) property

39. Which of the following was ultimately required of all athletes competing in the Olympics?
    (A) They must have completed military service.
    (B) They had to attend special training sessions.
    (C) They had to be Greek males with no criminal record.
    (D) They had to be very religious.

40. The word "halted" in line 16 means most nearly the same as
    (A) encouraged   (C) curtailed
    (B) started   (D) fixed

41. What is an "Olympiad"?
    (A) The time it took to finish the games
    (B) The time between games
    (C) The time it took to finish a war
    (D) The time it took the athletes to train

Questions 42 through 50 are based on the following passage.

Tampa, Florida, owes a great deal of its growth and prosperity to a Cuban cigar manufacturer named Vicente Martinez Ybor. When civil war broke out in 1869, he was forced to flee his country, and he moved his business to
(5) south Florida. Sixteen years later, labor union problems in Key West caused him to seek a better location along the west coast of the state. He bought a forty-acre tract of land and made plans to set up his cigar factory on the site. This original sixteen-block stretch of land later expanded to one
(10) hundred acres near Tampa. This newly developed area was called Ybor City in his honor. Spanish, Italian, and Cuban immigrants flocked to the area as the demand for workers in the cigar factory increased. One fifth of the city's twenty thousand residents enjoyed the high-paying jobs there. At
(15) the end of the 1800s, José Martí, a Cuban poet and freedom fighter, organized a revolution from Ybor City and managed to get considerable support for his movement. Teddy Roosevelt's "Rough Riders" were stationed there during the Spanish-American War in 1898. Much of the prosperity
(20) of this region is due to Ybor's cigar factory established more than one hundred years ago.

42. Where is Ybor City located?
    (A) South Florida   (C) West Florida
    (B) Cuba   (D) Martí

43. The word "flee" in line 4 means most nearly the same as
    (A) escape   (C) fight
    (B) return to   (D) disembody

44. The word "seek" in line 6 is closest in meaning to
    (A) purchase   (B) pursue   (C) elude   (D) develop

45. Why will people probably continue to remember Ybor's name?
    (A) He suffered a great deal.
    (B) An area was named in his honor.
    (C) He was a Cuban revolutionary.
    (D) He was forced to flee his homeland.

46. In line 12, the word "flocked" is closest in meaning to
    (A) came in large numbers
    (B) escaped hurriedly
    (C) increased rapidly
    (D) prospered greatly

47. In the early years, how many residents of Ybor City worked in the cigar factory?
    (A) 4,000   (B) 5,000   (C) 10,000   (D) 20,000

48. What is the best title for the passage?
    (A) The Spanish-American War
    (B) Cuban Contributions in the Development of Ybor City
    (C) Ybor's Contribution to Developing Part of the Tampa Area
    (D) The Process of Cigar Manufacturing

49. In line 8, "site" is closest in meaning to
    (A) location   (C) vision
    (B) view   (D) indebtedness

50. Who was José Martí?
    (A) A good friend of Ybor
    (B) One of Teddy Roosevelt's "Rough Riders"
    (C) A Cuban writer who sought to free his country
    (D) A worker in the cigar factory

STOP. THIS IS THE END OF THE EXAMINATION. IF YOU FINISH BEFORE TIME IS UP, CHECK YOUR WORK IN THIS SECTION ONLY. DO NOT WORK ON ANY OTHER SECTION OF THE TEST.

PRACTICE TEST 2

SECTION 1
LISTENING COMPREHENSION

Time: Approximately 30 Minutes
50 Questions

Section 1 has three parts. Each part has its own set of directions. Do not take notes while listening or make any marks on the test pages. Notetaking, underlining, or crossing out will be considered cheating on the actual TOEFL exam. Answer the questions following the conversations or talks based on what the speakers have *stated* or *implied*.

For Practice Test 2, restart your Listening Comprehension cassette immediately following Practice Test 1. On the actual TOEFL, you will be given extra time to go on to the next page when you finish a page in the Listening Comprehension section. In the following test, however, you will have only the 12 seconds given after each question. Turn the page as soon as you have marked your answer. Start the cassette now.

Part A

DIRECTIONS

In Part A, you will hear short conversations between two speakers. At the end of each conversation, a third voice will ask a question about what was said. The question will be *spoken* just one time. After you hear a conversation and the question about it, read the four possible answers and decide which one would be the best answer to the question you have heard. Then, on your answer sheet, find the number of the problem and mark your answer.

343

1. (A) Hand the man a drink.
   (B) Drink a diet soft drink.
   (C) Go to the store to buy a drink.
   (D) Go without a soft drink.

2. (A) They both liked it.
   (B) Neither liked it.
   (C) The mother didn't like it, but the father did.
   (D) The mother didn't like it because it wasn't in English.

3. (A) A supermarket.   (C) A pharmacy.
   (B) A department store.   (D) A car repair shop.

4. (A) The teacher postponed the conference.
   (B) There won't be a test this afternoon.
   (C) The students will be attending the conference.
   (D) The students took a science test that afternoon.

5. (A) The program was on too late.
   (B) The rain didn't let up until after the speech.
   (C) He doesn't like the president.
   (D) He had a late class.

6. (A) Lawyer-client.   (C) Dentist-patient.
   (B) Doctor-patient.   (D) Bank teller-customer.

7. (A) There is a quieter place available.
   (B) He doesn't care for tennis matches.
   (C) The noise should die down shortly.
   (D) It's even louder in the meeting room.

8. (A) She's not hungry.
   (B) She's at the orthodontist's.
   (C) The food tastes like an old shoe.
   (D) She's in too much pain.

9. (A) Packing her own groceries.
   (B) A lack of variety in meats.
   (C) The unreasonable prices.
   (D) The attitude of the employees.

10. (A) She does not feel well enough to return to work.
    (B) She hates her work.
    (C) She hasn't finished the assignment.
    (D) She is still unable to walk.

11. (A) Home economics.
    (B) Business administration.
    (C) Microbiology.
    (D) History.

12. (A) It is no longer delicious.
    (B) It makes delicious butter.
    (C) It is the best cheese.
    (D) There are many better cheeses.

13. (A) The game is temporarily delayed because of rain.
    (B) There will be no game if it rains.
    (C) There will be a game regardless of the weather.
    (D) It rains every time there is a game.

14. (A) She knew the answer to the question.
    (B) She had read the material, but she didn't know the answer.
    (C) She was not prepared for class.
    (D) Even though she hadn't read the material, she knew the answer.

15. (A) Thirty people returned the evaluation forms.
    (B) Sixty people filled out the evaluation forms.
    (C) Eight people returned their forms.
    (D) Only thirty people received the evaluation forms.

16. (A) He is a professional musician.
    (B) He is very talented, but he will never be a professional musician because he doesn't practice.
    (C) He practices every day, but he will never be a professional musician.
    (D) He doesn't want to be a professional musician because he wants to practice law.

17. (A) Stay home if the weather is nice.
    (B) Spend the weekend at the beach if the nice weather holds out.
    (C) Stay home because the weather will not be pleasant.
    (D) Go to the beach if the weather improves.

18. (A) Only he saw the terrible accident.
    (B) No one at all saw his terrible accident.
    (C) He saw no one in the accident.
    (D) No one in the terrible accident saw him.

19. (A) She writes and speaks Spanish equally well.
    (B) She both writes and speaks Spanish, but she writes it better.
    (C) Even though she writes Spanish, she speaks it better.
    (D) She doesn't like to write Spanish, but she speaks it.

20. (A) They missed the homework assignment, but they turned it in later.
    (B) They hate each other since their dispute.
    (C) They caught a baby squirrel, but they soon let it go.
    (D) They had an argument, but now they are friends again.

21. (A) A taxi.   (C) A boat.
    (B) A plane.   (D) A bus.

22. (A) He does not want to be helpful.
    (B) He does not understand the math problem.
    (C) He hasn't had a chance to work on the math calculation.
    (D) He has already figured out the problem.

23. (A) Mary works in a nursery.
    (B) Mary's children stay in a nursery while she works.
    (C) Mary takes her children to work with her.
    (D) Mary's children are ill today.

24. (A) He will move to Florida when he quits his job here.
    (B) As soon as his new job in Florida is confirmed, he will move there.
    (C) He wants to move to Florida, but he can't find a job there.
    (D) He plans to move to Florida when he retires.

25. (A) He doesn't like fishing on a hot, summer day.
    (B) Although he likes fishing, he doesn't want to do it on a hot, summer day.
    (C) Fishing is his favorite enjoyment on a hot, summer day.
    (D) He loves to eat hot fish for breakfast in the summer.

26. (A) When the production had begun, they realized that they should have practiced more.
    (B) Before the production began, they reviewed their lines one more time.
    (C) Although they had practiced for months, the production was a flop.
    (D) They went to the theater in two separate cars.

27. (A) She gave the class an assignment.
    (B) She gave the students a hand with their assignments.
    (C) She asked the students to turn in their assignments.
    (D) She asked the students to raise their hands if they wanted to ask a question about the assignment.

28. (A) Stacey will buy their dog.
    (B) After they return from vacation, they are going to buy a dog.
    (C) Stacey will take care of their dog while they are on vacation.
    (D) Stacey will be very tired after the long vacation.

29. (A) It originated in the United States.
    (B) It's very popular in Scotland.
    (C) It originated in the United States, but now it's more popular in Scotland.
    (D) It originated in Scotland, but now it's more popular in the United States.

30. (A) He saw them thirteen years ago.
    (B) They arrived thirty years ago.
    (C) He has not seen them for thirty years.
    (D) He sees them every thirteen years.

GO ON TO PART B

Part B

DIRECTIONS

In Part B, you will hear longer conversations. After each conversation, you will be asked some questions. The conversations and questions will be *spoken* just one time. They will not be written out for you, so you will have to listen carefully in order to understand and remember what the speaker says.

When you hear a question, read the four possible answers in your test book and decide which one would be the best answer to the question you have heard. Then, on your answer sheet, find the number of the problem and fill in the space that corresponds to the letter of the answer you have chosen.

31. (A) She was sick.
    (B) She couldn't make up her mind as to which countries she should visit.
    (C) She couldn't think of a topic for her composition.
    (D) She was totally disorganized.

32. (A) That she take a cruise.
    (B) That she try to get organized.
    (C) That she ride a camel.
    (D) That she write about her trip.

33. (A) Hungary.
    (B) North Africa.
    (C) Egypt.
    (D) The Holy Land.

34. (A) To pack his bags for his trip.
    (B) To write his own composition.
    (C) He's not feeling well.
    (D) To pick up some photographs.

35. (A) Type his paper.
    (B) Help him with his research.
    (C) Present his findings at the July conference.
    (D) Verify his findings.

36. (A) He's about to leave for a new job.
    (B) He wants to present it at a conference.
    (C) His employer has requested it.
    (D) It's very important for his livelihood.

37. (A) July.
    (B) September.
    (C) May.
    (D) February.

38. (A) He's completed typing his notes.
    (B) He's completed the research.
    (C) He's still performing research.
    (D) He's begun typing.

GO ON TO PART C

Part C

DIRECTIONS

In Part C, you will hear several talks. After each talk, you will be asked some questions. The talks and questions will be *spoken* just one time. They will not be written out for you, so you will have to listen carefully in order to understand and remember what the speaker says.

When you hear a question, read the four possible answers in your test book and decide which one would be the best answer to the question you have heard. Then, on your answer sheet, find the number of the problem and fill in the space that corresponds to the letter of the answer you have chosen.

39. (A) Nathaniel Bacon and his friends fought against Indian marauders.
    (B) Bacon and his friends were Piedmont farmers.
    (C) Bacon and a few farmers marched on the capital to protest the Indian raids.
    (D) Governor Berkeley did not listen to the demands of the farmers.

40. (A) Less than 1 year.   (C) 10 years.
    (B) 5 years.   (D) 23 years.

350

41. (A) He was killed by Indians.
    (B) Governor Berkeley had him hanged.
    (C) He succumbed to malaria.
    (D) He was accidently shot by one of the farmers.

42. (A) Death of its sculptor.
    (B) Lack of funds.
    (C) Disinterest in the project.
    (D) Too many Indian raids.

43. (A) Abraham Lincoln.   (C) Thomas Jefferson.
    (B) Franklin Roosevelt.   (D) George Washington.

44. (A) 27 years old.   (C) 60 years old.
    (B) 41 years old.   (D) 74 years old.

45. (A) They bear little resemblance to the people they represent.
    (B) The figures are gigantic, but too serious.
    (C) They portray the people they represent.
    (D) Because they are old and weatherbeaten, the faces are
        disfigured.

46. (A) This magnificent work of art is located very high in the
        Black Hills.
    (B) Four American presidents have been sculpted as a lasting
        memorial to their leadership.
    (C) It took fourteen years to complete the project.
    (D) Gutzon Borglum was near retirement age when he began
        this project.

47. (A) In a chemistry class.
    (B) At a gas station.
    (C) Near an oil well.
    (D) In a nuclear plant.

48. (A) Refined oil.
    (B) Unrefined oil.
    (C) A mixture of simple inorganic compounds.
    (D) The product of burning.

49. (A) By the percentage of nitrogen.
    (B) By the percentage of oxygen.
    (C) By the percentage of hydrogen and carbon.
    (D) By the percentage of sulfur.

50. (A) Oil that has been separated by distilling.
    (B) Oil that has greater than one percent sulfur content.
    (C) Oil that has less than one percent sulfur content.
    (D) Oil that is in its simplest form.

STOP. THIS IS THE END OF THE LISTENING COMPREHENSION SECTION.
GO ON TO SECTION 2.

SECTION 2
STRUCTURE AND WRITTEN EXPRESSION

Time: 25 Minutes
40 Questions

Part A

DIRECTIONS

Questions 1–15 are incomplete sentences. Beneath each sentence you will see four words or phrases, marked (A), (B), (C), and (D). Choose the *one* word or phrase that best completes the sentence. Then, on your answer sheet, find the number of the question and fill in the space that corresponds to the letter of the answer you have chosen. Fill in the space so that the letter inside the oval cannot be seen.

1. Captain Henry, _____ crept slowly through the under-brush.
   - (A) being remote from the enemy,
   - (B) attempting to not encounter the enemy,
   - (C) trying to avoid the enemy,
   - (D) not involving himself in the enemy,

2. Tommy was one _____.
   - (A) of the happy childs of his class
   - (B) of the happiest child in the class
   - (C) child who was the happiest of all the class
   - (D) of the happiest children in the class

3. _____ he began to make friends more easily.
   - (A) Having entered school in the new city, it was found that
   - (B) After entering the new school,
   - (C) When he had been entering the new school,
   - (D) Upon entering into the new school,

4. It is very difficult to stop the cultivation of marijuana because
_____.
   - (A) it grows very carelessly
   - (B) of it's growth without attention
   - (C) it grows well with little care
   - (D) it doesn't care much to grow

5. The fact that space exploration has increased dramatically in the past thirty years _____.
   - (A) is an evidence of us wanting to know more of our solar system
   - (B) indicates that we are very eager to learn all we can about our solar system
   - (C) how we want to learn more about the solar system
   - (D) is pointing to evidence of our intention to know a lot more about what is called our solar system

6. Many of the international problems we are now facing
_____.
   - (A) linguistic incompetencies
   - (B) are the result of misunderstandings
   - (C) are because of not understanding themselves
   - (D) lacks of the intelligent capabilities of understanding each other

7. Mr. Roberts is a noted chemist _____.
   - (A) as well as an effective teacher
   - (B) and too a very efficient teacher
   - (C) but he teaches very good in addition
   - (D) however he teaches very good also

8. Public television stations are different from commercial stations _____.
   - (A) because they receive money differently and different types of shows
   - (B) for money and program types
   - (C) in the areas of funding and programming
   - (D) because the former receives money and has programs differently from the latter

9. Manufacturers often sacrifice quality _____.
   - (A) for a larger profit margin
   - (B) in place of to earn more money
   - (C) to gain more quantities of money
   - (D) and instead earn a bigger amount of profit

10. Automobile production in the United States _____.
    - (A) have taken slumps and rises in recent years
    - (B) has been rather erratic recently
    - (C) has been erratically lately
    - (D) are going up and down all the time

11. A major problem in the construction of new buildings _____.
    - (A) is that windows have been eliminated while air conditioning systems have not been perfected
    - (B) is they have eliminated windows and still don't have good air conditioning
    - (C) is because windows are eliminated but air conditioners don't work good
    - (D) is dependent on the fact that while they have eliminated windows, they are not capable to produce efficient air conditioning systems

12. John said that no other car could go _____.
    (A) so fast like his car
    (B) as fast like his car
    (C) as fast like the car of him
    (D) as fast as his car

13. Her grades have improved, but only _____.
    (A) in a small amount
    (B) very slightly
    (C) minimum
    (D) some

14. While attempting to reach his home before the storm, _____.
    (A) the bicycle of John broke down
    (B) it happened that John's bike broke down
    (C) the storm caught John
    (D) John had an accident on his bicycle

15. The changes in this city have occurred _____.
    (A) with swiftness
    (B) rapidly
    (C) fastly
    (D) in rapid ways

GO ON TO PART B

Part B

DIRECTIONS

In questions 16–40, each sentence has four underlined words or phrases. The four underlined parts of the sentence are marked (A), (B), (C), and (D). Identify the *one* underlined word or phrase that must be changed in order for the sentence to be correct. Then, on your answer sheet, find the number of the question and fill in the space that corresponds to the letter of the answer you have chosen.

16. The officials object <u>to</u> <u>them</u> <u>wearing</u> long dresses for the
                        A   B   C

    inaugural dance <u>at the country club.</u>
                         D

17. Janet is finally used to <u>cook</u> on an electric stove <u>after having</u> a
                           A   B

    gas <u>one</u> <u>for so long.</u>
        C   D

18. He <u>knows</u> to repair <u>the</u> carburetor without <u>taking</u> the whole
         A   B   C

    car <u>apart.</u>
        D

19. Stuart stopped <u>to write</u> his letter <u>because</u> he had to <u>leave</u>
                  A   B   C

    <u>for the hospital.</u>
        D

20. She must <u>retyping</u> the report <u>before</u> she <u>hands it in</u>
            A   B   C

    <u>to the</u> director of financing.
      D

21. How <u>much</u> times <u>did Rick and Jennifer have to</u> do the
         A   B

    experiment before they <u>obtained the results</u> they had
                               C

    <u>been expecting?</u>
        D

22. Each of the <u>students</u> <u>in the</u> accounting class has to type <u>their</u>
               A   B   C

    <u>own</u> research paper this semester.
     D

23. Mrs. Stevens, along <u>with</u> <u>her cousins from</u> New Mexico,

                     A   B
    <u>are</u> planning <u>to attend</u> the festivities.

 C   D

24. They <u>are</u> going <u>to have to</u> <u>leave soon</u>, and <u>so do</u> we.

     A   B   C   D

25. All the <u>students</u> <u>are</u> looking <u>forward spending</u> <u>their</u> free time

         A   B   C   D
    relaxing in the sun this summer.

26. Dresses, skirts, shoes, and <u>children's clothing</u> <u>are advertised</u> <u>at</u>

                              A   B   C
    <u>great</u> reduced prices this weekend.

 D

27. Mary and <u>her sister</u> <u>just bought</u> <u>two new</u> <u>winters</u> coats at the

          A   B   C   D
    clearance sale.

28. <u>A</u> lunch <u>of</u> soup and sandwiches <u>do</u> not <u>appeal to all of</u> the

 A   B   C   D
    students.

29. Some of us <u>have to study</u> <u>their</u> lessons <u>more carefully</u> if we

          A   B   C
    expect <u>to pass</u> this examination.

       D

30. Mr. Peters used to <u>think</u> of <u>hisself</u> <u>as the only</u> president

                A   B   C
    <u>of the company</u>.

   D

31. The instructor advised the students <u>for</u> the <u>procedures</u> to
                                     A   B

    <u>follow</u> <u>in writing</u> the term paper.
     C   D

32. Although both <u>of them</u> <u>are trying</u> <u>to get</u> the scholarship, she
                  A   B   C

    has the <u>highest</u> grades.
         D

33. The new technique <u>calls</u> for <u>heat</u> the mixture before <u>applying</u>
                  A   B   C

    <u>it to the wood.</u>
       D

34. The pilot <u>and the crew</u> <u>distributed</u> the life preservers
               A   B

    <u>between</u> the twenty <u>frantic passengers.</u>
     C   D

35. A <u>five-thousand-dollars</u> reward <u>was offered</u>
     A   B   C

    <u>for the capture of</u> the escaped criminals.
         D

36. The <u>equipment</u> <u>in the office</u> <u>was badly</u> in need of
          A   B   C

    <u>to be repaired.</u>
      D

37. <u>A liter</u> is <u>one of the</u> metric <u>measurements,</u> <u>aren't they?</u>
     A   B   C   D

38. We thought he <u>is</u> planning <u>to go on vacation</u> <u>after</u>
             A   B   C

    <u>the first of</u> the month.
       D

39. There <u>are</u> a large supply <u>of pens</u> and notebooks
         A   B

    <u>in the storeroom</u> <u>to the left of</u> the library entrance.
         C   D

40. The president refuses <u>to accept</u> <u>either</u> of the four
                       A   B

    <u>new proposals</u> <u>made by</u> the contractors.
        C   D

STOP. THIS IS THE END OF THE STRUCTURE AND WRITTEN EXPRESSION SECTION. IF YOU FINISH BEFORE TIME IS UP, CHECK YOUR WORK ON PARTS A AND B OF THIS SECTION ONLY. DO NOT WORK ON ANY OTHER SECTION OF THE TEST.

SECTION 3
READING COMPREHENSION

Time: 55 Minutes
50 Questions

DIRECTIONS

In this section, you will read a number of passages. Each one is followed by approximately ten questions about it. For questions 1–50, choose the *one* best answer, (A), (B), (C), or (D), to each question. Then, find the number of the question on your answer sheet, and fill in the space that corresponds to the letter of the answer you have chosen. Answer all of the questions following a passage on the basis of what is *stated* or *implied* in that passage.

Questions 1 through 10 are based on the following passage.

Napoleon Bonaparte's ambition to control all the area around the Mediterranean Sea led him and his French soldiers to Egypt. After losing a naval battle, they were forced to remain there for three years. In 1799, while (5) constructing a fort, a soldier discovered a piece of stele (a stone pillar bearing an inscription) known as the Rosetta stone, in commemoration of the town near the fort. This famous stone, which would eventually lead to the deciphering of ancient Egyptian hieroglyphics dating to 3100 B.C., (10) was written in three languages: hieroglyphics (picture writing), demotic (a shorthand version of Egyptian hieroglyphics), and Greek. Scientists discovered that the characters, unlike those in English, could be written from right to left and in other directions as well. The direction in which they (15) were read depended on how the characters were arranged. Living elements (animals, people, and body parts) were often the first symbols, and the direction that they faced indicated the direction for reading them.

361

Twenty-three years after the discovery of the Rosetta
(20) stone, Jean François Champollion, a French philologist
fluent in several languages, was able to decipher the first
word—Ptolemy—the name of an Egyptian ruler. This name
was written inside an oval called a "cartouche." Further
investigation revealed that cartouches contained names of
(25) important people of that period. Champollion painstakingly
continued his search and was able to increase his growing
list of known phonetic signs. He and an Englishman,
Thomas Young, worked independently of each other to
unravel the deeply hidden mysteries of this strange lan-
(30) guage. Young believed that sound values could be assigned
to the symbols, while Champollion insisted that the pictures
represented words.

1. All of the following languages were written on the Rosetta
   stone EXCEPT
   (A) French   (C) Greek
   (B) demotic   (D) hieroglyphics

2. All of the following statements are true EXCEPT
   (A) cartouches contained names of prominent people of the
       period
   (B) Champollion and Young worked together in an attempt to
       decipher the hieroglyphics
   (C) one of Napoleon's soldiers discovered the Rosetta stone
   (D) Thomas Young believed that sound values could be
       assigned to the symbols

3. The word "deciphering" in line 8 is closest in meaning to
   (A) decoding   (C) discovery
   (B) downfall   (D) probing

4. The first word deciphered from the Rosetta stone was
   (A) cartouche   (C) demotic
   (B) Ptolemy   (D) Champollion

5. Napoleon's soldiers were in Egypt in 1799 because they were
   (A) celebrating a naval victory
   (B) looking for the Rosetta stone
   (C) waiting to continue their campaign
   (D) trying to decipher the hieroglyphics

6. The person responsible for deciphering the first word was
   (A) Champollion   (C) Ptolemy
   (B) Young   (D) Napoleon

7. Why was the piece of newly discovered stele called the Rosetta stone?
   (A) It was shaped like a rosette.
   (B) It was to honor Napoleon's friend Rosetta.
   (C) The town near the fort was called Rosetta.
   (D) The fort was called Rosetta.

8. In line 1, "ambition" is nearest in meaning to
   (A) aspiration   (C) indifference
   (B) indolence   (D) apathy

9. What is the best title for the passage?
   (A) Napoleon's Great Discovery
   (B) Deciphering the Hieroglyphics of the Rosetta Stone
   (C) Thomas Young's Great Contribution
   (D) The Importance of Cartouches

10. In which lines of the reading passage is the direction for reading hieroglyphics discussed?
    (A) Lines 5–8   (C) Lines 19–22
    (B) Lines 14–18   (D) Lines 25–27

Questions 11 through 20 are based on the following passage.

Sequoyah was a young Cherokee Indian, son of a white trader and an Indian squaw. At an early age, he became fascinated by "the talking leaf," an expression that he used to describe the white man's written records. Although many
(5) believed this "talking leaf" to be a gift from the Great Spirit, Sequoyah refused to accept that theory. Like other Indians of the period, he was illiterate, but his determination to remedy the situation led to the invention of a unique eighty-six-character alphabet based on the sound patterns
(10) that he heard.

His family and friends thought him mad, but while recuperating from a hunting accident, he diligently and independently set out to create a form of communication for his own people as well as for other Indians. In 1821, after
(15) twelve years of work, he had successfully developed a written language that would enable thousands of Indians to read and write.

Sequoyah's desire to preserve words and events for later generations has caused him to be remembered among the
(20) important inventors. The giant redwood trees of California, called "sequoias" in his honor, will further imprint his name in history.

11. What is the most important reason that Sequoyah will be remembered?
    (A) California redwoods were named in his honor.
    (B) He was illiterate.
    (C) He created a unique alphabet.
    (D) He recovered from his madness and helped humankind.

12. The word "squaw" in line 2 is closest in meaning to
    (A) woman   (B) teacher   (C) cook   (D) trader

13. How did Sequoyah's family react to his idea of developing his own "talking leaf"?
    (A) They arranged for his hunting accident.
    (B) They thought he was crazy.
    (C) They decided to help him.
    (D) They asked him to teach them to read and write.

14. What prompted Sequoyah to develop his alphabet?
    (A) People were writing things about him that he couldn't read.
    (B) He wanted to become famous.
    (C) After his hunting accident, he needed something to keep him busy.
    (D) He wanted the history of his people preserved for future generations.

15. In line 7, the word "illiterate" means most nearly the same as
    (A) fierce
    (B) poor
    (C) abandoned
    (D) unable to read or write

16. It is implied that Sequoyah called the written records "the talking leaf" because
    (A) they played music
    (B) when he observed white people reading, they seemed to understand what was written
    (C) he was going mad, and he thought the leaves were talking to him
    (D) it was the only way that the Great Spirit had of communicating with them

17. Sequoyah could best be described as
    (A) determined   (C) backwards
    (B) mad   (D) meek

365

18. What is the best title for the passage?
    (A) Sequoyah's Determination to Preserve the Cherokee Language
    (B) The Origin of the Cherokee Language
    (C) Sequoyah's Madness Leads to a New Language
    (D) The Origin of the "Sequoia" Trees in California

19. In line 3, "fascinated" is closest in meaning to
    (A) absorbed   (C) confused
    (B) exasperated   (D) imaginative

20. All of the following are true EXCEPT
    (A) Sequoyah developed a form of writing with the help of the Cherokee tribe
    (B) Sequoyah was a very observant young man
    (C) Sequoyah spent twelve years developing his alphabet
    (D) Sequoyah was honored by having some trees named after him

Questions 21 through 30 are based on the following passage.

   The mighty, warlike Aztec nation existed in Mexico from
1195 to 1521. The high priests taught the people that the sun
would shine, the crops would grow, and the empire would
prosper only if the gods were appeased by human sacrifices
(5) and blood offerings from all levels of their society. The
priests practiced forms of self-mutilation, such as piercing
their tongues with thorns and flagellating themselves with
thorn branches. They collected the small amount of blood
produced by these practices and offered it to Huitzilopochtli
(10) and Quetzalcoatl, their chief gods. They insisted that all
Aztecs needed to make some sort of daily sacrifice. Warriors
were promised a place of honor in the afterlife if they died
courageously in battle.
   The Aztecs were constantly at war in order to have
(15) enough captives from battle to serve as sacrificial victims.

366

The prisoners were indoctrinated before their deaths into believing that they, too, would find a place of honor in the afterlife and that their death insured the prosperity of the great Aztec nation. After being heavily sedated with mari-
(20) juana or a similar drug, they were led up the steps to the top of the ceremonial centers where they accepted their fate passively, and their palpitating hearts were removed from their bodies as an offering to the gods.

21. Why did the Aztecs offer human sacrifices?
    (A) They were cruel and inhuman.
    (B) They believed they had to pacify the gods.
    (C) They wanted to force the citizens to obey.
    (D) They wanted to deter crime.

22. Before the sacrifices, the victims were
    (A) tortured and harassed
    (B) fed and entertained
    (C) brainwashed and drugged
    (D) interrogated and drugged

23. In what manner did the victims accept their destiny?
    (A) Submissively   (C) Violently
    (B) Rebelliously   (D) Notoriously

24. The word "appeased" in line 4 is closest in meaning to
    (A) glorified   (C) angered
    (B) assaulted   (D) satisfied

25. What is the best title for the passage?
    (A) The Aztecs' Need to Offer Human Sacrifice
    (B) Aztec Victims
    (C) The History of the Mighty Aztec Nation
    (D) Aztec High Priests

26. What did the Aztecs believe the gods craved in order to ensure the people's survival?
    (A) Sunshine   (B) Blood   (C) Thorns   (D) Drugs

27. Which of the following is NOT given as a reason for offering human sacrifice?
    (A) The sun would not rise.
    (B) The crops would not grow.
    (C) The warriors would not be famous.
    (D) The empire would not be successful.

28. Why were the victims willing to accept their fate?
    (A) They liked to see the sun shine.
    (B) They wanted everyone to see them at the top of the ceremonial centers.
    (C) They were made to believe they would have a place of honor in eternity.
    (D) They liked to take drugs.

29. Which of the following is described as a form of self-torture that the high priests practiced?
    (A) Indoctrination
    (B) Heavy sedation
    (C) Piercing their tongues
    (D) Sacrificing victims

30. In line 1, the word "mighty" is closest in meaning to
    (A) primitive   (C) meticulous
    (B) unimposing   (D) powerful

Questions 31 through 41 are based on the following passage.

Petroleum products, such as gasoline, kerosene, home heating oil, residual fuel oil, and lubricating oils, come from one source—crude oil found below the earth's surface, as well as under large bodies of water, from a few hundred feet

(5) below the surface to as deep as 25,000 feet into the earth's interior. Sometimes crude oil is secured by drilling a hole into the earth, but more dry holes are drilled than those producing oil. Either pressure at the source or pumping forces crude oil to the surface.

(10) Crude oil wells flow at varying rates, from about ten to thousands of barrels per hour. Petroleum products are always measured in forty-two-gallon barrels.

Petroleum products vary greatly in physical appearance: thin, thick, transparent, or opaque, but regardless, their

(15) chemical composition is made up of only two elements: carbon and hydrogen, which form compounds called hydrocarbons. Other chemical elements found in union with the hydrocarbons are few and are classified as impurities. Trace elements are also found, but in such minute quantities that

(20) they are disregarded. The combination of carbon and hydrogen forms many thousands of compounds which are possible because of the various positions and unions of these two atoms in the hydrocarbon molecule.

The various petroleum products are refined by heating

(25) crude oil and then condensing the vapors. These products are the so-called light oils, such as gasoline, kerosene, and distillate oil. The residue remaining after the light oils are distilled is known as heavy or residual fuel oil and is used mostly for burning under boilers. Additional complicated

(30) refining processes rearrange the chemical structure of the hydrocarbons to produce other products, some of which are used to upgrade and increase the octane rating of various types of gasoline.

31. All of the following are true EXCEPT
    (A) crude oil is found below land and water
    (B) crude oil is always found a few hundred feet below the surface
    (C) pumping and pressure force crude oil to the surface
    (D) many petroleum products are obtained from crude oil

32. The word "minute" in line 19 is closest in meaning to
    (A) instant   (B) huge   (C) insignificant   (D) timely

33. Many thousands of hydrocarbon compounds are possible because
    (A) the petroleum products vary greatly in physical appearance
    (B) complicated refining processes rearrange the chemical structure
    (C) the two atoms in the molecule assume many positions
    (D) the pressure needed to force it to the surface causes molecular transformation

34. In line 32, the word "upgrade" is closest in meaning to
    (A) improve   (C) charge
    (B) counteract   (D) unite

35. Which of the following is true?
    (A) The various petroleum products are produced by filtration.
    (B) Heating and condensing produce the various products.
    (C) Chemical separation is used to produce the various products.
    (D) Mechanical means, such as centrifuging, are used to produce the various products.

36. The word "opaque" in line 14 means most nearly the same as
    (A) transparent   (B) turbid   (C) light   (D) crude

37. How is crude oil brought to the surface?
    (A) Expansion of the hydrocarbons
    (B) Pressure and pumping
    (C) Vacuum created in the drilling pipe
    (D) Expansion and contraction of the earth's surface

38. All of the following are listed as light oils EXCEPT
    (A) Distillate oil   (C) Lubricating oil
    (B) Gasoline   (D) Kerosene

39. What are the principal components of all petroleum products?
    (A) Hydrogen and carbon
    (B) Residual fuel oils
    (C) Crude oils
    (D) Refined substances

40. The word "condensing" in line 25 is nearest in meaning to
    (A) cooling   (C) diluting
    (B) expanding   (D) refuting

41. The word "they" in line 20 refers to
    (A) impurities   (C) hydrocarbons
    (B) minute quantities   (D) trace elements

Questions 42 through 50 are based on the following passage.

In the United States, presidential elections are held in years evenly divisible by four (1884, 1900, 1964, etc.). Since 1840, American presidents elected in years ending with zero have died in office, with one exception. William H. Harri-
(5) son, the man who served the shortest term, died of pneumonia only several weeks after his inauguration.

Abraham Lincoln was one of four presidents who were assassinated. He was elected in 1860, and his untimely death came just five years later. James A. Garfield, a former

371

(10) Union army general from Ohio, was shot during his first
year in office (1881) by a man to whom he wouldn't give a
job. While in his second term of office (1901), William
McKinley, another Ohioan, attended the Pan-American
Exposition in Buffalo, New York. During the reception, he
(15) was assassinated while shaking hands with some of the
guests. John F. Kennedy was assassinated in 1963 in Dallas
only three years after his election.

Three years after his election in 1920, Warren G. Harding
died in office. Although it was never proved, many believe
(20) he was poisoned. Franklin D. Roosevelt was elected four
times (1932, 1936, 1940, and 1944), the only man to serve so
long a term. He had contracted polio in 1921 and eventually
died of the illness in 1945.

Ronald Reagan, who was elected in 1980 and re-elected
(25) four years later, suffered an assassination attempt but did
not succumb to the assassin's bullets. He was the first to
break the long chain of unfortunate events. Will the
candidate in the election of 2000 also be as lucky?

42. All of the following were election years EXCEPT
(A) 1960   (B) 1930   (C) 1888   (D) 1824

43. Which president served the shortest term in office?
(A) Abraham Lincoln   (C) William McKinley
(B) Warren G. Harding   (D) William H. Harrison

44. Which of the following is true?
(A) All presidents elected in years ending in zero have died in
office.
(B) Only presidents from Ohio have died in office.
(C) Franklin D. Roosevelt completed four terms as president.
(D) Four American presidents have been assassinated.

45. How many presidents elected in years ending in zero since 1840
have died in office?
(A) 7   (B) 5   (C) 4   (D) 3

46. The word "inauguration" in line 6 means most nearly the same as
    (A) election
    (B) acceptance speech
    (C) swearing-in ceremony
    (D) campaign

47. All of the following presidents were assassinated EXCEPT
    (A) John F. Kennedy
    (B) Franklin D. Roosevelt
    (C) Abraham Lincoln
    (D) James A. Garfield

48. The word "whom" in line 11 refers to
    (A) Garfield
    (B) Garfield's assassin
    (C) a Union army general
    (D) McKinley

49. The word "assassinated" in line 8 is closest in meaning to
    (A) murdered
    (B) decorated
    (C) honored
    (D) sickened

50. In line 22, "contracted" is closest in meaning to
    (A) communicated about
    (B) developed
    (C) agreed about
    (D) notified

STOP. THIS IS THE END OF THE EXAMINATION. IF YOU FINISH BEFORE TIME IS UP, CHECK YOUR WORK IN THIS SECTION ONLY. DO NOT WORK ON ANY OTHER SECTION OF THE TEST.

PRACTICE TEST 3

SECTION 1
LISTENING COMPREHENSION

Time: Approximately 30 Minutes
50 Questions

Section 1 has three parts. Each part has its own set of directions. Do not take notes while listening or make any marks on the test pages. Notetaking, underlining, or crossing out will be considered cheating on the actual TOEFL exam. Answer the questions following the conversations or talks based on what the speakers have *stated* or *implied*.

For Practice Test 3, restart your Listening Comprehension cassette immediately following Practice Test 2. On the actual TOEFL, you will be given extra time to go on to the next page when you finish a page in the Listening Comprehension section. In the following test, however, you will have only the 12 seconds given after each question. Turn the page as soon as you have marked your answer. Start the cassette now.

Part A

DIRECTIONS

In Part A, you will hear short conversations between two speakers. At the end of each conversation, a third voice will ask a question about what was said. The question will be *spoken* just one time. After you hear a conversation and the question about it, read the four possible answers and decide which one would be the best answer to the question you have heard. Then, on your answer sheet, find the number of the problem and mark your answer.

1. (A) April.   (B) May.   (C) June.   (D) July.

374

2. (A) Philadelphia.   (C) Doctors.
   (B) Chapmans.   (D) Arizona.

3. (A) He'll see if he can get the computer going.
   (B) It's a very good computer.
   (C) Dana has a copy of the manual in the back office.
   (D) The woman was wise to have copied her data.

4. (A) A gas station.
   (B) A police station.
   (C) A lost-and-found department.
   (D) A bar.

5. (A) Jason Daniels isn't home right now.
   (B) The caller dialed the wrong number.
   (C) Jason Daniels can't come to the phone right now.
   (D) Jason Daniels doesn't want to speak to the caller.

6. (A) She's on a committee.
   (B) She's been working late.
   (C) She exercises too much.
   (D) She's trying to budget her sleep.

7. (A) Better.   (B) Sick.   (C) Fine.   (D) Tired.

8. (A) No, because it's not for sale.
   (B) Yes, because he has plenty of money.
   (C) Yes, if he borrows the money from the woman.
   (D) No, because he didn't bring enough money.

9. (A) Europe.   (C) Canada.
   (B) Where the speakers are.   (D) California.

10. (A) Her car is being repaired at the gas station.
    (B) Frank is going to the gas station to pick up her car.
    (C) She has gone to get her gas tank filled with gasoline.
    (D) Her car isn't working properly because of the type of gasoline that she is using.

11. (A) Although they knew there was going to be a meeting, they didn't come.
    (B) They didn't want to attend the meeting, but they did anyway.
    (C) They didn't know about the meeting.
    (D) They didn't let anybody know about the meeting, so nobody attended.

12. (A) He made the best grade in his class.
    (B) He is an exceptionally good student.
    (C) His classmates made good grades, but he didn't.
    (D) He is one of the better students in his class.

13. (A) The dean was asked to question several students.
    (B) The humanities professor questioned several students.
    (C) The humanities professor was able to answer the students' questions.
    (D) The humanities professor has asked the dean a question about some students.

14. (A) Refuse to work.
    (B) Leave early.
    (C) Request to work overtime.
    (D) Ask for assistance.

15. (A) He went to the concert because he didn't want to work.
    (B) He didn't go to the concert because he had too much work to do.
    (C) Although he had a lot of work to do, he went to the concert.
    (D) He never goes to a concert if he has work to do.

16. (A) He lost the library's new books.
    (B) He is going to the new library to look for some books.
    (C) He may keep the library books longer.
    (D) He had to pay a late fee for the books.

17. (A) He is afraid to start smoking because of the hazardous effects.
    (B) He is afraid he'll become fat if he stops smoking.
    (C) He is afraid that he will become more nervous if he stops smoking.
    (D) He doesn't realize the possible dangers of smoking.

18. (A) He studies regularly, but his grades are suffering.
    (B) He is so lazy that he never gets good grades.
    (C) He hasn't studied lately but will likely get good grades.
    (D) He probably will not pass because he hasn't studied.

19. (A) His meat wasn't tender.
    (B) The speaker did not have a good character.
    (C) It was difficult to meet new people in the crowd.
    (D) The meeting was cut short.

20. (A) He never forgets when he has a meeting.
    (B) It seems that he forgot about their meeting.
    (C) He should have canceled the meeting.
    (D) He has to come to the meeting.

21. (A) Vegetables.   (B) Fruit.   (C) Meat.   (D) Cookies.

22. (A) They couldn't afford a honeymoon.
    (B) They went to Puerto Rico.
    (C) They went to St. Augustine.
    (D) They are still planning on going to Puerto Rico.

23. (A) The first hot dog came from Germany.
    (B) Hot dogs originated in the United States.
    (C) Some hot dogs are made from reindeer meat.
    (D) Even countries like Finland have a food similar to hot dogs.

24. (A) His work is too simple to keep him interested.
    (B) He has no time to relax.
    (C) He has a flat tire.
    (D) He has no work to do.

25. (A) Tiffany is Stephanie's mother.
    (B) Tiffany and Stephanie are sisters.
    (C) Tiffany is older than Stephanie.
    (D) Tiffany is younger than Stephanie.

26. (A) To find out how long it will take to repair the car.
    (B) To find a different repairman.
    (C) To find out what it will probably cost before the work is done.
    (D) To repair it himself.

27. (A) She watched TV last night instead of working on her paper.
    (B) She didn't watch TV last night because she had to write a paper.
    (C) She wrote her paper last night while she was watching TV.
    (D) She is writing a TV script.

28. (A) Franklin admired the deer's beauty from his bedroom window.
    (B) Franklin closed the door quickly.
    (C) Franklin shot a deer with a rifle.
    (D) Franklin took a photograph of a deer.

29. (A) Start typing immediately.
    (B) Have her paper typed by somebody else.
    (C) Change her topic.
    (D) Find a different typing service.

30. (A) Yolanda injured Anna.
    (B) Yolanda had to run downtown last week.
    (C) Yolanda went downtown to exercise.
    (D) Yolanda met Anna downtown unexpectedly.

GO ON TO PART B

Part B

DIRECTIONS

In Part B, you will hear longer conversations. After each conversation, you will be asked some questions. The conversations and questions will be *spoken* just one time. They will not be written out for you, so you will have to listen carefully in order to understand and remember what the speaker says.

When you hear a question, read the four possible answers in your test book and decide which one would be the best answer to the question you have heard. Then, on your answer sheet, find the number of the problem and fill in the space that corresponds to the letter of the answer you have chosen.

31. (A) He was crazy.
    (B) They thought he was dead.
    (C) He had many broken bones.
    (D) He fell out of a plane.

32. (A) On a plane.
    (B) On television.
    (C) On the ground.
    (D) In a hospital.

33. (A) He fell out of a plane.
    (B) His two parachutes didn't open.
    (C) He fell while walking.
    (D) A parachute fell on him.

34. (A) He died.
    (B) He jumped from a plane again.
    (C) He broke his leg.
    (D) He went crazy.

35. (A) Dentist-patient.
    (B) Doctor-patient.
    (C) Teacher-student.
    (D) Pharmacist-customer.

36. (A) In a few days.
    (B) Before leaving the office.
    (C) Very slowly.
    (D) Soon enough.

37. (A) Some medicine.
    (B) Some tests.
    (C) Exhaling slowly.
    (D) Filling her lungs with air.

38. (A) She does not have enough air in her lungs.
    (B) She's exhaling too slowly.
    (C) She didn't do well in her tests.
    (D) She has a little congestion.

GO ON TO PART C

Part C

DIRECTIONS

In Part C, you will hear several talks. After each talk, you will be asked some questions. The talks and questions will be *spoken* just one time. They will not be written out for you, so you will have to listen carefully in order to understand and remember what the speaker says.

When you hear a question, read the four possible answers in your test book and decide which one would be the best answer to the question you have heard. Then, on your answer sheet, find the number of the problem and fill in the space that corresponds to the letter of the answer you have chosen.

39. (A) 2   (B) 5   (C) 3   (D) 7

40. (A) They attracted the attention of a private airplane.
    (B) They ran out of gas.
    (C) Some fishermen spotted them.
    (D) Their families finally found them.

41. (A) They knew that they had run out of fuel.
    (B) Their families had reported them missing.
    (C) They hadn't met the private airplane when it was due to arrive.
    (D) It was starting to get dark.

42. (A) 15 miles.   (B) 7½ miles.   (C) 2 miles.   (D) 5 miles.

43. (A) To plan a special diet for the patient to lose weight.
    (B) To show someone how to read an x-ray.
    (C) To get the patient to join an exercise class.
    (D) To inform the patient about how to deal with his illness.

44. (A) She talked with a chiropractor.
    (B) She read the x-rays.
    (C) She did some back stretching exercises.
    (D) She took some pain killers.

45. (A) Osteoarthritis.
    (B) Curvature of the spine.
    (C) Pinched nerves.
    (D) Muscle spasms.

46. (A) A painter.
    (B) A museum guide.
    (C) An art critic.
    (D) A friend of Dali.

47. (A) Perfume.
    (B) Leather goods.
    (C) Furniture.
    (D) Jewelry.

48. (A) A toreador.
    (B) Gala.
    (C) Columbus.
    (D) Lincoln.

49. (A) Landscapes.
    (B) Seascapes.
    (C) Hand craftsmanship.
    (D) Surrealism.

50. (A) Toreadors.
    (B) Slave markets.
    (C) Landscapes.
    (D) Limp watches.

STOP. THIS IS THE END OF THE LISTENING COMPREHENSION SECTION.
GO ON TO SECTION 2.

SECTION 2
STRUCTURE AND WRITTEN EXPRESSION

Time: 25 Minutes
40 Questions

Part A

DIRECTIONS

Questions 1–15 are incomplete sentences. Beneath each sentence you will see four words or phrases, marked (A), (B), (C), and (D). Choose the *one* word or phrase that best completes the sentence. Then, on your answer sheet, find the number of the question and fill in the space that corresponds to the letter of the answer you have chosen. Fill in the space so that the letter inside the oval cannot be seen.

1. The attorney told his client that _____.
   (A) they had little chance of winning the case
   (B) the case was of a small chance to win
   (C) it was nearly impossible to win him the case
   (D) the case had a minimum chance to be won by him

2. One of the professor's greatest attributes is _____.
   (A) when he gives lectures
   (B) how in the manner that he lectures
   (C) the way to give lectures
   (D) his ability to lecture

3. The bank sent a notice to its customers which contained
   _____.

   (A) a remembrance that interest rates were to raise the
   following month
   (B) a reminder that a raise in interest rates was the month
   following
   (C) to remember that the interest rates were going up next
   month
   (D) a reminder that the interest rates would rise the following
   month

4. _____ was the day before yesterday.
   (A) The France's Independence Day
   (B) The day of the French independence
   (C) French's Independence Day
   (D) France's Independence Day

5. It was not until she had arrived home _____ remem-
   bered her appointment with the doctor.
   (A) when she
   (B) that she
   (C) and she
   (D) she

6. George would certainly have attended the proceedings
   _____.
   (A) if he didn't get a flat tire
   (B) if the flat tire hadn't happened
   (C) had he not had a flat tire
   (D) had the tire not flattened itself

7. _____ received law degrees as today.
   (A) Never so many women have
   (B) Never have so many women
   (C) The women aren't ever
   (D) Women who have never

8. The students liked that professor's course because
_____.
   (A) there was few if any homework
   (B) not a lot of homework
   (C) of there wasn't a great amount of homework
   (D) there was little or no homework

9. George _____ he could improve his test scores, but he
did not have enough time to study.
   (A) knew to
   (B) knew how
   (C) knew how that
   (D) knew how to

10. _____, he would have come to class.
   (A) If Mike is able to finish his homework
   (B) Would Mike be able to finish his homework
   (C) If Mike could finish his homework
   (D) If Mike had been able to finish his homework

11. Lee contributed fifty dollars, but he wishes he could contribute
_____.
   (A) one other fifty dollars
   (B) the same amount also
   (C) another fifty
   (D) more fifty dollars

12. The people at the party were worried about Janet because no
one was aware _____ she had gone.
   (A) where that
   (B) of where
   (C) of the place where
   (D) the place

13. Since he changed professions, Fred's yearly income has
_____.
    (A) nearly tripled
    (B) got almost three times bigger
    (C) almost grown by three times
    (D) just about gone up three times

14. Nancy hasn't begun working on her Ph.D. _____
working on her master's.
    (A) still because she is yet
    (B) yet as a result she is still
    (C) yet because she is still
    (D) still while she is already

15. The director of this organization must know _____.
    (A) money management, selling, and able to satisfy the stock-
holders
    (B) how to manage money, selling his product, and be able to
satisfy stockholders
    (C) how to manage money, sell his product, and satisfy the
stockholders
    (D) money management, selling, the idea of being able to
satisfy the stockholders

Go on to Part B

Part B

DIRECTIONS

In questions 16–40, each sentence has four underlined words or
phrases. The four underlined parts of the sentence are marked (A),
(B), (C), and (D). Identify the *one* underlined word or phrase that
must be changed in order for the sentence to be correct. Then, on
your answer sheet, find the number of the question and fill in the
space that corresponds to the letter of the answer you have chosen.

16. She wishes that we <u>didn't send</u> <u>her the candy</u> yesterday
                                    A   B
    <u>because</u> she's <u>on</u> a diet.
      C   D

17. They are <u>planning on</u> <u>attending</u> the convention <u>next</u> month,
                  A   B   C
    and <u>so I am</u>.
        D

18. Today was <u>such beautiful</u> day that I couldn't bring <u>myself</u>
                      A   B
    <u>to complete</u> all <u>my chores</u>.
        C   D

19. <u>While</u> they <u>were</u> away at the beach, they allowed
      A   B
    <u>their neighbors</u> <u>use</u> their barbeque grill.
         C   D

20. The artist tried <u>stimulate</u> <u>interest in</u> painting <u>by taking</u> his
                      A   B   C
    students <u>to the</u> museums.
         D

21. Mumps <u>are</u> a very <u>common disease</u> <u>which</u> <u>usually</u> affects
         A   B   C   D
    children.

22. Nancy said <u>that</u> she <u>went</u> <u>to</u> the supermarket
              A   B C
    <u>before coming</u> home.
         D

23. Before she moved here, Arlene had been president
    A   B
    of the organization since four years.
       C   D

24. Each of the nurses report to the operating room when
         A   B
    his or her name is called.
        C   D

25. The athlete, together with his coach and several relatives,
         A   B   C
    are traveling to the Olympic Games.
    D

26. Professor Duncan teaches both anthropology as well as
                       A   B   C
    sociology each fall.
            D

27. My brother is in California on vacation, but I wish he was here
                 A   B   C
    so that he could help me repair my car.
                          D

28. I certainly appreciate him telling us about the delay in
       A   B   C
    delivering the materials because we had planned to begin work
    D
    tomorrow.

29. The chemistry instructor explained the experiment in
                                                      A
    such of a way that it was easily understood.
        B   C   D

30. Rudolph Nureyev <u>has become</u> one of the <u>greatest</u> <u>dancer</u> that
    　　　　　　　　　　　A　　　　　　　　　B　　　　C
    the ballet world has <u>ever known</u>.
    　　　　　　　　　　　　D

31. He has <u>less</u> friends in <u>his</u> classes now <u>than</u> he had <u>last year</u>.
    　　　　　A　　　　　　　B　　　　　　　C　　　　　　D

32. The town we visited <u>was</u> a <u>four-days</u> journey from our hotel, so
    　　　　　　　　　　　　A　　　　B
    we <u>took</u> the train instead <u>of the</u> bus.
    　　　C　　　　　　　　　　　D

33. The influence of the <u>nation's</u> literature, art, and <u>science</u>
    　　　　　　　　　　　　A　　　　　　　　　　　　　　　B
    <u>have</u> captured <u>widespread</u> attention.
    　　C　　　　　　　D

34. The leader emphasized <u>the need</u> <u>for justice</u> and equality
    　　　　　　　　　　　　　A　　　　　B
    <u>between</u> his <u>people</u>.
    　　C　　　　D

35. <u>Many</u> of the population in the <u>rural areas</u> <u>is</u>
    　A　　　　　　　　　　　　　　B
    <u>composed of</u> manual <u>laborers</u>.
    　　C　　　　　　　D

36. Several people <u>have</u> <u>apparent</u> tried to change
    　　　　　　　　　A　　　B
    <u>the man's mind</u>, but he refuses <u>to listen</u>.
    　　C　　　　　　　　　　　　D

37. Keith is one of <u>the</u> <u>most</u> intelligent boys <u>of</u> the <u>science</u> class.
    　　　　　　　　　A　　B　　　　　　　　　　C　　　　D

389

38. The girls <u>were sorry</u> to <u>had missed</u> the singers <u>when</u> they
             A   B   C

    <u>arrived at</u> the airport.
      D

39. When Keith visited Alaska, he <u>lived</u> in <u>a</u> igloo in the winter
                                 A   B

    months <u>as well as</u> in the spring.
       C   D

40. The harder he <u>tried</u>, the <u>worst</u> he <u>danced</u> before the
               A   B   C

    <u>large</u> audience.
      D

STOP. THIS IS THE END OF THE STRUCTURE AND WRITTEN EXPRESSION SECTION. IF YOU FINISH BEFORE TIME IS UP, CHECK YOUR WORK ON PARTS A AND B OF THIS SECTION ONLY. DO NOT WORK ON ANY OTHER SECTION OF THE TEST.

SECTION 3
READING COMPREHENSION

Time: 55 Minutes
50 Questions

DIRECTIONS

In this section, you will read a number of passages. Each one is followed by approximately ten questions about it. For questions 1–50, choose the *one* best answer, (A), (B), (C), or (D), to each question. Then, find the number of the question on your answer sheet, and fill in the space that corresponds to the letter of the answer you have chosen. Answer all questions following a passage on the basis of what is *stated* or *implied* in that passage.

Questions 1 through 10 are based on the following passage.

Elizabeth Blackwell was born in England in 1821 and emigrated to New York City when she was ten years old. One day she decided that she wanted to become a doctor. That was nearly impossible for a woman in the middle of the
(5) nineteenth century. After writing many letters seeking admission to medical schools, she was finally accepted by a doctor in Philadelphia. So determined was she that she taught school and gave music lessons to earn money for her tuition.
(10) In 1849, after graduation from medical school, she decided to further her education in Paris. She wanted to be a surgeon, but a serious eye infection forced her to abandon the idea.

Upon returning to the United States, she found it difficult
(15) to start her own practice because she was a woman. By 1857, Elizabeth and her sister, also a doctor, along with another female doctor, managed to open a new hospital, the first for women and children. Besides being the first female physi-

391

cian in the United States and founding her own hospital, she
(20) also established the first medical school for women.

1. Why couldn't Elizabeth Blackwell realize her dream of becom-
ing a surgeon?
(A) She couldn't get admitted to medical school.
(B) She decided to further her education in Paris.
(C) A serious eye infection halted her quest.
(D) It was difficult for her to start a practice in the United
States.

2. What main obstacle almost destroyed Elizabeth's chances for
becoming a doctor?
(A) She was a woman.
(B) She wrote too many letters.
(C) She couldn't graduate from medical school.
(D) She couldn't establish her hospital.

3. How many years elapsed between her graduation from medical
school and the opening of her hospital?
(A) 8   (B) 10   (C) 19   (D) 36

4. All of the following are "firsts" in the life of Elizabeth Blackwell
EXCEPT
(A) she became the first female physician in the United States
(B) she was the first woman surgeon in the United States
(C) she and several other women founded the first hospital for
women and children
(D) she established the first medical school for women

5. How old was Elizabeth Blackwell when she graduated from
medical school?
(A) 10   (B) 21   (C) 28   (D) 36

6. The word "abandon" in line 12 is closest in meaning to
(A) undertake   (C) continue
(B) give up   (D) look into

7. What is the main idea of this passage?
   (A) Elizabeth Blackwell overcame serious obstacles to become the first woman doctor in the United States.
   (B) Elizabeth Blackwell had to abandon her plans to become a doctor because of an eye infection.
   (C) Elizabeth Blackwell even taught music to pay for her medical studies.
   (D) Elizabeth Blackwell founded the first medical school for women.

8. The word "founding" in line 19 means most nearly the same as
   (A) locating   (C) establishing
   (B) looking for   (D) buying

9. Why was it nearly impossible for Elizabeth Blackwell to get into medical school?
   (A) She had a serious eye infection.
   (B) She had little or no money to pay tuition.
   (C) She wanted to be part of a profession that no woman had ever entered before.
   (D) Her family didn't want her to be a doctor.

10. The reason Elizabeth Blackwell could not become a surgeon is explained in lines
    (A) 4–5   (B) 8–9   (C) 11–13   (D) 14–15

Questions 11 through 21 are based on the following passage.

Glands manufacture and secrete necessary substances. Exocrine glands secrete their products through ducts, but endocrine glands, or ductless glands, release their products directly into the bloodstream.

(5)   One important endocrine gland is the thyroid gland. It is in the neck and has two lobes, one on each side of the windpipe. The thyroid gland collects iodine from the blood and produces thyroxine, an important hormone, which it

stores in an inactive form. When thyroxine is needed by the
(10) body, the thyroid gland secretes it directly into the bloodstream. Thyroxine is combined in the body cells with other
chemicals and affects many functions of the body.

The thyroid gland may be underactive or overactive,
resulting in problems. An underactive thyroid causes hypo-
(15) thyroidism, while an overactive one causes hyperthyroidism.
The former problem, called myxedema in adults and cretinism in children, causes the growth process to slow down. A
cretin's body and mind do not grow to their full potential.
Hyperthyroidism, on the other hand, results in extreme
(20) nervousness, an increase in heart action, and other problems.

Either hypothyroidism or hyperthyroidism may result in
goiter, or an enlarged thyroid gland. A goiter will appear
when the body is not getting enough iodine. Goiter is less
(25) common today, since most people use iodized salt.

11. The thyroid gland is called an endocrine gland because it
    (A) has ducts
    (B) has lobes
    (C) secretes directly into the bloodstream
    (D) is located in the neck

12. The word "it" in line 8 refers to
    (A) thyroxine   (C) iodine
    (B) blood   (D) thyroid gland

13. A cretin is
    (A) a child with hyperthyroidism
    (B) an adult with an underperforming thyroid gland
    (C) a young person with hypothyroidism
    (D) an extremely irritable child

14. Which of the following is a probable result of myxedema?
    (A) Sluggishness
    (B) Hyperactivity
    (C) Overproduction of thyroxine
    (D) Perspiration

15. The word "former" in line 16 refers to
    (A) hypothyroidism   (C) hyperthyroidism
    (B) overactive thyroid   (D) secretion

16. A goiter is
    (A) a person with myxedema
    (B) a swollen thyroid gland
    (C) an underactive thyroid gland
    (D) a chemical

17. Exocrine and endocrine glands are distinguished from each other by whether they
    (A) secrete through ducts or without ducts
    (B) cause hyperthyroidism or hypothyroidism
    (C) cause myxedema or cretinism
    (D) result in an enlarged or shrunken goiter

18. In line 1, the word "secrete" is closest in meaning to
    (A) indiscernible   (C) display
    (B) emit   (D) absorb

19. If a thyroid is not working enough, the illness is known as
    (A) hyperthyroidism   (C) excretion
    (B) hyperactivity   (D) hypothyroidism

20. The main idea of the passage is
    (A) how glands work
    (B) the function and illnesses of the thyroid gland
    (C) secretion with and without glands
    (D) the illnesses of an overactive thyroid gland

21. The function of the thyroid gland is described in lines
    (A) 2–4   (B) 7–9   (C) 13–15   (D) 22–25

Questions 22 through 30 are based on the following passage.

A recent investigation by scientists at the U.S. Geological Survey shows that strange animal behavior might help predict earthquakes. Investigators found such occurrences within a ten-kilometer radius of the epicenter of a fairly
(5) recent quake. Some birds screeched and flew about wildly; dogs yelped and ran around uncontrollably.

Scientists believe that animals can perceive environmental changes several hours or even days before the mishap. Animals were noted as being restless for several weeks
(10) before a Tashkent, Uzbekistan, earthquake. An hour before the disaster, domestic animals refused to go indoors, and dogs howled and barked furiously. In 1960, an earthquake struck Agadir in Morocco. Survivors recall that stray animals, including dogs, were seen streaming out of town
(15) before the earthquake. In a safari zoo near San Francisco, llamas would not eat the evening before a 1979 quake, and they ran around wildly all night.

Unusual animal behavior preceding earthquakes has been noted for centuries. British Admiral Robert Fitzroy
(20) reported huge flocks of screaming seabirds over Concepción, Chile, in 1835. An hour and a half later, dogs were seen fleeing, and ten minutes later the town was destroyed. Similar stories of chickens running around in apparent states of panic, horses trembling, and dogs barking inces-
(25) santly were recorded throughout the eighteenth and nineteenth centuries by survivors of earthquake destruction in India, Yugoslavia, Peru, Mexico, and the United States.

In 1976, after monitoring bizarre animal behavior, the Chinese predicted a devastating earthquake. Although
(30) hundreds of thousands of people were killed, the government was able to evacuate millions of other people and thus keep the death toll at a lower level.

22. What prediction may be made by observing animal behavior?
    (A) An impending earthquake
    (B) The number of people who will die
    (C) The ten-kilometer radius from the epicenter
    (D) The fact that an earthquake has occurred

23. The author implies that animals are aware of an impending earthquake because
    (A) of their superior intelligence
    (B) they have certain instinctive abilities to perceive that humans do not possess
    (C) they are generally closer to the epicenter than the human observers
    (D) they react to other animal behavior

24. The word "evacuate" in line 31 is closest in meaning to
    (A) remove   (B) exile   (C) destroy   (D) emaciate

25. All of the following statements are true EXCEPT
    (A) some animals may be able to sense an approaching earthquake
    (B) by observing animal behavior scientists perhaps can predict earthquakes
    (C) the Chinese have successfully predicted an earthquake and saved many lives
    (D) only dogs and horses seem to possess the special perception that allows them to predict earthquakes

26. In line 4, the word "epicenter" is nearest in meaning to
    (A) stratosphere   (C) periphery
    (B) contour   (D) core

27. The passage implies that if scientists can accurately predict
    earthquakes, there will be
    (A) fewer animals going crazy
    (B) a lower death rate
    (C) fewer people evacuated
    (D) fewer environmental changes

28. In line 29, "devastating" means most nearly the same as
    (A) destructive   (C) intense
    (B) voracious   (D) forthcoming

29. The main idea of this passage is that
    (A) earthquakes can be prevented by observing animal behav-
        ior
    (B) scientists can interpret animal behavior
    (C) observing animal behavior can help people prepare for
        earthquakes
    (D) people need to prepare animals for earthquakes

30. Where in the reading is it explained that the phenomena of
    animals' reacting to earthquakes has been reported for hun-
    dreds of years?
    (A) Lines 3–5   (C) Lines 18–19
    (B) Lines 7–8   (D) Lines 29–32

Questions 31 through 39 are based on the following passage.

As far back as 700 B.C., people have talked about children
being cared for by wolves. Romulus and Remus, the
legendary twin founders of Rome, were purported to have
been cared for by wolves. According to legend, Mars
(5) fathered the two boys. As a result, a relative of their mother
imprisoned her and ordered that the boys be drowned in the
Tiber River. However, a she-wolf saved them from this
horrible fate and took them back to her lair to care for them.
Legend has it that when a she-wolf loses her litter, she seeks

398

(10) a human child to take its place.

This seemingly preposterous idea did not become credible until the late nineteenth century when a French doctor actually found a naked ten-year-old boy wandering in the woods. He did not walk erect, could not speak intelligibly,
(15) nor could he relate to people. He only growled and stared at them. Finally, the doctor won the boy's confidence and began to work with him. After many long years of devoted and patient instruction, the doctor was able to get the boy to clothe and feed himself, recognize and utter a number of
(20) words, and write letters and form words.

31. The French doctor found the boy
(A) wandering in the woods
(B) at his doorstep
(C) growling at him
(D) speaking intelligibly

32. In line 9, the word "litter" means most nearly the same as
(A) garbage   (B) master   (C) offspring   (D) hair

33. The doctor was able to work with the boy because
(A) the boy was highly intelligent
(B) the boy trusted him
(C) the boy liked to dress up
(D) the boy was dedicated and patient

34. The word "utter" in line 19 is nearest in meaning to
(A) absolute   (B) speak   (C) scream   (D) read

35. All of the following statements are true EXCEPT
    (A) she-wolves have been said to substitute human children for their lost litters
    (B) examples of wolves' caring for human children can be found only in the nineteenth century
    (C) the French doctor succeeded in domesticating the boy somewhat
    (D) the young boy never was able to speak perfectly

36. The word "preposterous" in line 11 is closest in meaning to
    (A) dedicated   (C) wonderful
    (B) scientific   (D) absurd

37. The main idea of this passage is that according to legend
    (A) children who are raised by wolves can be rehabilitated
    (B) she-wolves replace their dead offspring with human children
    (C) Romulus and Remus were cared for by a she-wolf
    (D) a French doctor saved Romulus and Remus from drowning

38. According to the legend, Romulus and Remus were
    (A) found abandoned in Rome
    (B) the founders of Rome
    (C) discovered by a French doctor
    (D) drowned in the Tiber River in 700 B.C.

39. Where in the passage is it stated that, according to legend, Romulus and Remus founded Rome?
    (A) Lines 2–3   (C) Lines 9–10
    (B) Lines 5–7   (D) Lines 11–13

Questions 40 through 50 are based on the following passage.

Vibrio parahaemolyticus is a bacterial organism that has been isolated from sea water, shellfish, finfish, plankton, and salt springs. It has been a major cause of food poisoning in Japan, compelling the Japanese to do several studies on
(5) it. They have confirmed the presence of *V. parahaemolyticus* in the north and central Pacific, with the highest abundance in inshore waters, particularly in or near large harbors.

A man named Nishio studied the relationship between the chloride content of sea water and the seasonal distribu-
(10) tion of *V. parahaemolyticus* and concluded that while the isolation of the organism was independent of the sodium chloride content, the distribution of the bacteria in sea water was dependent on the water temperature. In fact, it has been isolated in high frequencies during summer, from
(15) June to September, but was not isolated with the same frequency in winter.

Within four or five days after eating contaminated foods, a person will begin to experience diarrhea, the most common symptom; this will very often be accompanied by
(20) stomach cramps, nausea, and vomiting. Headache and fever, with or without chills, may also be experienced.

40. Which of the following locations would be most likely to have a high concentration of *Vibrio parahaemolyticus*?
    (A) A bay
    (B) A sea
    (C) The middle of the ocean
    (D) Sediment

41. The word "inshore" in line 7 is closest in meaning to
    (A) near the coast   (C) active
    (B) deep   (D) cold

42. The word "it" in line 13 refers to
    (A) *Vibrio parahaemolyticus*
    (B) sea water
    (C) sodium chloride content
    (D) water temperature

43. The safest time for eating seafood in the north Pacific is probably
    (A) August
    (B) November
    (C) July
    (D) September

44. The most common symptom of *V. parahaemolyticus* poisoning is
    (A) nausea
    (B) diarrhea
    (C) vomiting
    (D) headache and fever

45. The word "this" in line 19 refers to
    (A) contaminated foods
    (B) symptoms
    (C) a person
    (D) diarrhea

46. The incubation period for this illness is
    (A) 2 to 3 days
    (B) 3 to 4 hours
    (C) 4 to 5 days
    (D) several months

47. In line 17, "contaminated" is closest in meaning to
    (A) ocean   (B) tainted   (C) salty   (D) cooked

48. Nishio's study showed that
    (A) the presence of *V. parahaemolyticus* was dependent on neither the salt content nor the water temperature
    (B) the presence of *V. parahaemolyticus* was dependent only on the salt content
    (C) the presence of *V. parahaemolyticus* was independent of both the water temperature and the salt content
    (D) the presence of *V. parahaemolyticus* was dependent on the water temperature

49. The word "cramps" in line 20 means most nearly the same as
   (A) noises
   (B) toxicity
   (C) severe pain
   (D) high temperature

50. The word "isolation" in line 11 is closest in meaning to
   (A) conjunction
   (B) impurity
   (C) separation
   (D) discovery

STOP. THIS IS THE END OF THE EXAMINATION. IF YOU FINISH BEFORE TIME IS UP, CHECK YOUR WORK IN THIS SECTION ONLY. DO NOT WORK ON ANY OTHER SECTION OF THE TEST.

PRACTICE TEST 4

SECTION 1
LISTENING COMPREHENSION

Time: Approximately 30 Minutes
50 Questions

Section 1 has three parts. Each part has its own set of directions. Do not take notes while listening or make any marks on the test pages. Notetaking, underlining, or crossing out will be considered cheating on the actual TOEFL exam. Answer the questions following the conversations or talks based on what the speakers have *stated* or *implied.*

For Practice Test 4, insert your Listening Comprehension cassette in your tape player. On the actual TOEFL, you will be given extra time to go on to the next page when you finish a page in the Listening Comprehension section. In the following test, however, you will have only the 12 seconds given after each question. Turn the page as soon as you have marked your answer. Start the cassette now.

Part A

DIRECTIONS

In Part A, you will hear short conversations between two speakers. At the end of each conversation, a third voice will ask a question about what was said. The question will be *spoken* just one time. After you hear a conversation and the question about it, read the four possible answers and decide which one would be the best answer to the question you have heard. Then, on your answer sheet, find the number of the problem and mark your answer.

1. (A) Something happened to her car.
   (B) She was broke and couldn't afford the bus.
   (C) She got up too late to catch the bus.
   (D) Her car got stuck in the driveway.

2. (A) She doesn't like other people brushing her clothes.
   (B) She doesn't like to drink.
   (C) She doesn't like to knit.
   (D) She doesn't like being snubbed at a party.

3. (A) He will buy the car as soon as he gets the money.
   (B) His friend is buying the car for him.
   (C) He can't afford to buy a new car.
   (D) He has already made the down payment on the car.

4. (A) She had to fly out of town.
   (B) She's sick.
   (C) She said that she'd come later.
   (D) She decided to stay home.

5. (A) 15   (B) 50   (C) 85   (D) 100

6. (A) The man doesn't have to study a foreign language.
   (B) The man just received an "A" on his test.
   (C) The man's adviser gave him some good advice.
   (D) He doesn't have to take the final exam.

7. (A) Rusty will lose his car because he hasn't made the payments.
   (B) The finance company is returning Rusty's car.
   (C) Rusty has a broken finger from falling on the pavement behind his car.
   (D) Rusty's car is being repaired.

8. (A) Reviewed a previous lesson.
   (B) Presented new material.
   (C) Tested the students.
   (D) Made the students write in class.

9. (A) The woman is getting another job.
   (B) The woman is disappointed at not getting the job.
   (C) The woman's boss is letting her have a better job.
   (D) The woman's job is much better than she had expected.

10. (A) They are pleased.   (C) They are undecided.
    (B) They dread it.   (D) They are frustrated.

11. (A) The bank closed before the woman could deposit her money.
    (B) If the woman hurries, she'll get to the bank before closing time.
    (C) The woman has to take some money out of the bank before it closes.
    (D) The bank is closing the woman's account because she hasn't deposited any money.

12. (A) They were total strangers.
    (B) He knew them only slightly.
    (C) He knew them very well.
    (D) He wasn't sure whether he knew them or not.

13. (A) Cut the sugar cubes into smaller pieces.
    (B) Put sugar in his coffee.
    (C) Reduce the amount of sugar he ingests.
    (D) Eat more sugar.

14. (A) They were pulled through the wreckage.
    (B) They were pulling each other through the wreckage.
    (C) None will survive.
    (D) All will probably survive.

15. (A) There were so many tickets left that they had to sell them again the next day.
    (B) Not many showed up to purchase tickets on opening day.
    (C) There were no tickets left by noon of the opening day.
    (D) A few tickets were left for the afternoon of opening day.

16. (A) Knowing that he lacked experience, he still applied.
    (B) Even though he was experienced, he didn't apply for the job.
    (C) He was highly qualified for the job, so he applied.
    (D) He didn't have much experience working in the fields.

17. (A) It could not be solved by anyone.
    (B) Everyone knew how to solve it.
    (C) Gary was the only one who couldn't solve it.
    (D) Only Gary could solve it.

18. (A) The people thanked her for her response.
    (B) The people were grateful because she had requested the information.
    (C) She was happy with the response to her first request.
    (D) She responded gratefully to their request.

19. (A) She can't attend the meeting because she has too much homework.
    (B) She completed her homework early so that she could attend the meeting.
    (C) Although she has homework due tomorrow, she plans to go to the meeting.
    (D) She refuses to attend this class because of the homework.

20. (A) Gil prefers that the woman wait for him.
    (B) Gil is happy because the woman didn't wait for him.
    (C) The woman is angry because Gil left before she arrived.
    (D) Gil doesn't want the woman to wait for him.

21. (A) Jogging.   (C) Taking a stroll.
    (B) At the store.   (D) Getting a newspaper.

22. (A) The woman will go home for dinner.
    (B) The woman won't go to the concert.
    (C) The man and woman will eat together.
    (D) Both of them will go home before going to the concert.

23. (A) Oscar pays his bills ahead of time.
    (B) Oscar has decided to get a loan to pay his bills.
    (C) Oscar has too many expenses and can't save any money.
    (D) Oscar's wife will have to go to work.

24. (A) His keys are lost forever.
    (B) He expects to find his keys soon.
    (C) His keys were lost, but now he has found them.
    (D) Someone showed up with his keys soon after he had lost
        them.

25. (A) They attended the concert even though the tickets were
        expensive.
    (B) They wanted to attend the concert, but the tickets were
        sold out.
    (C) The tickets were so inexpensive that they attended the
        concert.
    (D) They couldn't afford the tickets for the concert.

26. (A) Use a different type of viewing device.
    (B) Sit down.
    (C) Stand up.
    (D) Stop raising the sign.

27. (A) Melanie didn't wear the coat because she doesn't like red.
    (B) Melanie is allergic to wool.
    (C) Melanie wore the coat but broke out in a rash.
    (D) Melanie couldn't wear the coat because she was in a rush.

28. (A) He'd like to have a steak and salad now.
    (B) He thinks he'll run out and buy a steak and salad right now.
    (C) He just ate a steak and salad.
    (D) He's eating a steak and salad at the moment.

29. (A) She usually goes to the football games.
    (B) She hasn't seen a football game for a long time.
    (C) She doesn't like football.
    (D) She usually doesn't go to football games.

30. (A) The agent has sold no policies this week.
    (B) The agent has sold only one policy this week.
    (C) The agent hasn't sold too many policies this week.
    (D) Last week, the agent sold more policies than anybody else.

GO ON TO PART B

Part B

DIRECTIONS

In Part B, you will hear longer conversations. After each conversation, you will be asked some questions. The conversations and questions will be *spoken* just one time. They will not be written out for you, so you will have to listen carefully in order to understand and remember what the speaker says.

When you hear a question, read the four possible answers in your test book and decide which one would be the best answer to the question you have heard. Then, on your answer sheet, find the number of the problem and fill in the space that corresponds to the letter of the answer you have chosen.

31. (A) Department store.　　　(C) Produce market.
    (B) Supermarket.　　　　　(D) Variety store.

32. (A) Tuna fish.　(B) Eggs.　(C) Bleach.　(D) Detergent.

33. (A) It is a no-frills store.
    (B) The fresh food looked appetizing.
    (C) The lines are shorter.
    (D) There is a wide selection.

34. (A) The man did not enjoy the store.
    (B) Nothing was on sale.
    (C) He spent more than $50.
    (D) He found the food inexpensive.

35. (A) San Juan.　　　　　　(C) Miami.
    (B) Venus.　　　　　　　(D) Port-o-call.

36. (A) Morison.　　　　　　(C) Norrison.
    (B) Mowrison.　　　　　　(D) Morrison.

37. (A) Cash.　　　　　　　(C) Personal check.
    (B) Credit card.　　　　　(D) Traveler's checks.

38. (A) In three days.　　　　(C) March 15.
    (B) March 27.　　　　　　(D) June 20.

GO ON TO PART C

Part C

DIRECTIONS

In Part C, you will hear several talks. After each talk, you will be asked some questions. The talks and questions will be *spoken* just one time. They will not be written out for you, so you will have to listen carefully in order to understand and remember what the speaker says.

When you hear a question, read the four possible answers in your test book and decide which one would be the best answer to the question you have heard. Then, on your answer sheet, find the number of the problem and fill in the space that corresponds to the letter of the answer you have chosen.

39. (A) The high cost of gasoline.
    (B) Overcongestion of university areas.
    (C) Dangerous driving conditions.
    (D) Police roadblocks.

40. (A) State law only.
    (B) City law only.
    (C) Natural law.
    (D) City and state law.

41. (A) Roller skating in the streets is only a local problem.
    (B) Skaters are creating problems for motorists.
    (C) Police will ticket violators.
    (D) The problem is most common in college and university areas.

42. (A) New political ways.
    (B) New methods of fishing.
    (C) New means of water travel.
    (D) How to trap animals.

43. (A) They were plentiful in England.
    (B) They grew only in certain sections of the country.
    (C) They were preferred raw.
    (D) They did not exist in England.

44. (A) By canoe.
    (B) By blazing trails through the forest.
    (C) By toboggan and snowshoes.
    (D) On animals.

45. (A) Corn.
    (B) Domesticated animals.
    (C) Building shelters.
    (D) Trapping animals.

46. (A) The settlers were well prepared for the hardships that they
        would encounter.
    (B) The new settlers evidently found the winters severe.
    (C) The Indians taught the settlers how to build canoes.
    (D) The settlers brought tools and weapons to the New World.

47. (A) 6:45 in Baton Rouge.
    (B) 1:45 in Atlanta.
    (C) 1:45 in Dallas.
    (D) 2:45 in Dallas.

48. (A) Smoking cigars.
    (B) Drinking whiskey.
    (C) Smoking a pipe.
    (D) Smoking cigarettes.

49. (A) 3242   (B) 3224   (C) 2334   (D) 3442

50. (A) 1:45 P.M.   (B) 12 midnight.   (C) 1:45 A.M.   (D) 6:45 P.M.

STOP. THIS IS THE END OF THE LISTENING COMPREHENSION SECTION.
GO ON TO SECTION 2.

SECTION 2
STRUCTURE AND WRITTEN EXPRESSION

Time: 25 Minutes
40 Questions

Part A

DIRECTIONS

Questions 1–15 are incomplete sentences. Beneath each sentence you will see four words or phrases, marked (A), (B), (C), and (D). Choose the *one* word or phrase that best completes the sentence. Then, on your answer sheet, find the number of the question and fill in the space that corresponds to the letter of the answer you have chosen. Fill in the space so that the letter inside the oval cannot be seen.

1. The cyclist _____ he crossed the main street.
   (A) looked with caution after
   (B) had looked cautiously before
   (C) was looked cautious when
   (D) looks cautious when

2. Here _____ notebook and report that I promised you last week.
   (A) is the
   (B) are the
   (C) was the
   (D) has been a

3. Neither Jane nor her brothers _____ a consent form for tomorrow's field trip.
   - (A) need
   - (B) needs
   - (C) is needing
   - (D) has need

4. Cuba is _____ sugar-growing areas in the world.
   - (A) one of the larger
   - (B) one of largest
   - (C) one of the largest
   - (D) largest

5. The skiers would rather _____ through the mountains than go by bus.
   - (A) to travel on train
   - (B) traveled by train
   - (C) travel by train
   - (D) traveling by the train

6. That magnificent _____ temple was constructed by the Chinese.
   - (A) eight-centuries-old
   - (B) eight-century's-old
   - (C) old-eight-centuries
   - (D) eight-century-old

7. There were two small rooms in the beach house, _____ served as a kitchen.
   - (A) the smaller of which
   - (B) the smallest of which
   - (C) the smaller of them
   - (D) smallest of that

8. Pioneer men and women endured terrible hardships, and _____.
   - (A) so do their children
   - (B) neither did the children
   - (C) also the childs
   - (D) so did their children

9. Last year, Matt earned _____ his brother, who has a better position.
   - (A) twice as much as
   - (B) twice more than
   - (C) twice as many as
   - (D) twice as more as

10. _____, he would have been able to pass the exam.
   - (A) If he studied more
   - (B) If he were studying to a greater degree
   - (C) Studying more
   - (D) Had he studied more

11. Mr. Duncan does not know _____ the lawn mower after they had finished using it.
   - (A) where did they put
   - (B) where they did put
   - (C) where they put
   - (D) where to put

12. The facilities of the older hospital _____.
   - (A) is as good or better than the new hospital
   - (B) are as good or better that the new hospital
   - (C) are as good as or better than the new hospital
   - (D) are as good as or better than those of the new hospital

13. Our flight from Amsterdam to London was delayed _____ the heavy fog.
    (A) because of
    (B) because
    (C) on account
    (D) as result

14. The teacher suggested that her students _____ experiences with ESP.
    (A) write a composition on their
    (B) to write composition about the
    (C) wrote some compositions of his or her
    (D) had written any compositions for his

15. Of the two new teachers, one is experienced and _____.
    (A) the others are not
    (B) another is inexperienced
    (C) the other is not
    (D) other lacks experience

GO ON TO PART B

Part B

DIRECTIONS

In questions 16–40, each sentence has four underlined words or phrases. The four underlined parts of the sentence are marked (A), (B), (C), and (D). Identify the *one* underlined word or phrase that must be changed in order for the sentence to be correct. Then, on your answer sheet, find the number of the question and fill in the space that corresponds to the letter of the answer you have chosen.

16. While searching for the wreckage of a unidentified aircraft,
        A   B   C
    the Coast Guard encountered severe squalls at sea.
                                       D

416

17. Although a number of police officers <u>was guarding</u> the
                                         A
    priceless <u>treasures in</u> the museum, the director worried that
              B
    someone <u>would try</u> to <u>steal</u> them.
            C   D

18. Since it was <u>so difficult for</u> American Indians <u>to negotiate</u> a
                 A   B
    peace treaty or declare war <u>in their native language</u>, they used
                                C
    a <u>universal</u> understood form of sign language.
      D

19. Louis Braille designed a form of communication

    <u>enabling</u> people <u>to convey</u> and preserve their thoughts
    A   B
    <u>to incorporate</u> a series of dots which <u>were read</u> by the finger
    C   D
    tips.

20. While verbalization is <u>the most common form</u> of language in
                           A
    <u>existence</u>, humans make use of many <u>others systems</u> and
    B   C
    techniques <u>to express</u> their thoughts and feelings.
               D

21. The need <u>for</u> a <u>well-rounded education</u> was an idea
             A   B
    <u>espoused</u> by the Greeks <u>in time of</u> Socrates.
    C   D

417

22. Writers and media <u>personnel</u> sell <u>theirselves</u> best
                              A   B

    <u>by the</u> impression given in their verbal <u>expression</u>.
     C   D

23. <u>In the spirit</u> of the <u>naturalist</u> writers, that <u>author's</u> work
       A   B   C

    portrays man's struggle for <u>surviving</u>.
                              D

24. <u>Stephen Crane's story</u> is <u>a</u> clinical portrayal
            A   B

    <u>of man as an animal</u> trapped by <u>the fear</u> and hunger.
          C   D

25. Their silly, whiny conversation <u>on a child level</u> was meant
                                   A

    <u>to create</u> tension and <u>heighten</u> <u>Nancy's</u> fears and anxiety.
     B   C   D

26. For a long time, <u>this</u> officials <u>have been known</u> throughout the
                     A   B

    country <u>as</u> political bosses and <u>law enforcers</u>.
       C   D

27. Nora hardly <u>never</u> misses <u>an</u> opportunity <u>to play</u> <u>in</u> the tennis
             A   B   C D

    tournaments.

28. Air pollution, together <u>with</u> littering, <u>are</u> causing
                     A   B

    <u>many</u> problems <u>in our large</u>, industrial cities today.
      C   D

29. <u>Because of</u> the severe snow storm and the road blocks, <u>the</u> air
      A   B

    force <u>dropped food</u> and medical supplies <u>close the</u> city.
         C   D

30. Hummingbirds are <u>the only birds</u> capable <u>to fly</u> backward
            A   B

    <u>as well as</u> <u>forward</u>, up, and down.
      C   D

31. <u>The</u> news of the president's treaty negotiations with the
      A

    foreign government <u>were</u> <u>received with mixed emotions</u> by the
            B   C

    citizens <u>of both governments</u>.
        D

32. Angie's bilingual ability and previous experience <u>were</u> the
                  A

    qualities <u>that which</u> <u>helped her</u> get the job over all
         B   C

    <u>the other</u> candidates.
      D

33. <u>Joel</u> giving up <u>smoking has</u> caused <u>him to gain</u> weight and
      A   B   C

    <u>become irritable</u> with his acquaintances.
       D

34. They asked me <u>what did happen</u> <u>last night</u>, but I was <u>unable to</u>
          A   B   C

    <u>tell them</u>.
      D

35. The <u>test</u> administrator ordered <u>we</u> <u>not to open</u> our books until
       A   B   C

    he <u>told us to do so</u>.
      D

36. <u>Our new</u> neighbors <u>had been living</u> in Arizona <u>since</u> ten years
      A   B   C

    <u>before moving to</u> their present house.
       D

37. I would of attended the meeting of the planning committee
       A   B
    last week, but I had to deliver a speech at a convention.
                       C   D

38. We are suppose to read all of chapter seven and answer the
              A   B   C
    questions for tomorrow's class.
              D

39. The explanation that our instructor gave us was different
                          A   B
    than the one yours gave you.
     C   D

40. In the sixteenth century, Spain became involved in foreign
        A   B
    wars with several other European countries and could not find
               C
    the means of finance the battles that ensued.
                D

STOP. THIS IS THE END OF THE STRUCTURE AND WRITTEN EXPRESSION SECTION. IF YOU FINISH BEFORE TIME IS UP, CHECK YOUR WORK ON PARTS A AND B OF THIS SECTION ONLY. DO NOT WORK ON ANY OTHER SECTION OF THE TEST.

SECTION 3
READING COMPREHENSION

Time: 55 Minutes
50 Questions

DIRECTIONS

In this section, you will read a number of passages. Each one is
followed by approximately ten questions about it. For questions
1–50, choose the *one* best answer, (A), (B), (C), or (D), to each
question. Then, find the number of the question on your answer
sheet, and fill in the space that corresponds to the letter of the
answer you have chosen. Answer all questions following a passage
on the basis of what is *stated* or *implied* in that passage.

Questions 1 through 10 are based on the following passage.

Lichens, of which more than twenty thousand species
have been named, are complex associations between certain
fungi and certain algae. The lichen itself is not an organism;
rather it is the morphological and biochemical product of
(5) the association. Neither a fungus nor an alga alone can
produce a lichen.

The intimate relationship between these two living components of a lichen was once erroneously thought to
represent mutualism. In mutualistic relationships, both
(10) participants benefit. With lichens, however, it appears the
fungus actually parasitizes the algae. This is one of the
conclusions drawn from experiments in which the two
components of lichens were separated and grown apart.

In nature, lichen fungi may encounter and grow around
(15) several kinds of algae. Some types of algae the fungi may
kill; other types it may reject. Lichen algae are autotrophic,
meaning they make their own food through photosynthesis.
Lichen fungi are heterotrophic, meaning they depend upon

421

(20) the algae within the lichen to supply their food. Up to ninety percent of the food made by the green algal cells is transferred to the fungus. What, if anything, the fungus contributes to the association is not well understood.

Lichens are hardy. They grow in many habitats and are often pioneers in hostile environments where few other (25) organisms can flourish. They have been known to grow endolithically, having been discovered thriving inside of rocks in Antarctica. Lichens help reduce erosion by stabilizing soil. Several kinds of insects glue lichens to their exoskeletons for camouflage. Many species of birds use (30) lichens as building materials for nests. Humans have used lichens for dyes and antibiotics.

1. Which of the following best describes the lichen association?
   (A) Simple plants made of two different autotrophic organisms
   (B) A mutualistic association between a fungus and an alga
   (C) A parasitic association between two fungi, one autotrophic, the second heterotrophic
   (D) A union between a parasitic fungus and an autotrophic alga

2. The word "hardy" in line 23 is closest in meaning to
   (A) tender   (C) armed
   (B) durable   (D) beneficial

3. In biology, mutualism occurs when two different organisms live close together and
   (A) one organism parasitizes the other
   (B) both organisms benefit from the association
   (C) both organisms are harmed by the association
   (D) one organism benefits while the other does not or is harmed by the association

4. In line 7, the word "intimate" is nearest in meaning to
   (A) living   (C) biological
   (B) extraordinary   (D) close

5. Lichens serve as camouflage for which of the following?
   (A) Insects
   (B) Birds
   (C) Reptiles
   (D) Mammals

6. The true nature of the relationship between the lichen components was clarified by
   (A) examining lichens with a microscope
   (B) observing lichens placed in the dark
   (C) observing the lichen components when grown apart
   (D) decreasing the amount of nutrients available to the lichens

7. In line 24, the word "hostile" is closest in meaning to
   (A) unusual
   (B) cool
   (C) untraveled
   (D) inhospitable

8. An endolithic lichen is one that
   (A) grows in the canopies of trees
   (B) grows inside rocks
   (C) grows at very high altitudes
   (D) grows inside other organisms, including other lichens

9. Many lichens contribute to the communities they inhabit by
   (A) removing pollutants from the air
   (B) controlling wood-rotting fungi
   (C) slowing the spread of viruses
   (D) reducing soil erosion

10. In what part of the passage does the author indicate that scientists have changed their previous position on the makeup of lichens?
    (A) Lines 3–5
    (B) Lines 7–9
    (C) Lines 14–16
    (D) Lines 25–27

Questions 11 through 20 are based on the following passage.

When buying a house, you must be sure to have it checked for termites. A termite is much like an ant in its communal habits, although physically the two insects are distinct.

Like those of ants, termite colonies consist of different
(5) classes, each with its own particular job. The most perfectly formed termites, both male and female, make up the reproductive class. They have eyes, hard body walls, and fully developed wings. A pair of reproductive termites founds the colony. When new reproductive termites de-
(10) velop, they leave to form another colony. They use their wings only this one time and then break them off.

The worker termites are small, blind, and wingless, with soft bodies. They make up the majority of the colony and do all the work. Soldiers are eyeless and wingless but are larger
(15) than the workers and have hard heads and strong jaws and legs. They defend the colony and are cared for by the workers.

The male and female of the reproductive class remain inside a closed-in cell where the female lays thousands of
(20) eggs. The workers place the eggs in cells and care for them. Even if one colony is treated with poison, if a male and female of the reproductive class escape, they can form a new colony.

Pest control companies can inspect a house for infesta-
(25) tion of termites. Often, a lay person cannot spot the evidence, so it is critical to have the opinion of a professional. Treatments vary depending upon the type of termite.

11. How are termites like ants?
   (A) They live in communities, and each class has a specific duty.
   (B) Their bodies are the same shape.
   (C) The king and queen are imprisoned.
   (D) The females' reproductive capacities are the same.

12. The word "communal" in line 2 is closest in meaning to
    (A) eating
    (B) reproducing
    (C) organizational
    (D) social

13. Which of the following is NOT true?
    (A) All termites have eyes.
    (B) Some termites cannot fly.
    (C) Workers are smaller than soldiers.
    (D) Termites do not fly often.

14. In line 3, the word "distinct" is closest in meaning to
    (A) similar
    (B) different
    (C) genetically related
    (D) strong

15. In line 5, "classes" is closest in meaning to
    (A) sexes
    (B) colonies
    (C) courses
    (D) categories

16. Which of the following statements is probably true?
    (A) Thousands of termites may move together to develop a new colony.
    (B) The male and female reproductives do not venture outdoors except to form a new colony.
    (C) There are more soldiers than workers.
    (D) A worker could easily kill a soldier.

17. The word "founds" in line 9 is nearest in meaning to
    (A) establishes
    (B) destroys
    (C) controls
    (D) guards

18. The word "cells" in line 20 is closest in meaning to
    (A) combs
    (B) rows
    (C) compartments
    (D) placenta

19. Which of the following would be the best title for this passage?
    (A) Termites Destroy Houses
    (B) Termites Work Well Together
    (C) The Habits and Physical Characteristics of Termites
    (D) The Relationship of Soldier and Worker Termites

20. The word "each" in line 5 refers to
    (A) ants   (B) colonies   (C) jobs   (D) classes

Questions 21 through 31 are based on the following passage.

In recent years, there has been an increasing awareness of
the inadequacies of the judicial system in the United States.
Costs are staggering both for the taxpayers and the litigants—
and the litigants, or parties, have to wait sometimes many
(5) years before having their day in court. Many suggestions
have been made concerning methods of ameliorating the
situation, but as in most branches of government, changes
come slowly.

One suggestion that has been made in order to maximize
(10) the efficiency of the system is to allow districts that have an
overabundance of pending cases to borrow judges from
other districts that do not have such a backlog. Another
suggestion is to use pretrial conferences, in which judges
meet in their chambers with the litigants and their attorneys
(15) in order to narrow the issues, limit the witnesses, and
provide for a more orderly trial. The theory behind pretrial
conferences is that judges will spend less time on each case
and parties will more readily settle before trial when they
realize the adequacy of their claims and their opponents'
(20) evidence. Unfortunately, at least one study has shown that
pretrial conferences use more judicial time than they save,
rarely result in pretrial settlements, and actually result in
higher damage settlements.

Many states have now established another method, small-
(25) claims courts, in which cases over small sums of money can

426

be disposed of with considerable dispatch. Such proceedings cost the litigants almost nothing. In California, for
example, the parties must appear before the judge without
the assistance of counsel. The proceedings are quite infor-
(30) mal and there is no pleading—the litigants need to make
only a one-sentence statement of their claim. By going to
this type of court, the plaintiff waives any right to a jury trial
and the right to appeal the decision.

In coming years, we can expect to see more and more
(35) innovations in the continuing effort to remedy a situation
which must be remedied if the citizens who have valid claims
are going to be able to have their day in court.

21. The pretrial conference, in theory, is supposed to do all of the
following EXCEPT
    (A) narrow the issues
    (B) cause early settlements
    (C) save judicial time
    (D) increase settlement costs

22. The word "ameliorating" in line 6 is closest in meaning to
    (A) improving   (C) worsening
    (B) increasing   (D) distinguishing

23. In line 12, the word "backlog" is closest in meaning to
    (A) laziness   (C) overload
    (B) inefficiency   (D) dearth

24. What is the main topic of the passage?
    (A) All states should follow California's example in using
        small-claims courts in order to free judges for other work.
    (B) The legislature needs to formulate fewer laws so that the
        judiciary can catch up on its older cases.
    (C) Nobody seems to care enough to attempt to find methods
        for making the judicial system more efficient.
    (D) While there are many problems with the court system,
        there are viable suggestions for improvement.

427

25. In line 3, "litigants" is closest in meaning to
    (A) jury members   (C) parties in a lawsuit
    (B) commentators   (D) taxpayers

26. Which of the following is true about small-claims courts?
    (A) It is possible to have one's case heard by a jury if one is dissatisfied with the court's decision.
    (B) The litigants must plead accurately and according to a strict form.
    (C) The decision may not be appealed to a higher court.
    (D) The parties may not present their cases without an attorney's help.

27. The word "staggering" in line 3 is nearest in meaning to
    (A) up and down   (C) charged
    (B) decreasing   (D) astounding

28. The word "dispatch" in line 26 means most nearly the same as
    (A) transmittal   (B) haste   (C) clarity   (D) conflict

29. It is implied in the passage that
    (A) most people who feel they have been wronged have a ready remedy in courts of law
    (B) many people would like to bring a case to court but are unable to because of the cost and time required
    (C) the judicial system in the United States is highly acclaimed for its efficiency
    (D) someday pretrial conferences likely will replace trials completely

30. The word "remedy" in line 35 is closest in meaning to
    (A) correct   (B) review   (C) expose   (D) discover

31. The passage indicates that pretrial conferences may not actually produce positive results in lines
    (A) 3–5   (B) 16–19   (C) 20–23   (D) 29–31

Questions 32 through 39 are based on the following passage.

In an effort to produce the largest, fastest, and most luxurious ship afloat, the British built the *S.S. Titanic.* It was so superior to anything else on the seas that it was dubbed "unsinkable." So sure of this were the owners that they
(5)   provided only twenty lifeboats and rafts, less than one half the number needed for the 2,227 passengers on board.

Many passengers were aboard the night it rammed an iceberg, only two days at sea and more than halfway between England and its New York destination. Because
(10) the luxury liner was traveling so fast, it was impossible to avoid the ghostly looking iceberg. An unextinguished fire also contributed to the ship's submersion. Panic increased the number of casualties as people jumped into the icy water or fought to be among the few to board the lifeboats. Four
(15) hours after the mishap, another ship, the *Carpathia,* rescued the 705 survivors.

The infamous *S.S. Titanic* had enjoyed only two days of sailing glory on its maiden voyage in 1912 before plunging into 12,000 feet of water near the coast of Newfoundland,
(20) where it lies today.

32. All of the following are true EXCEPT
   (A) only a third of those aboard perished
   (B) the *Carpathia* rescued the survivors
   (C) the *S.S. Titanic* sank near Newfoundland
   (D) the *S.S. Titanic* was the fastest ship afloat in 1912

33. All of the following contributed to the large death toll EXCEPT
   (A) panic   (B) fire   (C) speed   (D) the *Carpathia*

34. How many days was the *S.S. Titanic* at sea before sinking?
   (A) 2   (B) 4   (C) 6   (D) 12

35. In line 11, the word "unextinguished" is closest in meaning to
    (A) indestructable
    (B) uncontrollable
    (C) undiscovered
    (D) unquenched

36. In line 18, "maiden voyage" is closest in meaning to
    (A) inaugural
    (B) most elegant
    (C) longest
    (D) final

37. The word "dubbed" in line 3 is closest in meaning to
    (A) called
    (B) initiated
    (C) christened
    (D) listed

38. What is the main idea of this passage?
    (A) The *S.S. Titanic* proved itself the most seaworthy vessel in 1912.
    (B) Attempts to rescue the *S.S. Titanic*'s survivors were not successful.
    (C) Overconfidence by builders and owners was greatly responsible for the sinking of the vessel.
    (D) A fire and panic were the only causes for the sinking of the ship.

39. In which lines does the author indicate that the *S. S. Titanic*'s owners were overly confident about its seaworthiness?
    (A) Lines 1–2
    (B) Lines 4–6
    (C) Lines 7–9
    (D) Lines 14–16

Questions 40 through 50 are based on the following passage.

One of the seven wonders of the ancient world, the Great Pyramid of Giza was a monument of wisdom and prophecy built as a tomb for Pharaoh Cheops in 2720 B.C. Despite its antiquity, certain aspects of its construction make it one of
(5) the truly great wonders of the world. The thirteen-acre structure near the Nile River is a solid mass of stone blocks covered with limestone. Inside are a number of hidden

430

passageways and the burial chamber for the pharaoh. It is
the largest single structure in the world. The four sides of
(10) the pyramid are aligned almost exactly on true north, south,
east, and west—an incredible engineering feat. The ancient
Egyptians were sun worshipers and great astronomers, so
computations for the Great Pyramid were based on astronomical observations.

(15)   Explorations and detailed examinations of the base of the
structure reveal many intersecting lines. Further scientific
study indicates that these represent a type of timeline of
events—past, present, and future. Many of the events have
been interpreted and found to coincide with known facts of
(20) the past. Others are prophesied for future generations and
are currently under investigation. Many believe that pyramids have supernatural powers, and this one is no exception. Some researchers even associate it with extraterrestrial
beings of the ancient past.

(25)   Was this superstructure made by ordinary beings, or one
built by a race far superior to any known today?

40. What has research of the base revealed?
    (A) There are cracks in the foundation.
    (B) Tomb robbers have stolen the pharaoh's body.
    (C) The lines represent important events.
    (D) A superior race of people built it.

41. Extraterrestrial beings are
    (A) very strong workers
    (B) astronomers in the ancient times
    (C) researchers in Egyptology
    (D) living beings from other planets

42. What was the most probable reason for providing so many hidden passages?
    (A) To allow the weight of the pyramid to settle evenly
    (B) To permit the high priests to pray at night
    (C) To enable the pharaoh's family to bring food for his journey to the afterlife
    (D) To keep grave robbers from finding the tomb and the treasure buried with the pharaoh

43. The word "intersecting" in line 15 is nearest in meaning to
    (A) crossing   (C) observing
    (B) aligning   (D) cutting

44. What do the intersecting lines in the base symbolize?
    (A) Architects' plans for the hidden passages
    (B) Pathways of the great solar bodies
    (C) Astrological computations
    (D) Dates of important events taking place throughout time

45. In line 20, the word "prophesied" is closest in meaning to
    (A) affiliated   (C) terminated
    (B) precipitated   (D) foretold

46. What is the best title for the passage?
    (A) Symbolism of the Great Pyramid
    (B) Problems with the Construction of the Great Pyramid
    (C) Wonders of the Great Pyramid of Giza
    (D) Exploration of the Burial Chamber of Cheops

47. On what did the ancient Egyptians base their calculations?
    (A) Observation of the celestial bodies
    (B) Advanced technology
    (C) Advanced tools of measurement
    (D) Knowledge of the earth's surface

48. Why was the Great Pyramid constructed?
    (A) As a solar observatory
    (B) As a religious temple
    (C) As a tomb for the pharaoh
    (D) As an engineering feat

49. Why is the Great Pyramid of Giza considered one of the seven wonders of the world?
    (A) It is perfectly aligned with the four cardinal points of the compass and contains many prophecies.
    (B) It was selected as the tomb of Pharaoh Cheops.
    (C) It was built by a super race.
    (D) It is very old.

50. The word "feat" in line 11 is closest in meaning to
    (A) accomplishment   (C) festivity
    (B) appendage   (D) structure

STOP. THIS IS THE END OF THE EXAMINATION. IF YOU FINISH BEFORE TIME IS UP, CHECK YOUR WORK IN THIS SECTION ONLY. DO NOT WORK ON ANY OTHER SECTION OF THE TEST.

PRACTICE TEST 5

SECTION 1
LISTENING COMPREHENSION

Time: Approximately 30 Minutes
50 Questions

Section 1 has three parts. Each part has its own set of directions. Do not take notes while listening or make any marks on the test pages. Notetaking, underlining, or crossing out will be considered cheating on the actual TOEFL exam. Answer the questions following the conversations or talks based on what the speakers have *stated* or *implied*.

For Practice Test 5, restart your Listening Comprehension cassette immediately following Practice Test 4. On the actual TOEFL, you will be given extra time to go on to the next page when you finish a page in the Listening Comprehension section. In the following test, however, you will have only the 12 seconds given after each question. Turn the page as soon as you have marked your answer. Start the cassette now.

Part A

DIRECTIONS

In Part A, you will hear short conversations between two speakers. At the end of each conversation, a third voice will ask a question about what was said. The question will be *spoken* just one time. After you hear a conversation and the question about it, read the four possible answers and decide which one would be the best answer to the question you have heard. Then, on your answer sheet, find the number of the problem and mark your answer.

1. (A) They were displeased.
   (B) They found it sad.
   (C) They thought it was shocking, but very funny.
   (D) They became angry at the promiscuity.

2. (A) To the beach.
   (B) To a play.
   (C) To a movie theater.
   (D) To a restaurant.

3. (A) He's dying.
   (B) He doesn't hear too well.
   (C) He was at a party.
   (D) He was reading something important.

4. (A) The class thought the demonstration was too complex.
   (B) Too many students showed up.
   (C) The professor didn't show up.
   (D) The professor canceled it.

5. (A) It's more direct.
   (B) There's a traffic jam.
   (C) It's faster.
   (D) It's less expensive.

6. (A) He got a one-way plane ticket.
   (B) He went the wrong direction on a one-way street.
   (C) He made an improper turn.
   (D) He slowed down at the wrong time.

7. (A) Susan Flannigan is in a bell-ringing group.
   (B) Her name sounds familiar.
   (C) Susan Flannigan is ringing the bell now.
   (D) Her name sounds melodic.

8. (A) Roy's standing in line for a gold medal.
   (B) Roy was the best, so he got a gold medal.
   (C) Nobody's better than Roy at getting gold medals.
   (D) Roy probably won't win a gold medal.

9. (A) The cartridge does not need to be replaced.
   (B) He does not intend to change the cartridge.
   (C) He already changed the cartridge.
   (D) He is uncomfortable because the woman is watching him.

10. (A) Every week, there are three direct flights from Atlanta to Chicago.
    (B) Next week, the three flights from Atlanta to Chicago will be stopped.
    (C) Three planes which travel from Atlanta to Chicago each week make nine stops enroute.
    (D) The number of planes that travel from Atlanta to Chicago will be reduced within the next three weeks.

11. (A) He is pleased because his family is coming up to see him.
    (B) He is considering several maps to decide where to go.
    (C) He is rather excited because he has a vacation soon.
    (D) He is coming up to see us on his vacation.

12. (A) She is angry because there is too much chlorine in the pool.
    (B) The chlorine in the swimming pool bothers her eyes.
    (C) She believes the correct amount of chlorine is essential to a clean swimming pool.
    (D) She doesn't believe that there is enough chlorine in the pool.

13. (A) She is uncomfortable telling the man that he is losing his job.
    (B) She misplaced the man's papers.
    (C) She is unsure when they will be moving.
    (D) She hasn't decided where his office will be located.

14. (A) Returned them and got a pair of pants instead.
    (B) Took them back to the store and got some different ones.
    (C) Got her money back because they didn't fit properly.
    (D) Received a refund because of a problem with the heel.

15. (A) He does not intend to go on the field trip.
    (B) Some people have not submitted a required form.
    (C) The trip has been canceled.
    (D) Everybody is likely to go on the trip.

16. (A) She was not able to read her assignment because she broke her glasses.
    (B) She could have read the assignment if she hadn't had to wash dishes.
    (C) She won't go to class tomorrow because she must go to the optometrist.
    (D) She cut herself on some broken glass, so she didn't do her homework.

17. (A) She has an easy schedule.
    (B) She doesn't pay attention in class.
    (C) Taking both courses together is a bad decision.
    (D) She is brilliant.

18. (A) It will be canceled as a result of mismanagement of funds.
    (B) They probably made an error in figuring the expenses.
    (C) They must give a complete report on the estimated costs.
    (D) They have to charge the calculations to the company office.

19. (A) She was able to go because her employer paid her expenses.
    (B) She couldn't go because her boss wouldn't pay her while she was away.
    (C) Although her employer had offered to pay her expenses, she didn't go.
    (D) Her boss refused to give her money, but she went anyway.

20. (A) Although June doesn't like television, her husband watches it every night.
    (B) June refuses to let her husband watch television.
    (C) June always asks her husband to watch television with her.
    (D) June's husband refuses to let her watch television.

21. (A) If it were a hot day, the trip would be difficult.
    (B) It is a very hot day for the long trip.
    (C) It's a magnificent day.
    (D) It's not as far as the woman thinks to their destination.

22. (A) The Kehoes got a bargain.
    (B) Chuck bought a new house.
    (C) The Kehoes bought a house out of the country.
    (D) Mr. Kehoe is a real estate agent.

23. (A) The food spoiled.
    (B) The group was shameful.
    (C) The weather was bad.
    (D) The program director wanted to have it on another day.

24. (A) Sebring High School.
    (B) Clark High School.
    (C) Melrose Community College.
    (D) Enrold College.

25. (A) A bicycle.   (C) A shirt.
    (B) A game.   (D) Baseball shoes.

26. (A) Please give me your hand.
    (B) Would you help me carry these packages?
    (C) Please remove your hands from those packages.
    (D) My hand is stuck under the packages.

27. (A) She is trying to find a new typing job.
    (B) She is looking for somebody to type her research paper.
    (C) She is trying to find somebody to move her typewriter to another table.
    (D) She has accepted employment as a typist.

28. (A) Harvey didn't go to class because he didn't know there was going to be a test.
    (B) Harvey didn't want to take the test, so he skipped class.
    (C) Harvey went to class although he didn't want to take the test.
    (D) Harvey was happy that yesterday's test was postponed.

29. (A) Joe uses some strange methods when he studies.
    (B) Joe receives very good grades although he doesn't study.
    (C) Joe is very fond of studying dangerous situations.
    (D) It's too bad that Joe dislikes studying.

30. (A) He has entered the university hospital for treatment.
    (B) He met his wife while she was working as a nurse at the university hospital.
    (C) He wants to find a place close to the university to keep his children during the day.
    (D) He likes the university because it has a good nursing program.

GO ON TO PART B

Part B

DIRECTIONS

In Part B, you will hear longer conversations. After each conversation, you will be asked some questions. The conversations and questions will be *spoken* just one time. They will not be written out for you, so you will have to listen carefully in order to understand and remember what the speaker says.

When you hear a question, read the four possible answers in your test book and decide which one would be the best answer to the question you have heard. Then, on your answer sheet, find the number of the problem and fill in the space that corresponds to the letter of the answer you have chosen.

31. (A) More than $195.
    (B) Less than $195.
    (C) $150.
    (D) Less than $150.

32. (A) One day.
    (B) Four days.
    (C) Several hours.
    (D) Ten hours.

33. (A) Mechanic.
    (B) Policeman.
    (C) TV repairman.
    (D) Car salesman.

34. (A) Broken fuel pump.
    (B) Dirty carburetor.
    (C) Dirty oil.
    (D) Leaky radiator.

35. (A) All her expenses will be paid.
    (B) She'll earn a great deal of money.
    (C) She can practice her Spanish.
    (D) She can spend her free time at the beach.

36. (A) One week.
    (B) Immediately.
    (C) Six weeks.
    (D) A few hours.

37. (A) Swimsuit.
    (B) A Spanish dictionary.
    (C) Passport.
    (D) Money.

38. (A) Interview local artists.
    (B) Photograph the craftsmen.
    (C) Write her story.
    (D) Listen to mariachi music.

GO ON TO PART C

Part C

DIRECTIONS

In Part C, you will hear several talks. After each talk, you will be asked some questions. The talks and questions will be *spoken* just one time. They will not be written out for you, so you will have to listen carefully in order to understand and remember what the speaker says.

When you hear a question, read the four possible answers in your test book and decide which one would be the best answer to the question you have heard. Then, on your answer sheet, find the number of the problem and fill in the space that corresponds to the letter of the answer you have chosen.

39. (A) He was struck by lightning.
    (B) He was very old.
    (C) He was in a car accident.
    (D) He fell down in his yard.

40. (A) His wife.   (B) A tree.   (C) A clock.   (D) Lightning.

41. (A) Edwards had been blind for nine years.
    (B) Edwards was unconscious for twenty minutes after the lightning had struck him.
    (C) Doctors believe that Edwards was never really blind or deaf.
    (D) Edwards awoke with his face in a puddle of water.

42. (A) Hiding from the storm under a tree.
    (B) Climbing a tree.
    (C) Driving a car.
    (D) Lying on the ground.

441

43. (A) He regained his sight from a head injury when he fell from a tree.
    (B) He was happy after his wife entered his room for the first time in nine years.
    (C) The lightning took the feeling from his legs and gave feeling in his eyes.
    (D) Because the blow that blinded him was very severe, it took another very severe blow to restore his sight.

44. (A) Cotton.   (B) Nylon.   (C) Grains.   (D) Rayon.

45. (A) It is the smallest state in size.
    (B) It was the first to discover lightweight fiber.
    (C) It was the first to ratify the Constitution.
    (D) It was the "bread basket" in colonial days.

46. (A) Irish.   (B) Swedish.   (C) English.   (D) Dutch.

47. (A) It was at the heart of the country.
    (B) It was extremely small.
    (C) Its inhabitants sold baskets which they made by hand.
    (D) Its inhabitants produced corn, wheat, and other grains, which were sold throughout the country.

48. (A) A duck.   (C) A chameleon.
    (B) A skunk.   (D) An Arctic fox.

49. (A) Their bite.   (C) Their odor.
    (B) Their pigmentation.   (D) Their quills.

50. (A) Claws.   (C) Bite.
    (B) Sting.   (D) Pigmentation.

STOP. This is the end of the listening comprehension section. Go on to section 2.

SECTION 2
STRUCTURE AND WRITTEN EXPRESSION

Time: 25 Minutes
40 Questions

Part A

DIRECTIONS

Questions 1–15 are incomplete sentences. Beneath each sentence you will see four words or phrases, marked (A), (B), (C), and (D). Choose the *one* word or phrase that best completes the sentence. Then, on your answer sheet, find the number of the question and fill in the space that corresponds to the letter of the answer you have chosen. Fill in the space so that the letter inside the oval cannot be seen.

1. I understand that the governor is considering a new proposal
   _____.
   (A) what would eliminate unnecessary writing in government
   (B) who wants to cut down on the amount of writing in government
   (C) that would eliminate unnecessary paperwork in government
   (D) to cause that the amount of papers written in government offices will be reduced

2. The doctor told his receptionist that he would return
   _____.
   (A) as early as it would be possible
   (B) at the earliest that it could be possible
   (C) as soon as possible
   (D) at the nearest early possibility

3. George belongs to the _____.
   (A) class of the upper middle
   (B) upper middle class
   (C) class from the center up
   (D) high medium class

4. A good student must know _____.
   (A) to study hard
   (B) to be a good student
   (C) how to study effectively
   (D) the way of efficiency in study

5. Jane changed her major from French to business, _____.
   (A) with hopes to be able easier to locate employment
   (B) hoping she can easier get a job
   (C) with the hope for being able to find better a job
   (D) hoping to find a job more easily

6. He has received several scholarships _____.
   (A) not only because of his artistic but his academic ability
   (B) for both his academic ability as well as his artistic
   (C) because of his academic and artistic ability
   (D) as resulting of his ability in the art and the academy

7. Harvey will wash the clothes, _____.
   (A) iron the shirts, prepare the meal, dusting the furniture
   (B) ironing the shirts, preparing the meal, and dusting the furniture
   (C) iron the shirts, prepare the meal, and dust the furniture
   (D) to iron the shirts, prepare the meal, and dust the furniture

8. _____ that new information to anyone else but the sergeant.
   (A) They asked him not to give
   (B) They asked him to don't give
   (C) They asked him no give
   (D) They asked him to no give

9. _____, he would have signed his name in the corner.
   - (A) If he painted that picture
   - (B) If he paints that picture
   - (C) If he had painted that picture
   - (D) If he would have painted that picture

10. The doctor insisted that his patient _____.
   - (A) that he not work too hard for three months
   - (B) take it easy for three months
   - (C) taking it easy inside of three months
   - (D) to take some vacations for three months

11. The manager was angry because somebody _____.
   - (A) had allowed the photographers to enter the building
   - (B) had let the photographers to enter into the building
   - (C) permitting the photographers enter the building
   - (D) the photographers let into the building without the proper documentations

12. Richard was asked to withdraw from graduate school because
   _____.
   - (A) they believed he was not really able to complete research
   - (B) he was deemed incapable of completing his research
   - (C) it was decided that he was not capable to complete the research
   - (D) his ability to finish the research was not believed or trusted

13. The committee members resented _____.
   - (A) the president that he did not tell them about the meeting
   - (B) the president not to inform them of the meeting
   - (C) the president's not informing them of the meeting
   - (D) that the president had failed informing themselves that there was going to be a meeting

14. _____ did Arthur realize that there was danger.
- (A) Upon entering the store
- (B) When he entered the store
- (C) After he had entered the store
- (D) Only after entering the store

15. The rabbit scurried away in fright_____.
- (A) when it heard the movement in the bushes
- (B) the movement among the bushes having been heard
- (C) after it was hearing moving inside of the bushes
- (D) when he has heard that something moved in the bushes

GO ON TO PART B

Part B

DIRECTIONS

In questions 16–40, each sentence has four underlined words or phrases. The four underlined parts of the sentence are marked (A), (B), (C), and (D). Identify the *one* underlined word or phrase that must be changed in order for the sentence to be correct. Then, on your answer sheet, find the number of the question and fill in the space that corresponds to the letter of the answer you have chosen.

16. Neither of the girls have turned in the term papers
         A   B
to the instructor yet.
   C   D

17. After studying all the new materials, the student was able to
    A   B   C
rise his test score by twenty-five points.
 D

18. The book that you see laying on the table belongs to the
            A   B   C   D

    teacher.

19. I suggest that he goes to the doctor as soon as he
            A   B   C

    returns from taking the exam.
        D

20. She is looking forward to go to Europe after she finishes her
            A   B   C

    studies at the university.
        D

21. They said that the man jumped off of the bridge and
             A   B   C

    plunged into the freezing water.
        D

22. Mr. Anderson used to jogging in the crisp morning air during
                    A   B   C

    the winter months, but now he has stopped.
        D

23. The volume four of our encyclopedia set has been missing
           A   B   C

    for two months.
     D

24. I do not know where could he have gone so early
                    A   B   C

    in the morning.
     D

25. The people tried <u>of defending</u> <u>their</u> village, but they were
                 A   B

    finally <u>forced</u> <u>to retreat.</u>
          C   D

26. The professor was <u>considering</u> <u>postponing</u> the examination
                  A   B

    until <u>the following week</u> <u>because</u> the students' confusion.
           C   D

27. <u>Having lost</u> the election, the presidential candidate intends
     A

    <u>supporting</u> the opposition <u>despite</u> <u>the objections of</u> his staff.
      B   C   D

28. The congressman, accompanied <u>by</u> secret service agents and
                         A

    aides, <u>are</u> preparing <u>to enter</u> the convention hall
        B   C

    <u>within the next</u> few minutes.
        D

29. <u>Because</u> the <u>torrential</u> rains that <u>had devastated</u> the area, the
     A   B   C

    governor sent the National Guard <u>to assist in</u> the clean-up
                         D

    operation.

30. Lack <u>of sanitation</u> in restaurants <u>are</u> a major <u>cause of</u> disease
         A   B   C

    <u>in some areas of</u> the country.
      D

448

31. Had the committee members considered the alternatives
    <u>_____</u>
           A
    more carefully, they would have realized that the
    <u>_____</u>
           B
    second was better as the first.
    <u>_____</u>   <u>_____</u>
         C   D

32. Malnutrition is a major cause of death
    <u>_____</u>
              A
    in those countries where the cultivation of rice have been
    <u>_____</u>   <u>____</u>
              B   C
    impeded by recurrent drought.
    <u>_____</u>
           D

33. The decision to withdraw all support from the activities of the
    <u>_____</u> <u>_____</u>
           A   B
    athletes are causing an uproar among the athletes' fans.
    <u>_____</u>   <u>_____</u>
            C   D

34. Underutilized species of fish has been proposed as a solution
    <u>_____</u>   <u>_____</u>   <u>__</u>
          A   B   C
    to the famine in many underdeveloped countries.
    <u>_____</u>
          D

35. Because the residents had worked so diligent to renovate the
    <u>_____</u>   <u>_____</u>   <u>_____</u> <u>_____</u>
       A   B   C   D
    old building, the manager had a party.

36. John's wisdom teeth were troubling him, so he went to a
                        <u>_____</u>
                              A
    dental surgeon to see about having them pull.
                   <u>_____</u>   <u>____</u> <u>____</u>
                        B   C   D

37. Hardly he had entered the office when he realized that he had
    <u>_____</u>   <u>_____</u>   <u>_____</u>
         A   B   C
    forgotten his wallet.
    <u>_____</u>
         D

449

38. Suzy <u>had</u> better <u>to change</u> her study habits if she
       A   B

    <u>hopes to be</u> admitted <u>to a good university.</u>
       C   D

39. The teacher <u>told</u> the students to <u>don't</u> <u>discuss</u> the take-home
         A   B   C

    exam <u>with each other.</u>
         D

40. Some bacteria <u>are extremely</u> harmful, but <u>anothers</u> are
             A   B

    <u>regularly</u> used in producing cheeses, crackers, and
      C

    <u>many other foods.</u>
      D

STOP. THIS IS THE END OF THE STRUCTURE AND WRITTEN EXPRESSION SECTION. IF YOU FINISH BEFORE TIME IS UP, CHECK YOUR WORK ON PARTS A AND B OF THIS SECTION ONLY. DO NOT WORK ON ANY OTHER SECTION OF THE TEST.

SECTION 3
READING COMPREHENSION

Time: 55 Minutes
50 Questions

DIRECTIONS

In this section, you will read a number of passages. Each one is followed by approximately ten questions about it. For questions 1–50, choose the *one* best answer, (A), (B), (C), or (D), to each question. Then, find the number of the question on your answer sheet, and fill in the space that corresponds to the letter of the answer you have chosen. Answer all questions following a passage on the basis of what is *stated* or *implied* in that passage.

Questions 1 through 11 are based on the following passage.

The food we eat seems to have profound effects on our health. Although science has made enormous steps in making food more fit to eat, it has, at the same time, made many foods unfit to eat. Some research has shown that
(5) perhaps eighty percent of all human illnesses are related to diet and forty percent of cancer is related to the diet as well, especially cancer of the colon. People of different cultures are more prone to contract certain illnesses because of the characteristic foods they consume.
(10)   That food is related to illness is not a new discovery. In 1945, government researchers realized that nitrates and nitrites (commonly used to preserve color in meats) as well as other food additives caused cancer. Yet, these carcinogenic additives remain in our food, and it becomes more
(15) difficult all the time to know which ingredients on the packaging labels of processed food are helpful or harmful.
    The additives that we eat are not all so direct. Farmers often give penicillin to cattle and poultry, and because of

451

this, penicillin has been found in the milk of treated cows.
(20) Sometimes similar drugs are administered to animals not
for medicinal purposes, but for financial reasons. The
farmers are simply trying to fatten the animals in order to
obtain a higher price on the market. Although the Food and
Drug Administration (FDA) has tried repeatedly to control
(25) these procedures, the practices continue.

A healthy diet is directly related to good health. Often we
are unaware of detrimental substances we ingest. Sometimes well-meaning farmers or others who do not realize the
consequences add these substances to food without our
(30) knowledge.

1. How has science done a disservice to people?
   (A) Because of science, disease caused by contaminated food
       has been virtually eradicated.
   (B) It has caused a lack of information concerning the value of
       food.
   (C) As a result of scientific intervention, some potentially
       harmful substances have been added to our food.
   (D) The scientists have preserved the color of meats, but not of
       vegetables.

2. The word "prone" in line 8 is nearest in meaning to
   (A) supine   (C) healthy
   (B) unlikely   (D) predisposed

3. What are nitrates used for?
   (A) They preserve flavor in packaged foods.
   (B) They preserve the color of meats.
   (C) They are the objects of research.
   (D) They cause the animals to become fatter.

4. FDA means
   (A) Food Direct Additives
   (B) Final Difficult Analysis
   (C) Food and Drug Administration
   (D) Federal Dairy Additives

5. The word "these" in line 13 refers to
   (A) meats
   (B) colors
   (C) researchers
   (D) nitrates and nitrites

6. In line 13, the word "carcinogenic" is closest in meaning to
   (A) trouble-making
   (B) color-retaining
   (C) money-making
   (D) cancer-causing

7. All of the following statements are true EXCEPT
   (A) drugs are always given to animals for medical reasons
   (B) some of the additives in our food are added to the food itself and some are given to the living animals
   (C) researchers have known about the potential hazards of food additives for more than forty-five years
   (D) food may cause forty percent of the cancer in the world

8. The word "additives" in line 13 is closest in meaning to
   (A) added substances
   (B) dangerous substances
   (C) natural substances
   (D) benign substances

9. What is the best title for this passage?
   (A) Harmful and Harmless Substances in Food
   (B) Improving Health Through a Natural Diet
   (C) The Food You Eat Can Affect Your Health
   (D) Avoiding Injurious Substances in Food

10. In line 3, the word "fit" is closest in meaning to
    (A) athletic   (B) suitable   (C) tasty   (D) adaptable

11. The fact that the topic has been known for some time is discussed in lines
(A) 2–4   (B) 10–11   (C) 17–19   (D) 26–27

Questions 12 through 21 are based on the following passage.

The ancient Egyptians firmly believed in the afterlife and spent their time on earth preparing for it. Elaborate burial rituals included preparing the burial site, providing for all of the deceased's material needs (food, clothing, jewels, and
(5) tools of their trade), and preserving the corpse so that it would not decay. This preservation was accomplished through a process of mummification. The ancients left no written accounts as to the execution of this process, so scientists have had to examine mummies and establish their
(10) own theories. The embalming process might have taken up to seventy days for the pharaohs and nobility and only a few days for the poor.

The embalmers spread a variety of compounds of salt, spices, and resins in and over the corpse to preserve it. They
(15) followed this with a prescribed wrapping, a procedure in which they wound strips of fine linen around, over, and under the body while placing various amulets within the wrappings to protect the deceased from harm on the long journey to the afterlife. They also painted resins over the
(20) wrapped linen. Finally, a pharaoh or noble would have been encased in a wooden box before being placed in a sarcophagus.

12. How have we been able to learn about the mummification process?
    (A) Accurate records have been handed down to us.
    (B) Interviews with embalmers who still use the process have revealed the secret.
    (C) After studying mummies, scientists have developed their own theories.
    (D) Chemical analysis of the compounds has led us to an explanation of the method used.

13. The word "they" in line 19 refers to
    (A) embalmers   (C) pharaohs
    (B) spices   (D) the poor

14. The embalming process can best be described as
    (A) lengthy and complicated
    (B) short and simple
    (C) strict and unfaltering
    (D) wild and terrifying

15. The word "decay" in line 6 is closest in meaning to
    (A) die   (C) embalm
    (B) deteriorate   (D) rejuvenate

16. All of the following statements are true EXCEPT
    (A) bodies were preserved as a matter of religious belief
    (B) all mummification took seventy days to complete
    (C) special compounds were used to embalm the bodies
    (D) it has been difficult to determine the process used

17. Why did the ancient Egyptians mummify the deceased?
    (A) To preserve the body from destruction
    (B) To scare tomb robbers
    (C) To encase the body in a sarcophagus
    (D) To protect the body from harm on the journey to the afterlife

18. It can be inferred that the Egyptians buried food, clothing, jewels, and tools with the deceased because
    (A) the family did not want anyone else to share them
    (B) that was the wish of the deceased
    (C) they were afraid
    (D) the deceased would need them while enroute to the afterlife

19. The word "amulets" in line 17 is closest in meaning to
    (A) weapons   (B) coins   (C) charms   (D) curses

20. In line 6, "accomplished" is closest in meaning to
    (A) performed   (C) reproduced
    (B) forsaken   (D) dwindled

21. The distinction between mummification of bodies from different classes is explained in lines
    (A) 2–6   (B) 10–12   (C) 13–14   (D) 15–17

Questions 22 through 30 are based on the following passage.

A tapeworm is a parasite that lives in the intestines of humans and animals. Some tapeworms attach themselves to the intestinal wall by means of suckers in their heads. Others float freely in the intestines and absorb food through
(5) the walls of their bodies.

A tapeworm consists of numerous segments. When a new segment forms, the older ones move to the back of the animal. Each segment contains hermaphroditic sexual organs (that is, male and female organs). The uterus of each
(10) segment fills with eggs, which develop into embryos. Generally, when the eggs are ready to hatch, the segment breaks off and is eliminated through the host's excretory system. These embryos hatch, develop into larvae, and grow to adults only if ingested by an intermediate host.
(15)   One may be infected by tapeworms by eating under-

cooked beef, pork, or fish. Symptoms include irregular appetite, abdominal discomfort, anemia, weakness, and nervousness.

22. The passage implies that all of the following are true EXCEPT
    (A) an embryo will cease to develop if not ingested by a host
    (B) a tapeworm will continue to live even when segments break off
    (C) the segment farthest back on the tail is the oldest
    (D) tapeworms always float freely in the digestive system

23. The word "eliminated" in line 12 is closest in meaning to
    (A) ingested   (B) expelled   (C) eaten   (D) grown

24. A hermaphrodite is
    (A) a tapeworm
    (B) a segment containing an embryo
    (C) a being that contains male and female sexual organs
    (D) an animal made of segments

25. The word "others" in line 4 refers to
    (A) segments
    (B) embryos
    (C) eggs
    (D) tapeworms

26. Which of the following is probably NOT a symptom of tapeworm infestation?
    (A) Unusual eating habits
    (B) Excitability
    (C) Deficiency of red blood cells
    (D) Euphoria

27. Which of the following statements is true?
    (A) A tapeworm uterus contains one egg.
    (B) Overcooked beef is a cause of tapeworms.
    (C) A male tapeworm must always be ingested before reproduction will occur.
    (D) Tapeworms vary in their methods of ingesting food.

28. What would be the best title for this reading passage?
    (A) Parasites
    (B) Reproduction of the Tapeworm
    (C) The Tapeworm, a Harmful Parasite
    (D) Segmented Parasites

29. A tapeworm attaches itself to the intestinal wall by
    (A) suction   (B) liquid   (C) food   (D) teeth

30. In line 6, the word "segments" is closest in meaning to
    (A) types   (B) sections   (C) organs   (D) worms

Questions 31 through 40 are based on the following passage.

After inventing dynamite, Swedish-born Alfred Nobel became a very rich man. However, he foresaw its universally destructive powers too late. Nobel preferred not to be remembered as the inventor of dynamite, so in 1895, just
(5) two weeks before his death, he created a fund to be used for awarding prizes to people who had made worthwhile contributions to humanity. Originally there were five awards: literature, physics, chemistry, medicine, and peace. Economics was added in 1968, just sixty-seven years after the first
(10) awards ceremony.

Nobel's original legacy of nine million dollars was invested, and the interest on this sum is used for the awards which vary from $30,000 to $125,000.

Every year on December 10, the anniversary of Nobel's
(15) death, the awards (gold medal, illuminated diploma, and money) are presented to the winners. Sometimes politics plays an important role in the judges' decisions. Americans have won numerous science awards, but relatively few literature prizes.

(20) No awards were presented from 1940 to 1942 at the beginning of World War II. Some people have won two prizes, but this is rare; others have shared their prizes.

31. The word "foresaw" in line 2 is nearest in meaning to
    (A) prevailed   (C) prevented
    (B) postponed   (D) predicted

32. The Nobel Prize was established in order to
    (A) recognize worthwhile contributions to humanity
    (B) resolve political differences
    (C) honor the inventor of dynamite
    (D) spend money

33. In which area have Americans received the most awards?
    (A) Literature   (C) Economics
    (B) Peace   (D) Science

34. All of the following statements are true EXCEPT
    (A) awards vary in monetary value
    (B) ceremonies are held on December 10 to commemorate
        Nobel's invention
    (C) politics plays an important role in selecting the winners
    (D) a few individuals have won two awards

35. In how many fields are prizes bestowed?
    (A) 2   (B) 5   (C) 6   (D) 10

36. It is implied that Nobel's profession was in
    (A) economics   (C) literature
    (B) medicine   (D) science

37. In line 6, "worthwhile" is closest in meaning to
    (A) economic   (C) trivial
    (B) prestigious   (D) valuable

38. How much money did Nobel leave for the prizes?
    (A) $30,000   (C) $155,000
    (B) $125,000   (D) $9,000,000

39. What is the main idea of this passage?
    (A) Alfred Nobel became very rich when he invented dynamite.
    (B) Alfred Nobel created awards in six categories for contributions to humanity.
    (C) Alfred Nobel left all of his money to science.
    (D) Alfred Nobel made a lasting contribution to humanity.

40. The word "legacy" in line 11 means most nearly the same as
    (A) legend   (B) bequest   (C) prize   (D) debt

Questions 41 through 50 are based on the following passage.

Ever since humans have inhabited the earth, they have made use of various forms of communication. Generally, this expression of thoughts and feelings has been in the form of oral speech. When there is a language barrier, communi-
(5) cation is accomplished through sign language in which motions stand for letters, words, and ideas. Tourists, the deaf, and the mute have had to resort to this form of expression. Many of these symbols of whole words are very picturesque and exact and can be used internationally;
(10) spelling, however, cannot.

Body language transmits ideas or thoughts by certain actions, either intentionally or unintentionally. A wink can be a way of flirting or indicating that the party is only joking. A nod signifies approval, while shaking the head indicates a
(15) negative reaction.

Other forms of nonlinguistic language can be found in Braille (a system of raised dots read with the fingertips), signal flags, Morse code, and smoke signals. Road maps and picture signs also guide, warn, and instruct people.
(20)   While verbalization is the most common form of language, other systems and techniques also express human thoughts and feelings.

460

41. Which of the following best summarizes this passage?
    (A) When language is a barrier, people will find other forms of communication.
    (B) Everybody uses only one form of communication.
    (C) Nonlinguistic language is invaluable to foreigners.
    (D) Although other forms of communication exist, verbalization is the fastest.

42. The word "these" in line 8 refers to
    (A) tourists
    (B) the deaf and the mute
    (C) thoughts and feelings
    (D) sign language motions

43. All of the following statements are true EXCEPT
    (A) there are many forms of communication in existence today
    (B) verbalization is the most common form of communication
    (C) the deaf and mute use an oral form of communication
    (D) ideas and thoughts can be transmitted by body language

44. Which form other than oral speech would be most commonly used among blind people?
    (A) Picture signs   (C) Body language
    (B) Braille   (D) Signal flags

45. How many different forms of communication are mentioned here?
    (A) 5   (B) 7   (C) 9   (D) 11

46. The word "wink" in line 12 means most nearly the same as
    (A) close one eye briefly
    (B) close two eyes briefly
    (C) bob the head up and down
    (D) shake the head from side to side

47. Sign language is said to be very picturesque and exact and can be used internationally EXCEPT for
    (A) spelling   (C) whole words
    (B) ideas   (D) expressions

48. People need to communicate in order to
    (A) create language barriers
    (B) keep from reading with their fingertips
    (C) be picturesque and exact
    (D) express thoughts and feelings

49. What is the best title for the passage?
    (A) The Importance of Sign Language
    (B) The Many Forms of Communication
    (C) Ways of Expressing Feelings
    (D) Picturesque Symbols of Communication

50. Who would be MOST likely to use Morse code?
    (A) A scientist   (C) An airline pilot
    (B) A spy   (D) A telegrapher

STOP. This is the end of the examination. If you finish before time is up, check your work in this section only. Do not work on any other section of the test.

PRACTICE TEST 6

SECTION 1
LISTENING COMPREHENSION

Time: Approximately 30 Minutes
50 Questions

Section 1 has three parts. Each part has its own set of directions. Do not take notes while listening or make any marks on the test pages. Notetaking, underlining, or crossing out will be considered cheating on the actual TOEFL exam. Answer the questions following the conversations or talks based on what the speakers have *stated* or *implied.*

For Practice Test 6, restart your Listening Comprehension cassette immediately following Practice Test 5. On the actual TOEFL, you will be given extra time to go on to the next page when you finish a page in the Listening Comprehension section. In the following test, however, you will have only the 12 seconds given after each question. Turn the page as soon as you have marked your answer. Start the cassette now.

Part A

DIRECTIONS

In Part A, you will hear short conversations between two speakers. At the end of each conversation, a third voice will ask a question about what was said. The question will be *spoken* just one time. After you hear a conversation and the question about it, read the four possible answers and decide which one would be the best answer to the question you have heard. Then, on your answer sheet, find the number of the problem and mark your answer.

1. (A) Mark is fond of rare meat.
   (B) Mark is angry at the chef.
   (C) Mark dislikes rare meat.
   (D) Mark doesn't want his meat cooked medium rare.

2. (A) The man doesn't like skim milk.
   (B) The milk has turned bad.
   (C) The man's check-cashing card has expired.
   (D) The milk may turn sour if they don't drink it within the next five days.

3. (A) He has other plans.
   (B) He has a bad personality.
   (C) He thinks it will be frightening.
   (D) He doesn't have enough time.

4. (A) It has been in her family a long time.
   (B) It is a family disgrace.
   (C) Her mother doesn't like it.
   (D) Her boyfriend gave it to her.

5. (A) It was cleaned.
   (B) There was a large sale.
   (C) The employees had to work very late.
   (D) There was a robbery.

6. (A) She has good taste in clothes.
   (B) Her choice is not suitable for the occasion.
   (C) The skirt is pretty, but not the blouse.
   (D) It is too elegant.

7. (A) Jack didn't visit them.
   (B) Jack will not visit them because it's not on his way.
   (C) They hope Jack will visit them.
   (D) They are sure that Jack will visit them if he doesn't run out of time.

8. (A) She'll count the votes on the proposal.
   (B) She'll support the man's proposal.
   (C) She'll make the proposal herself.
   (D) She'll back out of the proposal.

9. (A) At the jewelry store.   (C) From a machine.
   (B) From the purchaser.   (D) Down the hall.

10. (A) It will rain later.
    (B) It's probably not going to rain.
    (C) It's raining now, but will probably stop.
    (D) The rain has already stopped.

11. (A) The man should ask for advice.
    (B) The man needs to make his own decision.
    (C) The man should not buy the house.
    (D) The man should make an offer.

12. (A) Monday, Wednesday, and Friday.
    (B) Saturday and Sunday.
    (C) Tuesday, Thursday, and Sunday.
    (D) Monday, Friday, and Saturday.

13. (A) It was hard for her to learn so much material.
    (B) She learned the difficult extremes.
    (C) She wasn't able to materialize the difficulties.
    (D) She found the material after a difficult search.

14. (A) He studied because it was a nice day.
    (B) He didn't study because it was a very nice day.
    (C) He studied in spite of the beautiful weather.
    (D) He likes to study when the weather is nice.

15. (A) She found a hard seat because the theater was dark.
    (B) She couldn't find a seat in the dark.
    (C) She couldn't seat her friends.
    (D) She had some difficulty finding a seat.

16. (A) After the class had begun, some of the brazen students entered the room.
    (B) There were three dozen students in the class after it had begun.
    (C) There were 24 students in the class after it had begun.
    (D) The dozen people in the room were doubling as students.

17. (A) He expected the professor to contradict himself.
    (B) He had expected the professor to cancel the class.
    (C) He was contrary with the professor.
    (D) He hadn't expected the professor to cancel class, but he did.

18. (A) In a butcher shop.   (C) In a pharmacy.
    (B) In a bakery.   (D) In an ice-cream store.

19. (A) He won the trophy.
    (B) He's a minister.
    (C) He sprained his ankle.
    (D) He broke his arm.

20. (A) In the winter.   (C) In September.
    (B) In July.   (D) In April.

21. (A) The speakers may cause Katie to be late.
    (B) She will be here shortly.
    (C) The speakers will probably be late if she doesn't arrive soon.
    (D) She probably forgot the appointment.

22. (A) Go to a party either Friday or Saturday night.
    (B) Go to a party if the weather is good.
    (C) Go to a party on both Friday and Saturday nights.
    (D) Not go to a party because of the weather.

23. (A) Helen hates to eat fish.
    (B) Helen often fishes with her husband, but she doesn't like it.
    (C) Helen hates her husband after he has been fishing.
    (D) Helen likes to eat fish, but her husband likes to fish too much.

24. (A) Karl enjoys painting puzzles.
    (B) Karl's expression puzzled the woman.
    (C) Karl was confused.
    (D) Karl expressed the woman's face in a puzzle.

25. (A) He must exhaust the runner.
    (B) He was probably very tired after running.
    (C) The rum made him sleepy.
    (D) He must run after the thief.

26. (A) He can probably see her tomorrow afternoon.
    (B) Tomorrow at noon she will see him.
    (C) She may see him now, but she'll be too busy tomorrow.
    (D) He must pay his last bill if he wants to see her.

27. (A) Sally's friends have very bad habits.
    (B) Sally doesn't have many friends because she is spiteful.
    (C) Sally has many friends although she has bad habits.
    (D) Bad people are avoided by Sally.

28. (A) The houses are too simple to cost so much.
    (B) It is easy to pay for a nice house.
    (C) They don't have enough money for a new house because of the high prices.
    (D) They can afford a new house now, but not next year.

29. (A) It should have closed yesterday, but it will close in two days.
    (B) It closes two days from now.
    (C) It closed two days ago.
    (D) Registration for the class is late.

30. (A) She didn't know that they had changed plans.
    (B) Their change in plans didn't affect her plans.
    (C) She didn't tell them when she changed plans.
    (D) She didn't know that they had changed the schedule of the planes.

GO ON TO PART B

Part B

DIRECTIONS

In Part B, you will hear longer conversations. After each conversation, you will be asked some questions. The conversations and questions will be *spoken* just one time. They will not be written out for you, so you will have to listen carefully in order to understand and remember what the speaker says.

When you hear a question, read the four possible answers in your test book and decide which one would be the best answer to the question you have heard. Then, on your answer sheet, find the number of the problem and fill in the space that corresponds to the letter of the answer you have chosen.

31. (A) He's lost his job as a chef.
    (B) He can't keep up with new trends.
    (C) He hurt himself exercising.
    (D) He is overweight.

32. (A) Limit fats and keep working out in the gym.
    (B) Eat carbohydrates.
    (C) Stop eating dessert.
    (D) Do a breathing program.

33. (A) Eat yogurt.
    (B) Read a good book.
    (C) Snack on low-fat vegetables.
    (D) Take long walks.

34. (A) Take home leftovers from a salad bar.
    (B) Read books on dieting.
    (C) Bring lunch from home.
    (D) Skip lunch.

35. (A) Co-authors of a book.
    (B) Librarian-researcher.
    (C) Biographer-book buyer.
    (D) Professor-student.

36. (A) France.   (B) Chile.   (C) Mexico.   (D) Spain.

37. (A) Painter.   (C) Sociology professor.
    (B) World traveler.   (D) Writer.

38. (A) Chile.   (C) Germany.
    (B) France.   (D) Canada.

GO ON TO PART C

469

Part C

DIRECTIONS

In Part C, you will hear several talks. After each talk, you will be asked some questions. The talks and questions will be *spoken* just one time. They will not be written out for you, so you will have to listen carefully in order to understand and remember what the speaker says.

When you hear a question, read the four possible answers in your test book and decide which one would be the best answer to the question you have heard. Then, on your answer sheet, find the number of the problem and fill in the space that corresponds to the letter of the answer you have chosen.

39. (A) There was not much wind.
    (B) There was no way of controlling them.
    (C) It was hard to get off the ground.
    (D) They were too heavy.

40. (A) Germany.
    (B) France.
    (C) United States.
    (D) England.

41. (A) A French clockmaker.
    (B) Von Zeppelin.
    (C) A French count.
    (D) Blimp.

42. (A) Germany.
    (B) England.
    (C) United States.
    (D) France.

43. (A) The airships were used for wartime purposes.
    (B) They were afraid because of the tragedy of the *Hindenberg*.
    (C) The newer models were too small.
    (D) They were difficult to control.

44. (A) Elephants.
    (B) Rabbits.
    (C) Bears.
    (D) Tigers.

470

45. (A) Butterflies.
    (B) Mice.
    (C) Spiders.
    (D) Turtles.

46. (A) Disease.   (B) Speed.   (C) Size.   (D) Fur.

47. (A) Beasts.
    (B) Herbivorous.
    (C) Carnivorous.
    (D) Dinosaurs.

48. (A) 180 million years ago.
    (B) 60 million years ago.
    (C) 16 million years ago.
    (D) 150 million years ago.

49. (A) By excavating sites.
    (B) By reconstructing skeletons.
    (C) By observing them closely.
    (D) By living with them.

50. (A) Scientists have studied them for centuries.
    (B) They were meat eating as well as plant eating.
    (C) They wandered the earth for millions of years.
    (D) They lived on land, in the sea, and in the sky.

STOP. THIS IS THE END OF THE LISTENING COMPREHENSION SECTION.
GO ON TO SECTION 2.

SECTION 2
STRUCTURE AND WRITTEN EXPRESSION

Time: 25 Minutes
40 Questions

Part A

DIRECTIONS

Questions 1–15 are incomplete sentences. Beneath each sentence you will see four words or phrases, marked (A), (B), (C), and (D). Choose the *one* word or phrase that best completes the sentence. Then, on your answer sheet, find the number of the question and fill in the space that corresponds to the letter of the answer you have chosen. Fill in the space so that the letter inside the oval cannot be seen.

1. George did not do well in the class because _____.
   (A) he studied bad
   (B) he was not good studywise
   (C) he was a badly student
   (D) he failed to study properly

2. This university's programs _____ those of Harvard.
   (A) come second after
   (B) are second only to
   (C) are first except for
   (D) are in second place from

3. The more she worked, _____.
   (A) the less she achieved
   (B) she achieved not enough
   (C) she did not achieve enough
   (D) she was achieving less

472

4. _____ the best car to buy is a Mercedes Benz.
   - (A) Because of its durability and economy,
   - (B) Because it lasts a long time, and it is very economical,
   - (C) Because of its durability and it is economical,
   - (D) Because durability and economywise it is better than all the others,

5. When Henry arrived home after a hard day at work, _____.
   - (A) his wife was sleeping
   - (B) his wife slept
   - (C) his wife has slept
   - (D) his wife has been sleeping

6. He gave _____.
   - (A) to the class a tough assignment
   - (B) the class a tough assignment
   - (C) a tough assignment for the class
   - (D) an assignment very tough to the class

7. People all over the world are starving _____.
   - (A) greater in numbers
   - (B) in more numbers
   - (C) more numerously
   - (D) in greater numbers

8. It was not until she arrived in class _____ realized she had forgotten her book.
   - (A) and she
   - (B) when she
   - (C) she
   - (D) that she

9. John has not been able to recall where _____.
   (A) does she live
   (B) she lives
   (C) did she live
   (D) lived the girl

10. Ben would have studied medicine if he _____ to a medical school.
    (A) could be able to enter
    (B) had been admitted
    (C) was admitted
    (D) were admitted

11. He entered a university _____.
    (A) when he had sixteen years
    (B) when sixteen years were his age
    (C) at the age of sixteen
    (D) at age sixteen years old

12. The jurors were told to _____.
    (A) talk all they wanted
    (B) make lots of expressions
    (C) speak freely
    (D) talk with their minds open

13. Those students do not like to read novels, _____ text books.
    (A) in any case
    (B) forgetting about
    (C) leaving out of the question
    (D) much less

14. He _____ looked forward to the new venture.
    (A) eagerly
    (B) with great eagerness
    (C) eagernessly
    (D) in a state of increasing eagerness

15. The families were told to evacuate their houses immediately
    _____ .

    (A) at the time when the water began to go up
    (B) when the water began to rise
    (C) when up was going the water
    (D) in the time when the water raised

Go on to part b

Part B

DIRECTIONS

In questions 16–40, each sentence has four underlined words or phrases. The four underlined parts of the sentence are marked (A), (B), (C), and (D). Identify the *one* underlined word or phrase that must be changed in order for the sentence to be correct. Then, on your answer sheet, find the number of the question and fill in the space that corresponds to the letter of the answer you have chosen.

16. <u>Most</u> Americans would not be happy <u>without</u> <u>a</u> color
      A   B   C
    television, two cars, and <u>working at</u> an extra job.
                             D

17. <u>The</u> lion has <u>long</u> been <u>a</u> symbol of strength, power, and
     A   B   C
    <u>it is very cruel</u>.
         D

18. <u>All</u> the scouts got <u>theirselves</u> ready for <u>the</u> long camping trip
     A   B   C
    by spending their weekends <u>living</u> in the open.
                           D

19. Nobody <u>had known</u> before <u>the</u> presentation that Sue and her
          A   B
sister <u>will receive</u> <u>the</u> awards for outstanding scholarship.
          C   D

20. In 1927, Charles Lindbergh <u>was</u> the first <u>to fly</u> solo nonstop
                                A   B
from New York to Paris <u>in</u> <u>such</u> short time.
                        C   D

21. <u>Until</u> his last class at the university in 1978, Bob always
    A
<u>turns</u> in <u>all</u> of his assignments <u>on</u> time.
    B   C   D

22. When I <u>last</u> saw Janet, she <u>hurried</u> to her next class on
          A   B
<u>the other</u> side of the campus and <u>did not have</u> time to talk.
    C   D

23. <u>Before we returned</u> from swimming in the river near the camp,
    A
someone <u>had stole</u> our clothes, and we had to walk <u>back</u> with
          B   C
our towels <u>around</u> us.
            D

24. Patrick was very late <u>getting home</u> last night, and
                          A
unfortunately <u>for him</u>, the <u>dog</u> barking woke everyone <u>up</u>.
                B   C   D

25. He <u>has been hoped</u> for a raise for the <u>last</u> four months, but his
        A   B
boss is reluctant <u>to give</u> him <u>one</u>.
                    C   D

476

26. After driving for twenty miles, he suddenly realized that he
        A   B

    has been driving in the wrong direction.
          C   D

27. The Department of Foreign Languages are not located in the
     A   B   C

    new building opposite the old one.
              D

28. The Nobel Prize winner, accompanied by her husband and
                                    A

    children, are staying in Sweden until after the presentation.
          B   C   D

29. Neither of the scout leaders know how to trap wild animals
           A   B

    or how to prepare them for mounting.
    C   D

30. Those of you who signed up for Dr. Daniel's anthropology
       A   B

    class should get their books as soon as possible.
                C   D

31. I put my new book of zoology here on the desk a few minutes
                    A   B

    ago, but I cannot seem to find it.
    C   D

32. Marta being chosen as the most outstanding student on her
     A   B   C

    campus made her parents very happy.
             D

33. Jane said she would <u>borrow</u> <u>me</u> her new movie camera if I
                                    A   B

    <u>wanted</u> to use it <u>on my trip</u> to Europe.
     C   D

34. When <u>Cliff was sick</u> with the flu, his mother made <u>him</u>
             A   B

    <u>to eat</u> chicken soup and <u>rest</u> in bed.
     C   D

35. My cousin <u>composes not only</u> the music, <u>but</u> also sings
                A   B

    <u>the songs for</u> the <u>major</u> Broadway musicals.
      C   D

36. <u>The</u> geology professor showed <u>us</u> a sample <u>about</u> volcanic rock
  A   B   C

    which dated <u>back</u> seven hundred years.
            D

37. The girl <u>whom</u> my cousin married <u>was used</u> to be a chorus girl
  A   B   C

    for <u>the</u> Rockettes in Radio City Music Hall in New York.
       D

38. Ralph <u>has called</u> his lawyer last night <u>to tell</u> him about his
             A   B

    problems, but was told <u>that</u> the lawyer <u>had gone</u> to a lecture.
                     C   D

39. Some bumper stickers <u>are</u> very funny and make us <u>laugh</u>, yet
                  A   B

    <u>another</u> can make us angry because of their <u>ridiculousness</u>.
     C   D

40. <u>The</u> results of the test proved <u>to</u> Fred and <u>me</u> that we needed
      A   B   C

to study harder and watch <u>less</u> movies on television if we
                                 D

wanted to receive scholarships.

STOP. THIS IS THE END OF THE STRUCTURE AND WRITTEN EXPRES-SION SECTION. IF YOU FINISH BEFORE TIME IS UP, CHECK YOUR WORK ON PARTS A AND B OF THIS SECTION ONLY. DO NOT WORK ON ANY OTHER SECTION OF THE TEST.

SECTION 3
READING COMPREHENSION

Time: 55 Minutes
50 Questions

DIRECTIONS

In this section, you will read a number of passages. Each one is followed by approximately ten questions about it. For questions 1–50, choose the *one* best answer, (A), (B), (C), or (D), to each question. Then, find the number of the question on your answer sheet, and fill in the space that corresponds to the letter of the answer you have chosen. Answer all questions following a passage on the basis of what is *stated* or *implied* in that passage.

Questions 1 through 10 are based on the following reading passage.

The First Amendment to the American Constitution declares freedom of the press to all people. Although this right was not officially adopted until 1791, the famous Zenger trial of 1735 laid the groundwork for insuring this
(5) precious freedom.

John Peter Zenger emigrated as a teenager from Germany. In 1733, he began publishing the *New York Weekly Journal.* The following year, he was arrested for writing a story about the crown-appointed governor of New York.
(10) While Zenger was imprisoned for nine months, his wife dutifully published the newspaper every day, bravely telling the truth about the corrupt government officials sent by the king to govern the colonies.

Finally Zenger's long-awaited trial took place. The hos-
(15) tile judge dismissed Zenger's local lawyers, making it necessary for his wife to seek out Andrew Hamilton, a prominent Philadelphia lawyer. Persuaded by Hamilton,

the jury bravely returned a not-guilty verdict, defying the judge's orders for a conviction.

(20)   As a result of determination and bravery on the part of the colonists, a lasting victory for freedom of the press was gained by a young immigrant.

1. John Peter Zenger was a
    (A) corrupt governor of New York
    (B) famous lawyer
    (C) brave newspaper publisher
    (D) hostile judge

2. What political problem existed in the colonies at that time?
    (A) Government officials were corrupt.
    (B) Newspapers exaggerated the truth about the political officials.
    (C) Lawyers were hostile to witnesses.
    (D) All newspaper publishers were imprisoned.

3. How long did it take after the Zenger trial before the concept of freedom of the press was officially adopted?
    (A) 9 months   (C) 56 years
    (B) 1 year   (D) 58 years

4. All of the following are true EXCEPT
    (A) despite Zenger's imprisonment, his newspaper continued to be published
    (B) Andrew Hamilton encouraged the jury to fight for freedom
    (C) the jury obeyed the judge's orders and convicted Zenger
    (D) the king controlled the colonies through his own appointed rulers

5. Why was Peter Zenger arrested?
    (A) He emigrated from Germany.
    (B) His wife published his newspaper for him.
    (C) He wrote a story about the governor of New York.
    (D) He persuaded a jury to defy the judge's orders.

481

6. It can be inferred that the judge was hostile toward Peter Zenger because the judge
   (A) represented the ideas of the king
   (B) hated newspaper publishers
   (C) didn't like interference with the Constitution
   (D) had appointed the governor about whom Zenger wrote

7. The word "defying" in line 18 is closest in meaning to
   (A) altering
   (B) defecting
   (C) disregarding
   (D) defending

8. In line 11, the word "dutifully" is closest in meaning to
   (A) faithfully
   (B) carelessly
   (C) unfortunately
   (D) vigorously

9. The main idea of this passage is
   (A) Andrew Hamilton gave Americans freedom of the press
   (B) Peter Zenger's persistent fight paved the way for freedom of the press
   (C) judges don't always get juries to agree with them
   (D) Peter Zenger's trial prepared the way for jurors to defy judges' orders

10. The passage indicates that the governor was appointed by the monarch of another country in lines
    (A) 3–5   (B) 6–8   (C) 8–9   (D) 14–16

Questions 11 through 20 are based on the following passage.

    The period commonly known as the Renaissance (1400–1600) began in Florence, Italy. It represented a renewed interest in Greek and Roman art and literature. The greatest achievements in art during this period were the
(5) perfection of depth perspective, use of colors, and effects of light and shadow. Artists across Europe improved on the ancient artists' techniques as no other period had done. The

learned were studying Greek and Roman to read the
ancient literary classics. There were many advances in
(10) science and technology, discoveries in the New World, and
changes in religion. The growth of universities throughout
Europe helped create a more educated middle class that
was to take over running the government within the following centuries. Europe had come out of the Dark Ages. This
(15) idea of rebirth in learning characterized other epochs in
history in different parts of the world.

In A.D. 800, Charlemagne became king of the Franks and
initiated the Carolingian renaissance, which lasted until the
end of the ninth century. This period saw beautiful and
(20) more modern cities patterned on Roman architecture.
Charlemagne stimulated learning and the development of
the arts, sponsored a palace academy, established a curriculum in schools for the nobility, created libraries (a carryover
from Alexandrian Egypt of 323 B.C.), and changed writing to
(25) an improved style of script.

Kievan Russia also enjoyed a century of rebirth some two
hundred years later under the able rule of Yaroslav the
Wise. Like Charlemagne, he founded schools, established
libraries, and brought about many architectural achieve-
(30) ments.

11. Which was the earliest period of rebirth mentioned?
   (A) Russian   (C) Carolingian
   (B) Italian   (D) Roman

12. Which city did Charlemagne look upon as a model for his
   architectural improvements?
   (A) Kiev   (B) Rome   (C) Carolingian   (D) Frank

13. All of the following are mentioned as characteristics of periods of renaissance EXCEPT
    (A) maintaining the status quo
    (B) improved education
    (C) architectural advances
    (D) the creation of libraries

14. What can we assume about Yaroslav?
    (A) He was demented.
    (B) He was a competent leader.
    (C) He was inept.
    (D) He was cruel.

15. The word "carryover" in line 23 means most nearly the same as
    (A) remnant   (C) innovation
    (B) residue   (D) barbarism

16. According to the passage, what do all three periods have in common?
    (A) A concern for education and learning
    (B) A desire for advanced science and technology
    (C) An aversion to new libraries
    (D) An interest in traveling throughout the world

17. What does the word "renaissance" mean in the context of these three civilizations?
    (A) Improving on the basic principles of past cultures
    (B) Trying to do everything as the ancients had done
    (C) Helping to maintain Roman culture at any cost
    (D) Tearing down existing buildings and using Roman architectural techniques for new ones

18. Which of the renaissance periods lasted the longest?
    (A) Italian   (C) Alexandrian
    (B) Carolingian   (D) Kievan

484

19. Which renaissance had the most widespread and lasting effect on future generations?
    (A) Italian
    (B) Kievan
    (C) Alexandrian
    (D) Carolingian

20. The main idea of this passage is that
    (A) throughout history there has been a rebirth of ideas and an effort to copy without creating anything new
    (B) only western Europe was interested in rebirth
    (C) the periods of rebirth saw greater advances for each culture
    (D) rebirth of a culture does not depend on outside influences

Questions 21 through 29 are based on the following passage.

Gelatin is a protein substance that comes from the skins and bones of animals. Most people know it as the substance used to make a jellylike salad or dessert. Not only is it useful in making these foods, but it is also beneficial to the
(5) consumer because of its high protein content. Gelatin is also commonly used in the photographic industry and in making medicinal capsules.

The process for producing gelatin is a long and complex one. In the processing of gelatin made from bones (which
(10) varies slightly from that of gelatin made from skin), the grease first must be eliminated. Then the bones are soaked in a solution of hydrochloric acid in order to rid them of minerals and washed several times in water. Next, the bones are placed in distilled water, heated to over 90°F for a few
(15) hours, placed in fresh distilled water, and then heated again at a little over 100°F. A fluid forms from this heating, and it is concentrated, chilled, and sliced. Finally, it is dried and ground. In its final form, gelatin is white, tasteless, and odorless.

21. It can be inferred from this reading passage that
    (A) one could easily make gelatin at home
    (B) it is necessary to add minerals to the gelatin
    (C) fat aids in making good gelatin
    (D) gelatin is useful for elderly and ill people because it is easy to chew and high in protein

22. The word "fluid" in line 16 is closest in meaning to
    (A) liquid   (C) hard material
    (B) distilled water   (D) substance

23. Which of the following is true?
    (A) Gelatin made from skin is produced in the same way as that made from bones.
    (B) Grease probably does not aid in producing gelatin.
    (C) The chemical used in making gelatin comes off the surface of the bones by rinsing with water.
    (D) When the gelatin is dried, it is in powder form.

24. Which of the following would be the best title for this passage?
    (A) The Process of Making Gelatin
    (B) Protein Foods
    (C) Uses for Bones
    (D) A Great Dessert

25. All of the following industries are mentioned as using gelatin EXCEPT
    (A) the lawn care industry
    (B) the photographic industry
    (C) the pharmaceutical industry
    (D) the food industry

26. According to the passage, why is eating gelatin healthy?
    (A) It does not damage the teeth.
    (B) It is low fat.
    (C) It is protein rich.
    (D) It has no animal byproducts.

27. The word "ground" in line 18 is closest in meaning to
    (A) refrigerated   (C) putrified
    (B) pulverized   (D) dirtied

28. Why would gelatin be useful for medicine capsules?
    (A) It tastes good.
    (B) It is a natural substance that is easy to digest.
    (C) It is easy to make and thus inexpensive.
    (D) It won't melt at high temperatures.

29. The word "that" in line 10 refers to
    (A) gelatin   (B) processing   (C) skin   (D) bones

Questions 30 through 41 are based on the following passage.

        In recent years, scientific and technological developments
    have drastically changed human life on our planet, as well as
    our views both of ourselves as individuals in society and of
    the universe as a whole. Perhaps one of the most profound
(5) developments of the 1970s was the discovery of recombinant
    DNA technology, which allows scientists to introduce ge-
    netic material (or genes) from one organism into another.
    In its simplest form, the technology requires the isolation of
    a piece of DNA, either directly from the DNA of the
(10) organism under study or artificially synthesized from an
    RNA template by using a viral enzyme called reverse
    transcriptase. This piece of DNA is then ligated to a
    fragment of bacterial DNA which has the capacity to
    replicate itself independently. The recombinant molecule
(15) thus produced can be introduced into the common intesti-
    nal bacterium *Escherichia coli,* which can be grown in very
    large amounts in synthetic media. Under proper conditions,
    the foreign gene will not only replicate in the bacteria, but
    also express itself, through the process of transcription and
(20) translation, to give rise to large amounts of the specific
    protein coded by the foreign gene.

The technology has already been successfully applied to the production of several therapeutically important biomolecules, such as insulin, interferon, and growth hormones.
(25) Many other important applications are under detailed investigation in laboratories throughout the world.

30. Recombinant DNA technology consists primarily of
    (A) producing several therapeutically important biomolecules
    (B) giving rise to large amounts of protein
    (C) introducing genetic material from one organism into another
    (D) using a viral enzyme called reverse transcriptase

31. The word "profound" in line 4 is closest in meaning to
    (A) significant   (C) dangerous
    (B) boring   (D) secret

32. In line 8, the word "isolation" is closest in meaning to
    (A) destruction   (C) segregation
    (B) duplication   (D) study

33. Recombinant DNA technology has been used in the production of all of the following biomolecules EXCEPT
    (A) growth hormones   (C) interferon
    (B) *Escherichia coli*   (D) insulin

34. In line 10, "artificially" is closest in meaning to
    (A) correctly   (C) artistically
    (B) synthetically   (D) carefully

35. The word "ligated" in line 12 is closest in meaning to
    (A) intersected   (B) cut   (C) elevated   (D) bound

36. Which of the following is NOT true?
    (A) The foreign gene will replicate in the bacteria, but it will not express itself through transcription and translation.
    (B) The bacterium *Escherichia coli* can be grown in large amounts in synthetic media.
    (C) Research continues in an effort to find other uses for this technology.
    (D) Recombinant DNA technology is a recent development.

37. In line 13, the word "fragment" is nearest in meaning to
    (A) particle
    (B) reproduction
    (C) opposite
    (D) large piece

38. The word "capacity" in line 13 is nearest in meaning to
    (A) hormones
    (B) technology
    (C) ability
    (D) space

39. Expression of a gene in *Escherichia coli* requires
    (A) the viral enzyme reverse transcriptase
    (B) the processes of transcription and translation
    (C) production of insulin and other biomolecules
    (D) that the bacteria be grown in a synthetic media

40. The term "recombinant" is used because
    (A) by ligation, a recombinant molecule is produced, which has the capacity of replication
    (B) the technique requires the combination of several types of technology
    (C) by ligation, a recombinant protein is produced; part of whole amino acids come from each different organism
    (D) *Escherichia coli* is a recombinant organism

41. The word "replicate" in line 14 is closest in meaning to
    (A) reproduce   (B) join   (C) reside   (D) coexist

Questions 42 through 50 are based on the following passage.

Of the six outer planets, Mars, commonly called the Red Planet, is the closest to Earth. Mars, 4,200 miles in diameter and 55 percent of the size of Earth, is 34,600,000 miles from Earth, and 141,000,000 miles from the Sun. It takes this
(5) planet, along with its two moons, Phobos and Deimos, 1.88 years to circle the Sun, compared to 365 days for the Earth.

For many years, Mars had been thought of as the planet with the man-made canals, supposedly discovered by an Italian astronomer, Schiaparelli, in 1877. With the United
(10) States spacecraft Viking I's landing on Mars in 1976, the man-made canal theory was proven to be only a myth.

Viking I, after landing on the soil of Mars, performed many scientific experiments and took numerous pictures. The pictures showed that the red color of the planet is due
(15) to the reddish, rocky Martian soil. No biological life was found, though it had been speculated by many scientists. The Viking also monitored many weather changes including violent dust storms. Some water vapor, polar ice, and permafrost (frost below the surface) were found, indicating
(20) that at one time there were significant quantities of water on this distant planet. Evidence collected by the spacecraft shows some present volcanic action, though the volcanoes are believed to be dormant, if not extinct.

42. All of the following are true EXCEPT
   (A) Mars has two moons
   (B) it takes longer for Mars to circle the sun than it takes Earth
   (C) Martian soil is rocky
   (D) Mars is larger than Earth

43. Man-made canals were supposedly discovered by
   (A) Viking I
   (B) Schiaparelli
   (C) Phobos
   (D) Martian

490

44. The word "supposedly" in line 8 is closest in meaning to
    (A) actually
    (B) presumably
    (C) formerly
    (D) unquestionably

45. Mars has been nicknamed
    (A) Viking I
    (B) the Red Planet
    (C) Deimos
    (D) Martian

46. In line 11, the word "myth" is closest in meaning to
    (A) fact   (B) event   (C) legend   (D) enigma

47. The Viking I exploration accomplished all of the following EXCEPT
    (A) performing scientific experiments
    (B) collecting information showing volcanic action
    (C) monitoring weather conditions
    (D) discovering large quantities of polar ice and permafrost

48. What is the main idea of this passage?
    (A) Fairly recent studies of this planet reveal data that contradict previously held theories.
    (B) Very little of the Martian landscape has changed over the years.
    (C) Scientists are only speculating about the Red Planet.
    (D) Scientists are no longer interested in the planet because there is no life on it.

49. The word "monitored" in line 17 is nearest in meaning to
    (A) programmed
    (B) televised
    (C) censored
    (D) observed

50. The word "dormant" in line 23 is closest in meaning to
    (A) dangerous
    (B) inactive
    (C) erupting
    (D) significant

STOP. THIS IS THE END OF THE EXAMINATION. IF YOU FINISH BEFORE TIME IS UP, CHECK YOUR WORK IN THIS SECTION ONLY. DO NOT WORK ON ANY OTHER SECTION OF THE TEST.

**PART V: Listening Comprehension Scripts,
Answers, and Explanations
for Practice Tests 1 through 6**

HOW TO USE PART V

Part V contains answers and explanations for the six practice tests, scripts for the listening comprehension sections, answer keys that are cross-referenced to grammar review pages in Part III, and scoring charts to help you see your strengths and weaknesses. In order to improve your score, you MUST analyze your mistakes and strive to avoid making the same errors again. MAKE FULL USE OF THE FOLLOWING PAGES TO IMPROVE YOUR PERFORMANCE. Follow this step-by-step procedure.

• First turn to the *answer keys* to check your results. Then turn to the *Analysis-Scoring Sheet* for the test you have taken and fill in the number of questions that you got CORRECT in each section. Follow the directions to figure your total converted score. Which section did you do best in? Which section did you do worst in? The section in which you received your lowest score is the section which you must work hardest on improving.

• If you did poorly on the listening comprehension, *study the script carefully,* comparing the questions that you heard to what you read on paper. *Listen to the tape again* to see if you can now hear more clearly. If there are vocabulary items, idiomatic expressions, or grammatical constructions that are causing you to make mistakes in listening, look them up and study them again. Use your dictionary for expressions that were not covered in this guide.

• If you did poorly in the grammar section, you must *look back at the rule and study it again* until you can recognize such a problem immediately. Most grammar explanations contain a shortened version of the rule, and the answer keys are cross-referenced by page number. The page numbers refer to rules and examples in Part III that you should study again. Sometimes there are several page numbers because the sentence contains several different problems.

• For the reading comprehension questions, *look at the explanations and refer back to the reading* itself to understand why you missed the question. The explanation will often tell you in which sentence the material necessary to answer the question can be found. Remember that generally the words in the questions and the words in the text are not exactly the same. Be sure that you understand the meaning of each reading selection and question and that you learn any new vocabulary words that you run across.

• *Always look back at questions that you missed* to see whether you could answer them correctly now that you have restudied.

CONVERTED SCORE SHEET

To use this chart, find the number in the raw score column that corresponds to your total CORRECT answers on each section. The converted score in each section is listed to the right of the raw score. Transfer each of the three converted scores to the Practice Test Analysis-Scoring Sheet that precedes the explanation section for each practice test. Follow the directions given there to determine your total converted score. The highest possible score on the tests in this guide is 673; the lowest is 223. On the actual TOEFL the scores may range from 700 to 200.

	Converted Scores					Converted Scores		
Raw Score	Section 1	Section 2	Section 3		Raw Score	Section 1	Section 2	Section 3
50	68		67		40	56	67	55
49	66		66		39	56	66	54
48	64		65		38	55	64	53
47	63		63		37	54	63	52
46	62		61		36	53	61	51
45	61		60		35	52	59	50
44	60		59		34	52	58	49
43	59		58		33	51	57	49
42	58		57		32	50	55	48
41	57		56		31	50	54	48

	Converted Scores		
Raw Score	Section 1	Section 2	Section 3
30	49	53	47
29	49	52	47
28	48	51	46
27	48	50	45
26	47	49	45
25	46	48	44
24	46	47	43
23	45	46	42
22	44	45	41
21	44	44	41
20	43	43	40
19	43	42	39
18	42	41	38
17	41	40	37
16	41	39	36

	Converted Scores		
Raw Score	Section 1	Section 2	Section 3
15	40	38	35
14	39	37	34
13	38	36	33
12	37	35	32
11	36	34	31
10	34	33	30
9	33	32	29
8	32	30	28
7	31	29	28
6	30	28	27
5	29	26	26
4	28	25	25
3	27	24	24
2	26	22	23
1	25	20	22

PRACTICE TEST 1

ANSWER KEY FOR PRACTICE TEST 1

After some answers in this answer key, you will find numbers in italic type. These are page numbers in Part III where you will find review material for these questions. Although any one question may involve several different rules and concepts, these page numbers refer to important areas you should review if you have missed a question or are not sure of the material involved. Make full use of these page number references and of the index to direct your personal review.

Section 1: Listening Comprehension

1. (B)	11. (C)	21. (C)	31. (B)	41. (D)
2. (A)	12. (B)	22. (B)	32. (B)	42. (C)
3. (B)	13. (D)	23. (D)	33. (B)	43. (B)
4. (C)	14. (D)	24. (A)	34. (B)	44. (B)
5. (C)	15. (C)	25. (B)	35. (C)	45. (C)
6. (B)	16. (A)	26. (B)	36. (A)	46. (A)
7. (A)	17. (A)	27. (C)	37. (B)	47. (B)
8. (C)	18. (C)	28. (C)	38. (D)	48. (A)
9. (B)	19. (D)	29. (C)	39. (A)	49. (C)
10. (D)	20. (C)	30. (B)	40. (D)	50. (A)

Section 2: Structure and Written Expression

1. (C) *39*
2. (D) *52*
3. (D) *74–75*
4. (C) *102–103*
5. (C) *132*
6. (B) *112, 153–154*
7. (B) *212–215*
8. (D) *52–53, 100–101*
9. (D) *183–184*
10. (D) *98*
11. (C) *204–206*
12. (B) *44–49, 74–75*
13. (C) *94*
14. (C) *44–49*
15. (D) *96–98*
16. (C) *280–281*
17. (A) *44–49*
18. (D) *229*
19. (D) *62*
20. (A) *102–103*
21. (D) *62*
22. (B) *44–49*
23. (B) *65–67*
24. (D) *204–206, 212–215*
25. (D) *100–101*
26. (A) *167–170*
27. (B) *224–226*
28. (C) *104*
29. (C) *54*
30. (D) *100–101*
31. (D) *123–124*
32. (A) *47*
33. (D) *44–49*
34. (A) *76*
35. (A) *44–49*
36. (A) *152*
37. (B) *44–49*
38. (B) *277–278*
39. (A) *280–281*
40. (A) *39*

Section 3: Reading Comprehension

1. (B)
2. (A)
3. (B)
4. (A)
5. (D)
6. (B)
7. (B)
8. (C)
9. (A)
10. (B)
11. (D)
12. (D)
13. (A)
14. (B)
15. (A)
16. (B)
17. (C)
18. (C)
19. (B)
20. (B)
21. (D)
22. (D)
23. (B)
24. (B)
25. (D)
26. (C)
27. (A)
28. (B)
29. (D)
30. (B)
31. (A)
32. (A)
33. (A)
34. (B)
35. (D)
36. (B)
37. (A)
38. (A)
39. (C)
40. (C)
41. (B)
42. (C)
43. (A)
44. (B)
45. (B)
46. (A)
47. (A)
48. (C)
49. (A)
50. (C)

PRACTICE TEST 1: ANALYSIS-SCORING SHEET

Use the chart below to spot your strengths and weaknesses in each test section and to arrive at your total converted score. Fill in your number of correct answers for each section in the space provided. Refer to the Converted Score Sheet on page 496 to find your converted score for each section and enter those numbers on the chart. Find the sum of your converted scores, multiply that sum by 10, and divide by 3.

Example: If raw scores are then converted scores are

Section 1:   33   51
Section 2:   26   49
Section 3:   38   53

Sum of Converted Scores   153
Times 10 = 1,530
Divided by 3 =   510 = Total Converted Score

This will give you the approximate score that you would obtain if this were an actual TOEFL. Remember that your score here may possibly be higher than the score that you might receive on an actual TOEFL simply because you are studying the elements of the test shortly before taking each test. The score is intended only to give you a general idea of approximately what your actual score will be.

	Total Possible	Total Correct	Converted Score
Section 1: Listening Comprehension	50		
Section 2: Structure and Written Expression	40		
Section 3: Reading Comprehension	50		
TOTALS	140		

Sum of Converted Scores _____
Times 10 = _____
Divided by 3 = _____ = Total Converted Score

SECTION 1: LISTENING COMPREHENSION SCRIPT

Part A

1. Man: I hear Jan isn't teaching here this term.
   Woman: That's right. She was fired.
   Third Voice: What does the woman say about Jan?

2. Man: Nancy, I heard you were late for class this morning.
   Woman: I overslept and missed the bus.
   Third Voice: Why does the woman say she was late?

3. Woman: I heard on the radio that the eastbound lanes of Interstate 4 are closed.
   Man: Yes, a tractor-trailer jackknifed and caused a huge pileup.
   Third Voice: What are the speakers discussing?

4. Man: What do you think of Professor Conrad's class?
   Woman: Well, his lectures are interesting enough, but I think he could choose more appropriate questions for the tests.
   Third Voice: What does the woman say about Professor Conrad's class?

5. Woman: Are you going to watch the movie on TV tonight?
   Man: No, I think I'll watch the soccer game and then the documentary on volcanoes.
   Third Voice: What does the man say is the first program he is planning to watch?

6. Man: Where did Suzanne come from?

   Woman: She was born in Switzerland and grew up in Sweden, but she's a citizen of England.

   Third Voice: Which country does the woman say is Suzanne's present home?

7. Woman: Karen is entering Stetson University this fall.

   Man: So she did apply.

   Third Voice: What had the man assumed about Karen?

8. Man: Why are you wearing that cream all over your arms?

   Woman: I ate wild berries at the picnic last week, and I broke out in a rash.

   Third Voice: What does the woman say happened to her?

9. Woman: Would you please spell your name for me, sir?

   Man: Sure. W-I-double T-N-E-R.

   Third Voice: How does the man say he spells his last name?

10. Woman: I have to go out of town for a meeting tomorrow, and I need somebody to work for me.

    Man: Sure. I could use the extra hours!

    Third Voice: What is the man probably going to do?

11. Woman: Louie, how did your football team do last season?

    Man: We won three, lost five, and tied twice.

    Third Voice: How many games does the man say his team tied?

12. Woman: Do you know what happened to Sally?

    Man: She couldn't find the classroom until after the class had begun.

    Third Voice: What does the man say happened to Sally?

13. Woman: Did April visit you in the hospital when you were ill?

    Man: No, but it was certainly kind of her to send me flowers.

    Third Voice: What does the man say about the flowers?

14. Man: William looked very tired this morning.

    Woman: He drove George's car from Georgia to New York without stopping to sleep.

    Third Voice: What does the woman mean?

15. Woman: How was the turnout at the meeting last night?

    Man: Fewer people came than I had expected.

    Third Voice: What does the man say about attendance at the meeting?

16. Woman: Was Harry successful at his new venture?

    Man: He spent five hours knocking on doors, but he didn't sell a single magazine.

    Third Voice: What does the man say about Harry?

17. Man: Did Frank have his house repaired?

    Woman: The contractor said the repairs would be very expensive, but he decided to have the work done.

    Third Voice: What does the woman say about the repairs to Frank's house?

18. Woman: What did you do last night?

    Man: I should have studied, but I was too tired.

    Third Voice: What does the man say he did last night?

19. Man: Do you think Gloria will come with us?

    Woman: I understand she hasn't gone to a movie in years.

    Third Voice: What does the woman say about Gloria?

20. Man: What happened to Harvey today?

  Woman: His face turned bright red when the teacher asked him a question.

  Third Voice: What does the woman say about Harvey?

21. Woman: Good afternoon, I'm Roseanne, your flight attendant. Welcome aboard.

  Man: Hello. I've got seat A8. I hope it's by a window so that I can see the view.

  Third Voice: Where did this conversation most probably take place?

22. Man: I heard Jane isn't going to be working this summer.

  Woman: That's right. She's taking sick leave.

  Third Voice: What does the woman say about Jane?

23. Man: A change has sure come over you.

  Woman: I finally had my annual review meeting with my boss. It couldn't have gone better.

  Third Voice: What does the woman mean?

24. Man: Doesn't Professor Jones realize there are only two days before the test?

  Woman: He apologized for not announcing the test earlier.

  Third Voice: What does the woman say about the professor?

25. Woman: Stacey had a disagreement with her boss yesterday, didn't she?

  Man: She says she is leaving her job for good.

  Third Voice: What does the man say about Stacey?

26. Man: Did John stop at the store?

    Woman: No, he had some money, but not enough to buy groceries.

    Third Voice: What does the woman say about John?

27. Man: I can't believe there were no empty seats at the rally.

    Woman: They expected eighty people, but twice that many showed up.

    Third Voice: How many people does the woman say attended the rally?

28. Woman: Are we doing anything today?

    Man: We were supposed to meet Fred and Mary at the movies, but we're broke.

    Third Voice: What does the man mean?

29. Man: I understand Ana is mad at Ted.

    Woman: Yes, he refused to go to the banquet even though he was going to receive an award.

    Third Voice: Why does the woman say Ana is angry at Ted?

30. Woman: How does Mike like his coffee?

    Man: He likes sugar in it, but nothing else.

    Third Voice: What does the man say about Mike?

Part B

Questions 31 through 34 are based on the following conversation.

Man: How long have you been out of the country, miss? Where did you go?

Woman: I spent three weeks in Switzerland and one week in Greece.

Man: Did you spend any time in agricultural areas there?

Woman: No, I stayed mostly in the cities and spent one day at the beach in Corinth.

Man: Do you have any plants, meat, or alcoholic beverages to declare?

Woman: I have only two bottles of wine.

Man: What else did you buy?

Woman: A couple of festive costumes, books, and native arts and crafts.

Man: How much did you spend on your purchases while you were away?

Woman: About $300.

Man: Please open this small suitcase for me. . . . OK, give this card to the official at the red desk.

31. Where did this conversation most likely take place?
32. How many countries did the woman visit?
33. What does the man ask the woman to do?
34. What did the woman have to declare?

Questions 35 through 38 are based on the following conversation.

Woman: I hear that Paul Schmidt has written a new novel.

Man: Yes, it's a science fiction piece called *Martian Renaissance*.

Woman: Sounds intriguing. What's the plot like?

Man: It deals with a five-man, one-woman crew on a three-year mission to Mars.

Woman: Is their mission successful?

Man: Well, in some respects it is. They have a series of incredible adventures once they land.

Woman: Do they meet any real Martians?

Man: Yes, they are even held captive by them.

Woman: What do the Martians look like? Are they little green men?

Man: You'll have to read the book to find out.

35. What is the name of Paul Schmidt's new book?
36. What type of book is it?
37. How long did the mission to Mars take?
38. Which of the following is NOT mentioned?

Part C

Questions 39 through 42 are based on the following lecture about the game of jai alai.

Although played quite well in Florida and Latin America, jai alai is not an American game. This handball type game originated in the Basque region of Spain. Jai alai is one of the fastest-moving ball games. In Florida it is legal to place bets on the players, somewhat similar to betting in horse racing. Bets are placed on a win, place, show basis—that is, first, second, and third.

Sports experts agree that jai alai requires more skill, speed, endurance, and nerve than any other ball game.

39. Where did jai alai originate?
40. Betting on jai alai players is compared to what other sport?
41. Which of the following is NOT true?
42. To what game is jai alai compared in the reading?

Questions 43 through 47 are based on the following lecture about Alexander Graham Bell.

Alexander Graham Bell was born in Edinburgh, Scotland, in the nineteenth century and later came to the United States. Several members of his family did a great deal to encourage him in the field of science. His father was most instrumental in supervising his work with the deaf. While he dealt with the deaf and investigated the science of acoustics, his studies eventually led to the invention of the multiple telegraph and his greatest invention—the telephone. The last quarter of a century of his life was dedicated to advances in aviation.

43. What was considered to be Alexander Graham Bell's greatest achievement?
44. To what did Bell dedicate the last years of his life?
45. What can we conclude about Alexander Graham Bell?
46. Which of the following statements is NOT true?
47. How many years did Bell dedicate to aviation?

Questions 48 through 50 are based on the following explanation of life insurance products to a customer.

Now that you know you want to purchase life insurance, you must choose from two types. The amount of money paid periodically for an insurance policy is a premium. The type of life insurance you choose will affect the amount of the premium you pay.

Term life insurance is purchased for a given period of time, or term. At the end of the term, the insurance expires. It insures your life based on a formula that considers how long you are expected to live. This product provides the greatest coverage for the least amount of money. You do not pay any money as an investment in addition to the insurance cost. If you choose to purchase insurance after the expiration, the premium will be higher because it is calculated on your attained age, and at that point, you will be older than you are now. The longer the premium is guaranteed to remain constant, the greater the premium will be because it reflects the average cost of insurance for all years being covered.

Cash value life insurance, on the other hand, has a component fund in which the life insurance company deposits part of the premium and pays interest earned on its investments in mortgages, bonds, stocks, and other investments. The balance of the premium purchases term insurance, which is calculated in the same way as if you purchase term life insurance. Consequently, the premium is significantly higher than that of term life insurance. However, most cash value life insurance products have a fixed premium schedule and remain in effect throughout your life. In many cases, the interest earned on the investment portion of the premium will ultimately pay the premiums so that at some point you can discontinue making payments out of pocket.

Once the fund has started to accumulate, you may borrow some of the funds at a low interest rate, receive retirement income, or even stop paying premiums. This type of policy also builds up a cash value so that if you want to cancel the policy, some money is actually returned, unlike the term policy, which has no value other than the insurance.

48. Which of the following is NOT a reason to buy cash value insurance?
49. Why is cash value life insurance more expensive than term life insurance?
50. Which of the following is a benefit of term life insurance?

EXPLANATIONS FOR PRACTICE TEST 1

SECTION 2: STRUCTURE AND WRITTEN EXPRESSION

Part A

1. (C) The word order should be: subject + verb + complement + modifier of manner + modifier of time.

2. (D) Choice (A) is incorrect because *another* is singular and *pants* is plural. (B) and (C) are incorrect because *other* cannot be used in the plural form when it is functioning as an adjective. (D) is correct; *pair* is preceded by the singular article (*an + other* pair).

3. (D) *Committee* is singular, so the pronoun that follows it must be *it* and the verb must be *has.* Choice (B) is verbose and uses a plural reflexive pronoun, *themselves,* incorrectly. (C) is passive and thus not parallel. It also contains an unnecessary preposition, *at.*

4. (C) Choice (A) is incorrect because *lonelynessly* is not a word, and the expression *in times previous* should read *in previous times* (or better, *previously*). Choice (B) creates a double negative, *not never,* and *sole* means *only.* It does not mean *alone.* (D) is verbose.

5. (C) *Must* + perfective indicates a logical conclusion. (He made the highest score, so we assume that he studied.)

6. (B) Modal + [verb in simple form]. (Will be teaching = future progressive.) Choice (A) is incorrect because *must* should not be followed by the infinitive. (C) is incorrect because *because of* cannot be followed by a complete sentence. (D) is incorrect because *have* cannot be followed by a [verb + *ing*].

7. (B) Choices (A), (C), and (D) all have dangling participles (suggesting that the *problem, it,* or the *discussion* may have been served lunch). The subject of the participial phrase must be *the committee members.*

8. (D) Follow the negative agreement rule: *neither* + auxiliary + subject. Choice (A) is incorrect because *states* is plural and *hasn't* is singular. (B) is incorrect for the same reason, and it has *others* before a noun. (C) is incorrect because *also* is redundant when used with *either.*

9. (D) This sentence requires the subjunctive form: *requested that* + [verb in simple form]. In choice (A) the verb is in the past tense (*studied*) rather than in the simple form (*study*), and the modifier (*more carefully*) is incorrectly placed before the complement (*the problem*). (B) also contains the verb in past tense and *carefulnessly,* which is not a word.

10. (D) Use the affirmative agreement rule: *so* + auxiliary + subject. Choices (A) and (B) do not have an auxiliary, and (C) has an incorrect auxiliary (*is* instead of *does*).

11. (C) The sequence of tenses should be *said . . . could* (past . . . past). In choice (A) *can* is present tense, and *the* usually cannot precede a day of the week. Choice (B) is passive. The passive construction is not necessary here and makes the sentence verbose. Choice (D) contains incorrect word order.

12. (B) *Organization* is singular and requires a singular verb, *has*. *Less* is used with non-count nouns and *fewer* with count nouns. Choice (A) contains a plural pronoun and verb, and *volunteers* should be preceded by *fewer*. (C) uses incorrect word order. (D) is incorrect because you should use *than,* not *that,* in a comparative.

13. (C) This is an embedded question: question word + subject + verb. Choices (A), (B), and (D) do not follow this order. (D) also has the expression *the time when,* which is redundant.

14. (C) Use *much* + non-count nouns. Choice (A) uses *many* instead of *much*. (B) and (D) are verbose and use *the* incorrectly (*sugar* here is general, not specific).

15. (D) This is a tag question. *Has* is the auxiliary in the main clause; therefore, *has* must be used in the tag. The main clause is negative, so the tag should be affirmative. When *there* is used as the subject of the main clause, it must also be the subject of the tag.

Part B

NOTE: $\emptyset$ = nothing, indicating that this word or phrase should be deleted.

16. (C) should be *on. On* + the name of a street.

17. (A) should be *fewer. Members* is a count noun and must be preceded by *fewer.*

18. (D) should be *very*. *Really* is slang and not appropriate in formal written English.

19. (D) should be *since*. Use *since* + beginning time (the action began in the 1960s and continues up to the present). *During* or *in* would also be correct if the sentence were taken to mean that the progress took place *only* in the 1960s.

20. (A) should be *rarely*. *Rarely* is negative and cannot be used with another negative. *Not rarely* is a double negative.

21. (D) should be *yet*. Use *yet* in negative sentences. *Already* is used only in positive sentences.

22. (B) should be ∅ or *some*. *News* is a non-count noun and *a* means *one*.

23. (B) should be *remembered*. He gave the assignment first (past perfect), and then he remembered (simple past) that Monday was a holiday.

24. (D) should be *cried out*. The correct sequence of tenses requires past tense. (*Having* + [verb in past participle] means past time.)

25. (D) should be *either*. Correct negative agreement is: subject + auxiliary + *not* + *either*.

26. (A) should be *was hit*. Passive voice is necessary here. *Be* + [verb in past principle]. (The ship *hit* the bridge.)

27. (B) should be *the manager*. Subject + verb + indirect object + direct object. There should be *no* preposition.

28. (C) should be *not to allow*. This is a negative indirect command: verb + (*not*) + infinitive.

29. (C) should be *those*. It is incorrect to say *these ones* or *those ones* although it is possible to say *this one* or *that one*.

30. (D) should be *doesn't either*. *Seldom* is negative and must be followed by negative agreement, not positive agreement.

31. (D) should be *didn't it*. *Used to* indicates a past habit and uses *did* when an auxiliary is needed.

32. (A) should be *a*. Use this indefinite article before words beginning with a consonant sound.

33. (D) should be *much homework*. *Homework* can never be plural, and it is non-count, so it must be preceded by *much*.

34. (A) should be *are*. *Scissors* is plural and must be used with a plural verb.

35. (A) should be *information*. This noun can never be plural. It is non-count.

36. (A) should be *intelligent enough*. Adjective + *enough*.

37. (B) should be *many*. *People* is a plural count noun.

38. (B) should be *from*. *From* a time *to* a time.

39. (A) should be *on*. Always use this preposition with the floor of a building because a floor is a surface.

40. (A) should be *a new sports car last week*. The complement (*a new sports car*) should precede the modifier (*last week*).

SECTION 3: READING COMPREHENSION

1. (B) The three periods are the Paleolithic, Mesolithic, and Neolithic.

2. (A) The sentence indicates that the name "Stone Age" was "derived from," or "came from," the tools and weapons that were used.

3. (B) The hatchet was developed between 2 million B.C. and 8000 B.C., during the first period.

4. (A) Farming was never mentioned.

5. (D) The reading implies that the items made were not sophisticated, so the reader can infer that the word "crude" is related to that concept.

6. (B) Sentence 2 says, "Its name was derived from the stone tools and weapons that modern scientists found."

7. (B) The sentence indicates that the people began domesticating animals and establishing permanent governments, indicating that those actions were less "nomadic" than in previous times, which should lead you to understand that "nomadic" means "wandering."

8. (C) The subject described in the introductory sentence of the passage is the Stone Age. The Neolithic (A) and Paleolithic (B) ages are discussed as subdivisions of the Stone Age. The Ice Age (D) is mentioned in just one sentence as being an important influence on ancient societies.

9. (A) The passage describes the numerous developments, or inventions, of the Mesolithic Age (pottery, fish hooks, hunting dogs, and the bow and arrow). Hunting and fishing would not keep people indoors all the time (B), and no mention was made of people being warriors (C) or crude (D).

10. (B) The sentence indicates that the age being discussed is different from previous "eras," so that should provide you with a hint that "era" means "period" of time.

11. (D) The sentence indicates that the need to preserve energy has become more evident, or "highlighted."

12. (D) Choices (A), (B), and (C) were drawbacks (disadvantages) of the "conventional method" of boning. Only choice (D), toughness of meat, was given as a drawback of hot boning.

13. (A) The sentence indicates that there is some "urgency" to preserve energy.

14. (B) The first paragraph concerns the fact that hot boning is an energy-saving technique, and the last paragraph says that refrigeration space and costs are minimized by hot boning.

15. (A) A "carcass" is a "body," and "to chill" means "to cool."

16. (B) "Early excision" means "hot boning." Paragraph 3 says "early excision, or hot boning," which indicates that they mean the same thing.

17. (C) The last paragraph states, ". . . hot boning following electrical stimulation has been used to reduce the necessary time of rigor mortis."

18. (C) There is no contextual clue to assist you if you do not know what "bovine" means, other than that it is an adjective modifying "carcass."

19. (B) The sentence preceding this sentence is discussing the advantage of hot boning following electrical stimulation, rather than hot boning alone. So "this" refers to that concept. Notice that "rigor mortis" (C) is not a "method" at all.

20. (B) The entire reading is about treatment of the body of the dead animal, which is what a "carcass" is.

21. (D) The word "considerable" modifies "amount of refrigerated space." What can modify an amount? It must mean a large amount or a small amount. Answers (A) and (B) make no sense in that context, and "lesser" is not followed by words indicating it is a comparison.

22. (D) The reading states that hot boning actually results in tougher meat, so answer (A) is not correct. The reading does not say anything about what the bones can be used for, so (B) is incorrect. (C) is incorrect because increasing chilling time certainly would not be a benefit and would not be recommended.

23. (B) This word is related to the verb "trim," which means to cut or remove.

24. (B) The last sentence says that the United States currently controls the canal.

25. (D) Locks are enclosures of the canal governed by gates that allow the interior water level to be raised or lowered so ships can pass from one elevation of the canal to another.

26. (C) Sentence 2 says that it costs fifteen thousand dollars to travel through the canal and ten times that amount ($150,000) to go around Cape Horn.

27. (A) Sentence 1 suggests that 1920 was thirty-nine years after the canal construction was begun (1920 − 39 = 1881).

28. (B) Because of lower costs and shorter traveling time, we can assume that the project has been beneficial.

29. (D) The fact that the sentence indicates the Atlantic and Pacific Oceans are "linked" indicates that they have been "joined."

30. (B) "Initiated" means "commenced," or "launched."

31. (A) The passage states that more than fifteen thousand ships pass through the canal each year, so (A) cannot be true. Choices (B), (C), and (D) are all facts from the passage.

32. (A) They did not place the olive wreaths on their "own" heads.

33. (A) The sentence states that the games were open to all free males with no criminal record, but that previously that was not the case, which indicates that "elite" means "aristocracy."

34. (B) The first sentence says that "the first Olympic Games were held . . . to honor the Greeks' chief god, Zeus."

35. (D) Add a B.C. date to an A.D. date to get the total length of time. The question asks for the approximate number of years, and the answer choices are in round numbers, so round off 776 B.C. to 800 B.C. and add it to the approximate modern date of 2000. 800 + 2000 = 2,800.

36. (B) This is an inference question. Choice (A) is incorrect because the passage does not indicate the Greeks were pacifists; in fact, it states that they were sometimes involved in wars. Choice (C) is incorrect because nothing in the reading passage suggests that they were "simple." Because they "calculated time in four-year cycles," it could not be inferred that they couldn't count (choice D). Because the whole passage concerns athletics, choice (B) is the logical answer.

37. (A) The passage specifically states that "the Greeks emphasized physical fitness and strength in their education of youth." Choice (B) is not mentioned in the passage. Choice (C) is incorrect because only the elite and military could participate at first, and then only free Greek males. Pleasing the gods was the goal of competing during religious festivities, not returning to war (D).

38. (A) The sentence indicates that winners were honored for their "deeds," so it can be inferred that "deeds" are "accomplishments."

39. (C) The third sentence states that the "games were open to all free Greek males who had no criminal record."

40. (C) The sentence indicates that the games were very important, so it is implied that a war would be stopped, or "curtailed."

41. (B) The passage states that the winners of local athletic contests competed every four years at Mount Olympus, so an "Olympiad" spans the time between the Olympic Games.

42. (C) Sentence 3 states that Ybor moved his business from south Florida to west Florida.

43. (A) The sentence states that he was "forced to flee" as a result of a revolution, so "flee" means "escape."

44. (B) The sentence indicates that the problems where he was living caused him to "seek," "look for," or "pursue" another location.

45. (B) It can be inferred from the reading that Ybor will be remembered because Ybor City was named in his honor.

46. (A) The sentence states that people "flocked" because of the demand for workers, which implies that many people traveled to the location.

47. (A) One fifth of the city's twenty thousand residents means that four thousand people worked at the cigar factory.

48. (C) The passage is about Ybor, so it would be logical to use his name in the title. The passage is not about the Spanish-American War (A), nor is it a technical article about cigar making (D). Choice (B) is feasible; however, the passage focuses on Ybor's contribution to the Tampa area and not the broad contributions of many Cubans.

49. (A) A "site" is a "location," and this is implied in the sentence that states Ybor bought a tract of land on which he built his factory.

50. (C) The passage states that Martí was a Cuban poet and freedom fighter who organized a revolution. None of the other choices is mentioned in the passage.

PRACTICE TEST 2

ANSWER KEY FOR PRACTICE TEST 2

After some answers in this answer key, you will find numbers in italic type. These are page numbers in Part III where you will find review material for these questions. Although any one question may involve several different rules and concepts, these page numbers refer to important areas you should review if you have missed a question or are not sure of the material involved. Make full use of these page number references and of the index to direct your personal review.

Section 1: Listening Comprehension

1. (D)	11. (B)	21. (D)	31. (C)	41. (C)
2. (C)	12. (C)	22. (B)	32. (D)	42. (B)
3. (C)	13. (C)	23. (B)	33. (A)	43. (B)
4. (B)	14. (C)	24. (B)	34. (B)	44. (D)
5. (D)	15. (A)	25. (C)	35. (A)	45. (C)
6. (A)	16. (B)	26. (B)	36. (B)	46. (C)
7. (A)	17. (B)	27. (C)	37. (C)	47. (C)
8. (D)	18. (A)	28. (C)	38. (B)	48. (B)
9. (A)	19. (A)	29. (D)	39. (C)	49. (D)
10. (A)	20. (D)	30. (C)	40. (A)	50. (B)

Section 2: Structure and Written Expression

1. (C) *229*
2. (D) *46, 148–149, 229*
3. (B) *212–215*
4. (C) *80, 229*
5. (B) *44–49*
6. (B) *209–210*
7. (A) *134–135, 186–187*
8. (C) *221–223*
9. (A)
10. (B) *67, 134–135*
11. (A) *84–85, 134–135, 209*
12. (D) *138–139*
13. (B) *135*
14. (D) *212–215*
15. (B) *135, 229*
16. (B) *89–90*
17. (A) *123–124*
18. (A) *188*
19. (A) *84–85*
20. (A) *112*
21. (A) *45*
22. (C) *71*
23. (C) *69–70*
24. (D) *98*
25. (C) *86*
26. (D) *135*
27. (D) *150–151*
28. (C) *68–69*
29. (B)
30. (B) *82*
31. (A)
32. (D) *147–148*
33. (B) *85–86*
34. (C) *269*
35. (B) *150–151*
36. (D) *91*
37. (D) *97*
38. (A) *205–206*
39. (A) *69–70*
40. (B)

Section 3: Reading Comprehension

1. (A)	11. (C)	21. (B)	31. (B)	41. (D)
2. (B)	12. (A)	22. (C)	32. (C)	42. (B)
3. (A)	13. (B)	23. (A)	33. (C)	43. (D)
4. (B)	14. (D)	24. (D)	34. (A)	44. (D)
5. (C)	15. (D)	25. (A)	35. (B)	45. (A)
6. (A)	16. (B)	26. (B)	36. (B)	46. (C)
7. (C)	17. (A)	27. (C)	37. (B)	47. (B)
8. (A)	18. (A)	28. (C)	38. (C)	48. (B)
9. (B)	19. (A)	29. (C)	39. (A)	49. (A)
10. (B)	20. (A)	30. (D)	40. (A)	50. (B)

PRACTICE TEST 2: ANALYSIS-SCORING SHEET

Use the chart below to spot your strengths and weaknesses in each test section and to arrive at your total converted score. Fill in your number of correct answers for each section in the space provided. Refer to the Converted Score Sheet on page 496 to find your converted score for each section and enter those numbers on the chart. Find the sum of your converted scores, multiply that sum by 10, and divide by 3.

Example: If raw scores are   then   converted scores are
Section 1:   33   51
Section 2:   26   49
Section 3:   38   53
              Sum of Converted Scores   153
                        Times 10 = 1,530
                    Divided by 3 =   510 = Total Converted
                                                  Score

This will give you the approximate score that you would obtain if this were an actual TOEFL. Remember that your score here may possibly be higher than the score that you might receive on an actual TOEFL simply because you are studying the elements of the test shortly before taking each test. The score is intended only to give you a general idea of approximately what your actual score will be.

	Total Possible	Total Correct	Converted Score
Section 1: Listening Comprehension	50		
Section 2: Structure and Written Expression	40		
Section 3: Reading Comprehension	50		
TOTALS	140		

Sum of Converted Scores _____
            Times 10 = _____
        Divided by 3 = _____ = Total Converted Score

SECTION 1: LISTENING COMPREHENSION SCRIPT

Part A

1. Man: We have diet soda, but no regular cola.

   Woman: I'll pass, thanks.

   Third Voice: What is the woman probably going to do?

2. Man: How did your parents like the play they attended last week?

   Woman: My mother thought the language was terrible, but my father liked it.

   Third Voice: What does the woman say about her parents' reaction to the play?

3. Woman: I need to have this prescription filled, please.

   Man: All right, but you'll have a fifteen-minute wait.

   Third Voice: Where did this conversation most probably take place?

4. Woman: I thought we were going to have a science test this afternoon.

   Man: It was postponed because the teacher had to attend a conference.

   Third Voice: What does the man mean?

5. Woman: The president's State of the Union message last night was quite inspiring.

   Man: I couldn't watch it because my political science lecture let out too late.

   Third Voice: What does the man mean?

6. Man: Do you think I have a chance of proving my case?

   Woman: Definitely, and we're going to sue for punitive damages as well.

   Third Voice: What is the probable relationship between the man and the woman?

7. Woman: I can't even think with all that racket.

   Man: It won't get any better. Why don't you work inside the meeting room.

   Third Voice: What does the man imply?

8. Man: Marie's not eating her supper tonight. What's the matter with her?

   Woman: She went to the orthodontist and had braces put on her teeth. She says it hurts too much to chew.

   Third Voice: What does the woman say about Marie?

9. Man: Have you been to that new supermarket that just opened?

   Woman: Yes. The prices are quite reasonable. They have a great variety of meats and vegetables, but you have to bag your own groceries.

   Third Voice: What does the woman say she dislikes about the store?

10. Man: I hope you'll be ready to return to work soon.

    Woman: I'm not quite up to it yet.

    Third Voice: What does the woman mean?

11. Man: I heard Marilyn's entered college.

    Woman: Yes, she's taking courses in statistics, economics, and accounting.

    Third Voice: What career does Marilyn probably plan to follow?

12. Woman: Would you like Swiss cheese or American?

    Man: There's no better cheese than Swiss cheese.

    Third Voice: What does the man say about Swiss cheese?

13. Woman: I hope the game's not canceled.

    Man: It will be held rain or shine.

    Third Voice: What does the man say about the game?

14. Woman: I hear Martha was criticized in class.

    Man: Had she read the material, she would have been prepared.

    Third Voice: What does the man say about Martha?

15. Man: Did everyone return the evaluation forms?

    Woman: Sixty people received them, but only half returned them.

    Third Voice: What does the woman say about the evaluation forms?

16. Woman: Charlie has the potential to be a professional musician, but he is too lazy to practice.

    Man: What a shame!

    Third Voice: What does the woman say about Charlie?

17. Man: How long are you going to be away?

    Woman: I'm planning on spending the weekend at the beach as long as the weather stays nice.

    Third Voice: What is the woman probably going to do?

18. Woman: Are there any witnesses to the terrible accident?

    Man: No one but the seven-year-old boy saw it.

    Third Voice: What do the speakers say about the boy?

19. Woman: Louise writes in Spanish very well.

    Man: She writes it as well as she speaks it.

    Third Voice: What does the man say about Louise?

20. Woman: How are Peter and Lucy doing lately?

    Man: They had a quarrel, but they soon made up.

    Third Voice: What does the man say about Peter and Lucy?

21. Woman: Do you make connections with the Maple Avenue line?

    Man: Yes, ma'am. Pay your fare and I'll give you a free transfer and call you before we get to Maple Avenue.

    Third Voice: Where did this conversation most probably take place?

22. Woman: I need some help with this math calculation.

    Man: I've already looked at it. It's over my head too.

    Third Voice: What does the man mean?

23. Man: What does Mary do with her children while she works?

    Woman: She takes them to a nursery on her way to work.

    Third Voice: What does the woman mean?

24. Woman: Do you know where Dan is moving?

    Man: He will move to Florida if his job confirmation comes through.

    Third Voice: What does the man say about Dan?

25. Man: Does your father fish even in this heat?

    Woman: Sure. He likes nothing better than fishing on a hot, summer day.

    Third Voice: What does the woman say about her father?

26. Man: Have the actors finished with rehearsals?

    Woman: They went over their lines one more time before
                 the production began.

    Third Voice: What does the woman say about the actors?

27. Man: We are supposed to turn in our assignments
                 tomorrow, right?

    Woman: No. Ms. Daly asked us to hand them in today.

    Third Voice: What does the woman say about Ms. Daly?

28. Woman: What are we doing with the dog while we are on
                 vacation?

    Man: Stacey will look after him.

    Third Voice: What does the man say?

29. Man: A lot of people play golf here in the United
                 States.

    Woman: Yes. Although the game originated in Scotland,
                 it's more popular here than anywhere else.

    Third Voice: What do the speakers say about golf?

30. Woman: When was the last time you saw them?

    Man: It's been thirty years.

    Third Voice: What does the man mean?

Part B

Questions 31 through 34 are based on the following conversation.

Man: You don't look too happy. What seems to be the prob-
        lem?

Woman: I've got to write a long composition for my English class,
        and I just can't come up with any ideas; it's due tomorrow.

Man: That shouldn't be too difficult. Remember those pictures you were showing me last week, the ones from your cruise last winter?

Woman: Sure. I've got them someplace.

Man: Why don't you write about your impressions of the pyramids in Egypt and the camel ride you took.

Woman: That sounds like a good idea. I can also tell about our visit to North Africa, the Holy Land, and all of the historical, biblical places we visited.

Man: Well, now that you're feeling better about this, I think I'll be on my way. I've got to finish my composition too.

Woman: Thanks for your help. Once I get organized, it won't be so difficult.

31. What was the woman's problem?
32. What does the man suggest?
33. Which of the following places did the woman NOT visit?
34. Why does the man have to leave?

Questions 35 through 38 are based on the following conversation.

Woman: Alan, you've been so busy lately that we don't see you anymore.

Man: I've been trying to finish this research project so that I can present my findings at the annual conference in July.

Woman: But that's two months away. You've still got lots of time.

Man: Not really. You see, I've finished all the research, and I've just about organized all my notes, but it will take me almost two months to type them.

Woman: I can type up your paper in less than two weeks.

35. What does the woman offer to do for the man?
36. Why does the man need to finish the paper?
37. According to the conversation, what month is it now?
38. What stage of completing the project has the man reached?

Part C

Questions 39 through 41 are based on the following talk in a history class.

Nathaniel Bacon was a man determined to protect his property against Indian raids. He encouraged other Piedmont farmers to do likewise. After Governor William Berkeley of Virginia had refused to help them, Bacon and his friends banded together and destroyed a group of attackers in April of 1676. Governor Berkeley declared them traitors, and they assembled a group of some five hundred people and marched on Jamestown, the capital, to insist on the governor's assistance. Berkeley later ordered them all arrested. Because of this, the farmers burned Jamestown and took control of the government. The governor fled.

The fight, which was known as Bacon's Rebellion, lasted almost a year. Bacon contracted malaria and died in October of 1676, leaving the farmers at the mercy of Governor Berkeley. Twenty-three men were hanged at his request. King Charles II was very much upset by the governor's treatment of the farmers and forced him out of office.

39. Which of the following is NOT true?
40. Approximately how long were Bacon and the farmers able to fight off the governor?
41. How did Nathaniel Bacon die?

Questions 42 through 46 are based on the following talk about Mount Rushmore.

Towering over the Black Hills of South Dakota at six thousand feet above sea level can be seen the majestic and lifelike figures of four of America's greatest presidents. Gutzon Borglum spent fourteen years carving these gargantuan busts in Mount Rushmore as a lasting tribute to American leadership. In 1927, Borglum began this monumental task when he was sixty years old, a time when most men are preparing for their retirement, and not for a lengthy project. Upon Borglum's death, his son continued the project until the funding ran out.

Of the four presidents, George Washington's bust is the most prominent, looking as serious as we tend to think of him. Behind him is Thomas Jefferson, who bears a friendlier visage. Teddy Roosevelt is tucked off into the corner next to the last of the four, Abraham Lincoln, whose bust is the least complete.

It is unbelievable that such a monumental masterpiece should sit in a now quiet area, once the scene of deadly battles between the Sioux Indians and the white man.

42. Why was work on Mount Rushmore finally discontinued?
43. Which of the following presidents is NOT represented in this magnificent sculpture?
44. How old was Gutzon Borglum when he died?
45. How can the figures of Mount Rushmore best be described?
46. Which of the following is NOT true?

Questions 47 through 50 are based on the following talk about crude oil.

What you see below you is crude oil. Crude oil is the source of all petroleum products: gasoline, fuel oil, jet fuel, asphalt, lubricants, and chemicals. The modern world cannot exist without the energy derived from petroleum products, for industrial operations as well as transportation. These products are burned to produce energy or used as lubricants to reduce friction.

Many years ago, crude oil could be found close to the surface, and it would ooze from the ground without a recovery operation. That supply was very limited. Today oil wells must be drilled to depths of hundreds and even thousands of feet. Generally, crude oil must be pumped to the surface.

Crude oils are classified into two types determined by the percentage of sulfur they contain. "Sweet" crude oil has less than one percent sulfur, while "sour" crude has greater than one percent sulfur content. Crude oil is a mixture of many complex organic compounds. Though the chemical elements involved are mostly carbon and hydrogen, with traces of sulfur, nitrogen, and oxygen, the complicated structures of these organic chemicals create a multitude of different compounds.

47. Where did this talk most probably take place?
48. What is crude oil?
49. How are crude oils classified?
50. What does "sour" crude oil refer to?

EXPLANATIONS FOR PRACTICE TEST 2

SECTION 2: STRUCTURE AND WRITTEN EXPRESSION

Part A

1. (C) In choice (A), the verb *being* is incorrect because it suggests that Captain Henry is *now* remote from the enemy. If this were true, he would not need to creep through the underbrush. (B) is incorrect because the infinitive *to encounter* is split by the particle *not*. (D) uses incorrect vocabulary. One can "involve oneself in something," but one cannot "involve oneself in a person or people."

2. (D) Choice (A) incorrectly uses *childs. Children* is the correct plural of *child.* (B) is incorrect because a plural noun is required after *one of the.* Choice (C) is verbose.

3. (B) Choice (A) is in error because it contains a dangling participle, suggesting that *it* entered school. (C) contains an improper use of the past perfect progressive (*had been entering*). (D) incorrectly uses *enter into;* use *enter* + noun. (Exception: It is correct to *enter into* an agreement or contract.)

4. (C) In choice (A) *carelessly* is misused. *Carelessly* is the opposite of *carefully* and can be used only with people or animals. In (B) *it's* is an error. *It's* means *it is.* It is not the same as the possessive pronoun *its.* (D) is incorrect because only a person can *care* about something. *Care* indicates the presence of feelings, which plants (marijuana) do not have.

5. (B) Choice (A) is incorrect because *evidence* is a non-count noun, so a singular article cannot be used with it. Also, you should use a possessive form before a gerund (*our wanting*). (C) is incorrect because it is an incomplete sentence. After *the fact,* which is the subject of the sentence, a verb is necessary (the verb *has* in this case is part of a relative clause). Choice (D) is verbose.

6. (B) Choice (A) is a sentence fragment. It has no main verb. (C) uses *themselves* incorrectly. It has no antecedent. Choice (D) has no sensible meaning.

7. (A) Choice (B) contains an incorrect inclusive (*too*). *Also* would be correct here. Choices (C) and (D) should say *teaches well.* A verb is modified by an adverb.

8. (C) Choice (A) uses improper word choice and is not parallel. The verb *receive* refers only to *money.* Another verb would be necessary for *different types of shows* (such as, *broadcast* different types of shows). (B) uses improper word choice and order. (D) is verbose, and *differently from* should be *different from.*

9. (A) Choice (B) is incorrect because the proper form is: preposition + [verb + *ing*]. Choice (C) has improper word choice. We do not speak of *quantities of money.* Choice (D) is incorrect because *amount of profit* is redundant, and *bigger* is too informal for written English. It would be correct if it said *earn a larger profit.*

10. (B) The subject of this sentence is singular (*production*). Choice (A) incorrectly uses a plural verb (*have*). Choice (C) is incorrect because *be* is a linking verb and cannot be modified by the adverb *erratically.* (D) also uses a plural verb with a singular subject. Also, *going up and down* is too informal for written English.

11. (A) In choice (B), the pronoun *they* has no antecedent. Choice (C) is incorrect because verbs are modified by adverbs. In this case, the word should be *well*, not *good*. (D) is verbose, has no antecedent for the pronoun *they*, and should read *capable of producing*. *Capable* + *of* + [verb + *ing*].

12. (D) In an equal comparison use *as . . . as*.

13. (B) *Improved* is a verb and must be modified by an adverb.

14. (D) Choices (A), (B), and (C) all contain dangling participles, suggesting that the *bicycle, it*, or the *storm* is attempting to reach home.

15. (B) Choices (A) and (D) are verbose. Choice (C) uses *fastly*, which is not a word.

Part B

16. (B) should be *their*. Use a possessive adjective before a gerund.

17. (A) should be *cooking*. *Be used to* + [verb + *ing*].

18. (A) should be *knows how*. *Know how* + [verb in infinitive].

19. (A) should be *writing*. *Stop* + [verb + *ing*].

20. (A) should be *retype*. Modal + [verb in simple form].

21. (A) should be *many*. *Times* is a plural count noun and thus cannot be modified by *much*.

22. (C) should be *his*. *Each* is singular and must be followed by a singular verb and pronoun.

23. (C) should be *is*. *Mrs. Stevens* is a singular subject and requires a singular verb. The phrase beginning with *along with* has no effect on the number of the verb.

24. (D) should be *so are*. The auxiliary in the main sentence is *are*. The positive agreement must contain the same auxiliary.

25. (C) should be *forward to spending. Look forward to* + [verb + *ing*].

26. (D) should be *greatly*. Adverb + adjective + noun.

27. (D) should be *winter*. When a noun functions as an adjective, it cannot be plural. (*Winter* is the adjective and *coats* is the noun.)

28. (C) should be *does*. The singular subject *lunch* requires the singular verb *does*.

29. (B) should be *our*. For agreement of pronouns use *us . . . our*.

30. (B) should be *himself. Hisself* is not a word.

31. (A) should be *on*. One *advises* someone *on* something.

32. (D) should be *higher*. Use the comparative, not the superlative, when only two entities are mentioned.

33. (B) should be *heating*. Use a gerund [verb + *ing*] after a preposition (*for*).

34. (C) should be *among*. Use *among* for three or more entities and *between* for two entities.

35. (B) should be *dollar*. When a noun functions as an adjective, it cannot be plural.

36. (D) should be *repair. In need of* + noun.

37. (D) should be *isn't it. A liter* is singular, so the tag must also be singular.

38. (A) should be *was*. The correct sequence of tenses is *thought* (past) . . . *was* (past).

39. (A) should be *is*. The subject is singular (*supply*) and must take a singular verb (*is*).

40. (B) should be *any*. *Either* is used for only two items, *any* for three or more.

SECTION 3: READING COMPREHENSION

1. (A) Three languages, hieroglyphics, demotic, and Greek, are mentioned in paragraph 1, sentence 4. The only choice not mentioned is (A), French.

2. (B) Paragraph 2, sentence 5, states that they worked "independently of each other." "Independently" means the opposite of "together."

3. (A) In the passage, "deciphering" is done to ancient Egyptian hieroglyphics, so choices (B) and (C) can be eliminated immediately. Later in the passage, mention is made of "unraveling" the language mysteries, which should lead you to choose "decoding" rather than "probing."

4. (B) Paragraph 2, sentence 1, says that the word was "Ptolemy."

5. (C) The words "they were forced to remain there for three years" indicate that they were waiting to continue their campaign. This is an inference question. Note that choice (A) is contradicted by paragraph 1, sentence 2, which tells us they lost a naval battle. Choices (B) and (D) are contradicted by the fact that the stone was discovered by accident during the construction of a fort.

6. (A) Paragraph 2, sentence 1, states that Champollion deciphered the first word.

7. (C) Sentence 3 states the stele was "known as the Rosetta stone, in commemoration of the town near the fort."

8. (A) The sentence states that he had an "ambition to control all the area around the Mediterranean Sea," which should lead you to understand that "ambition" is a desire, or "aspiration."

9. (B) Choice (A) is not inaccurate; however, one might expect a passage so titled to concentrate on the details of Napoleon and how he discovered the stone, which it doesn't. Choice (C) covers a detail of the passage, as does choice (D). Determining what was written on the stone was the chief subject of the passage.

10. (B) Lines 14–18 state that "the direction in which they were read depended on how the characters were arranged." The following sentence continues the description.

11. (C) The entire reading, especially the last paragraph, indicates that Sequoyah will be remembered because he created a new alphabet. Although he will also be remembered because the redwoods were named after him, that simply manifests the result of his accomplishment.

12. (A) The first sentence states that he was the "son of a white trader and an Indian squaw." This is a description of his parents. If you are unfamiliar with the word, answers (A) through (C) could describe a person, but (A) is the correct answer. Choice (D) would not be a good guess since his other parent has been identified as a trader. It would be unlikely that "squaw" would also mean "trader."

13. (B) Paragraph 2, sentence 1, says, "His family and friends thought him mad."

14. (D) Paragraph 3, sentence 1, says that he desired "to preserve words and events for later generations." Those words and events would be the history of his people.

15. (D) "Illiterate" means "not literate," or not able to read or write.

16. (B) No mention of music was made in the passage (A), nor was any made of Sequoyah actually going mad and listening to leaves (C). The passage states that some thought written material was from the Great Spirit, but no mention was made of avenues of supernatural communication (D). Sequoyah was fascinated with reading, writing, and the idea of recording and storing information for future generations.

17. (A) The fact that he spent twelve years developing this written alphabet, despite obstacles, demonstrates his determination.

18. (A) The passage is about Sequoyah, so it would be logical for the title to contain his name. This would make choice (A) preferable to choice (B). Choice (C) is inaccurate, and choice (D), although mentioned, is not what the passage is about.

19. (A) The reading implies that he was very interested in the "leaf," so you should be able to guess that "fascinated" means that. A synonym for "fascinated" in this context is "absorbed."

20. (A) Paragraph 2, sentence 1, says that he worked "independently," which means that he had the help of no one. Choice (A) is the only choice that is not true. Choices (C) and (D) are specifically stated in the passage. Choice (B) should be inferred from the facts given, such as Sequoyah's basing his alphabet on sound patterns he heard, and his early observation of the "talking leaf."

21. (B) Sentence 2 indicates that the Aztecs believed that they must offer human sacrifices to appease, or pacify, the gods.

22. (C) Paragraph 2, sentences 2 and 3, tell us that the victims were indoctrinated (brainwashed) and heavily sedated (drugged).

23. (A) The last sentence says that "they accepted their fate passively," or "submissively."

24. (D) From the context you can gather that the gods needed to be pleased. This eliminates choices (B) and (C). "Glorified" (A) appears to be a possibility, but the definition of "appease" is to soothe and satisfy (D).

25. (A) Making sacrifices to the gods is the subject of the reading passage. Choices (B) and (D) are details in the passage, and choice (C) is too broad in scope.

26. (B) The priests offered their collected blood to the gods, warriors killed in battle gained favor with the gods, and victims' palpitating hearts were removed for the gods, so choice (B) is correct.

27. (C) The list of reasons human sacrifices were necessary is contained in sentence 2. The need for sacrifices as a requirement of fame is not mentioned in the passage.

28. (C) The second paragraph explains that the priests made the victims believe that they would occupy a place of honor in the afterlife if they would allow themselves to be sacrificed.

29. (C) Sentence 3 states, "The priests practiced forms of self-mutilation, such as piercing their tongues . . ."

30. (D) Aztecs were both "mighty" and "warlike." That should provide a clue that "mighty" means "powerful."

31. (B) Paragraph 1, sentence 1, says that crude oil is found "from a few hundred feet beneath the surface to as deep as 25,000 feet." Thus (B), "always found a few hundred feet," is not true.

32. (C) The sentence in which "minute" appears indicates that "minute" means a small amount because the trace elements are "disregarded." This should give you the hint that "minute" means "insignificant" in this sentence.

33. (C) Paragraph 3, last sentence, specifically states this as the reason for the many thousands of compounds. Complicated refining processes (B) are mentioned as producing other products, but not thousands of compounds.

34. (A) The sentence states that other products are produced, "some of which are used to upgrade and increase the octane rating." This implies that to "upgrade" means to "improve."

35. (B) Paragraph 4, sentence 1, gives heating and condensing as the methods of producing products.

36. (B) The sentence implies that "opaque" is a physical appearance, just like "thin," "thick," and "transparent." Furthermore, "thin" and "thick" are opposites, so you should assume that "transparent" and "opaque" are opposites as well. Answer choice (A) is the opposite of "opaque." Choice (C) is incorrect because "light" is not a characteristic of "opaque." "Crude" (D) is raw oil, not a description of its appearance.

37. (B) The last sentence of paragraph 1 says, "Either pressure at the source or pumping forces crude oil to the surface." Although choices (A), (C), and (D), might conceivably produce pressure, they are not as complete as (B) because they do not include pumping and are not specifically mentioned in the reading.

38. (C) Paragraph 4, sentence 2, lists examples of light oils as gasoline, kerosene, and distillate oil. Lubricating oil is mentioned in the first sentence of the reading, but we are not told whether it is classified as a light or heavy oil.

39. (A) The third paragraph explains that the chemical composition of petroleum products is carbon and hydrogen.

40. (A) A reduction in temperature (cooling) changes vapors to liquids, thus creating gasoline, kerosene, and distillate oil. Expanding (B) or diluting (C) the vapors, or gases, would not

create one of the liquid oil products mentioned. To refute is to prove false, so choice (D) is incorrect.

41. (D) The sentence states, "Trace elements are also found, but in such minute quantities that they are disregarded." The subject of the sentence is clearly the reference for the pronoun.

42. (B) Paragraph 1, sentence 1, says that an election year is one that is evenly divisible by four. Of the choices given, only (B), 1930, is not evenly divisible by four, leaving a remainder of two.

43. (D) The last sentence of paragraph 1 tells us that William H. Harrison served the shortest term.

44. (D) Paragraph 2 gives the names of the four American presidents assassinated. Choice (A) is not true because the reading gives information only about presidents since 1840. Ronald Reagan also did not die in office. Choice (C) is not true because, although Roosevelt was elected four times, he died during the fourth term.

45. (A) The entire reading answers this question. The presidents mentioned are Harrison, Lincoln, Garfield, McKinley, Kennedy, Harding, and Roosevelt.

46. (C) "Inauguration" means "swearing-in ceremony," a ceremonial induction into office.

47. (B) Paragraph 3 tells us that Roosevelt died of polio; he was not assassinated.

48. (B) This form of the relative pronoun is the objective or complement form, meaning it must replace the complement of the sentence rather than the subject. Analyze the sentence. "James A. Garfield . . . was shot . . . by a man . . ." (He would not give a job to the man.) So the reference is to the man to whom Garfield would not give a job, and that is the same man who assassinated him.

49. (A) The entire passage is about presidents who died or were murdered in office. There are clues throughout the passage that "assassinated" means "murdered."

50. (B) The sentence states "He had contracted polio . . . and eventually died . . ." The fact that polio is a disease should lead you to presume that "contracted" means "caught" or "developed."

PRACTICE TEST 3

ANSWER KEY FOR PRACTICE TEST 3

After some answers in this answer key, you will find numbers in italic type. These are page numbers in Part III where you will find review material for these questions. Although any one question may involve several different rules and concepts, these page numbers refer to important areas you should review if you have missed a question or are not sure of the material involved. Make full use of these page number references and of the index to direct your personal review.

Section 1: Listening Comprehension

1. (D)	11. (C)	21. (B)	31. (D)	41. (B)
2. (A)	12. (C)	22. (C)	32. (B)	42. (B)
3. (D)	13. (A)	23. (B)	33. (B)	43. (D)
4. (A)	14. (D)	24. (B)	34. (B)	44. (B)
5. (B)	15. (B)	25. (C)	35. (B)	45. (B)
6. (B)	16. (C)	26. (C)	36. (B)	46. (B)
7. (C)	17. (B)	27. (A)	37. (A)	47. (B)
8. (C)	18. (C)	28. (D)	38. (D)	48. (B)
9. (C)	19. (A)	29. (B)	39. (C)	49. (D)
10. (C)	20. (B)	30. (D)	40. (A)	50. (C)

Section 2: Structure and Written Expression

1. (A)
2. (D)
3. (D) *191–193*
4. *(D) 48–50*
5. (B)
6. (C) *118*
7. (B) *227–228*
8. (D) *45, 153–154*
9. (B) *118*
10. (D) *118*
11. (C) *52–53*
12. (B) *219–220*
13. (A)
14. (C) *62–63*
15. (C) *88, 221–223*
16. (A) *121–122*
17. (D) *98–99*
18. (A) *157*
19. (D) *83–84*
20. (A) *83–84*

21. (A) *45*
22. (B) *65–67, 205*
23. (D) *62*
24. (B) *71*
25. (D) *69–70*
26. (B) *187*
27. (C) *120–123*
28. (B) *89–90*
29. (B) *157*
30. (C) *149*
31. (A) *45*
32. (B) *150–151*
33. (C) *70*
34. (C) *269*
35. (A) *45*
36. (B) *100*
37. (C) *148*
38. (B)
39. (B) *47*
40. (B) *146*

Section 3: Reading Comprehension

1. (C)
2. (A)
3. (A)
4. (B)
5. (C)
6. (B)
7. (A)
8. (C)
9. (C)
10. (C)

11. (C)
12. (D)
13. (C)
14. (A)
15. (A)
16. (B)
17. (A)
18. (B)
19. (D)
20. (B)

21. (B)
22. (A)
23. (B)
24. (A)
25. (D)
26. (D)
27. (B)
28. (A)
29. (C)
30. (C)

31. (A)
32. (C)
33. (B)
34. (B)
35. (B)
36. (D)
37. (B)
38. (B)
39. (A)
40. (A)

41. (A)
42. (A)
43. (B)
44. (B)
45. (D)
46. (C)
47. (B)
48. (D)
49. (C)
50. (C)

PRACTICE TEST 3: ANALYSIS-SCORING SHEET

Use the chart below to spot your strengths and weaknesses in each test section and to arrive at your total converted score. Fill in your number of correct answers for each section in the space provided. Refer to the Converted Score Sheet on page 496 to find your converted score for each section and enter those numbers on the chart. Find the sum of your converted scores, multiply that sum by 10, and divide by 3.

Example: If raw scores are   then   converted scores are
Section 1:   33   51
Section 2:   26   49
Section 3:   38   53
            Sum of Converted Scores   153
                    Times 10 = 1,530
                Divided by 3 =   510 = Total Converted
                                                Score

This will give you the approximate score that you would obtain if this were an actual TOEFL. Remember that your score here may possibly be higher than the score that you might receive on an actual TOEFL simply because you are studying the elements of the test shortly before taking each test. The score is intended only to give you a general idea of approximately what your actual score will be.

	Total Possible	Total Correct	Converted Score
Section 1: Listening Comprehension	50		
Section 2: Structure and Written Expression	40		
Section 3: Reading Comprehension	50		
TOTALS	140		

Sum of Converted Scores _____
        Times 10 = _____
        Divided by 3 = _____ = Total Converted Score

SECTION 1: LISTENING COMPREHENSION SCRIPT

Part A

1. **Man:** I thought Mike and Francie were getting married in June.

   Woman: No, that's when his cousin's wedding is. They're getting married the following month.

   Third Voice: When does the woman say Mike and Francie are getting married?

2. **Man:** Did you hear that the Chapmans sold their house and are moving to Arizona?

   Woman: Yes, and the man who bought the house is a doctor from Philadelphia.

   Third Voice: According to the speakers, from where will the new owner come?

3. **Woman:** My computer won't boot up this morning.

   Man: Good thing you backed up your data last night.

   Third Voice: What does the man mean?

4. **Woman:** This doesn't look at all familiar. We must be lost. We'd better get some directions.

   Man: Let's pull in here. While I'm filling the tank, you can ask for directions.

   Third Voice: Where will the man and woman go for assistance?

5. **Man:** May I speak to Jason Daniels, please?

   Woman: Nobody by that name works here.

   Third Voice: What does the woman mean?

6. Man: Kelly, you look tired.

   Woman: I am. I've been working on the budget report for the finance committee for three days and nights.

   Third Voice: Why does the woman say she's tired?

7. Woman: John, how are you? I heard you were sick.

   Man: They must have confused me with somebody else. I've never felt better.

   Third Voice: How does the man say he feels?

8. Man: I'd like to buy this table, but I'm $20 short.

   Woman: I'll lend you the money if you can pay me back by Friday.

   Third Voice: Can the man buy the table?

9. Man: Has Dave returned from Europe yet?

   Woman: Yes, but he was here for only three days before his company sent him to Canada.

   Third Voice: Where does the woman say Dave is now?

10. Man: Have you seen Ann Marie in the past fifteen minutes?

    Woman: She went to the gas station to have her tank filled.

    Third Voice: What does the woman say about Ann Marie?

11. Woman: George and Jeff were not at the meeting.

    Man: They would have come if they had known about it.

    Third Voice: What does the man say about George and Jeff?

12. Woman: Are the test results posted yet?

    Man: Yes. Most of the students scored eighty percent and above, but Michael is the exception.

    Third Voice: What does the man imply about Michael?

13. Man: Have they found out who took the answer sheets?

    Woman: The humanities professor asked the dean to question several students.

    Third Voice: What does the woman mean?

14. Man: I'm afraid I'll have to work late again tomorrow night.

    Woman: Why don't you ask for some extra help?

    Third Voice: What does the woman suggest the man do?

15. Man: If Henry hadn't had so much work to do, he would have come to the concert with us.

    Woman: It's too bad he missed such a great show.

    Third Voice: What do the speakers say about Henry?

16. Man: Did James return the books to the library?

    Woman: No, he had them renewed.

    Third Voice: What does the woman say about James?

17. Man: Has Harry stopped smoking yet?

    Woman: He is afraid he'll gain weight.

    Third Voice: What do the speakers say about Harry?

18. Man: Does Jonathan spend much time studying?

    Woman: He hasn't studied in weeks, but he'll do well.

    Third Voice: What does the woman imply about Jonathan?

19. Woman: How was your meal at the banquet?

    Man: My meat was so tough I could hardly cut it.

    Third Voice: What does the man say about his experience at the banquet?

20. Man: Where could Rick be?

    Woman: He must have forgotten about our meeting.

    Third Voice: What does the woman say about Rick?

21. Man: What's in that bag over there?

    Woman: I bought some apples, peaches, pears, and grapes.

    Third Voice: What is the woman talking about?

22. Woman: Where did Joe and Nancy go for their honey-moon?

    Man: They were going to go to Puerto Rico, but they couldn't afford it, so they went to St. Augustine instead for one week.

    Third Voice: What does the man say about the couple's honey-moon?

23. Woman: Did you know that the hot dog did not originate in the United States but in Germany?

    Man: Yes, and they've even had something similar to it in Finland. It's made out of reindeer meat.

    Third Voice: Which of the following is NOT true about the hot dog?

24. Woman: You ought to take it easy for a few days.

    Man: I have no time to spare.

    Third Voice: What problem does the man have?

25. Man: Tiffany is already walking, but Stephanie isn't.

    Woman: Tiffany was born before Stephanie was.

    Third Voice: What does the woman say about Tiffany and Stephanie?

26. Man: I am taking my car downtown to be repaired.

    Woman: Be sure you get an estimate.

    Third Voice: What does the woman advise the man?

548   ANSWERS AND EXPLANATIONS FOR PRACTICE TEST 3

27. Woman: Why did Professor Nelson get angry with Jane?
    Man: She should have worked on her paper last night, but she watched TV instead.
    Third Voice: What does the man say about Jane?

28. Man: Franklin focused on the deer and snapped the shutter.
    Woman: What a great shot!
    Third Voice: What are the speakers talking about?

29. Woman: I need to complete my paper this weekend.
    Man: If I were you, I'd have it typed by a service.
    Third Voice: What does the man suggest the woman do?

30. Man: I hear Yolanda ran into Anna downtown last week.
    Woman: I haven't seen either of them for months.
    Third Voice: What does the man mean?

Part B

Questions 31 through 34 are based on the following conversation.

Man: Did you see that TV program last night about the sky diver whose parachutes didn't open after he had jumped from his plane?

Woman: No, I didn't. Did he die?

Man: No. It's really unbelievable how he could have survived such a free fall, much less live to tell about it on television!

Woman: What happened?

Man: Neither of his chutes opened as he plummeted to the ground. When they found him, they thought he was dead. Doctors said he'd never walk again, but he proved them wrong.

Woman: How long was he recuperating?

Man: He spent eighteen months in the hospital while his broken bones were mending. He was no sooner discharged than he jumped out of a plane again.

Woman: Gee, some people sure do crazy things!

31. Why was the man in the hospital?
32. Where did the interview take place?
33. What caused the man's accident?
34. What did the man do soon after he was released from the hospital?

Questions 35 through 38 are based on the following conversation.

Man: What's the matter?

Woman: I can't sleep lying down. I feel a lot of pressure in my chest.

Man: Well, there is some congestion. I want to do some tests.

Woman: How soon will I get the results?

Man: Oh, you'll have the results before you leave the office, and I'll prescribe some antibiotics that I believe will help you.

35. What is the probable relationship between these two speakers?
36. When will the woman receive the results of the tests?
37. What does the man think will help the woman?
38. What is the woman's problem?

Part C

Questions 39 through 42 are based on the following news story.

Two men and a thirteen-year-old boy are safe now after being rescued from their tiny boat which had been adrift in the Gulf of Mexico for twenty-four hours. After their families had reported them missing, the Coast Guard began searching, but the group was rescued after waving frantically at a private airplane flying over-head. It turned out that they had drifted only seven and a half miles from where their engine had broken down.

39. How many people were in the boat?
40. How were the boaters finally rescued?
41. Why did the authorities begin to search for the boat?
42. How far had the boat drifted?

Questions 43 through 45 are based on the following commentary by a doctor to a patient.

Mr. Davis, I've just finished reading your x-rays, and I would like to discuss them with you. You have osteoarthritis in the middle of your back and scoliosis, which is a curvature of the spine. I can also feel the muscle spasms and pinched nerves from your shoulders to the base of your spine. While this may sound terrible to you, it is not life-threatening, nor is it something to worry about. At present, there is no cure for these problems, but you can control them with proper treatment. First of all, we need to adjust your diet a little. The nurse will provide you with information on some foods to avoid completely and others whose consumption should be restricted. Here is an explanation of some back exercises that you can do. They will help to stretch and strengthen the muscles and to relieve the pain. Use a heating pad and an ice pack to alleviate soreness in the joints. I'm going to prescribe some muscle relaxers and pain killers. Take them as indicated. In about six weeks we'll see how you are progressing and then begin some chiropractic treatment. I'd like to see you again in three weeks. Please have the nurse make an appointment for then.

43. What is the purpose of this talk?
44. What did the speaker do before talking with Mr. Davis?
45. According to the speaker, what is scoliosis?

Questions 46 through 50 are based on the following talk about Salvador Dali.

Ladies and gentlemen, please move in a little closer as we begin our tour this afternoon. Today you will enjoy the largest collection of Salvador Dali's works under one roof. They include several hundred oil paintings, drawings, and watercolors, more than a thousand graphics, and a variety of sculptures as well as jewelry. As you will see, Dali was multitalented. He designed furniture, created exquisite works with fine jewels, and concocted perfumes with tantalizing aromas. He developed his talents over a span of six decades, leaving an indelible imprint on the world of art.

Here we see some of his early paintings, mostly landscapes of the town of his birth—Figueras in Catalonia, Spain—and the seascapes of a neighboring town called Cadaqués. While these represent a more traditional art form, it was at this time that Dali's controversial career began. He was expelled from a prestigious art school in Madrid because he disagreed with his professors on their techniques. He once threw himself down several flights of steps just to get attention. At the age of twenty-one, he had his first one-man show.

Four years later in Paris, he fell madly in love with Gala Eluard, the wife of a French poet. She became his lover, and later they married. She was the inspiration and model for many of his works. *The Discovery of America by Christopher Columbus,* his monumental masterpiece, shows Gala appearing on Columbus's banner. She also served as his model for other works, such as the *Crucifixion, Ecumenical Council,* and *Hallucinogenic Toreador.*

Dali's themes varied from one period to the next, but many contained recurring images of ants, crutches, limp watches, grasshoppers, and sexual symbols. All of these were, in some way, a carryover from his childhood and adolescence. He often placed familiar and outrageous imaginary objects side by side. A number of paintings, such as *Slave Market; Old Age, Adolescence, Infancy; Hallucinogenic Toreador;* and *Lincoln in Dalivision* portray double images. Depending on how you look at these works, you can see two entirely different views.

Surrealistic paintings are what Dali is best known for, and in most of them he left everything to the viewer's interpretation. As you wander around on your visit today, look at the paintings up close and then move back about twenty feet and ponder them again from that distance.

Before leaving, stop at our gift shop to browse and perhaps to purchase some of the Dali memorabilia—posters, books, clothing, perfume, and post cards. On your next trip to St. Petersburg, come back to visit us. We are open Tuesday through Saturday from 10 A.M. to 5 P.M., on Sunday from noon to 5 P.M., and we are closed on Mondays and holidays.

46. Who is the speaker?
47. Which of the following was not mentioned as a Dali creation?
48. Who was one of Dali's frequent models?
49. What was the artist's most renowned art form?
50. What kind of paintings were the artist's earliest?

EXPLANATIONS FOR PRACTICE TEST 3

SECTION 2: STRUCTURE AND WRITTEN EXPRESSION

Part A

1. (A) Choice (B) includes improper word choice and order. (C) is incorrect because it is not possible to say "win him the case." Correct form is "win the case for him." (D) is incorrect because *minimum* is a noun and cannot modify another noun (*chance*); it is not clear to whom *him* refers, and the order is not correct.

2. (D) Choices (A) and (B) are in error because it is not correct to say "an attribute is *when*" or "an attribute is *how*"; an attribute is a static quality. Choice (C) would be correct if it were "the way he gives lectures."

3. (D) Choice (A) uses incorrect vocabulary choice. *Remembrance* has a sentimental meaning; it should be *reminder*. Also, the verb *rise*, not *raise* should be used. (B) should read *the following*

month, not *the month following.* (The adjective precedes the noun.) Also, *rise,* not *raise,* is required. (C) is incorrect because the verb *contained* must be followed by a noun, not a verb.

4. (D) Choice (A) incorrectly uses *the* before a singular country name. (B) uses improper word order and also uses *the* incorrectly. (C) is in error because *French* when used as an adjective cannot be made possessive.

5. (B) The expression should read, "It was *not until . . . that.*" To use *when* (choice A) is redundant.

6. (C) In choice (A) there is improper use of the past conditional. (B) includes improper vocabulary choice. A flat tire does not *happen.* (D) makes improper use of the reflexive *itself.* A tire, being inanimate, could not flatten itself.

7. (B) The correct structure is adverbial (*never*) + auxiliary (*have*) + subject (*so many women*) + verb (*received*).

8. (D) Choice (A) is incorrect because *homework* is a non-count noun and *few* cannot be used with non-count nouns. (B) is incorrect because a complete sentence is required after *because.* Choice (C) is verbose. Also, *because of* cannot be followed by a complete sentence.

9. (B) *Know how* in this sentence means "to have a practical understanding of something." It is not correct to use *to* after *know how* unless it is followed by a verb.

10. (D) Choices (A), (B), and (C) are all incorrect past conditions.

11. (C) Choice (A) includes improper word choice. *One other* should be *another.* Choice (B) uses *also. Also* does not mean the same as *again,* which is the meaning conveyed by the sentence. (D) uses incorrect word order. It should say *fifty dollars more.*

12. (B) Choices (A) and (D) are incorrect because the adjective *aware* must be followed by *of* before a noun or noun phrase. Choice (C) uses *of,* but *the place where* is redundant.

13. (A) Choices (B), (C), and (D) are all too informal for written English and are verbose.

14. (C) *Still, yet,* and *already* are misused in the other answer choices.

15. (C) Choices (A) and (D) omit the word *how,* which must follow *know* before a verb. Only choice (C) uses parallel construction (*how to manage . . . sell . . . satisfy*).

Part B

NOTE: Ø = nothing, indicating that this word or phrase should be deleted.

16. (A) should be *hadn't sent.* A past wish must be followed by the past perfect.

17. (D) should be *so am I.* For affirmative agreement use *so* + auxiliary + subject.

18. (A) should be *such a beautiful.* Cause and effect: *such + a +* adjective + singular count noun.

19. (D) should be *to use. Allow* + indirect object + infinitive.

20. (A) should be *to stimulate.* Use *try* + infinitive.

21. (A) should be *is. Mumps* is a non-count noun.

22. (B) should be *had gone.* The past perfect is necessary to show that this action (going to the supermarket) occurred before the other action (coming home).

23. (D) should be *for*. Use *for* + duration of time.

24. (B) should be *reports*. *Each* + singular verb.

25. (D) should be *is*. *Athlete* is the subject and is singular.

26. (B) should be Ø. *Both* and *as well as* are redundant if they are used together; use either *both . . . and* or *as well as* alone.

27. (C) should be *were*. This is a present wish. The verb *be* must be in the plural past tense form in a present wish because it is contrary to fact.

28. (B) should be *his*. Possessive forms must be used before a gerund.

29. (B) should be *such a way*. Cause and effect: *such* + *a* + singular count noun + *that*.

30. (C) should be *dancers*. After *one of the* there must be a plural noun.

31. (A) should be *fewer*. *Friends* is a plural count noun, so *less* is incorrect.

32. (B) should be *four-day*. *Four-day* here functions as an adjective modifying the noun *journey,* so it cannot be plural.

33. (C) should be *has*. The subject, *influence,* is singular and thus requires a singular verb, *has*.

34. (C) should be *among*. Use *between* when there are only two entities, *among* when there are more than two.

35. (A) should be *Much*. *Population* is a non-count noun, so *many* cannot modify it.

36. (B) should be *apparently*. Verbs are always modified by adverbs, not adjectives.

37. (C) should be *in*. After *one of the* + superlative + noun + . . . , use *in* + singular count noun.

38. (B) should be *to have missed*. This is a perfect infinitive.

39. (B) should be *an*. Use *an* before words beginning with vowel sounds.

40. (B) should be *worse*. This is a double comparative: *the harder . . . the worse. Worst* is superlative.

SECTION 3: READING COMPREHENSION

1. (C) Paragraph 2, sentence 2, says that "a serious eye infection forced her to abandon the idea." Choice (A) is contradicted by the information given. She *did* get admitted to medical school because the first paragraph says "she was finally accepted." Choices (B) and (D) are true statements, but they have nothing to do with her not becoming a surgeon.

2. (A) Paragraph 1 says that it was "nearly impossible" for a woman at this time to become a doctor. This answer can also be inferred from the fact that she was the first female physician in the United States.

3. (A) Paragraph 2 tells us that she graduated in 1849 and paragraph 3 that the hospital was opened in 1857. 1857 − 1849 = 8.

4. (B) The question asks for the one choice that was *not* a first in Elizabeth Blackwell's life. The passage states that she did *not* become a surgeon because of an eye infection.

5. (C) Paragraph 2 tells us that she graduated in 1849, and paragraph 1 that she was born in 1821. 1849 − 1821 = 28.

6. (B) The sentence states that she had to "abandon" her dream of being a surgeon because of a serious eye infection. That indicates that "abandon" means "give up."

7. (A) Answer choice (B) is incorrect because she did not abandon her plans to become a "doctor," only her plans to become a "surgeon." Answer choices (C) and (D) are details but not the main idea of the entire passage.

8. (C) The passage states that she "managed to open a new hospital," and then says "Besides being the first female physician and *founding* her own hospital . . ." This means that *opening* and *founding* are the same thing. The answer is further hinted at later in the last sentence, where it says "she also *established,*" which indicates that *founding* and *establishing* are synonyms.

9. (C) Answer choice (A) prevented her from becoming a surgeon, not a doctor. She may not have had a lot of money (she taught school and gave music lessons for money), but she evidently did pay her tuition (B). Her sister was also a doctor, so there is no reason to think she was not supported by her family (D). However, it required many letters to medical schools before she found one that would accept women, so (C) is the best answer choice.

10. (C) Line 11 specifically states that a serious eye infection forced Blackwell to abandon the idea of becoming a surgeon.

11. (C) We are told in paragraph 1 that endocrine glands have no ducts and release their products directly into the bloodstream.

12. (D) The sentence states "The thyroid gland collects . . . , which *it* stores . . ." The pronoun precedes a verb (stores) and thus is a subject, so "it" relates back to the "thyroid gland" in the subject position of the sentence.

13. (C) Paragraph 3, sentences 2 and 3, says that cretinism occurs in children as a result of hypothyroidism, or underactive thyroid gland.

14. (A) Paragraph 3, sentence 3, tells us that myxedema occurs in adults and causes the growth process to slow down. We can infer that this would result in sluggishness, or lethargy.

15. (A) "Former" means the first of two, while "latter" refers to the second. The two items mentioned in the previous sentence are "underactive thyroid" and "overactive thyroid." The sentence also states that "underactive thyroid" is the same as "hypothyroidism." So "former" refers to an "underactive thyroid," also known as "hypothyroidism."

16. (B) We are told in paragraph 4, sentence 1, that a goiter is an enlarged, or swollen, thyroid gland.

17. (A) The first paragraph states that "exocrine glands secrete their products through ducts, but endocrine glands, or ductless glands, release their products directly into the bloodstream." Thus the answer is (A).

18. (B) The sentence states that glands of this type "secrete" and the other "release." "Emit" is a synonym for "release" or "secrete."

19. (D) Paragraph 3 states that an "underactive thyroid causes hypothyroidism."

20. (B) The passage does not address all glands, only some specific types of glands, so choice (A) is incorrect. The passage does not involve secretion in general, so (C) is incorrect. The passage deals with both an underactive and an overactive thyroid gland, not just an overactive one, so choice (D) is wrong.

21. (B) The "function" of a thing is its purpose or the job it is to perform. The function of the thyroid gland—to collect iodine and produce and store thyroxine—is described only in lines 7–9.

22. (A) Paragraph 2 says that "animals can perceive environmental changes . . ." The fact that observing animal behavior can predict earthquakes does not indicate that the number of deaths nor the location of the epicenter can be predicted, so answer choices (B) and (C) are incorrect. The entire reading regards learning of an impending earthquake in advance and not after it has occurred, so answer choice (D) is incorrect.

23. (B) Reasons for the animals' perceptions are not specifically given in the reading, but we can assume that animals are able to predict these occurrences because they have some instincts that humans do not possess. No other choice is reasonable or is suggested in any way by the reading.

24. (A) Even if you are not familiar with the word "evacuate," you would know that to keep the death toll down, people would have to be moved away, or "removed," from the area.

25. (D) The reading gives examples of other animals, such as llamas, seabirds, and chickens.

26. (D) The root word "center" in "epicenter" is the clue that "core" is the word nearest in meaning.

27. (B) It can be inferred that if scientists can predict earthquakes, they will have enough warning to lead people to safety, thus lowering the death rate.

28. (A) The phrase "although hundreds of thousands of people were killed" implies that the event was destructive.

29. (C) This is an inference question. The passage is about earthquakes and animals, so choice (B) is too broad for the main idea. Earthquakes can't be prevented by observing animal behavior, so choice (A) is incorrect, and choice (D) was not mentioned in the passage.

30. (C) In the third paragraph, the author states that "Unusual animal behavior preceding earthquakes has been noted for centuries." Later in the same paragraph, the author states that such behavior was observed "throughout the eighteenth and nineteenth centuries."

31. (A) Paragraph 2, sentence 1, states that the boy was found "wandering in the woods." While it is true that the boy growled at people, choice (C), we are not told that he growled at the doctor when he was found.

32. (C) The word "offspring" means "children." "Litter" is used to indicate the offspring of multiparous animals (animals that give birth to a number of offspring each pregnancy).

33. (B) Paragraph 2, sentence 4, says that "the doctor won the boy's confidence and began to work with him." You should infer that the ability to work with him was the result of the boy's confidence (trust).

34. (B) "Utter" does mean "absolute," but not in this context, so choice (A) is incorrect. The word is found in a list of the doctor's accomplishments with the boy, and *screaming* a number of words" most likely would not be considered a positive development, so choice (C) is incorrect. Since reading may be done silently, and "utter" means to pronounce words using the voice, choice (B) is better than (D).

35. (B) Sentence 1 indicates that wolves have been said to care for human children as far back as 700 B.C. Choice (C) is true. "Domesticating" means to "tame" or "make fit for living in human society." The doctor was successful in getting the boy to clothe and feed himself and speak and write to some degree. Choice (D) is true because "utter a number of words" does not indicate that he could speak "perfectly."

36. (D) In this sentence, the word "preposterous" is being contrasted with the word "credible." Since "credible" means "believable," you can determine that "preposterous" means the opposite, "absurd" (totally unbelievable).

37. (B) Answer choice (A) is incorrect because the passage is about some specific children (Romulus, Remus, and another boy), and not children in general. No general statement is made about children raised by wolves. Choice (C) is only one part of the reading. Romulus and Remus are discussed in paragraph 1, but another child is discussed in paragraph 2. Choice (D) is incorrect because it confuses the attempted drowning of Romulus and Remus with the French doctor, who is mentioned in paragraph 2.

38. (B) Rome did not exist when Romulus and Remus were children because they were the founders (A). A French doctor encountered a boy wandering in the woods, but that happened 2,500 years after the lives of Romulus and Remus (C). The twins were ordered to be drowned, but they were not (D). Legend has it that Romulus and Remus founded the city of Rome.

39. (A) The reading states that Romulus and Remus were the "legendary twin founders of Rome" on line 3.

40. (A) The last sentence of paragraph 1 states that *V. parahaemolyticus* is found in highest abundance in inshore waters, particularly near harbors (a harbor is similar to a bay).

41. (A) "Inshore" means "close to shore" or "near the coast."

42. (A) The entire reading passage concerns *Vibrio parahaemolyticus*. The word "it" in paragraph 1, sentence 2, refers to that organism, and so does the word "it" in line 13. The preceding sentence refers to the organism by name and then calls it an "organism." When it refers to it as an "organism," it discusses "isolation." Thus, the only thing "it" can be referring to is the "organism."

43. (B) The last sentence of paragraph 2 states that a Japanese scientist has not isolated *V. parahaemolyticus* as frequently in winter as during warmer months. November is the coldest month listed for the north Pacific.

44. (B) The first sentence of paragraph 3 gives diarrhea as the most common symptom.

45. (D) The word "this" refers to "diarrhea, the most common symptom," which appears just before it.

46. (C) An incubation period means the time between a microorganism's entry into a body and the exhibiting of the first symptoms. The first sentence of paragraph 3 says that the first symptom occurs "within four or five days."

47. (B) The fact that a person becomes ill after eating "contaminated" food should lead you to the conclusion that it means "tainted." If you don't know the meaning of "tainted," it is still possible to eliminate the other three choices from the way "contaminated" is used.

48. (D) Paragraph 2, sentence 1, states, "the distribution of the bacteria in sea water was *dependent* on the water temperature," but "*independent* of the sodium chloride content." Sodium chloride is salt.

49. (C) Since stomach cramps are given as a symptom of the infection, you can assume they would be unpleasant. Choice (C) is the most logical. Although high temperature would also be unpleasant, it would not normally be associated with the stomach.

50. (C) "Isolation" means "separation." Another form of the word, "isolated," appears in the following sentence.

PRACTICE TEST 4

After some answers in this answer key, you will find numbers in italic type. These are page numbers in Part III where you will find review material for these questions. Although any one question may involve several different rules and concepts, these page numbers refer to important areas you should review if you have missed a question or are not sure of the material involved. Make full use of these page number references and of the index to direct your personal review.

Section 1: Listening Comprehension

1. (A)	11. (C)	21. (B)	31. (B)	41. (A)
2. (D)	12. (B)	22. (C)	32. (D)	42. (A)
3. (C)	13. (C)	23. (C)	33. (B)	43. (D)
4. (B)	14. (D)	24. (B)	34. (D)	44. (C)
5. (C)	15. (C)	25. (D)	35. (A)	45. (B)
6. (A)	16. (A)	26. (D)	36. (D)	46. (A)
7. (A)	17. (D)	27. (B)	37. (B)	47. (C)
8. (A)	18. (C)	28. (A)	38. (C)	48. (D)
9. (B)	19. (C)	29. (A)	39. (A)	49. (B)
10. (A)	20. (D)	30. (A)	40. (D)	50. (C)

Section 2: Structure and Written Expression

1. (B) *57, 59, 205, 229*
2. (B) *70*
3. (A) *72–73*
4. (C) *148–149*
5. (C) *125–127*
6. (D) *150–151*
7. (A) *148, 175*
8. (D) *45, 99*
9. (A) *45, 145*
10. (D) *118*
11. (C) *94*
12. (D) *68, 142–143*
13. (A) *153–154*
14. (A) *183–184*
15. (C) *52–53*
16. (C) *47*
17. (A) *75–76*
18. (D) *135*
19. (C)
20. (C) *52–53*
21. (D) *48–50*
22. (B) *82*
23. (D)
24. (D) *48–50*
25. (A)
26. (A) *45*
27. (A) *103*
28. (B) *69–70*
29. (D)
30. (B) *85*
31. (B) *45, 68*
32. (B) *175*
33. (A) *89–90*
34. (A) *94–95*
35. (B) *79, 104*
36. (C) *62*
37. (A) *113, 118*
38. (A) *129*
39. (C) *139–140*
40. (D) *86, 289*

Section 3: Reading Comprehension

1. (D)
2. (B)
3. (B)
4. (D)
5. (A)
6. (C)
7. (D)
8. (B)
9. (D)
10. (B)
11. (A)
12. (D)
13. (A)
14. (B)
15. (D)
16. (B)
17. (A)
18. (C)
19. (C)
20. (D)
21. (D)
22. (A)
23. (C)
24. (D)
25. (C)
26. (C)
27. (D)
28. (B)
29. (B)
30. (A)
31. (C)
32. (A)
33. (D)
34. (A)
35. (D)
36. (A)
37. (A)
38. (C)
39. (B)
40. (C)
41. (D)
42. (D)
43. (A)
44. (D)
45. (D)
46. (C)
47. (A)
48. (C)
49. (A)
50. (A)

PRACTICE TEST 4: ANALYSIS-SCORING SHEET

Use the chart below to spot your strengths and weaknesses in each test section and to arrive at your total converted score. Fill in your number of correct answers for each section in the space provided. Refer to the Converted Score Sheet on page 496 to find your converted score for each section and enter those numbers on the chart. Find the sum of your converted scores, multiply that sum by 10, and divide by 3.

Example: If raw scores are   then   converted scores are
Section 1:   33   51
Section 2:   26   49
Section 3:   38   53
                   Sum of Converted Scores   153
                        Times 10 = 1,530
                   Divided by 3 =   510 = Total Converted
                                                Score

This will give you the approximate score that you would obtain if this were an actual TOEFL. Remember that your score here may possibly be higher than the score that you might receive on an actual TOEFL simply because you are studying the elements of the test shortly before taking each test. The score is intended only to give you a general idea of approximately what your actual score will be.

	Total Possible	Total Correct	Converted Score
Section 1: Listening Comprehension	50		
Section 2: Structure and Written Expression	40		
Section 3: Reading Comprehension	50		
TOTALS	140		

Sum of Converted Scores _____
Times 10 = _____
Divided by 3 = _____ = Total Converted Score

SECTION 1: LISTENING COMPREHENSION SCRIPT

Part A

1. Man: You're so late. I thought you'd never get here.

   Woman: My car broke down on the highway, and I had to walk.

   Third Voice: Why does the woman say she had to walk?

2. Man: We missed you at Dale's party last night.

   Woman: I'm not going to any celebrations with that group because they're so tightly knit that they brush everyone else off.

   Third Voice: Why does the woman say she didn't attend Dale's party?

3. Woman: Bill, are you still planning to buy that nice red sports car you looked at last week?

   Man: I'm afraid that's impossible because I haven't been able to come up with the cash, and someone else has already made a down payment on it.

   Third Voice: What does Bill say about buying a car?

4. Man: Gail is supposed to be here at the meeting tonight. Where is she?

   Woman: She came down with the flu and had to stay home.

   Third Voice: Why does the woman say Gail didn't attend the meeting?

5. Man: How many people will be coming to the reunion on Saturday?

   Woman: We had to cross fifteen names off our original list of one hundred.

   Third Voice: How many people does the woman say they expect to attend the reunion?

6. Woman: You look happy this morning.

   Man: I just came from my adviser's office and found out that the college board has done away with the foreign language requirement for graduation.

   Third Voice: What does the man mean?

7. Man: I hear that Rusty's car is being repossessed by the finance company.

   Woman: Yes, he's fallen behind on the payments.

   Third Voice: What does the woman mean?

8. Woman: What did you do in class today?

   Man: The teacher went over last Friday's lesson.

   Third Voice: What does the man say the teacher did in class?

9. Woman: Not getting that job was a big letdown.

   Man: Don't worry. Something better will come along.

   Third Voice: What are the speakers talking about?

10. Man: How do the Finleys feel about moving to New Mexico?

    Woman: They're really looking forward to it.

    Third Voice: What does the woman say about the Finleys' reaction to moving?

11. Man: Where are you going in such a rush?

    Woman: I have to deposit my paycheck before the bank closes, or else I won't have any funds to pay these bills.

    Third Voice: What does the woman mean?

12. Woman: Dan, how was your visit with your sister's friends?

    Man: I hardly knew the people.

    Third Voice: What did the man say about his sister's friends?

13. Woman: You need to cut down on your sugar intake.

    Man: I find it very hard to resist.

    Third Voice: What does the woman suggest the man do?

14. Man: Was anyone seriously injured in the accident?

    Woman: It looks as if all the victims will pull through.

    Third Voice: What does the woman say about the victims of the accident?

15. Woman: Did many people buy tickets for the rock concert?

    Man: So many people showed up to purchase the tickets on opening day that they were sold out by noon.

    Third Voice: What does the man mean?

16. Woman: Did Phil apply for the accounting position that was advertised in the paper?

    Man: Despite his inexperience in the field, Phil applied for the job.

    Third Voice: What does the man say about Phil?

17. Man: Who solved that difficult physics problem?

    Woman: No one but Gary knew how to solve it.

    Third Voice: What does the woman say about the problem?

18. Man: What sort of response did you get on your request for additional funding?

    Woman: The response to my initial request was gratifying.

    Third Voice: What does the woman mean?

19. Man: Will Amy be attending tonight's meeting?

    Woman: She plans to attend the meeting in spite of the homework she needs to complete for tomorrow.

    Third Voice: What does the woman say about Amy's plans?

20. Man: Are you going to wait for Gil?

    Woman: He would rather that I didn't wait for him, but I plan to anyway.

    Third Voice: What does the woman mean?

21. Man: Where is Diane?

    Woman: She ran out of milk and went out to get some.

    Third Voice: Where does the woman say that Diane is?

22. Woman: I want to go to the concert tonight, but it starts at seven, and I have to work until five. There won't be enough time to go home for dinner.

    Man: I've got an idea. I'll pick you up after work and we'll eat downtown. That'll give us plenty of time to get to the concert.

    Third Voice: If the speakers follow the man's suggestion, what will happen?

23. Man: I understand Oscar's been a little depressed.

    Woman: He's got so many bills that his wife says he'll never get ahead.

    Third Voice: What does the woman mean?

24. Woman: Where are your keys?

    Man: I can't find them, but I'm sure they'll show up soon.

    Third Voice: What does the man say about his keys?

25. Man: Did you and Stanley go to the concert last week?

    Woman: We would have attended if the tickets had not been too expensive.

    Third Voice: What does the woman mean?

26. Man: I'm sorry to bother you, but I can't see when you
                   hold the banner up.

    Woman: Sorry. I didn't realize it blocked your view.

    Third Voice: What will the woman probably do?

27. Woman: I thought Melanie was going to wear that pretty
                   red wool coat you bought her.

    Man: She couldn't wear it because it made her break
                   out in a rash.

    Third Voice: What do we learn from this conversation?

28. Woman: Are you hungry now?

    Man: I could sure go for a steak and salad.

    Third Voice: What does the man mean?

29. Woman: Does Jeanette like football?

    Man: She rarely misses a game.

    Third Voice: What does the man say about Jeanette?

30. Woman: How is business?

    Man: Our best agent hasn't sold a single policy this
                   week.

    Third Voice: What does the man mean?

Part B

Questions 31 through 34 are based on the following conversation.

Man: I can't believe it. Today I went shopping at the store near
        my house instead of my usual store, and the prices were
        fantastic!

Woman: Is it one of those no-frills stores?

Man: No, they just had some good sales, and the produce
        looked better than it has recently at my regular store.

Woman: What kinds of things were on sale?

Man: I got a dozen large eggs for 85¢, beer for $2.75, tuna fish for 99¢, and bleach for 80¢. I bought a lot of food for less then $50.

Woman: Where is this store? I might try it too.

Man: It's the one on the corner of 16th Avenue and Main Street.

31. To what type of store did the man go?
32. Which of the following items did the man NOT buy on sale?
33. What was one advantage of this store over the man's regular store?
34. Which of the following is true about the man's shopping experience?

Questions 35 through 38 are based on the following conversation.

Woman: Good morning, Friendly Travel Agency. May I help you?

Man: My wife and I are planning a trip to San Juan and are interested in a package deal. What can you recommend?

Woman: Well, sir, we have a very special seven-day cruise including San Juan and another port of call, tourist class accommodations, all inclusive for $699 each from Miami.

Man: We don't care much for cruises.

Woman: In that case, how about a twelve-day trip, including air fare, accommodations at the Venus Hotel, several trips to the outer islands, and two meals per day for only $749 each?

Man: That sounds more like what we had in mind. What else does it include?

Woman: A sightseeing tour of Old San Juan and El Yunque Rain Forest, and an afternoon at Luquillo Beach.

Man: My wife would certainly love that!

Woman: When would you like to leave?

Man: March 15th.

Woman: Shall I make reservations for you?

Man: Yes. Please make them now. My name is James Morrison,
          that's M-O-double R-I-S-O-N. I'd like to charge them to
          my VISA card. My number is 4555-2000-9361-8788. The
          expiration date is in June.

Woman: After verifying your credit, we'll mail your tickets directly
          to you. You should have them in three days. That will give
          you plenty of time before your departure.

35. Where are the man and his wife going?
36. What is the man's name?
37. How does the man plan to pay for the trip?
38. When does the man wish to leave?

Part C

*Questions 39 through 41 are based on the following talk about roller
skating.*

In an effort to fight the soaring costs of gasoline and public
transportation, many athletic students have taken to roller skating.
This means of transportation is creating traffic problems and is
presenting a safety hazard for skaters as well as motorists in college
and university areas throughout the country.

If skaters do not return to the sidewalk, but insist on causing a
dilemma for drivers and risking their own safety, the police will
issue the violators $15 citations for disregarding a city as well as a
state ordinance. In the past month, seven careless students have
been injured, three seriously, as they darted into oncoming traffic.
Many of them refuse to wear helmets and are suffering head injuries
as a result. One student was thrown 50 feet and suffered a
concussion requiring a three-week hospital stay.

39. What problem has caused students to take up skating as a
    means of transportation?
40. What law forbids roller skating in the streets?
41. Which of the following is NOT true?

Questions 42 through 46 are based on the following talk about early life in North America.

When the early settlers, especially the English, arrived in the New World, the hardships and dangers awaiting them were totally unexpected. Had it not been for some friendly Indians, the colonists never would have survived the terrible winters. They knew nothing about planting crops, hunting animals, building shelters, nor making clothing from animal skins. Life in England had been much simpler, and this new life was not like what the Spanish explorers had reported.

The settlers introduced iron tools, muskets for hunting, domesticated animals, and political ways to the Indians. In exchange, the settlers learned to build canoes for water transportation and to use snowshoes and toboggans for winter traveling. The Indians taught them to blaze trails through the forest, to hunt large animals and trap smaller ones, and to spear fish in the lakes and streams. The natives also introduced to the settlers typical foods such as turkey, corn, squash, beans, and pumpkin.

The early settlers did everything possible in order to make their new settlements resemble the homes they had left behind.

42. Which of the following did the new settlers teach the Indians?
43. What does the speaker imply about corn, squash, and pumpkin?
44. How did the Indians teach the settlers to travel in the winter?
45. Which of the following was NOT introduced to the settlers by the Indians?
46. Which of the following is NOT true?

Questions 47 through 50 are based on the following announcement by a bus driver.

Welcome aboard the Luxury Cruise bus to Dallas, Baton Rouge, and Atlanta. We are scheduled to arrive in Dallas at 1:45 this afternoon. There will be a fifteen-minute rest stop at that time. We will have a thirty-minute dinner stop in Baton Rouge at 6:45 for those of you who are continuing on to Atlanta. We should arrive in

Atlanta at 1:45 tomorrow morning. Please remember the number of your bus for reboarding. That number is 3224.

This coach is air-conditioned for your comfort. Please remember that smoking of cigarettes is permitted only in the last six rows, and the smoking of any other material is prohibited, as is the drinking of alcoholic beverages.

Thank you for traveling with us. Have a pleasant trip.

47. At what time and in what city will the passengers have a fifteen-minute rest stop?
48. Which of the following is permitted in the last six rows?
49. What is the number of the bus?
50. At what time is the bus supposed to arrive at its final destination?

EXPLANATIONS FOR PRACTICE TEST 4

SECTION 2: STRUCTURE AND WRITTEN EXPRESSION

Part A

1. (B) Choice (A) is verbose, using *with caution* rather than *cautiously*. Also, it would make no sense to look cautiously *after* crossing the street. Choice (A) also uses simple past when past perfect is required. Choice (C) is passive and the sentence does not call for a passive meaning. Also, using the adjective *cautious* would indicate that *look* in the sentence is a stative verb meaning *appear,* and that is not the meaning of the sentence. (D) uses an incorrect sequence of tenses. The verb *crossed* is in the past.

2. (B) The subject *notebook and report* is plural, and choices (A), (C), and (D) all contain singular verbs.

3. (A) The plural verb *need* is required here because if there is a plural noun after *nor,* the verb must be plural.

4. (C) Choice (A) is incorrect because the superlative, not the comparative, must be used when more than two are expressed. Choices (B) and (D) are incorrect because the definite article *the* must be used before the superlative.

5. (C) The correct form is *would rather* + [verb in simple form].

6. (D) *Eight-century-old* is functioning as an adjective and cannot be plural.

7. (A) Use the comparative when only two entities are involved. Choice (B) incorrectly uses the superlative. Choice (C) would be correct if *the smaller of them* began a new sentence, but it is not correct after the comma. (D) incorrectly uses the relative pronoun *that,* which cannot be used with the preposition.

8. (D) Choice (A) includes an incorrect sequence of tenses; *do* should be *did* to agree with *endured.* (B) uses negative agreement, and the sentence is positive. Choice (C) includes incorrect use of affirmative agreement. Also, the correct plural of *child* is *children.*

9. (A) This is a multiple number comparative. Choice (C) is also a multiple number comparative, but one earns *money. Money* is a non-count noun, and thus the sentence requires *much.*

10. (D) This is a past condition. The correct sequence is *had studied . . . would have been able.* (B) is verbose.

11. (C) The correct structure for an embedded question is question word + subject + verb. Choices (A) and (B) incorrectly include *did,* and choice (D) incorrectly uses the infinitive *to put.*

12. (D) Choice (A) is incorrect because the subject *facilities* is plural and requires a plural verb. Choice (B) uses an incorrect comparative. It should be *better than.* Choices (A), (B), and (C) all use an illogical comparison. They seem to compare the *facilities* with the *new hospital.* Choice (D) is correct; *those of* = *the facilities of.*

13. (A) Choices (B), (C), and (D) are all missing necessary prepositions, because *of,* on account *of,* as *a* result *of* (notice that a necessary article was left out here as well).

14. (A) In this subjunctive construction use *suggest that* + [verb in simple form].

15. (C) Choice (A) incorrectly uses *others,* which implies that there are more than one other. The sentence says there are two teachers. Choice (B) incorrectly uses *another,* which indicates the indefinite. A specific is required here. (D) is incorrect because in this sentence *other* requires the article *the*.

Part B

16. (C) should be *an.* Use *an* before a word beginning with a vowel sound.

17. (A) should be *were guarding.* Use *a number of* + plural verb.

18. (D) should be *universally.* An adjective (*understood*) is always modified by an adverb, never by another adjective.

19. (C) should be *by incorporating.* This indicates the method by which they convey and preserve their thoughts.

20. (C) should be *other systems. Other* cannot be plural when it appears before a noun.

21. (D) should be *in the time of.* This sentence calls for specific time, *the* time of Socrates.

22. (B) should be *themselves.* The word *theirselves* does not exist.

23. (D) should be *survival.* A noun, not a gerund, is necessary here after the preposition *for.*

24. (D) should be *fear*. In this sentence *fear* is indefinite and cannot be modified by the definite article *the*.

25. (A) should be *on a child's level* or *on a childish level*. Before a noun, *child* must be possessive (*child's*) or it must be in adjective form (*childish*).

26. (A) should be *these*. *These* is the plural of *this*. The plural form is required here before the plural noun *officials*.

27. (A) should be *hardly ever*. *Hardly never* is a double negative and should be avoided.

28. (B) should be *is*. *Air pollution* is a singular subject and requires a singular verb.

29. (D) should be *close to the city*. *Close to* means *near*.

30. (B) should be *of flying*. The adjective *capable* requires the preposition *of* + [verb + *ing*].

31. (B) should be *was*. *News* is a non-count noun and requires a singular verb.

32. (B) should be *which* or *that*. *That which* is redundant here because they are both relative pronouns. One or the other should be used, but not both.

33. (A) should be *Joel's*. Use the possessive before a gerund.

34. (A) should be *what happened*. For embedded questions, use question word + subject + verb. This is a subject question, so the question word (*what*) is also the subject.

35. (B) should be *us*. Use the object pronoun after a verb. The sentence is an indirect command.

36. (C) should be *for*. Use *for* + duration of time.

37. (A) should be *would have*. The conditional perfect uses *would* + *have* + [verb in past participle]. *Would of* is never correct.

38. (A) should be *supposed to*. Use *be* + *supposed to* (means *should*).

39. (C) should be *from*. Always use *different from*.

40. (D) should be *of financing*. The noun *means* requires the preposition *of* + [verb + *ing*].

SECTION 3: READING COMPREHENSION

1. (D) Lichens are not considered to be plants, so choice (A) is incorrect. In mutualistic associations, both life forms benefit. The passage explains that the algae are parasitized in lichens, so choice (B) is incorrect. Choice (C) is wrong because the association is between a fungus and an alga, not two fungi.

2. (B) The sentences following the sentence in which "hardy" is used describe some of the hostile places lichens can thrive, so you should realize that "hardy" means "tough," or "durable."

3. (B) The passage states that lichens were mistakenly thought to be mutualistic associations where both participants benefit, so choice (B) correctly defines the relationship.

4. (D) Any of the answer choices could describe the relationship of the fungi and algae in lichens; however, you should know that "intimate" means in "close" association.

5. (A) In the last paragraph, it's explained that insects glue lichens on their exoskeletons for camouflage.

6. (C) Paragraph 2 explains that lichens were once thought to represent mutualistic relationships, but this was tested by growing different lichen fungi and algae apart.

7. (D) According to the passage, a "hostile" environment is one in which few other organisms can flourish, so "inhospitable" would be the best answer.

8. (B) The sentence in which lichens are described as being endolithic goes on to explain that lichens have been found inside of rocks in Antarctica.

9. (D) "Reducing soil erosion" is the only one of the four answer choices that was stated in the reading passage.

10. (B) Paragraph 2 explains that experiments were conducted that showed the fungi parasitize the algae in the lichen relationship, but that this was not what scientists had originally thought.

11. (A) The first paragraph says that termites and ants have similar communal habits, but that they are physically different. Choice (B) is incorrect because there is no comparison of ants' and termites' bodies in the passage. Answer choices (C) and (D) are not suggested in the reading.

12. (D) The word "communal" is related to "commune" and "community," both of which relate to how living things function in "social" groups.

13. (A) We are told that the reproductive termites have eyes, but that the workers are blind and the soldiers are eyeless. Choices (B), (C), and (D) are true because only the reproductives fly, and fly only one time, and soldiers are larger than workers.

14. (B) The sentence states that termites and ants are alike in some respects, "although physically the two insects are distinct." The word "although" should lead you to understand that "distinct" is the opposite of "like"; thus it means "different."

15. (D) The passage indicates that each "class" has its own job, and the word "class" is used throughout the reading passage to describe different "types" and "categories."

16. (B) The male and female reproductives, it is implied in paragraph 2, fly only to develop a new colony. Choice (A) is not true because the reading indicates that a pair of reproductives flies alone. Choice (B) is not true because the author states in paragraph 3 that the workers make up the majority of the colony. Choice (D) is not correct because a worker is smaller than a soldier and does not have the hard head and strong jaws and legs of a soldier.

17. (A) To "found" means to "establish."

18. (C) A "cell" is an enclosed "compartment."

19. (C) Answer choice (A) is incorrect because the majority of the reading is not concerned with the destruction of houses. Choice (B) is incorrect because only a portion of the reading is related to how termites work together. Answer choice (D) is incorrect because the reading passage is not significantly concerned with the relationship of these two types of termites. Choice (C) is a general statement about the topic of the reading.

20. (D) The sentence says, "Like those of ants, termite colonies consist of different classes, each . . ." The word "each" refers to the word immediately before it, "classes."

21. (D) In sentences 2 and 3 of paragraph 2, all of the other choices are given as purposes of the pretrial conference.

22. (A) The passage starts out indicating that there are problems in the court system. The sentence containing the word "ameliorating" should lead you to understand that it means becoming "better" or "improving."

23. (C) The sentence states that one suggestion is to allow districts with too many cases to borrow judges from those that do not have a "backlog," which should lead you to understand that "backlog" means too many cases, or an "overload."

24. (D) The word "viable" means "workable" or "practical." Although the pretrial conference, according to the reading, has not been as beneficial as had been hoped, the small-claims court is given as a viable suggestion for improvement. Also, the last paragraph suggests that more innovations will be proposed in a continuing effort to find remedies. Nowhere in the passage is it suggested that all states should follow California's example (A), that the legislature should formulate fewer laws (B), or that no one cares (C). In fact, the entire reading concerns suggested remedies of those who are concerned.

25. (C) Paragraph 1, sentence 2, says, ". . . and the litigants, or parties, have to wait. . ." This indicates that "litigants" is another way of saying "parties in a lawsuit" in this context.

26. (C) The last sentence of paragraph 3 indicates that a litigant waives (gives up) his or her right to a jury trial and the right to appeal.

27. (D) The reading passage indicates that one of the problems is costs, which should lead you to understand that "staggering" means "very high," "shocking," or "astounding."

28. (B) The sentence indicates that small-claims courts can be beneficial, which should lead you to understand that "dispatch" means speed, or "haste."

29. (B) The second sentence of paragraph 1 says that "costs are staggering" (overwhelming) and litigants "have to wait sometimes many years." Also, the last sentence of the reading says that the problems "must be remedied if the citizens who have valid claims are going to be able to have their day in court."

30. (A) You can gather from the entire passage that the "situation" needs to be "fixed" or "improved." To "correct" the situation is closest in meaning to "remedy."

ANSWERS AND EXPLANATIONS FOR PRACTICE TEST 4

31. (C) Lines 12–23 discuss pretrial conferences. The sentence beginning "The theory behind pretrial conferences . . ." shows the apparent benefits of the pretrial conference, and the sentence beginning with "Unfortunately" is the sentence indicating that pretrial conferences may not work.

32. (A) The last sentence of paragraph 2 tells us that 705 survivors were rescued by the *Carpathia*. The last sentence of paragraph 1 tells us there were 2,227 passengers at the start of the voyage. Rounding off, 700 divided by 2,000 is about one third (700 × 3 = 2,100 is another way to estimate) that survived and were rescued, so it could not be true that only one third of the people perished (died).

33. (D) The panic of the people, the fire on the ship, and the speed at which the ship was moving are all mentioned as contributing to the disaster. The *Carpathia,* however, was the rescue ship.

34. (A) Paragraph 2, sentence 1, and paragraph 3 indicate choice (A) is true. "Only two days at sea" and "two days of sailing glory on its maiden voyage" both indicate that it had traveled only two days.

35. (D) To "extinguish" is to put out a fire; "unextinguished" means that the fire was not stopped (was "unquenched").

36. (A) In this context, "maiden" means "first" or "inaugural." Paragraph 3 states that the "*S.S. Titanic* had enjoyed only two days of sailing glory."

37. (A) From the reading you can infer that people believed the *S.S. Titanic* was "unsinkable," so you could assume that they "called" it "unsinkable." The ship was christened (C) and probably listed (D) in the naval registry as the *S.S. Titanic,* its formal name. Ships are launched, not "initiated" (B).

38. (C) Answer choice (C) is the only correct answer. The *S.S. Titanic* sank; therefore, it was not seaworthy (A). Choice (B) is incorrect because the *Carpathia* successfully rescued one third

of the passengers. Choice (D) is incorrect because the cause of the disaster was the ship's striking an iceberg.

39. (B) The last sentence of paragraph 1 states that the owners provided less than one half the number of lifeboats and rafts necessary for all of the passengers.

40. (C) The passage states, "Explorations and detailed examinations of the base of the structure reveal many intersecting lines. Further scientific study indicates that these represent a type of timeline of events." None of the other three answer choices is supported by the passage.

41. (D) The prefix "extra-" means "outside" or "beyond." "Terrestrial" refers to the earth, so "extraterrestrial" refers to beings from somewhere beyond earth. The use of the word "even" in the sentence might help you to conclude that "extraterrestrial beings" are something out of the ordinary.

42. (D) The author implies that there are a number of passages in order to protect the tomb and its treasures.

43. (A) "Intersecting" lines are lines that cross one another, choice (A).

44. (D) The passage states that researchers have found that the intersecting lines represent historical and future events.

45. (D) To "prophesy" is to tell of the future, so choice (D) is correct. The "future generations" in the sentence is a contextual clue.

46. (C) The passage is essentially a listing of the amazing things about the Great Pyramid, so choice (C) is accurate. Choice (A) covers a fraction of the passage. That the Great Pyramid was a massive construction project is briefly described; however, the passage is not about construction problems, so choice (B) is incorrect. Choice (D) is too limited because it refers only to the burial chamber rather than the entire pyramid.

47. (A) The last sentence of paragraph 1 says that they based their calculations on astronomical observations (observation of the celestial bodies).

48. (C) Paragraph 1, sentence 1, tells us that it was built "as a tomb for Pharaoh Cheops." Although the Egyptians did observe the solar system (A), a tomb would have some connection with religious observances (B), and the pyramid was an engineering feat (D), none of these are given as the reason for the pyramid's construction.

49. (A) The passage implies that the pyramid is one of the seven wonders of the world for many reasons. Two of the reasons are 1) the alignment of the pyramid's four sides with true north, south, east, and west and 2) the timeline on the base that stretches into the future.

50. (A) A "feat" is a notable "achievement," so "accomplishment" is the correct answer. In the sentence, the adjectives describing "feat" are "incredible" and "engineering," both referring to the perfect alignment of the Great Pyramid with the compass points. That contextual information should help you eliminate the other answer choices.

PRACTICE TEST 5

After some answers in this answer key, you will find numbers in italic type. These are page numbers in Part III where you will find review material for these questions. Although any one question may involve several different rules and concepts, these page numbers refer to important areas you should review if you have missed a question or are not sure of the material involved. Make full use of these page number references and of the index to direct your personal review.

Section 1: Listening Comprehension

1. (C)	11. (C)	21. (B)	31. (B)	41. (C)
2. (D)	12. (B)	22. (A)	32. (B)	42. (A)
3. (B)	13. (A)	23. (C)	33. (A)	43. (D)
4. (D)	14. (B)	24. (C)	34. (C)	44. (B)
5. (C)	15. (B)	25. (A)	35. (B)	45. (C)
6. (B)	16. (A)	26. (B)	36. (A)	46. (A)
7. (B)	17. (C)	27. (A)	37. (D)	47. (D)
8. (D)	18. (B)	28. (A)	38. (D)	48. (A)
9. (B)	19. (A)	29. (D)	39. (C)	49. (D)
10. (A)	20. (A)	30. (C)	40. (C)	50. (A)

Section 2: Structure and Written Expression

1. (C) *175*
2. (C) *229*
3. (B)
4. (C) *188*
5. (D) *135, 204–205*
6. (C) *185–186*
7. (C) *221–223*
8. (A) *104*
9. (C) *118*
10. (B) *183–184*
11. (A) *173*
12. (B) *87, 209*
13. (C) *81, 84–85, 89–90*
14. (D) *227–228*
15. (A) *59–61, 204–205, 221–223*
16. (B) *71*
17. (D) *191–193*
18. (C) *193–194*
19. (B) *183–184*
20. (B) *86*
21. (C)
22. (A) *123–124*
23. (A) *48–50*
24. (A) *94*
25. (A) *84*
26. (D) *153–154*
27. (B) *84*
28. (B) *69–70*
29. (A) *153–154*
30. (B) *68–69*
31. (D) *140*
32. (C) *68–69*
33. (C) *69–69*
34. (B) *68–69*
35. (C) *135*
36. (D) *171*
37. (A) *227–228*
38. (B) *129*
39. (B) *104*
40. (B) *52–53*

Section 3: Reading Comprehension

1. (C)	11. (B)	21. (B)	31. (D)	41. (A)
2. (D)	12. (C)	22. (D)	32. (A)	42. (D)
3. (B)	13. (A)	23. (B)	33. (D)	43. (C)
4. (C)	14. (A)	24. (C)	34. (B)	44. (B)
5. (D)	15. (B)	25. (D)	35. (C)	45. (C)
6. (D)	16. (B)	26. (D)	36. (D)	46. (A)
7. (A)	17. (A)	27. (D)	37. (D)	47. (A)
8. (A)	18. (D)	28. (C)	38. (D)	48. (D)
9. (C)	19. (C)	29. (A)	39. (D)	49. (B)
10. (B)	20. (A)	30. (B)	40. (B)	50. (D)

PRACTICE TEST 5: ANALYSIS-SCORING SHEET

Use the chart below to spot your strengths and weaknesses in each test section and to arrive at your total converted score. Fill in your number of correct answers for each section in the space provided. Refer to the Converted Score Sheet on page 496 to find your converted score for each section and enter those numbers on the chart. Find the sum of your converted scores, multiply that sum by 10, and divide by 3.

Example: If raw scores are   then   converted scores are
Section 1:   33   51
Section 2:   26   49
Section 3:   38   53
                 Sum of Converted Scores   153
                         Times 10 = 1,530
                     Divided by 3 =   510 = Total Converted
                                                    Score

This will give you the approximate score that you would obtain if this were an actual TOEFL. Remember that your score here may possibly be higher than the score that you might receive on an actual TOEFL simply because you are studying the elements of the test shortly before taking each test. The score is intended only to give you a general idea of approximately what your actual score will be.

	Total Possible	Total Correct	Converted Score
Section 1: Listening Comprehension	50		
Section 2: Structure and Written Expression	40		
Section 3: Reading Comprehension	50		
TOTALS	140		

Sum of Converted Scores _____
Times 10 = _____
Divided by 3 = _____ = Total Converted Score

SECTION 1: LISTENING COMPREHENSION SCRIPT

Part A

1. **Woman:** There were tears of laughter on the faces of everyone in the theater.

   Man: The play certainly raised some eyebrows, but it was nothing less than hilarious.

   Third Voice: According to the man and woman, how did the audience react to the play?

2. **Man:** The Green Dolphin sounds like a nice place to eat.

   Woman: OK, let's go there. I hear that they have a complete menu and a warm atmosphere.

   Third Voice: Where are the man and woman going?

3. **Man:** Do you think your grandfather heard our plans for the surprise party?

   Woman: No, he's partially deaf.

   Third Voice: Why does the woman say her grandfather doesn't know about the party?

4. **Woman:** Why didn't you have your geology class today?

   Man: Only three out of a class of twenty-five showed up. Since the professor had planned to present a complex demonstration, he decided to cancel the class until everybody was present.

   Third Voice: Why does the man say the geology class didn't meet today?

5. Woman: Since it's the rush hour, let's take the subway.

   Man: OK. It's not as direct as the bus, but it's faster and there'll be no chance of a traffic jam.

   Third Voice: Why do the man and woman decide to take the subway?

6. Man: I heard Doug got a ticket yesterday.

   Woman: He did. He drove down a one-way street the wrong way.

   Third Voice: What does the woman say about Doug's receiving a ticket?

7. Woman: Do you know Susan Flannigan?

   Man: The name rings a bell, but I'm not sure.

   Third Voice: What does the man mean?

8. Man: Roy doesn't stand a chance of winning a gold medal in the Olympics.

   Woman: True, but he's doing his best.

   Third Voice: What do the speakers mean?

9. Woman: Somebody needs to change the cartridge in the copy machine.

   Man: Don't look at me!

   Third Voice: What does the man mean?

10. Woman: I need to go to Chicago next week. What do you have available?

    Man: There are three nonstop flights from Atlanta to Chicago each week.

    Third Voice: What does the man say about the flights from Atlanta to Chicago?

11. Man: Mr. Roberts is preparing for his upcoming vaca-
                  tion.
    Woman: Yes, he's looking forward to it.
    Third Voice: What does the woman mean?

12. Man: Why are Maria's eyes so red?
    Woman: They're irritated from the chlorine in the pool.
    Third Voice: What does the woman say about Maria?

13. Man: I'm really looking forward to moving to the new
                  building.
    Woman: Uh, I'm not quite sure how to put this. Your
                  position is being eliminated.
    Third Voice: What is the woman's problem?

14. Woman: Did Sandra like the shoes you bought her for her
                  birthday?
    Man: She exchanged them for a different pair.
    Third Voice: What does the man say that Sandra did with the
                  shoes?

15. Woman: It seems that everyone will be going on the field
                  trip.
    Man: Don't be too sure. Not everyone has turned in a
                  consent form.
    Third Voice: What does the man imply?

16. Man: Why didn't Janet finish her homework?
    Woman: Her glasses broke, so she couldn't read her
                  assignment.
    Third Voice: What does the woman say happened to Janet?

17. Man: Leslie is taking biochemistry and advanced calculus next semester.

    Woman: She's got to be out of her mind!

    Third Voice: What does the woman imply about Leslie?

18. Man: We're way over budget on this project.

    Woman: They must have miscalculated the cost of the new equipment.

    Third Voice: What does the woman say about the project?

19. Woman: I thought Naomi couldn't afford to go to the conference.

    Man: She couldn't have attended if her boss hadn't paid her way.

    Third Voice: What does the man say about Naomi's attending the conference?

20. Man: Does June like the new television programs this fall?

    Woman: She dislikes television, but her husband watches it nightly.

    Third Voice: What does the woman mean?

21. Woman: It sure is a long way up to the peak.

    Man: Especially on such a hot day!

    Third Voice: What does the man mean?

22. Woman: Did you hear about the house that the Kehoes bought in the country?

    Man: Yes, and Chuck said that they got a very good deal on it.

    Third Voice: What does the man mean?

23. Man: The program director said that we'd have to postpone the outing until Saturday because of inclement weather.

    Woman: It's a shame. The food has already been ordered and will probably spoil.

    Third Voice: Why does the man say the outing was postponed?

24. Man: I thought you said that Rob went to Sebring High School.

    Woman: No, he used to attend Clark High School, but after graduation last year, he enrolled in Melrose Community College where he's presently studying.

    Third Voice: Where does the woman say Rob goes to school?

25. Man: Have you bought Jerry's birthday gifts yet?

    Woman: I've found the baseball shoes, a shirt, and a game, but not the bicycle.

    Third Voice: Which of the following items has the woman NOT bought?

26. Man: Do you need some help, miss?

    Woman: Yes, could you give me a hand with these packages?

    Third Voice: What does the woman mean?

27. Woman: Has Louise found another job yet?

    Man: She's searching for a new job as a typist.

    Third Voice: What does the man say about Louise?

28. Woman: Did Harvey know about the physics test when he skipped class the other day?

    Man: No, had he known about the test, he wouldn't have missed class.

    Third Voice: What does the man mean?

29. Man: I understand that Joe is not doing well in school.
    Woman: It's a pity that he hates to study.
    Third Voice: What does the woman mean?

30. Woman: What is Scott doing with his children while he's in school?
    Man: He's trying to find a nursery near the university.
    Third Voice: What does the man say about Scott?

Part B

Questions 31 through 34 are based on the following conversation.

Woman: I've been hearing some strange noises under the hood for the past two weeks. What do you think is wrong?

Man: Well, your radiator is leaking, your fuel pump is broken, and your carburetor is dirty.

Woman: How long will the repairs take?

Man: I can probably have it as good as new in four days.

Woman: How much will all of this cost?

Man: About $195.

Woman: Do you accept these ten-percent discount coupons for work over $150?

Man: Yes, we do. If you leave it now, I'll have it ready by Friday afternoon.

31. What do the speakers imply about what the woman will probably pay?
32. How long will it take to complete the repairs?
33. What can we assume the man does for a living?
34. Which of the following was NOT mentioned as a problem?

Questions 35 through 38 are based on the following conversation.

Woman: Have you heard that Nancy's boss wants her to accept a six-week assignment in Acapulco?

Man: Yes, but what exactly will she be doing there all that time?

Woman: Her boss wants her to write a feature story on the regional arts and crafts. She'll be photographing and interviewing the local artists.

Man: She'll really like that, especially since all of her expenses will be paid and she can practice her Spanish.

Woman: Yes, but most of all, she'll get to spend her leisure hours soaking up the sun on those lovely beaches.

Man: At night she'll be eating that great food and listening to the mariachi music. When will she be leaving?

Woman: Since she doesn't need a passport, it'll probably be in about a week.

Man: That doesn't give her much time to get organized.

35. Which of the following was NOT mentioned as a reason for Nancy's enjoying her new assignment?
36. How soon will Nancy be leaving?
37. What is the one thing Nancy will NOT need for this trip?
38. What does the man suggest Nancy can do at night?

Part C

Questions 39 through 43 are based on the following talk about a medical miracle.

Robert Edwards was blinded in an automobile accident nine years ago. He was also partially deaf because of old age. Last week, he was strolling near his home when a thunderstorm approached. He took refuge under a tree and was struck by lightning. He was knocked to the ground and woke up some twenty minutes later, lying face down in water below the tree. He went into the house and lay down in bed. A short time later, he awoke; his legs were numb and he was trembling, but, when he opened his eyes, he could see the clock across the room fading in and out in front of him. When his wife entered, he saw her for the first time in nine years. Doctors confirm that he has regained his sight and hearing, apparently from the flash of lightning, but they are unable to explain the occurrence. The only possible explanation offered by one doctor was that, since Edwards lost his sight as a result of trauma in a terrible accident, perhaps the only way it could be restored was by another trauma.

39. What caused Robert Edwards's blindness?
40. What was the first thing that Edwards saw after being struck by lightning?
41. Which of the following statements is NOT true?
42. What was Edwards doing when he was struck by lightning?
43. What was the reason given by one doctor that Edwards regained his sight?

Questions 44 through 47 are based on the following talk about Delaware.

Delaware is considered the first state of the United States because it was the first to accept the Constitution, in December, 1787. It is a very small state, second only to Rhode Island. Another important fact about Delaware is that nylon, that lightweight, yet strong fiber of the twentieth century, was invented there. In colonial days, Delaware was part of the "bread basket" area, raising wheat, corn, and other grains for national consumption.

In 1638, a group of Swedish settlers set up a colony along the Delaware River and lived there peacefully until 1655 when the Dutch, who disliked the Swedes, settled there. Later, it was taken over by the English, and finally became independent in 1776.

44. What important twentieth-century fiber was invented in Delaware?
45. Why is Delaware considered the first state of the United States?
46. Which of the following did NOT at any time control the Delaware territory?
47. Why was this area known as the "bread basket"?

Questions 48 through 50 are based on the following talk about animals.

Adaptation is the process by which living things adjust to changes in their environment—ways of finding food, protecting themselves from their enemies, and reproducing. The protective adaptations vary with each species of animal, depending on its individual needs and environment.

Many animals possess colors that help them blend in with their surroundings. Polar bears and Arctic foxes can easily move undetected amidst the winter snows. Many butterflies' colors make it difficult to find them among the trees. Chameleons can change colors to disguise themselves on rocks, trees, and wood chips.

Snakes bite; wasps and bees sting; skunks emit a pungent odor; and porcupines release painful quills into their attackers.

48. Which of the following was NOT mentioned as possessing a protective device?
49. What makes porcupines unique?
50. Which of the following protective devices was NOT mentioned in this talk?

EXPLANATIONS FOR PRACTICE TEST 5

SECTION 2: STRUCTURE AND WRITTEN EXPRESSION

Part A

1. (C) Choice (A) is incorrect. *What* is not a relative pronoun, and thus cannot follow a noun in this way. Choice (B) incorrectly uses the pronoun *who,* which may be used only for people. The noun immediately before it is *proposal.* (D) is verbose.

2. (C) Choices (A), (B), and (D) are all verbose.

3. (B) To speak of societal classes we have only the following choices: lower class, lower-middle class, middle class, upper-middle class, and upper class.

4. (C) Choices (A) and (B) are incorrect because the correct form is *know how* + [verb in infinitive]. Choice (D) is verbose, using a poor choice of vocabulary in "way of efficiency in study."

5. (D) Choice (A) uses improper word order. Also, *easier* should be *easily* (the adverb) to modify the verb, and "with hopes *to be* able" should be "with hopes *of being* able." (B) uses an improper sequence of tenses; *can* should be *could*. And, as in (A), *easier* should be *easily*. Choice (C) is incorrect because the proper idiom is *hope of*, not *hope for*.

6. (C) Choice (A) should read *not only . . . but also*. (B) is redundant. You should not say *both . . . as well as*, and the choice does not include the necessary noun (*ability, skill, talent,* etc.) after *artistic*. (D) is verbose and uses poor vocabulary choice.

7. (C) Choices (A), (B), and (D) lack parallel structure. Correct structure is *will* + [verb in simple form]: *will wash . . . iron . . . prepare . . . dust*.

8. (A) The correct form for the negative indirect command is verb + indirect object + *not* + infinitive.

9. (C) The past condition requires *if . . .* past perfect . . . modal + perfective.

10. (B) For the subjunctive use *insisted that* + [verb in simple form]. Choice (A) would be correct if it did not include *that he,* which is redundant when used with *that his patient*.

11. (A) Choice (B) is incorrect because it says *let . . . to enter*. It must be *let* + [verb in simple form], "*let* the photographers *enter*." In choice (C), *permitting* is in the gerund form, and a verb in the past perfect is needed. Also *permit*, like *allow*, must be followed by the infinitive, not the simple form. (D) uses incorrect word order; the verb is after the complement.

12. (B) Choice (A) is incorrect because there is no antecedent for the pronoun *they*. Choice (C) is verbose and should read either *capable of completing* or *able to complete*. (D) is also verbose and uses improper word choice. You cannot "trust" ability.

13. (C) Choice (A) is incorrect because the committee members did not resent the *president;* they resented *his not informing them.* If the sentence meant that they resented the president, it would have to say, ". . . resented the president *for not informing* . . ." (B) is not correct because this wording would also indicate that they resented the president himself, but *resent* here must be followed by [verb + *ing*]. (D) is verbose. It also should use *fail* + infinitive (*failed to inform*). Also, in choice (D), *themselves* is an improper use of the reflexive; *them* would be correct.

14. (D) This sentence involves the use of an adverbial at the beginning of a sentence. Correct form is adverbial + auxiliary + subject + verb. The auxiliary *did* is in the main sentence before the subject *Arthur,* so (D) is the only possible answer, as it begins with the adverbial *only.*

15. (A) Choice (B) is incorrect because it does not use parallel structure. Active voice . . . active voice is needed. Choice (C) makes improper use of the past progressive. (D) is verbose and makes improper use of the present perfect. Correct sequence of tense is *scurried . . . heard.*

Part B

NOTE: Ø = nothing, indicating that this word or phrase should be deleted.

16. (B) should be *has. Neither* must be followed by a singular verb.

17. (D) should be *raise.* Use *raise* + complement (*his test score* is the complement). *Rise* does not take a complement.

18. (C) should be *lying*. Use *lay* + complement. There is no complement in this sentence, so the verb *lie,* not *lay,* is required.

19. (B) Should be *go*. The correct subjunctive form is *suggest that* + [verb in simple form].

20. (B) should be *going. Look forward to* + [verb + *ing*].

21. (C) should be ∅. The preposition *of* is not necessary after the preposition *off.*

22. (A) should be *jog*. Correct usage is *used to* + [verb in simple form] (Mr. Anderson *used to jog* . . .) or *be used to* + [verb + *ing*] (Mr. Anderson *was used to jogging* . . .).

23. (A) should be *volume*. Use noun + cardinal number or *the* + ordinal number + noun. It is correct to say *volume four* or *the fourth volume.*

24. (A) should be *he could have*. This is an embedded question: question word + subject + verb.

25. (A) should be *to defend*. Use *try* + infinitive.

26. (D) should be *because of.* Use *because* + sentence and *because of* + noun phrase. *The students' confusion* is only a noun phrase.

27. (B) should be *to support. Intend* + infinitive.

28. (B) should be *is. Congressman* is a singular subject and requires a singular verb.

29. (A) should be *because of.* Use *because of* + noun phrase. Note that "that had devastated the area" is a relative clause; therefore, "the torrential rains" is only a noun phrase, not a sentence.

30. (B) should be *is*. *Lack* is a singular subject and requires a singular verb.

31. (D) should be *than the first*. The correct comparison is *better than*.

32. (C) should be *has*. *Cultivation* is a singular subject and requires a singular verb.

33. (C) should be *is causing*. *Decision* is a singular subject and requires a singular verb.

34. (B) should be *have been*. *Species* (in this sentence) is a plural subject and requires a plural verb. *Species* may also be singular, but if that had been the case in this sentence, *underutilized* would have been preceded by *an*.

35. (C) should be *diligently*. The verb *had worked* should be modified by an adverb, not an adjective.

36. (D) should be *pulled*. The correct construction is *have* + complement + [verb in past participle]. This is the rule for passive causatives.

37. (A) should be *Hardly had he*. For an adverbial at the beginning of a sentence use adverbial + auxiliary + subject + verb.

38. (B) should be *change*. *Had better* + [verb in simple form].

39. (B) should be *not to*. For the negative indirect command use verb + *not* + infinitive.

40. (B) should be *others*. *An* means *one;* here *others* must be plural because it is functioning as a pronoun. It is *never* possible to say *anothers*.

SECTION 3: READING COMPREHENSION

1. (C) A "disservice" is a harmful action. Sentence 2 says that science has "made many foods unfit to eat." The reading later gives nitrates and nitrites as harmful substances that have been added to food.

2. (D) "Prone" in this context means the different cultures are more "likely" to contract certain illnesses because of their food choices. Choice (B) can be eliminated because it's the opposite of "likely." Choice (C) doesn't make sense, and choice (A) means lying face down, the other definition of "prone." "Predisposed" is the synonym for "prone" in this use.

3. (B) Paragraph 2, sentence 2, says that nitrates are used as color preservers in meat.

4. (C) In the last sentence of the third paragraph, the letters FDA follow the title Food and Drug Administration.

5. (D) "These" is specifying the "carcinogenic additives" that follow it. "These carcinogenic additives" refers to the previous sentence's "nitrates and nitrites" that caused cancer. Therefore, "nitrates and nitrites" is the answer.

6. (D) "Carcinogenic" means "cancer-causing." Paragraph 2, sentence 2, states that nitrates and nitrites cause cancer. The following sentence begins, "Yet, these carcinogenic additives. . . ." You can assume that the word "these" refers to the cancer-causing additives mentioned in the previous sentence.

7. (A) Paragraph 3, sentences 3 and 4, tell us that drugs are not always administered for medicinal reasons.

8. (A) The root "add" should lead you to choose answer choice (A).

9. (C) The whole passage discusses illnesses and the benefits of a healthy diet. Answer choices (A) and (B) are too general. Choice (D) is incorrect because the passage does not deal only with "avoiding" injurious substances.

10. (B) The word "fit" is contrasted with "unfit." The fact that the sentence says "science has made enormous steps in making food more fit to eat" should provide a clue that "fit" is "suitable."

11. (B) The passage states "That food is related to illness is not a new discovery" in line 10 and goes on to describe a 1945 study.

12. (C) Choice (A) is not correct because the passage states that the Egyptians left "no written accounts." Modern embalmers still using these methods (B) are not mentioned at all, nor is chemical analysis (D). Sentence 4 does state specifically that "scientists have had to examine mummies and establish their own theories," choice (C).

13. (A) The subject of this paragraph is the "embalmers."

14. (A) This is an inference question. The reading does not specifically describe the embalming process in any of these ways. However, you can assume that the process was not "short and simple" (B) because in some cases it took seventy days. A process would not be "strict and unfaltering" (C); those would be qualities more likely ascribed to a person. There is nothing at all in the reading to suggest that the embalming would be either "wild" or "terrifying" (D). Because of the several steps involved and the time mentioned, however, it would seem logical that the process is "lengthy and complicated," choice (A).

15. (B) Choice (A) is incorrect because the passage is discussing the treatment of bodies that are already dead. To embalm (C) is to preserve *against* decay. To rejuvenate (D) means to restore youth. "Decay" is nearest in meaning to "deteriorate."

16. (B) You are asked for the one choice that is *not* true. Choice (A) is true because the Egyptians "firmly believed in the afterlife." Choice (C) is true. The compounds are listed as being made up of salt, spices, and resins. Choice (D) is not specifically mentioned, but you should assume that it has been difficult to determine the process since there are no written

accounts available. Choice (B), however, is false. Sentence 5 says, "up to seventy days for the pharaohs and nobility and *only a few days* for the poor," so embalming did not *always* take seventy days to complete.

17. (A) It was important to the Egyptians that corpses did not decay (sentence 2), so choice (A) is correct. Scaring robbers away (B) is not mentioned in the passage. Encasing a body in a sarcophagus (C) was part of the entire burial ritual for a pharaoh or noble, but it followed mummification and was not the reason for it. Amulets are described as protecting the body from harm on its journey (D), not the mummification process.

18. (D) In the first paragraph, it's stated that food, clothing, jewels, and tools provide for the deceased's material needs. In the second paragraph, the need for protection on the long journey to the afterlife is mentioned. It can be inferred from these two statements that the Egyptians believed material items were still needed by the deceased because they were on a long journey to the afterlife.

19. (C) "Amulets" are charms that protect against injury or evil. "Curses," choice (D), can be eliminated because the entire passage relates the respect the Egyptians had for the deceased. Curses are also not tangible. There are no clues to eliminate choices (A) and (B) if you do not know the meaning of "amulets."

20. (A) Substitute the answer choices for "accomplished" in the sentence. "Performed" is the only verb that makes sense.

21. (B) The passage states that "the embalming process might have taken up to seventy days for the pharaohs and only a few days for the poor."

22. (D) The second sentence states that some tapeworms attach themselves to the intestinal wall; thus they do *not* float freely.

23. (B) The excretory system is responsible for removing waste from a body. Only choice (B) relates to elimination.

24. (C) Paragraph 2, sentence 3, explains that a hermaphrodite has both male and female sexual organs.

25. (D) The subject of the previous sentence is "some tapeworms." So "others" means "other tapeworms."

26. (D) Euphoria is not mentioned as a symptom. Irregular appetite, nervousness, and anemia, which mean the same as answers (A), (B), and (C), are mentioned.

27. (D) We are told in paragraph 1 that some tapeworms attach themselves to the intestinal wall to feed, while others float freely and absorb food through their body walls.

28. (C) The reading gives general information about a particular parasite, the tapeworm. Choices (A) and (D) are too broad in scope, and choice (B) is too narrow.

29. (A) Sentence 2 of paragraph 1 mentions that some tapeworms attach themselves by means of suckers in their heads.

30. (B) "*A* tapeworm consists of numerous segments" is the statement, so choices (A) and (D) do not make sense. The only organs mentioned in the passage are hermaphroditic sexual organs, and they are located *in* each segment, so choice (C) does not make sense. "Segments" is nearest in meaning to "sections."

31. (D) "Foresaw" means to have known beforehand, which is nearest in meaning to "predicted."

32. (A) The third sentence of paragraph 1 says that the prize was established to recognize "worthwhile contributions to humanity."

33. (D) The last sentence of paragraph 3 says that Americans have won "numerous science awards."

34. (B) Choice (A) is true. The awards vary from $30,000 to $125,000. We are told specifically that politics sometimes plays an important role in the selection (C) and that some people have won two prizes, although that is rare (unusual). If it is rare, then only *a few* will have done so (D). Choice (B) is not true. The date December 10 is not important in commemorating Nobel's invention, but rather the anniversary of his death.

35. (C) Paragraph 1, sentence 4, says that there were originally five awards, and economics was added in 1968. The total, then, is six.

36. (D) An inventor of dynamite would most likely be working in the field of science.

37. (D) The contributions that the Nobel Prize winners make to humanity are most likely "valuable."

38. (D) Nobel's original legacy was $9,000,000 (paragraph 2).

39. (D) Choices (A) and (B) are details of the passage, not the main idea. Choice (C) is not stated in the passage. Leaving $9,000,000 to support people who make valuable contributions to humanity is in itself a great contribution to humanity (D).

40. (B) A "legacy" is the property or money given to another at death, so "bequest" has most nearly the same meaning.

41. (A) You are asked to choose the best summary of the passage, which means the statement that best tells the general idea. Choice (B) is the opposite of what the reading says. Choices (C) and (D) *may* be true, but they are too specific to give the general idea of the entire passage. And while you might assume that verbalization is the fastest form of communication (D), the reading does not mention this.

42. (D) "These" is an adjective describing "symbols," and "symbols" is a term that can be used to describe the motions of sign language explained two sentences earlier.

43. (C) The deaf, although they cannot hear, sometimes can speak, but the mute, by definition, cannot speak. Therefore, they could not themselves use *oral* communication.

44. (B) Blind people cannot see, so choices (A), (C), and (D) would not be used by them. Braille is read with the fingertips (paragraph 3).

45. (C) There are nine forms of communication listed in the reading: oral speech, sign language, body language, Braille, signal flags, Morse code, smoke signals, road maps, and picture signs.

46. (A) Choices (C) and (D) are described in the following sentences, so they can be eliminated. To "wink" is to close one eye briefly, and to "blink" is to close both eyes briefly.

47. (A) The last sentence of paragraph 1 says that these symbols (sign language) *cannot* be used internationally for spelling.

48. (D) Sentence 2 describes the expression of thoughts and feelings as the reason for communication, which is introduced in sentence 1.

49. (B) Since the passage focuses on communication, it would be appropriate to use that word in the title. Choice (B) covers the passage's topic while choice (D) is too narrow.

50. (D) A nonlinguistic code would most likely be used by a telegrapher.

PRACTICE TEST 6

After some answers in this answer key, you will find numbers in italic type. These are page numbers in Part III where you will find review material for these questions. Although any one question may involve several different rules and concepts, these page numbers refer to important areas you should review if you have missed a question or are not sure of the material involved. Make full use of these page number references and of the index to direct your personal review.

Section 1: Listening Comprehension

1. (C)	11. (B)	21. (C)	31. (D)	41. (A)
2. (B)	12. (C)	22. (A)	32. (A)	42. (A)
3. (C)	13. (A)	23. (B)	33. (C)	43. (B)
4. (A)	14. (B)	24. (B)	34. (C)	44. (B)
5. (D)	15. (D)	25. (B)	35. (D)	45. (D)
6. (B)	16. (C)	26. (A)	36. (B)	46. (D)
7. (B)	17. (D)	27. (C)	37. (D)	47. (D)
8. (B)	18. (A)	28. (C)	38. (D)	48. (B)
9. (C)	19. (C)	29. (C)	39. (B)	49. (B)
10. (C)	20. (B)	30. (A)	40. (C)	50. (A)

Section 2: Structure and Written Expression

1. (D) *135, 229*
2. (B)
3. (A) *146*
4. (A) *221–223, 229–230*
5. (A) *59–61*
6. (B) *224–226*
7. (D)
8. (D)
9. (B) *94*
10. (B) *118*
11. (C)
12. (C) *229*
13. (D)
14. (A) *229*
15. (B) *192, 219–220*
16. (D) *221–223*
17. (D) *221–223*
18. (B) *82*
19. (C) *205*
20. (D) *157*

21. (B) *59*
22. (B) *59–60*
23. (B) *65–66*
24. (C) *89–90*
25. (A) *64*
26. (C) *205*
27. (B) *68*
28. (B) *69–70*
29. (B) *72–73*
30. (C) *212*
31. (A)
32. (A) *89–90*
33. (A) *273*
34. (C) *171*
35. (A) *185–186*
36. (C) *289*
37. (C) *123–124*
38. (A) *59, 61–62*
39. (C) *52–53*
40. (D) *45*

Section 3: Reading Comprehension

1. (C)	11. (C)	21. (D)	31. (A)	41. (A)
2. (A)	12. (B)	22. (A)	32. (C)	42. (D)
3. (C)	13. (A)	23. (B)	33. (B)	43. (B)
4. (C)	14. (B)	24. (A)	34. (B)	44. (B)
5. (C)	15. (A)	25. (A)	35. (D)	45. (B)
6. (A)	16. (A)	26. (C)	36. (A)	46. (C)
7. (C)	17. (A)	27. (B)	37. (A)	47. (D)
8. (A)	18. (A)	28. (B)	38. (C)	48. (A)
9. (B)	19. (A)	29. (B)	39. (B)	49. (D)
10. (C)	20. (C)	30. (C)	40. (A)	50. (B)

PRACTICE TEST 6: ANALYSIS-SCORING SHEET

Use the chart below to spot your strengths and weaknesses in each test section and to arrive at your total converted score. Fill in your number of correct answers for each section in the space provided. Refer to the Converted Score Sheet on page 496 to find your converted score for each section and enter those numbers on the chart. Find the sum of your converted scores, multiply that sum by 10, and divide by 3.

Example: If raw scores are   then converted scores are
Section 1:   33   51
Section 2:   26   49
Section 3:   38   53
          Sum of Converted Scores   153
                    Times 10 = 1,530
                    Divided by 3 =   510 = Total Converted
                                                  Score

This will give you the approximate score that you would obtain if this were an actual TOEFL. Remember that your score here may possibly be higher than the score that you might receive on an actual TOEFL simply because you are studying the elements of the test shortly before taking each test. The score is intended only to give you a general idea of approximately what your actual score will be.

	Total Possible	Total Correct	Converted Score
Section 1: Listening Comprehension	50		
Section 2: Structure and Written Expression	40		
Section 3: Reading Comprehension	50		
TOTALS	140		

Sum of Converted Scores _____
Times 10 = _____
Divided by 3 = _____ = Total Converted Score

SECTION 1: LISTENING COMPREHENSION SCRIPT

Part A

1. Woman: Mark can't stand rare meat.

   Man: I know. I ordered medium well. We'll send it back.

   Third Voice: What do the speakers mean?

2. Man: Ugh, this milk is sour!

   Woman: It should be good. The expiration date is five days away.

   Third Voice: What are the man and woman talking about?

3. Woman: Have you seen that movie about the girl who had sixteen different personalities?

   Man: No, and I don't plan to. It sounds scary.

   Third Voice: Why does the man say he doesn't want to see the movie?

4. Man: I haven't seen you wear that lovely necklace before.

   Woman: It was packed away until last week. It's a family heirloom.

   Third Voice: What does the woman say about the necklace?

5. Woman: The neighborhood convenience store was held up last night.

   Man: Yes, I heard it on the radio this morning.

   Third Voice: What does the woman say happened at the convenience store last night?

6. Woman: Do you think this skirt goes well with this blouse?

   Man: Yes, but I think your red dress would be more elegant for the reception.

   Third Voice: What does the man say about the woman's choice of clothing?

7. Woman: I wish Jack were coming to visit us.

   Man: He won't be able to because it's out of his way.

   Third Voice: What do the speakers mean?

8. Man: I hope you will back me up on this new curriculum proposal.

   Woman: You can count on me!

   Third Voice: What does the woman mean?

9. Man: Miss, can you give me change for a dollar?

   Woman: I'm sorry, sir. I'm not allowed to give change without a purchase. If you go across the hall, you'll find a change machine in front of the jewelry store.

   Third Voice: Where does the woman suggest that the man get change?

10. Man: It wasn't supposed to rain today.

    Woman: It'll let up, won't it?

    Third Voice: What can be inferred about the weather?

11. Man: I should submit an offer on the house today, shouldn't I?

    Woman: You'll have to decide that for yourself.

    Third Voice: What does the woman mean?

12. Woman: I hear your son is working part-time at the department store.

    Man: Yes. He works Monday, Wednesday, and Friday from three to seven and all day Saturday.

    Third Voice: Which days does the man imply that his son does NOT work?

13. Man: Are you prepared for the test, Cindy?

    Woman: I found it extremely difficult to learn all that material.

    Third Voice: What does the woman say about her preparation for the test?

14. Woman: Did Bob study yesterday?

    Man: He would have if it hadn't been such a nice day.

    Third Voice: What does the man say Bob did yesterday?

15. Woman: Why was Susan so late the other night?

    Man: She could hardly find a seat in the dark theater.

    Third Voice: What does the man say happened to Susan?

16. Woman: Were there a lot of students in the class?

    Man: Before the class began, a dozen students were in the room, but soon the number doubled.

    Third Voice: What does the man mean?

17. Woman: How was your class?

    Man: Contrary to what I had expected, the professor canceled it.

    Third Voice: What does the man mean?

18. Man: How would you like your two pounds of pork
                    chops sliced?

    Woman: Medium thin will be fine.

    Third Voice: Where does this conversation probably take place?

19. Man: Which of the boys is Henry Adams?

    Woman: The one with the green sweater, using the
                    crutches.

    Third Voice: What does the woman imply about Henry Adams?

20. Woman: That famous science fiction writer Isaac Asimov's
                    new book is coming out in July.

    Man: We probably won't be able to find a library copy
                    until September.

    Third Voice: When does the woman say Asimov's book will be
                    published?

21. Man: Where's Katie?

    Woman: I don't know, but if she doesn't get here soon, we
                    will probably be late.

    Third Voice: What does the woman say about Katie?

22. Man: What are you doing this weekend?

    Woman: I can't remember whether Tony and I are going to
                    a party on Friday or Saturday night.

    Third Voice: What are the woman and Tony planning to do?

23. Woman: Do Helen and her husband go fishing together?

    Man: Helen dislikes going fishing with her husband,
                    even though she goes quite often.

    Third Voice: What does the man mean?

24. Man: Have you seen Karl?

    Woman: Yes. I was puzzled by the expression on his face.

    Third Voice: What does the woman mean?

25. Man: Clint looked worn out.

    Woman: He must have been exhausted after that run.

    Third Voice: What does the woman say about Clint?

26. Man: When can I see Dr. Jones?

    Woman: She should be free to see you after noon tomorrow.

    Third Voice: When does the woman say the man can have an appointment?

27. Woman: Sally's not very sociable, is she?

    Man: In spite of her bad habits, she has a lot of friends.

    Third Voice: What does the man say about Sally?

28. Man: Ramona, are you and your husband going to buy a new house this year?

    Woman: Houses are so expensive now that we simply can't afford to buy one.

    Third Voice: What does the woman say about the cost of houses?

29. Woman: Can I still register for the economics class?

    Man: It's too late. Registration closed the day before yesterday.

    Third Voice: What does the man say about registration for classes?

30. Man: Why isn't Elaine going to the country with us?

    Woman: I forgot to tell her about our change in plans.

    Third Voice: What do the speakers say about Elaine?

Part B

Questions 31 through 34 are based on the following conversation.

Man: Well, that's the last straw. I've reached 200 pounds, I'm out of breath, and nothing fits me anymore. How in the world can I break this cycle?

Woman: I lost thirty pounds last year, and I can't tell you how much better I feel.

Man: I lost fifteen once but gained it right back. You look great. How did you do it?

Woman: It requires a change in lifestyle, permanently. I cut down on fat intake and other problem foods, including sweets and alcohol, and I got into a regular program of exercise.

Man: I'm a member of a gym, but it's so boring. I feel inadequate next to those muscular and slim bodies.

Woman: That's how they got perfect, by going to the gym and watching what they ate. If you don't want to go there, swim or ride a bicycle. Take a brisk walk after each meal. Here, let me lend you these two books. One has information on the fat content of certain foods—so you know what to avoid. And the other has menus and recipes for a great number of healthy, low-fat meals. But remember, the change in food is not enough. You must get the exercise too.

Man: I guess I'll just have to draw the line and do without the foods I love, as you recommend. No more heavy meals, desserts, or nightly cocktails. I'll also have to force myself to get that exercise. Maybe I'll even go back to the gym.

Woman: Right. And brown bag it instead of going out to lunch at work. Stock up on harmless goodies. If you get hungry, nibble on some celery or carrots. If you follow the recipes in this book, you'll see that dieting doesn't have to be unpleasant.

31. What is the man's problem?
32. How does the woman suggest that he solve his problem?
33. What does the woman suggest that he do when he's hungry?
34. What does the woman mean by the expression "brown bag it"?

Questions 35 through 38 are based on the following conversation.

Man: Yesterday, we were discussing the famous poet, Gabriela Mistral. Who can tell me something about her?

Woman: She was from Chile and lived in poverty in her early years. She became a teacher and then a writer.

Man: What was her claim to fame?

Woman: She won the Nobel Prize in literature in 1945. She was the first Latin American woman to do so.

Man: Why are her works so significant?

Woman: She addresses social issues such as maternity, love, children, gender equity, and the plight of the downtrodden. Her themes have been nourished by her own personal sorrow.

Man: Did she teach only in her native country?

Woman: No, she was invited by the governments of Mexico, Spain, France, the United States, and Germany to teach in several universities.

Man: She was well loved by her colleagues and readers and has left us a treasure of poetic works.

35. What is the probable relationship between the man and the woman?
36. Where was Gabriela Mistral born?
37. What was Gabriela Mistral's profession?
38. According to this conversation, which country was NOT mentioned as one where Gabriela Mistral had taught?

Part C

Questions 39 through 43 are based on the following talk about early air transportation.

Almost two centuries ago, humans enjoyed their first airborne ride in a cloth balloon. Passengers rode in a basket fastened below the balloon. These brave adventurers depended solely on the wind velocity and direction to move them about because of the lack of a steering mechanism.

In 1852, a French clockmaker flew the first controllable balloon a distance of seventeen miles. Germany began producing and using airships about forty-six years later with its famous zeppelins, named in honor of their inventor, Count von Zeppelin. The largest and probably most famous of Germany's airships was the *Hindenberg*, which could travel at eighty-five miles per hour.

Later, the two countries bordering on the English Channel, Great Britain and France, built smaller airships called "blimps." The latter airships were intended for patrolling the coast and observing submarine activity, while the former served as passenger and cargo ships.

After the *Hindenberg* burned in 1937, more and more people shied away from this form of transportation.

39. Why was it difficult to fly in the air-filled balloons of two hundred years ago?
40. Which of the following countries was NOT involved in the production of airships?
41. Who flew the first controllable balloon?
42. Which country used these airships for passenger and cargo transport?
43. Why did fewer people travel on airships after 1937?

Questions 44 through 46 are based on the following talk about animal life spans.

All living, self-propelled beings do not enjoy the same life span. Scientists have discovered that the faster a living thing grows and moves during its life, the shorter its life will be. Animals producing many offspring will have shorter lives than those that produce only a few. Larger animals live longer than smaller ones. Some species live several weeks, while others can enjoy more than a one-hundred-year existence.

Disease and other environmental conditions are capable of wiping out a particular species in a given area.

44. Based on the information in this talk, which of the following will probably live only a short time?

45. Which of the following can be expected to live the longest?
46. Which was NOT mentioned as a cause for shortening an animal's life span?

Questions 47 through 50 are based on the following lecture about dinosaurs.

It was not until 1822 that scientists learned about the existence of dinosaurs. Thanks to an English doctor and his wife, the door was opened to this zoological study. Reasoning that the reptiles' tremendous size must have made them terrible creatures, scientists combined two Greek words, *deimos,* meaning *terrible,* and *sauros,* meaning *lizards,* to form the word *dinosaur.*

After many years of study, they determined that these beasts roamed the earth for millions of years, and ceased to exist some sixty million years ago.

Unbelievable as it may seem, not all dinosaurs were carnivorous, that is, meat eating. Many were herbivorous, or vegetarian.

By reassembling the bones found at excavation sites, scientists have been able to reconstruct the skeletons and learn a great deal about the dinosaurs' living conditions. They have learned that dinosaurs inhabited not only the land, but also the water and sky.

47. By what name did scientists refer to these creatures?
48. When do scientists believe that the last of the dinosaurs disappeared?
49. How have scientists been able to learn of the living conditions of these animals?
50. Which of the following is NOT true of these animals?

EXPLANATIONS FOR PRACTICE TEST 6

SECTION 2: STRUCTURE AND WRITTEN EXPRESSION

Part A

1. (D) Choice (A) is incorrect because the verb *studied* should be modified by an adverb, *badly*. (B) is in error because it is never correct to say *wise* with a noun or verb to mean *in relation to*. (C) uses *badly*, which is an adverb and cannot modify the noun *student*.

2. (B) The expression *second only to* here means that Harvard's programs are the best, and this university's programs are second best.

3. (A) This is a double comparative. The correct form is *the more . . . the less.*

4. (A) Choice (A) contains correct parallel structure: *durability* (noun) . . . *economy* (noun). Choice (B) is verbose. *Lasts a long time* means it is *durable*. It is not necessary to use so many words. When there is a shorter answer that means the same and is grammatically correct, choose the shorter answer. Choice (C) would be correct if it said "its *durability* and *economy*" (noun/noun). Choice (D) uses *economy-wise*. It is always incorrect to use *wise* with a noun in this way.

5. (A) Past progressive: *when* . . . simple past . . . past progressive. Choice (D) would be correct if it said *had been sleeping.*

6. (B) The form should be subject + verb + indirect object + direct object. There should be *no* preposition.

7. (D) The correct expression is *in greater numbers.* This is an expression that you should memorize.

8. (D) Always after the phrase *it was not until* must appear the word *that.* To use *when* here would be redundant.

9. (B) For an embedded question, use question word + subject + verb.

10. (B) Past condition. When the conditional perfect is used in the result clause, the past perfect must be used in the *if* clause.

11. (C) There are only a few possibilities for expressing age in English: (1) when he was sixteen (years old), (2) at (age) sixteen, and (3) at the age of sixteen. Choice (C) follows rule (3) and is the only correct answer.

12. (C) Choice (A) is verbose and too informal for written English. Choice (B) uses *make . . . expressions,* which has to do with facial features, not speech, and makes no sense here. In choice (D) *with their minds open* (having open minds) is an idiom meaning to be willing to have no biases. When used in this context with *talk,* it is not logical.

13. (D) *Much less* is used in this context in a negative sentence to indicate that the second item mentioned is disliked even more than the first. The students dislike reading novels and dislike reading textbooks even more.

14. (A) Choices (B) and (D) are verbose. *Eagerly* is much more concise than either of these choices. Choice (C) uses *eagernessly,* which is not a word. It is not possible to add an adverb affix (*-ly*) to a noun affix (*-ness*).

15. (B) Choices (A), (C), and (D) are all verbose. In addition, choice (D) includes the wrong verb (*raised*); (A) and (D) incorrectly use *the time when.* It should be *the time that* because *the time when* is redundant; choice (C) uses incorrect word order.

Part B

NOTE: $\emptyset$ = nothing, indicating that this word or phrase should be deleted.

16. (D) should be $\emptyset$. Parallel structure would be adjective/noun, adjective/noun, adjective/noun. The phrase *working at* is not necessary because the verb is in the main clause.

17. (D) should be *cruelty*. Parallel structure requires noun (*strength*), noun (*power*), and noun (*cruelty*).

18. (B) should be *themselves*. The form *theirselves* does not exist.

19. (C) should be *would receive*. The sequence of tenses should be past . . . past.

20. (D) should be *such a short time*. Cause/effect: *such* + *a* + adjective + singular count noun.

21. (B) should be *turned*. He finished taking classes in 1978; therefore, the verb must be in the past tense.

22. (B) should be *was hurrying*. Past progressive: *when* . . . past tense . . . past progressive.

23. (B) should be *had stolen*. Use the past perfect: *had* + [verb in past participle].

24. (C) should be *dog's*. Use the possessive form before a gerund.

25. (A) should be *has been hoping*. Use the present perfect progressive: *has been* + [verb + *ing*].

26. (C) should be *had been driving*. The correct sequence of tenses is *after driving* . . . *had been driving*. *After driving* is past in this sentence, and *has been driving* is present.

27. (B) should be *is*. *The Department of Foreign Languages* is singular so the verb must be singular.

28. (B) should be *is*. *Accompanied by* is a prepositional phrase and therefore is not part of the subject. The subject is *winner*, which is singular.

29. (B) should be *knows*. *Neither* is singular and requires a singular verb.

30. (C) should be *your*. *Those of you* is the subject, so we must keep the same person pronoun for the possessive (*your*).

31. (A) should be *zoology book*. It is not correct to say *a book of* _____ for textbooks.

32. (A) should be *Marta's*. Use the possessive form before a gerund.

33. (A) should be *lend* or *loan*. This is incorrect vocabulary choice. (I am the receiver and Jane is the giver.)

34. (C) should be *eat*. Causative: *make* + [verb in simple form].

35. (A) should be *not only composes*. The actor does two different things, using two different verbs, *composes* and *sings*. *Not only* must precede the first verb because there are two verbs.

36. (C) should be *of*. *About* is an incorrect preposition with *sample*. It should be a *sample of* something.

37. (C) should be *used*. Use *be* + *used to* + gerund and *used to* + simple form.

38. (A) should be *called*. *Last night* is a specific time and requires the simple past tense, not the present perfect.

39. (C) should be *others*. *Another* is singular. *Others* must be plural to agree with *their*.

40. (D) should be *fewer*. *Movies* is a count noun, so it requires *fewer* not *less*.

SECTION 3: READING COMPREHENSION

1. (C) Paragraph 2 tells us that he published the *New York Weekly Journal,* a newspaper his wife continued to publish while he was imprisoned.

2. (A) Paragraph 2, last sentence, specifically speaks of "corrupt government officials."

3. (C) Paragraph 1, last sentence, says that the right (freedom of the press) was adopted in 1791 and that the Zenger trial was in 1735. $1791 - 1735 = 56$.

4. (C) You are asked for the one choice that is *not* true. Choice (A) is true. It is mentioned in paragraph 2. Choice (B) is true. We are told that the jury was "persuaded" by Hamilton. And it should be obvious that they were fighting "for freedom" because the entire reading concerns freedom of the press. Choice (D) is true. We are told in paragraph 2 that the king sent corrupt officials "to govern the colonies."

5. (C) Paragraph 2, sentence 3, specifically states that he was arrested for "writing a story about the crown-appointed governor of New York."

6. (A) Choice (A) is the answer because the governor was crown appointed, and if the judge wanted to stay in office, he would represent the king. Choice (B) is incorrect because it was not mentioned in the passage. Choice (C) is incorrect because the Constitution was adopted 56 years *after* the trial. Choice (D) is incorrect because the governor is described as "crown appointed." Choices (C) and (D) are tricky because of the facts (C) and the vocabulary "crown appointed" (D).

7. (C) Substitute the answer choices for "defying" in the sentence. "Disregarding" is closest in meaning to "defying." If you are not familiar with the word "defying," you can infer that it means "disregarding" because the passage says the judge ordered a guilty verdict, but the jury found Zenger not guilty.

8. (A) Zenger's wife continued to publish the newspaper every day, including articles about corrupt government officials, which was the very act that landed her husband in prison. That context should tell you that "dutifully" is closest in meaning to "faithfully."

9. (B) The passage is about Peter Zenger and the right to publish information freely, so look for those key words and ideas. Andrew Hamilton played an important role in the trial; however, he did not give Americans freedom of the press, so answer choice (A) is not correct. Choices (C) and (D) focus on law rather than publishing, so they can be eliminated.

10. (C) Line 9 specifically states that the governor was "crown appointed," which means he was appointed by a monarch.

11. (C) Paragraph 2 says, "In A.D. 800, Charlemagne . . . initiated the Carolingian renaissance . . ." Although the Roman civilization is mentioned in the passage, and is older, it is not given as an example of a civilization involving rebirth.

12. (B) Paragraph 2 says that during the Carolingian period, modern cities were "patterned on Roman architecture." You could eliminate choices (C) and (D) immediately, as the question asks for a "city" and these two choices are not city names.

13. (A) Choices (B), (C), and (D) are specifically mentioned in the reading. If you know that "status quo" means the "existing condition," you could realize that this would not be appropriate for a time of rebirth.

14. (B) This is an inference question. From the fact that we are told of the "able rule" of Yaroslav, we can assume that he was in general a competent leader. Also, given his name, Yaroslav the *Wise,* one would not assume he was demented, inept, or cruel, all negative qualities.

15. (A) The word "carryover" means most nearly the same as "remnant." One can assume from the context that the libraries were something that *came from* Alexandrian Egypt. The only other choice that is close is (B), "residue." But "residue" has the connotation of a chemical process and thus is not the best choice.

16. (A) Education and learning are mentioned in the descriptions of all three renaissance periods. Choice (C) is incorrect, and choices (B) and (D) are not common to all three periods.

17. (A) "Renaissance" means "rebirth" in the three civilizations, specifically a rebirth of Greek and Roman culture. Art techniques, patterns of architecture, and educational systems are all mentioned as being borrowed and improved upon.

18. (A) The Italian renaissance lasted from 1400 until 1600, or 200 years. The Carolingian renaissance lasted throughout the 800s, or 100 years. The Kievan renaissance also lasted a century, or 100 years. Therefore, the answer is (A), the Italian renaissance.

19. (A) The Italian renaissance was most recent and lasted twice as long as the other two periods of rebirth. It also spread throughout Europe, and the New World through exploration.

20. (C) Choice (A) is incorrect because all of the cultures *improved* on what they knew of previous cultures, rather than merely copying what predecessors had accomplished. Choice (B) is incorrect because Russia is not in western Europe. Choice (D) is incorrect because other cultures, namely the Greek and Roman, were studied. The ways in which the several cultures advanced during their periods of rebirth is the focus of the entire passage.

21. (D) Sentences 2 and 3 in paragraph 1 state that the foods made from gelatin are *jellylike* (which would be easy to chew) and high in protein, so we can assume that gelatin would be beneficial for elderly and ill people.

22. (A) If you don't know the meaning of "fluid," this question could be difficult. The two sentences following "fluid" tell you that it is concentrated, chilled, sliced, and finally dried and ground. A "fluid" is closest in meaning to "liquid." When the "liquid" in this passage is concentrated and chilled, it becomes a firmer substance.

23. (B) Paragraph 2, sentence 2, says that the grease must first be eliminated, so it probably does not aid in producing gelatin. The reading passage specifically contradicts choice (A) because it says in the first sentence of paragraph 2 that processing gelatin made from bones "varies slightly from that of gelatin made from skin." The reading indicates that a much more detailed procedure of producing gelatin is required than what is described in choice (C). Answer choice (D) is incorrect because the reading indicates gelatin is "dried and ground." Only after the grinding would gelatin be in powder form.

24. (A) The whole reading deals with the process of making gelatin. Choice (B) is too general, and the other choices suggest only details of the passage.

25. (A) This is the only answer choice not listed in the passage.

26. (C) The passage states that gelatin is beneficial to the consumer because it is high in protein.

27. (B) Substitute the answer choices for "ground" in the sentence. One would not "putrify" (C) or "dirty" (D) a commercial or food product, so eliminate those choices. The gelatin has already been chilled, or "refrigerated," choice (A), in the previous sentence. That leaves "pulverized," choice (B). To "pulverize" is to "grind."

28. (B) The last sentence says that gelatin is tasteless, so choice (A) is incorrect. Gelatin is not easy to make, so choice (C) is not true. One can infer that gelatin does melt at high temperatures because it has to be refrigerated to be sliced and ground, so choice (D) is untrue.

29. (B) The sentence states, "In the processing of gelatin made from bones (which varies slightly from *that* of gelatin made from skin), the grease must first be eliminated." "That" refers to the "processing" at the beginning of the sentence.

30. (C) Paragraph 1, sentence 2, says that the technology "allows scientists to introduce genetic material (or genes) from one organism into another." The key word in this question is "primarily." Choice (D) is a small part of the technology. Choice (A) is a result of the technology. Choice (B) is the function of the foreign gene and also involves only a part of the technology.

31. (A) Substitute the answer choices for "profound" in the sentence. From the context, you can infer that recombinant DNA technology is incredible. The development is not "boring," choice (B), or "secret," choice (D). The technology may be "dangerous," choice (C), but that is not the focus of this sentence. "Profound" means "significant" in this use.

32. (C) In the sentence, "isolation" applies to a piece of DNA from an organism under study. "Destruction" (A) of the DNA doesn't make sense, nor does the "study" of what is already being studied, choice (D). "Duplication" is addressed in the last half of the sentence by "artificially synthesized." "Isolation" is closest in meaning to "segregation."

33. (B) Paragraph 1, sentence 5, tells us that *Escherichia coli* is a bacterium into which the recombinant molecule can be introduced. It is not itself produced by DNA technology.

34. (B) The word "artificially" means "not naturally," or "synthetically."

35. (D) In the sentence, a piece of DNA is being "ligated" *to* a fragment of bacterial DNA. The only answer choice that makes sense is (D).

ANSWERS AND EXPLANATIONS FOR PRACTICE TEST 6

36. (A) Sentence 6 states that "the foreign gene will not only replicate in the bacteria, but also express itself." Thus choice (A) is the one choice that is *not* true. Choices (B), (C), and (D) are specifically mentioned in the passage.

37. (A) The "fragment" in the sentence is some bacterial DNA. Choices (B) and (C) do not make sense, and it's highly unlikely that scientists would be dealing with a "large piece" (D) of DNA. "Particle" is the best answer choice.

38. (C) The sentence states that bacterial DNA has the "capacity" to replicate itself independently. DNA doesn't have "hormones," choice (A), "technology," choice (B), or "space," choice (D). It does have the "ability" to replicate, however, so that is the best choice.

39. (B) The last sentence of paragraph 1 states that the expression of a gene requires the processes of transcription and translation. Choice (D) is not true because, while the reading states that *Escherichia coli* may be produced in large amounts in synthetic media, it does not say that it *requires* synthetic media.

40. (A) Sentence 4 says, "This piece of DNA is then *ligated* to a fragment of bacterial DNA which has the capacity to replicate itself independently." Sentence 5 continues, "The recombinant molecule *thus* produced. . . ." This means that two different molecules are ligated (joined) to produce "a recombinant molecule." Choice (B) is not true, since, although several technologies are combined, the reading does not say that the technologies are *re*combined. Choice (C) is not true because recombination of molecules is at the level of DNA, and not at the level of their products, the proteins. Choice (D) is not true because *Escherichia coli* is used to obtain expression of the recombinant molecule, but it is a "common intestinal bacterium," and not a recombinant.

41. (A) The only answer choice that makes sense for the synonym of "replicate" is "reproduce."

42. (D) Mars is 55 percent the size of Earth; therefore, it is smaller.

43. (B) The first sentence of paragraph 2 tells us that the canals were thought to have been discovered by Schiaparelli.

44. (B) "Supposedly" modifies Schiaparelli's discovery of man-made canals on Mars. The next sentence states that the man-made canal theory was proved to be a myth. The context casts doubt on the discovery, so "presumably" is closest in meaning to "supposedly."

45. (B) If Mars is "commonly called" the Red Planet, that is how it is "nicknamed."

46. (C) A "myth" is either something untrue or a culture's world view. In this use, "myth" is closest in meaning to "legend," which is a popular story or theory that is unverified.

47. (D) This is the only choice that is *not* true. The last paragraph states that some polar ice and permafrost were found, indicating that at one time there were significant quantities. Now, however, only traces are left, not large quantities.

48. (A) Most of the passage is spent telling the reader what Viking I discovered when it landed on Mars and how the data refutes some of the beliefs people had about Mars. The other three answer choices are incorrect.

49. (D) The sentence states that weather changes are being "monitored," so the word nearest in meaning to that is "observed."

50. (B) The fact that the volcanoes on Mars are believed to be "dormant," though some show signs of activity, should lead you to choose "inactive" as the synonym for "dormant" and the condition of most of the volcanoes.

PART VI: Test of Written English

THE TEST OF WRITTEN ENGLISH

The Test of Written English is available on some administrations of the TOEFL. If you take the TOEFL at an administration where the writing test is offered, you must take that portion of the test as well. The writing test is scored by two separate readers on a scale of 1 to 6, with 1 being the poorest score and 6 being the best. If the scores given by the two readers differ by more than one point, a third reader also reviews the paper. The scores are based upon the essay as a whole; such items as vocabulary, grammar, use of examples, and organization are not scored separately. The score is reported as a separate number on the TOEFL score report.

Ability Tested

The writing test analyzes your ability to respond to an essay question under time constraints. A topic will be presented, and the student must use proper organization, grammar, vocabulary, and spelling and must provide sufficient examples.

Basic Skills Necessary

You must be able to organize and write an effective essay, using correct grammar and spelling.

General Information

The TOEFL Bulletin indicates that during the writing test, students will have the opportunity to write an essay of 200 to 300 words in 30 minutes. Examinees will not need specific or detailed knowledge of the topic presented. A lined page will be attached to the answer sheet for writing the essay. Additional paper will be provided for making notes before writing the actual essay.

In order to score well on the Test of Written English, you should keep the following points in mind:

1. Address the assigned topic completely, being sure to answer all parts of the question asked.
2. Write a good introductory paragraph and conclusion.

3. Organize your thoughts before beginning writing and organize your paragraphs well.
4. Use correct grammar, vocabulary, and spelling. Use vocabulary and grammatical constructions that you are sure of. It is better to write simply and correctly than to try to write eloquently but make errors.
5. Keep your essay to no more than 200 or 300 words.
6. Allow enough time to write the essay well. Don't take so much time organizing your thoughts that you do not have time left to write.
7. Use specific details and avoid too many generalizations.

PLANNING YOUR ESSAY

If you have learned in composition classes a good way to organize your thoughts quickly, use the method that you already know. You should use a standard outline, a cluster outline, or some other method to organize your thoughts before you begin to write. An essay that is not properly planned will not be organized sufficiently to receive a good score. You should spend no more than 10 minutes organizing so that you have at least 20 minutes to write the essay. You will not be required to turn in your outline or other planning format, so you may use whatever is useful for you.

There are various methods of planning, and you should use the method that works best for you. The most common method is the standard outline. Each major category will be a paragraph in the essay. Study the following sample question and outline:

Some people purchase a home and others rent. Describe one or two benefits of owning a home and one or two benefits of renting. Compare the two options and explain which you think might be better for someone your age and in your situation.

Questions that must be addressed:

1. What are the benefits of owning?
2. What are the benefits of renting?
3. Which is the best for someone your age and in your situation?

STANDARD OUTLINE

I. Benefits of owning

  A. It is yours and you can do what you want
    1. Do not have to worry too much about noise
    2. Can redecorate without worrying about losing the deposit

  B. Financial reasons
    1. Interest is tax deductible
    2. Home appreciates in value

II. Benefits of renting

  A. Not tied down—if need to move, just have to worry about lease

  B. Financial reasons
    1. Do not have to come up with down payment
    2. Do not have to qualify for credit

III. Renting better for foreign student in early 20s

  A. Not tied down
    1. May transfer to another school
    2. Will return to own country after school

  B. Financial reasons
    1. Cannot afford to buy
    2. No credit

Another way of planning such an essay is with the "cluster outline." Study the following example:

CLUSTER OUTLINE

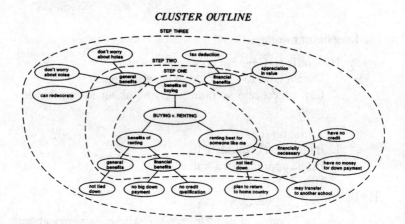

Introductory Paragraph

Every good essay has a strong opening paragraph. One method that is useful for constructing an opening paragraph is the *Generalize-Focus-Survey* structure. This is a three- or four-sentence paragraph in which the first sentence makes a generalization about the topic, the second sentence focuses on what will be discussed, and the last one or two sentences survey the details you will present in the body of the essay. Consider the following examples on the topic presented in the preceding pages:

1. *Generalize:*

   Many find it advantageous to purchase a home, but others find renting more suited to their needs.

2. *Focus:*

   While there are advantages for both options, renting is generally the best choice for young foreign students.

3. *Survey:*

   Foreign students often do not have good credit histories or enough money to buy a home and need to know that it will not be necessary to find a buyer for the home if they decide to transfer to another school or return home.

Body

The body of the essay should follow the form of your outline with separate paragraphs for each major topic. Try to avoid very short paragraphs or very long paragraphs.

Conclusion

The conclusion should sufficiently restate, but not simply repeat, the major points that you have stated in the body of the essay. Consider the following example:

> At various times of their lives, people have different needs. While purchasing a home is often the best choice for somebody with an adequate income and roots in a community, for the reasons discussed, it is often not the most feasible choice for young foreign students.

SAMPLE ESSAYS

SAMPLE ESSAY 1

Introduction

Many find it advantageous to purchase a home, but others find renting more suited to their needs. While there are advantages for both options, renting is generally the best choice for young foreign students. Foreign students often do not have good credit histories or enough money to buy a home and need to know that it will not be necessary to find a buyer for the home if they decide to transfer to another school or return home.

Body Paragraph 1: Benefits of owning home

Owning a home provides a number of benefits. For example, a homeowner can make more noise than someone who lives in an apartment without having to worry that every small noise might disturb neighbors. Unlike apartment dwellers, homeowners can also put holes in walls and redecorate without being concerned about losing part or all of a security deposit. Owning is also an advantage because the interest on mortgage payments can be deducted on their income tax. In addition, real estate generally appreciates in value over the years.

Body Paragraph 2:
Benefits of renting

There are also benefits to renting. A renter is tied down only by the terms of the rental agreement or lease. If a renter wants to move, it is not necessary to find a buyer. In addition, a renter does not have to provide a large down payment as does a home owner and does not have to have a good credit history.

Body Paragraph 3:
Best choice for one in
student's situation

A foreign student who plans to return home after college or who wishes to transfer to another school often cannot be tied down to a house. The foreign student often does not have enough money for a down payment or a credit history sufficient to borrow money to purchase a home. Consequently, renting is the answer for most young foreign students.

Conclusion

At various times of their lives, people have different needs. While purchasing a home is often the best choice for somebody with an adequate income and roots in a community, for the reasons discussed, it is often not the most feasible choice for young foreign students.

Topic

A writer has accused teachers and parents of causing children to develop *calcuholism*—a reliance on calculators and resulting loss of mathematical ability. Describe what you believe the writer means by *calcuholism* and what you believe causes it. Also state what you believe can be done to alleviate the problem.

Questions to Answer

1. What is *calcuholism*?
2. What causes it?
3. What can be done to alleviate it?

Standard Outline

   I. What the writer means by *calcuholism*

     A. The term indicates an addiction or dependency

     B. Generally such a dependency is unhealthy

     C. Problem—if children rely too much on calculators, they lose ability to do mathematics easily without it

  II. What causes it—more technology

     A. Emphasis in schools on more advanced math and technical classes that require calculators

     B. Emphasis in offices on speed and efficiency—word processors and computers

     C. Emphasis in industry on technologically advanced machines

III. What can be done to alleviate it

     A. Schools should avoid causing students to rely on calculators

     B. All should avoid becoming too dependent on the calculator
       1. Restrict use of calculators
       2. Keep up practice with actual math

Cluster Outline

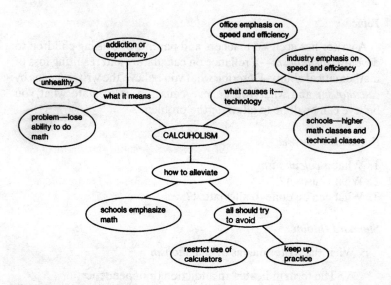

Introductory Paragraph

The type of introductory paragraph used in this essay, instead of one using the *Generalize-Focus-Survey* method, is one which follows the form of the outline in a general way.

I. It has been said that many people are victims of *calcuholism,* a dependence on the use of calculators, causing a diminished ability to do mathematics on one's own.

II. Technology in schools, offices, and industry has resulted in an unfortunate overdependence on all types of modern devices, but particularly on calculators.

III. Calcuholism can be avoided if schools and individuals concentrate on using the mind to do mathematics rather than relying on calculators for simple tasks.

Conclusion

Calcuholism has increased in recent years and will continue to increase due to advances in technology. To avoid dependency, we must do mathematics with our minds from time to time rather than with a machine.

Complete Essay

Introduction

It has been said that many people are victims of *calcuholism,* a dependence on the use of calculators, causing a diminished ability to do mathematics on one's own. Technology in schools, offices, and industry has resulted in an unfortunate overdependence on all types of modern devices, but particularly on calculators. Calcuholism can be avoided if schools and individuals concentrate on using the mind to do mathematics rather than relying on calculators for simple tasks.

Body Paragraph 1:
What is it?

Obviously the term *calcuholism* has been coined with the intent to compare it to other addictions such as alcoholism. While it is not nearly as serious as alcoholism, dependence on the calculator can be harmful. Abuse of something normally beneficial may lead to a harmful reliance on it. It is not that calculators are harmful, but that overuse may cause harm by causing people to forget how to do mathematics with their own minds.

Body Paragraph 2:
What causes it?

The problem arises from modern technological advances. In schools, classes become more complicated because of the technology for which students must be prepared when they graduate. Calculators are permitted and essential in many such classes. In offices, calculators, computers, and word processing systems are commonplace because they increase speed and improve efficiency. Business people may spend hours working with numbers and rarely calculate mentally. In industry as well, the emphasis on advanced machines results in individuals' solving fewer mathematical problems on their own.

Body Paragraph 3: What can be done to alleviate?

To alleviate the problem, schools should avoid allowing students to use calculators too early and should require sufficient in-class work without them. All of us should restrict our use of calculators and strive to do math on our own so that we will not lose our basic math skills.

Conclusion

Calcuholism has increased in recent years and will continue to increase due to advances in technology. To avoid dependency, we must do mathematics with our minds from time to time rather than with a machine.

SAMPLE ESSAY 3

Topic

The chart below shows the number of barrels of oil produced and the number consumed by various regions of the world. What does the chart tell you? Write one or more paragraphs that convey the information displayed in the chart.

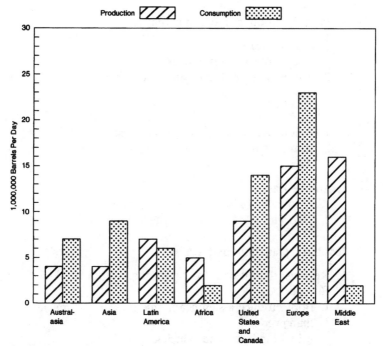

(This chart is not a completely accurate reflection of fact, but is a close representation for illustration purposes.)

Standard Outline

I. Regions that use more than they produce

    A. Australasia and Asia—each uses about 50% more than produced

B. Europe
1. Uses about 75% more than produced
2. Almost the largest producer, but also the largest user

C. U.S. and Canada
1. Produce ⅗ of what is used
2. Produce twice what many other regions produce, but use the most with exception of Europe

II. Regions that produce more than they use

A. Latin America
1. Uses ⅚ of what it produces
2. Biggest user of the regions that produce more than they use

B. Africa
1. Produces more than twice what it uses
2. It and Middle East use less than any other region on chart

C. Middle East
1. Produces more than any other region
2. Tied with Africa for using smallest amount

III. Possible explanations and results

A. Regions that use a lot more than produce—U.S. and Europe
1. Both produce a significant amount, but use much more than produce
2. A lot of industry and vehicles

B. Regions that produce a lot more than they use—Africa and Middle East
1. Little industry and few vehicles using petroleum products

C. Regions that produce more than they use can make a profit selling to countries that consume more than they produce

Introductory Paragraph

Generalize:

A graph of world petroleum consumption compared to petroleum use shows a tremendous difference among regions.

Focus:

Some use more than they produce, while others produce more than they use.

Survey:

Certain regions have large petroleum production but lack the industry and transportation to utilize it. They are able to make a profit by selling to regions that need it.

Conclusion

As the chart describes, certain regions produce more petroleum than they consume, and others consume more than they produce. Those with a surplus can profit by selling it to the large consumers that cannot produce all that they need.

Complete Essay

Introduction	A graph of world petroleum consumption compared to petroleum use shows a tremendous difference among regions. Some use more than they produce, while others produce more than they use. Certain regions have large petroleum production but lack the industry and transportation to utilize it. They are able to make a profit by selling to regions that need it.
Body Paragraph 1: Regions that use more	Four regions shown consume more petroleum than they produce. Both Australasia and Asia consume about fifty percent more than they produce. Europe consumes about

seventy-five percent more than it produces. It is one of the largest producers but also is the largest consumer of all the regions. The United States and Canada together produce about three fifths of what they consume; while they produce more than twice as much as many other regions, they consume the most with the exception of Europe.

Body Paragraph 2:
Regions that use less than
they produce

Three regions shown on the chart produce more than they consume. Latin America produces approximately ten percent more than it consumes. It is the biggest consumer among the regions that produce more than they consume. Africa produces more than twice what it consumes, and the Middle East is the biggest producer of all. However, those two regions are tied for consuming the smallest amount.

Body Paragraph 3:
Possible explanation

The United States, Canada, and Europe use a great deal more than they produce, but each produces a considerable amount. The high usage probably results from their industrial and transportation requirements. On the other hand, Africa and the Middle East produce much more than they use, which probably indicates low petroleum needs in industry and transportation.

Conclusion

As the chart describes, certain regions produce more petroleum than they consume, and others consume more than they produce. Those with a surplus can profit by selling it to the large consumers that cannot produce all that they need.

A PATTERNED PLAN OF ATTACK

Essay Writing

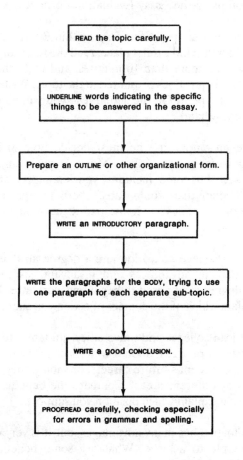

READ the topic carefully.

↓

UNDERLINE words indicating the specific things to be answered in the essay.

↓

Prepare an OUTLINE or other organizational form.

↓

WRITE an INTRODUCTORY paragraph.

↓

WRITE the paragraphs for the BODY, trying to use one paragraph for each separate sub-topic.

↓

WRITE a good CONCLUSION.

↓

PROOFREAD carefully, checking especially for errors in grammar and spelling.

SAMPLE TOPICS

Following are sample topics for practice. You should find a composition teacher who is fluent in English to grade your practice essays for you using the Essay Evaluation Form at the end of this section.

Write each of your practice essays within 30 minutes without doing any research. Find a quiet place, read the topic, organize your thoughts using no more than 10 minutes, and write the essay. Be sure to answer all questions presented in the topic. Write your essay by hand; do not type it. On the actual test, you will be required to write the essay by hand.

1. You are an employer who must decide how to handle the smoking issue in your office. Many of your employees are nonsmokers, but some, including your managers, are smokers. Devise a plan that would satisfy both groups. Explain the benefits of the plan you choose and its advantages over other options.

2. Is having a college education and a degree all that important today? Explain advantages and disadvantages to seeking a college degree as opposed to beginning work after high school and explain which of the courses of action you support.

3. In American colleges and universities, students study material from a variety of areas. Should courses concentrate only in the area of the student's future careers, or should they continue to be in many different areas? Compare the benefits of the two options and explain which position you support.

4. Being bilingual has many advantages, but it is very difficult for many people to achieve. What are some benefits of being bilingual or multilingual?

5. Some major companies in the United States are discussing the idea of having their employees work ten-hour days, forty hours a week, with three days off instead of two. What are the advantages and disadvantages of such a plan? Decide whether

this plan or the standard eight-hour day and five-day week would be better for a business that you are familiar with and support your choice.

6. The four charts below show various information regarding farming in the United States for the years 1900, 1925, 1950, and 1975. What do the charts tell you? Write one or more paragraphs that convey the information in the four charts.

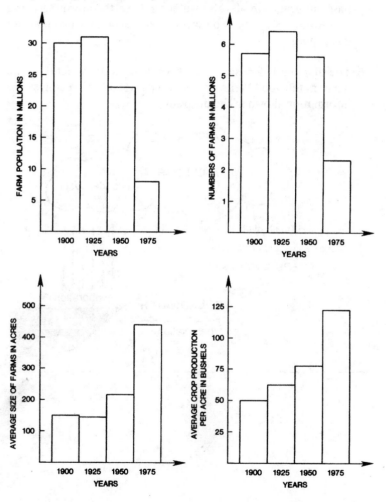

7. Students who live away from home while attending classes face the task of choosing housing accommodations. Some live in dormitories; others prefer living alone in apartments. Explain the benefits and disadvantages of the different options and support the option you prefer.

8. Some educators believe that students should receive letter grades in the courses in their major areas of concentration and pass-fail grades in all other subjects. Give the advantages and disadvantages of the two positions and explain which position you support.

9. The diagram below shows the hydrologic cycle. What does the diagram tell you? Write one or two paragraphs that convey the information shown in the diagram.

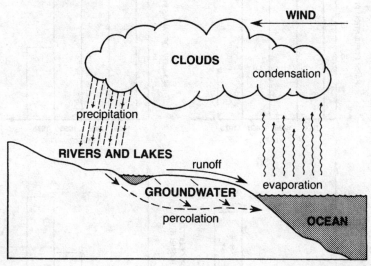

10. The four charts below show percentages of manufactured products, agricultural products, and mineral products produced in four states. What do the charts tell you? Write one or more paragraphs that convey the information in the four charts.

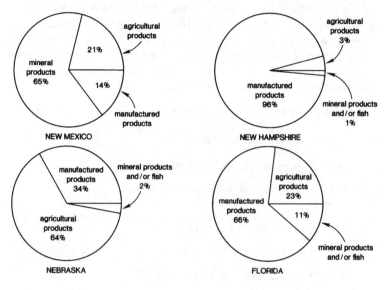

ESSAY EVALUATION FORM

Use a scale of 1 through 6 to rate the essay in each area. A rating of 1 is the lowest score possible, while a rating of 6 is the highest. In general an overall evaluation of 4, 5, or 6 may be considered a passing score by many institutions. TOEFL essays are given an *overall* score of from 1 to 6. However, this form will allow grading of your essay in a more detailed way in order for you to better analyze the areas in which you have problems.

HOW EFFECTIVELY DOES YOUR ESSAY. . .   EVALUATION

Address the Topic?

1. Does it focus on the assigned topic?   1. _____

2. Does it complete all tasks set forth by the assignment?   2. _____

Organize Its Thoughts?

3. Is there an effective introduction?   3. _____

4. Are the paragraphs logically arranged?   4. _____

5. Does each paragraph focus on one main idea?   5. _____

6. Are there smooth transitions between paragraphs?   6. _____

7. Is there an effective closing?   7. _____

Support Its Points?

8. Are there sufficient specific details for each point?   8. _____

9. Are the examples given relevant to the issue?   9. _____

10. Are the examples fully developed?   10. _____

Use Language Correctly?

11. Are grammar and usage correct?   11. _____

12. Is punctuation correct?   12. _____

13. Is spelling correct?   13. _____

14. Is vocabulary correct?   14. _____

TOTAL SCORE _____

TOTAL SCORE ÷ 14 = AVERAGE SCORE _____

FINAL PREPARATION: "The Final Touches"

1. Make sure that you are familiar with the testing center location and nearby parking facilities.
2. The last week of preparation should be spent primarily on reviewing strategies, techniques, and directions for each area.
3. Don't cram the night before the exam. It's a waste of time! RELAX.
4. Remember that you will be in the exam room for three hours or more, and you may bring no food with you. You may wish to eat a good breakfast. Remember that you will probably not have a break to visit a restroom, so don't drink too much before the exam.
5. Dress comfortably so that you will not be distracted. Take a light jacket if you are sensitive to cold in case the room is chilly.
6. Leave home in plenty of time to get to the exam. If you have to rush, you will feel nervous when you arrive.
7. Start off crisply, working the problems you know first, and then coming back and trying the others.
8. If you can eliminate one or more of the choices, make an educated guess. *Do not leave any spaces blank because there is no penalty for guessing.*
9. In reading passages, actively note main points, definitions, names, important conclusions, places, and numbers.
10. Make sure that you are answering "what is being asked" and that your answer is reasonable.
11. Using the SUCCESSFUL OVERALL APPROACH is the key to getting the ones right that you should get right—resulting in a good score on the TOEFL.

INDEX TO THE REVIEWS

$ 3.49 (SHIPPING & HANDLING)
+ $ 12.00
_____
$ 15.49